The APB
Dooley & Me

By

Peter Muir

This book is **COPYRIGHT** and apart from fair dealing for the purpose of private study, research, criticism, or review, as permitted under the **COPYRIGHT ACT**, no part may be reproduced by any process without the written permission of the publisher: **KADO MUIR, PO BOX 13, LEONORA WA 6438.**

Limited Edition For Collectors

Book Number: _____

Author's Signature: _____

Comments:

This is a limited edition print prepared by the son of Peter and Dolly - Kado Muir. It is substantially as written by Peter with the occasional reformatting and corrections.

Kado Muir, Leonora, WA, 6438
www.kadomuir.com

All enquiries
Ph. +61 89467 6046
m. +61 477 184 957
e. kadomuir@gmail.com

PREVIOUS BOOKS BY THE AUTHOR

DUNMORE IN THE WEST [Muir Family Genealogy]	1984	
VAN DIEMENS LAND ANCESTORS [Hunt Families]	1985	
GENEALOGY OF A NGALIA FAMILY	1985	Pukungka & Muir
PITURI PETE [Vol. 1 The Stockman]	1985	
KUTUNATU [Darlot Families]	1986	Pukungka & Muir
ROBERT MUIR [1839-51 NSW Journals]	1986	
PITURI PETE [Vol. 2 The Legend]	1987	
PITURI PETE [Vols. 1 & 2 combined]	1987	
PACK SADDLE [Station Diary & Bush Verse]	1988	
SAND SOAKS & DESERT OAKS [1965-68 Desert Explorations]	1988	
SHATTERED ROCKS & SHADED WATERS [Ashburton Fall]	1988	
BLUE PEAKS & RED RIDGES [Carnarvon Ranges]	1989	
STAGNANT WELLS & SANDHILL STAGES [Canning Route]	1989	
DEWDROP FRESH & BITTER BRINE [Savory Creek]	1990	
KANGARALPI NGALIAKU [Aboriginal Tales]	1990	Pukungka & Muir
EMPRESS SPRING A DIMINISHED AURA	1991	

The APB Dooley & Me
Recollections of Our First Two Years Together
1968-1970

Second Edition
2016

Contents

WHAT DOES THE COLOUR MEAN 9
INTRODUCE THE APB 10
INTRODUCE - DOOLEY 12
INTRODUCE - ME 16
LEAD-UP TO THE PREAMBLE 21
PREAMBLE 26
INTRODUCTION 36
Chapter One - CHERISHED REFLECTIONS 41
Chapter Two - THE ELOPERS RETURN 52
Chapter Three - EVEN LOVERS MUST WORK 58
Chapter Four - CONTRACT DOGGER ON KALUWIRI 66
Chapter Five - YUNDAMINDRA 78
Chapter Six - BACK IN THE SADDLE AGAIN 88
Chapter Seven - MOTORISED RIDERS OF THE OPEN RANGE 106
Chapter Eight - THOSE GREEN EYES 118
Chapter Nine - SEARCH PARTIES & EVENTS AT THE PUB 121
Chapter Ten - CHILDHOOD RECOLLECTIONS REVISITED 131
Chapter Eleven - CYCLONE INGRID 139
Chapter Twelve - APB CONVOY - KARONIE TO LAVERTON 145
Chapter Thirteen - A NEW LANDROVER AT LAST 151
Chapter Fourteen - WIDESPREAD TRAVELS & A SHIFT OF CAMP 162
Chapter Fifteen - HOSPITAL ATTITUDE v. NUPTIAL AMPLITUDE 176
Chapter Sixteen - AND KADO MAKES THREE 184
Chapter Seventeen - A RANGE OF DRAGS & TRACKS SO STRANGE 189
Chapter Eighteen - THE RED WELL CAMP 198
Chapter Nineteen - AN AXE KILLER ALLEGED 205
Chapter Twenty - BREAK NEW TRACKS - OR SCREW A FEW NECKS .. 216
Chapter Twenty One - THE MUIR GORGE & AN ANNUAL BREAK 226
Chapter Twenty Two - THE GUILE OF BUREAUCRATS DOTH PREVAIL 230
EPILOGUE 235

Images

Figure 1 a & b Dooley and Peter, above 1968 below 2004 8

Figure 2 APB Dingo Bounty 11

Figure 3 Nyiruru Soak 1970 15

Figure 4 Robert Muir 1815 - 1851 20

Figure 5 Windich Springs 1962 25

Figure 6 APB Supervisors inspect Rabbit Proof Fence 1968 40

Figure 7 Wittenoom 1968 77

Figure 8 Our Old Stone House "Hometead Palms" Leonora 1969 86

Figure 9 Rutter Soak 105

Figure 10 Camels on Road 117

Figure 11 A Doggers Bounty 117

Figure 12 APB Landrover 138

Figure 13 APB Trap Setting Demonstration 161

Figure 14 A Doggers Camp 175

Figure 16 Kado makes Three 183

Figure 15 Dooley and Kado at Gnamma hole N of Ingitjingi 183

Figure 17 Homestead Palms "Town House" 197

Figure 18 Peter Hill and Joey Munro 204

Figure 19 a & b The Strange Track 1970 215

Figure 20 Filling in the Blanks – Duketon Mapsheet 225

Figure 21 Dooley and Peter 233

Figure 1 a & b Dooley and Peter, above 1968 below 2004

WHAT DOES THE COLOUR MEAN

If your girl is lithe and dusky and your heart is full of ache
Her love can be both ardent or serene
Hot passionate embraces and tranquil love caress
Do you stop to think what does the colour mean

It's a myth and it's a fable white supremacy is dead
All is equal now for white and black or brown
She will proudly share her life with you no matter what's ahead
And she'll help you to your feet when you are down.

I ask the question clearly just what does the colour mean
When two lovers have their future life to share
No longer like the old days, now it's normal to be seen
And people on the street no longer stare

All humans now can share their life with anyone they choose
True love is free to prosper in the sun
Let white and dark blood mingle it is good to see it so
So much better for our country to be one

Oh long dark drooping lashes cover eyes so clear and bright
Neath silky raven tresses of her hair
Soft caresses show her fond love as dark arms hold you tight
For to her it does not matter that you're fair

A romance so ecstatic, though you've broken old folklore
But you need not stop to wonder what it means
For you both will share one future, love, affection and much more
In a fantasy beyond the wildest dreams

Oh tell me kindly tell me what does the colour mean
If it's not there to provide variety
If there were no dusky damsels and not one coloured man
What a dreary pallid place this world would be.

Composed in the stockcamp
on Landor Station WA
by The Author
1959

INTRODUCE THE APB

My personal knowledge of the APB extends only from the time when I initially heard of that illustrious organisation during the hot months of January 1959. I had recently arrived in WA from the then wilds of the Northern Territory to have a look-see at the even more remote wilds of Western Australia's western desert regions, if and when I could find ways and means of doing so.

There was no way I could finance such a venture myself in those days but I did hear of a way my ambition could be achieved if I got a job as a government dogger [controller of wild dogs] with the Department responsible for such things. The Agriculture Protection Board of WA or the APB as it was better known. Five years after arrival in WA I eventually got the opportunity and was employed by the APB as a government dogger in 1964. I remained with the APB for the best part of twelve years give or take a month or two, my period of employment being broken for a few months between the latter parts of 1968 and 1969 as described in the foregoing narrative of events.

During my years of employment with the APB I seldom saw a supervisor in the flesh from one year to the next. Doggers were in a position of trust and nobody could be more independent than a government dogger. However behind the scenes, ensconced in their plush head office in Perth, I somehow gained the firm impression that my benefactor the APB was overburdened with top brass, and like the armed forces, there was a hierarchy of self important officials of the upper echelon who were inclined to hand down the strangest of decisions through a regular conduit of less important officials. It was all somewhat like happens in the army. Orders come down from the Generals and Colonels or Majors etc. and from those proud bearers of shoulder pips, and red piping on coat lapels and around their hat brims; filter further downstream to Sergeant Majors, Sergeants and Corporals, until finally it reach the lower ranks of Private, Trooper, or whatever, or in the context of our narrative, to the lowest rank of the lot, the common government dogger.

Not that this system hierarchical system bothered any of us doggers though, it did not. We were always away out in the open country, far removed from the perils of top brass and shiny backsides, who spent their days in swivel chairs behind a desk in some far-off office.

We dust-coated doggers of the outback solitude were riders of the open range, or to be more precise, riders of the open spinifex and red sand. We were supplied with strychnine with which to lace poison baits for dingoes and steel jawed traps to catch them in, as well as a copious supply of 303 bullets and an ex army rifle to fire these missiles with. The nearest thing we had to what could be termed as supervisors, were pompous and often quite ignorant individuals, whom we seldom encountered in the flesh, each of these petty officials were known as a Regional Vermin Control Officer or RVCO for short.

Pseudo bosses who for the most part would only arrange to meet us in town, if perchance we travelled thence periodically for stores, fuel, vehicle maintenance, or to post away an obligatory report of the previous month's activities. Us Doggers were indeed an independent lot, make no mistake. The outback regions we travelled in the line of work, were ours, undisturbed by outside visitors in those halcyon days of yore.

I am writing this short introduction to the APB during the month of December 2000 and now find it somewhat sad to relate, that the APB I knew so well during those exotic days of literal desert exploration, savoured so much by me between the years of 1964 to 1976, no longer exists as I knew it. Possibly many readers of this book have never heard of the APB - yet it was such a notable and important organisation in its heyday and even if that official body did not intend to do me any favours, I cannot deny that the APB, despite its short-comings in respect to the unapproachable upper brass, did in fact provide me with almost twelve full years of a most interesting and adventurous life.

Figure 2 APB Dingo Bounty

INTRODUCE - DOOLEY

When the Ngalia first came in to the settled areas not all of them stayed. Some went back to their own country again soon afterwards and stopped out there for a long time until one day they start to think about all the good things they'd seen in town. The blankets, tea-leaf and sugar, Golden Syrup, clothes, and things like that. They would tell the other people who still lived out Mangkili way, all about those things and the desert people would soon want to come in to have a look for themselves so, the first lot what had been in before, would bring them in to show them all those wonderful things. They would walk back to places like Coxes Find and of course the new arrivals would get a taste for the new sort of food, especially the sweet things, and before long, they too would begin to wander around the settled country instead of return to their own tribal land.

Others would go to Cosmo Newberry. The manager at Cosmo was a grumpy old man named Donnegan. He had a big savage dog that followed him everywhere and he always carried a stockwhip over one arm when he rode his horse to supervise the Aboriginal people he was in charge of. They all had to work for rations at Cosmo and Donnegan was a hard boss.

One day Donnegan rode into our camp near Coxes Find to tell us we were welcome to come and sit down at Cosmo Newberry if we wanted to. He said we would get plenty of rations every week. My people thought that was good news so we all walked across country to Cosmo to have a look at the place. We arrived there early one morning and when Donnegan saw us newcomers he rode up to our camp on his big horse.

First thing he tell us kids: "Hey! come on you lot, come into the homestead and get some tucker and clothes." Then he tell the old people, "You fellas gotta leave all the kids here with me now, they gotta go to school while you fellas work." Well us kids didn't like the idea at all. We didn't want to stop with Donnegan and his funny old school. The old people didn't want to leave us there either. But we did stay for a little while just to see what it was like and the old people camped to one side of the settlement. There was two halfcaste girls with us that time, Muriel Barnes and Phyllis Polak. The rest of us was all fullbloods. We all stopped there together and Donnegan gave us blankets, tucker, clothes, and a few other things. Once he got us kids settled in he then give the old people a job. First they had to build a big bough shed near the homestead then he made them chop wood for the kitchen stove. Some had to build a brush yard and others were sent out a few miles to build brush fences and make paddocks for the cattle and horses. No wire or posts, just bushes heaped up in long rows for miles and miles, and while they worked, Donnegan would ride up and down on his horse to watch them, with the whip on his arm and the big dog close behind.

The big dog was always there ready to bite anyone who might get cheeky with Donnegan. They built brush fences like that all around the north side of Cosmo Newberry country, right around east to the Warburton Road and also some distance to the south. There was another long brush fence on the west side too. Yes there was brush fences everywhere on Cosmo country. You can still see what's left of them out there today. There are brush fences right out as far as Mount Shenton country near Jutson Soak. Donnegan was a proper hard boss. He used to ride up and down all day long just like you see on the pictures about the days when people had Negro slaves.

Well Donnegan would watch and see who was a good worker and who was lazy, and when ration day come round he would go up to the people and say: "Alright you fellas, you sit down here and wait for your stores now." All the best workers would get their rations first, they would get a good share. But the people what never done much work, well they wouldn't get anything right away, they would have to wait until last and sometimes Donnegan would tell them to go away and come back in the afternoon. Just as punishment I suppose.

One old lady he told to wait was my father's aunt. I called that old lady granny. Well Donnegan made a mistake to pick on her because she was a good worker. When Donnegan told her to wait she got wild about it and they had a row: "I bin workin hard too you know Donnegan, I bin cleanin all that sticks and puttin bushes on the fence every day and now you can't givem tucker." Donnegan he tell her, "Oh no old lady you just gotta wait a bit yet, no rations for you now, you gotta come back after dinner."

That was enough for my granny, she turned away from Donnegan then called me over and said my name: "Hey Pukungka, you wanta come along with me eh? We all goin huntin and campin out bush today, no use to stop here in this puckin place with no puckin tucker." So I went with her but not only me, a lot of other kids and big people followed her too. We all set off along the Warburton Road. It was only a wheel track in those days, not a big graded road like it is now. We walked all the way past Lake Throssel to Nulleye Soak before we slowed down. The party split up there at Nulleye. Most of the people continued along the track north-east to Warburton and took all the kids with them except me. My granny and her lot turned off the road north into the desert. I was the only kid with them. My old granny tell me: "You know what Pukungka, I take you away because Donnegan can't givem rations. We go for a long walkabout in our own country now." Well we went on a long walkabout alright, through spinifex and sandhills all the way. We musta been out there for about one year I reckon because I was only little when we left Cosmo but was much bigger by the time we got back to Mulga Queen again and my relations there didn't recognise me at first.

I had grown into a big girl but we'd been in the dry country so long, that my hair was all matted and full of lice, and the old government dress I wore all that time was so hard and stiff it used to rustle like paper when I walked along. While we was away the old people looked for dingo pups to scalp and take back to Mulga Queen to sell to old Jack Shepherd.

We didn't go back by way of Cosmo Newberry, oh no, we didn't want to run into Donnegan again. Instead we went away around by the north side through a big saltpan called Lake Wells. This is a long wide lake that pinches in to a narrow neck in the middle. That narrow place we call *Watuta* is where the old bush people used to walk across from Mangkili side in the early days. That was the traditional road or blackfella highway.

I remember we was short of water when we got there because a soakage we'd called into the day before had a rotten dead dog in it and the water was so stinkin we couldn't drink it. That 'dead dog soak' *Wakamurru* was east of the lake near a place called Peterswald Hill. I learned the name of that hill later from my husband Peter. I didn't know the English name for it in those days though. It was late in the day when we reached that bad water but we had to keep on walking after dark so we could get across the lake to another water on the west side. We burnt spinifex as we walked along to light our way in the dark and I can still remember the smell of that smoke even now after all these years. I was almost perished for want of a drink but had to put up with a dry mouth, and the smoke only made it worse.

Somehow the old people missed that *watuta* narrow neck in the dark and we had to cross the lake at a wide place with water up to their knees. In some deeper places they had to carry me on their shoulders. That night we camped on an island about half way across the lake. Next day there was miles of bog and the salt was so hot it burned my skin and made me cry with pain but we got over it alright and later in the day we came to a big rockhole. It must have been deep but I didn't see the water because the old people wouldn't let me go anywhere near it. I remember they had to join a number of dog chains together and lower a billycan down to the water. They always carried chains for the dogs so they could tie them up of a night time. We got used to doing that in the station country so the dogs wouldn't get poisoned, and of course we still had the chains with us when we went out bush on that trip. The old people always chained the dogs up out there too in case they might run off with a dingo.

Many years later after I met my husband, we went back to that country with a Landrover because Peter wanted to find a place that the explorer Carnegie had named Empress Spring. Peter was a government dogger in those days and we used to go out together all over the desert country in search of dingoes. We tried to find that big rockhole west of Lake Wells too. We found the narrow neck alright but I couldn't work out which way to go from there because in those earlier years we had not crossed the lake at the right place and I still don't know whether our night time crossing was north or south of the narrow neck. I just can't remember where it might be. We did find a lot of other rockholes though, and Peter did eventually find the Empress Spring he was after, although I didn't really know what he was looking for at the time. Peter knew of the place by its English name; which of course that was unknown to me, but after he'd found it, we camped there that night and by next morning I remembered the place from years before. I only knew it by its native name of *Reti*. It wasn't the big rockhole the old people had kept me away from though, so I was a bit disappointed about that because I'd wanted so much for my husband to see the rockhole of my younger days. We must go out there and have another look. I'd love to find it again.

One year Peter went up in an aeroplane with Tony Drake Brockman who had taken up country to run cattle south of Lake Wells. They saw a real big rockhole away to the north of Gregory Hills and I think that might be the one I was at when little but Peter said it was a long way off and would be hard to find with a Landrover unless we had plenty of time to spare because it appeared to be in difficult country. One day we might try.

Well, getting back to that walkabout trip when I was little, I do remember, that from the big rockhole on west side of Lake Wells where the billycan was lowered on dog chains, we still had a long dry walk before we reached the next water. This was situated in thick mulga scrub country surrounded by dark stony hills. The water there is called *Nyiruru* and from what I remembered of it I had the impression it was a springwater. Me and Peter found *Nyiruru* alright and I recognised it straight away, but it didn't look the same as when I was a small girl and I was rather disappointed with it. The first time I'd seen it about thirty years before, I'd thought it was a wonderful place, and while the old people camped close by to rest up after the long dry walkabout we'd just finished, I used to spend all my time beside the water. It was at that time a deep hole full of saturated sand in a small creek with water just under the surface. I used to sit there beside it for hours and sift the wet sand through my fingers to watch water collect in the small basins I scooped out of the sand.

It seemed such a beautiful spot at the time and I always believed it was a permanent spring but my illusions were shattered when Peter and I relocated the place. The little girl's beautiful image of tranquil waters could never be related to what we found. *Nyiruru* turned out to be only a small sandfilled catchment that happened to be full all those years ago after a chance thunder storm had passed through the area, but when found by Peter and myself thirty years later, was dry and devoid of moisture.

These big English words are not part of my vocabulary. Peter has put them into my story in order to show how disillusioned and disappointed I was to come back as an adult eager to see an enchantment of younger days, only to find a bone dry parched and insignificant depression in a rough little storm gutter that runs off the ugly scrub covered stone hills behind it. My earlier picture of *Nyiruru* was no doubt enhanced by the long dry walk and near perish experienced before we reached it. The place must have saved our lives all those years ago, and I know we camped there to rest for at least a week before we tackled the final long dry stage south to Mulga Queen.

Once started on that last part of our year long journey we kept going without a stop until well inside Bandya Station country wherein Mulga Queen is situated, and arrival there ended the longest walkabout of my girlhood days. The only time I have ever seen and lived in my tribal land as a nomad like my ancestors.

Figure 3 Nyiruru Soak 1970

INTRODUCE - ME

I admit to more than a little pride in being a fifth or sixth generation Australian with at least one convict ancestor. The convict was my great-great grandfather William Hunt, who arrived in Van Diemens Land aboard the convict ship Elizabeth on 6 July 1832. He was transported for a period of fourteen years penal servitude for some minor offence. William Hunt obtained permission to marry a free immigrant of Irish descent, one Fanny Mason. Their union took place in Launceston on 14 July 1845. To them a child was born on 18 April 1846 and named William Hunt after his father.

William Hunt the younger, my distaff great grandfather, worked his way successfully through various government departments to eventually become Deputy Sheriff and Clerk of the Peace for what was by this time Tasmania. He was also connected with the defence force of that colony as a gunner in the Launceston Artillery. Much later in 1906 he was appointed Commissioner of Police, but unfortunately took ill soon after the appointment and died 17 May of that year just a fortnight before taking up his post.

Another of my Van Diemens Land distaff ancestors, great-great-great grandfather James Houghton, was a shipwright by trade. He was appointed superintendent of government boat builders by the authorities in Van Diemens Land and a notice to that effect appeared in the Hobart Town Gazette, issue of 6 July 1822. Research indicates that he came out to these shores, possibly on a naval vessel, circa 1819. In later life he became a prosperous farmer.

A bit more genealogical research shows that my paternal great-great grandfather Robert Muir sailed from Plymouth aboard the barque Alfred. He arrived at the age of twenty-four years in Port Jackson after a voyage of one hundred and twenty-one days, on Wednesday 16 January 1839. The next morning he had his first view of what was then known as Sydney Town, which he described as a most disagreeable place. The most notable remark recorded in his diary being that George Street was about two miles long. Unimpressed by Sydney Town, he returned to the ship that night to dine on board. Next day he purchased horses, pack and riding saddles and stores, then left immediately for the bush where a partner named Campbell had a cattle station called Glenmore in the Hunter Valley. Great-great grandfather Robert, over the following few years had much experience with local bush natives, and on one rare occasion met a bushranger on the run from police troopers. He made a note in his diary to the effect that the said bushranger had riding alongside him on horseback, a young black gin dressed in boy's clothing, Robert Muir later took up a cattle selection of his own and called it Brezia, or Breezo for short. He married Isabella Ninian Lang my great-great grandmother. The couple settled on Dunmore, the property of his Lang family in-laws, where Elizabeth died shortly after the birth of my paternal great grandfather in 1847, to be followed later by Robert Muir at the early age of thirty-six years in 1851.

Along with other deceased members of the family both my great-great grand parents are buried in a vault or sarcophagus near Dunmore House.

The controversial character and would-be republican Dr John Dunmore Lang, whose statue now stands in Wynyard Park in Sydney, was my great-great grandmother Elizabeth Lang's uncle. The Lang family arrived in Van Diemens Land aboard the good ship Brixton in 1821. Dunmore House the Muir-Lang family home, still stands near Maitland in the Upper Hunter River district of NSW, but the property, now much reduced in size, is currently occupied by other owners. After reading my great-great grandfather Robert Muir's diary I know I would have been quite at home with him, and in my former drinking days, would have been quite happy to share a bottle of rum with him beside some lonely campfire, even though I realise that could never be, considering the several generations that separate his time from mine.

I have gone to some lengths to provide the above details as a bit of background for my dearly beloved grandmother Florence Hunt who was born in Launceston Tasmania during February 1882. Florence Hunt was a daughter of William Hunt the younger, referred to in paragraph two of this text. She later moved to the mainland and married into the Rothwell family to produce two daughters and one son. The youngest daughter Bertha born in 1911 was my mother who later married John Muir. In 1929 I came along, although I don't recall all the circumstances of that illustrious event, me being a bit young at the time. To cut a long story short as that overworked saying goes, my parents parted when I was still a toddler. My old grandmother became the woman of my life after the separation of my parents and I remained with gran until the age of twelve.

There is no doubt in my mind that those first twelve fascinating years of my early youth laid the groundwork for even more interesting times ahead. I never knew my grandfather, he died long before I was born. My father didn't want anything to do with me, his first born, and my mother, because of the separation, had to work for a living. I only ever had fleeting glimpses of mum, she played little part in my upbringing being always away somewhere else.

Grandma as I always called her, grew up in the atmosphere of what people these days refer to as the Victorian Era. Grandma always sought work in far-off places of outback NSW, pastoral properties, wheat farms, country towns, grandma went from one housekeeping job to another. We always travelled by train. These early years of my life were back in the 1930s when steam engines ruled the rails. Oh what nostalgic recollections I have of those journeys by steam train. The deep throated roar of the engine's whistle blasting the cold night air. Boyhood nose stuck to a frosty window pane as the train clicketty clacked over uneven rails, with carriages swaying to and fro all the while. We mostly travelled overnight. Sometimes we had to change trains in the wee small hours. This nearly always meant a cold shivering delay at some wayside stop. The passenger waiting room would have a big open fireplace with back logs ablaze, around which the adults would sit and chat, but I never seemed able to get close to the fireside. A porter or station attendant would come in every now and again to stoke the fire and keep the waiting adult passengers cosy and warm.

The expected transfer train would eventually herald its arrival at the lonely stop with yet another deep throated roar through the darkness outside. The train would huff and puff to a halt at the lonely station and blow off steam with an even greater roar than the whistle blast. Then with a bit more huffing and puffing we would soon be off again to yet another exotic destination.

Those train travelling days certainly did gladden the heart and provide fodder for fanciful boyhood dreams. Once arrived at our destination, the owner of whatever property we were bound for, would meet the train and transport us thence in a vintage vehicle of one kind or another. On rare occasions we were sometimes met by a horse drawn buggy and pair.

Our eventual arrival at yet another strange and often decrepit well-weathered homestead, was a source of never ending adventure for me. The scented aroma of candlesticks, hurricane lamps and woodfire stoves would waft on the early morning air as we took stock of our new abode in the pre-dawn light. Such lifestyle was the norm during my childhood out in the backblocks.

Hospitality to all travellers was obligatory in those days. The homestead dining tables would seldom seat less than eight or ten. All food was home cooked, and roast legs of mutton or beef followed by fresh hot scones, were a regular part of daily fare.

I enjoyed a quite diverse education. At age twelve I lay in bed one night and counted a total of thirty-two different country schools attended during those early years. Most of them were the single room variety staffed by only one teacher who had to handle several primary classes all day without assistance. I was never a scholar, and never aspired to be one. My only real ambition in life during childhood was to be with horses and cattle. I intended to be another Clancy of the overflow or man from Snowy River when I grew up. I often too, had thoughts of one day going bush with a tribe of nomadic Aborigines. I would make toy spears and boomerangs to play with when without the company of other kids, as I mostly was on some of the properties where grandma worked.

Grandma eventually decided to bundle me off to complete the last two years of elementary education at a high school. By this time it was 1941 and I surmise, that the 1939 War may have played some part in her unwelcome decision to pack me off. I also suspect that her twelve year old grandson might have become a bit too much for the old lady to handle. Anyway I did complete school, right up until the day I turned fourteen. School holidays were on at the time and I never went back to school after that break.

During that same end of term school break the smell of horse dung one day wafted across my nostrils and the bellow of bullocks in a nearby paddock hit my ears. Then a travelling horse dealer came along. The dealer had a mob of forty or more horses and was walking them all over the country, or droving if you like, from place to place in search of sales. He agreed to take me along as offsider at £1-0-0 a week and keep. A one pound note is the official oldtime equivalent of our current two dollars, but of course back then it was a huge sum of money. One pound then could buy a hundred times or maybe more, than what two dollars does now.

I spent twelve months with that horse dealer, riding in the saddle all over the country, and learned more from him in that one year than some so-called horsemen learn in a lifetime. The long and short of it is that I left the travelling horse dealer and headed for cattle country out along the Birdsville Track, north of Marree in South Australia. For the next twenty years I followed full time cattle and horse work, either on foot in a stockyard, or riding in the saddle all the time. In addition to South Australia, I roamed all over the Northern Territory and Western Queensland before coming across to WA in 1959 in search of the last vestiges of real horse and cattle work. Those twenty years of full time stockwork as a ringer, put me in regular contact with tough whites and tribal Aborigines. It may sound corny but I really did love the lifestyle of camping on the ground out under the stars each night. Exotic is too weak a word to describe the richness of regular life in the unfenced bush and whole days spent in the saddle.

As a youngster I never had much opportunity to enjoy female company and if the opportunity had arisen, I must admit my first preference would have been for a fullblood Aboriginal girl. Someone I could relate to and who would be accustomed to life in the bush. Work on cattle stations or droving the stockroutes with bullocks on the hoof though does not provide much contact with female company of any kind. It is hard work performed by tough men, with long hours and little time for rest.

As diesel road trains took over from the drovers and modern methods made inroads on the cattle properties, pure saddle work became increasingly hard to get, so that men like me began to seek those few places further out, the last frontiers where mechanisation did not yet prevail. My search brought me to Western Australia and after a couple of years in the Gascoyne, I ended up in the little township of Wiluna. By this time the stations around Lake Carnegie east of Wiluna were also on the verge of displacing stockmen with vehicles. Drovers had already vanished, due to the advent of road trains not long prior to my arrival on the scene. I was by this time somewhat disheartened to see a horse mounted era literally vanish in front of my eyes.

The only genuine bush work of any appeal to me after demise of the stockhorse, was to become a dogger with the Agriculture Protection Board, the APB. The only catch being that in those days of 1964, a prospective applicant to that august government department for a dogger's job, had first to produce a four wheel drive vehicle of his own. In other words a man had to outlay a considerable sum of money just to get the job.

Being fortunate in that I was never one to waste my meagre resources, I had sufficient in the bank to buy a second-hand Landrover, so hopped on the local mail plane which was at that time one of the last Douglas DC3's in regular flight. After a bumpy ride to Perth, I purchased the vehicle and set off that same day back to Wiluna. Because I was not accustomed to city traffic, the salesman had to drive me out to the Great Northern Highway and put me on the road, he then caught a Taxi back to town. That was my first ever trip to Perth.

The allocated dogging area was along the Ashburton Fall, in a stretch of rugged untracked and totally unoccupied country, behind the pastoral properties known as Mount Augustus, Dooley Downs, Elliott Creek (now called Wanna) at western end and southern side of the run, and Mount Vernon at the extreme eastern end. That was a most fascinating fifteen months. I eventually wrote a book about the Pingandy experience based on comprehensive field notes kept during that 1964-65 period.

In the early part of 1965 I was offered the opportunity to literally explore a virgin wilderness of isolated desert breakaway systems, sandhills, and open spinifex beyond all station boundaries. This was called a wild dog survey. It covered pure desert country from a salt lake north of Wiluna known as Nabberu, north to the inland flowing channel of Savory Creek and on to Jiggalong.

The western side of this area was bounded by the long abandoned and quite derelict Rabbit Proof Fence. I was to extend the explorations and survey of wild dog movements east from that fenceline, to the then untracked Canning Stockroute. There wasn't even a bullock pad visible on the Canning then. As mentioned earlier in this Introduction, my childhood, and later teenage stockwork days of full time work in the bush, fitted me well for such a task. I wrote four books about that wondrous three year exploration phase. The books were based on detailed field notes recorded beside numerous smoky campfires at the end of each long interesting day, between the years 1965-68.

I said before that my one romantic ambition in life was to some day wed a fullblood Aboriginal girl. My ingrained psyche would never consider any other option. I was three full years on that exploration job and during that time met the desired fullblood woman of my dreams. In her own sphere she was as widely travelled in the bush as myself. Known far and wide as Dooley, she was and still is, highly respected by both black and white. Before we met, she was already a notable character in her own right. A real daughter of the Dreaming. As a child Dooley knew the nomadic desert life of her old people from personal experience, before settling down on the inside pastoral country later as an adult. We were a perfect match when we first got together and still are. The following narrative describes only the first two of our wonderful thirty odd years together.

I dedicate this book to Dooley, who remains the only real love of my life, and to our children and their offspring.

The Author
February 2000

Figure 4 Robert Muir 1815 - 1851

LEAD-UP TO THE PREAMBLE

Wednesday 25th - September 1968 (10283) A cool night beside the pool and for once, no mosquitoes. Travelled west further into Ken Hall's cattle country this morning in search of any established motor tracks that might run north into the guts of the new dog control area. Seven miles at first then north along a wide grass flat decorated with scattered flood gums. Got onto a faint set of wheel marks there and followed them one mile to a clayhole with small quantity of water. Saw two turkeys near a windmill on a bore hole nearby. Continued north past the mill and through a fence with gate at one mile, to a cattle yard half a mile further on. The track ended there so returned from yard to the gum creek where I'd camped last night. Followed the gum creek next, northward along its east side for two miles to a second windmill on yet another bore hole where, the creek was crossed and travel continued north along the creek's west side for about seven miles, crossed the creek then and followed the motor track east for three miles to a magnificent large open pool in yet another creek with two ducks and a lot of young ones on the water. The ducks didn't fly away when the vehicle approached but instead continued to enjoy themselves as wild ducks with little ones always do when not disturbed. I watched them dive and swim around for some time, then left them to their pleasures and went for a walk around the area.

All the country covered this morning is well grassed but prone to flood wash, and not much sign of game was seen either, apart from those ducks on the big pool, and turkeys seen earlier. I found a puzzle. A sort of old pump stand or whatever, on clear bare ground atop a small rise above the waterhole banks. Perhaps the frame once supported equipment used in the old days to pump water from the creek, or maybe it is the frame of a small two stamp battery. Yes that's what it is. The dismantled remains of a small stamp-mill. I remember now there is supposed to be a place somewhere around this west side of the fence known as Battery Claypan.

I didn't take much notice at the time John Roach told me the yarn, but recall now that it was about a couple of prospectors who were alleged to have treated stolen gold ore out this way many years ago, but were caught red-handed, and that is all I know. This must be that battery. It is said their guilt was obvious, because the (at that time) remote spot selected to treat the ill-gotten gains, was not gold country and thus they couldn't explain their presence with gold at a gold-less site. From Battery Pool I continued east by south to yet a third windmill with tank at five miles. Both dry. Drove south-east from the dry tank back to Grasscutter Mill which was struck at nine miles from the pool. Returned west then for six or seven miles and followed another long unused motor track north for three miles.

It turned out to be only a wet weather deviation around flood country so I left it and went back to the main track, then followed that to another waterhole nine miles west of Grasscutter. I think this must be Pinyerinya Pool as marked on the map.
I pulled up for dinner beside the pool and could see Yowereena Hill (also marked on map) about two miles north-north-west. Continued west after dinner. Reached the gum creek again at four miles and followed it south back to the main track from which I then followed another faint set of wheel marks south-west, but they vanished after a short distance and couldn't be found again, so were left. No doubt it is much more fun to explore open virgin country than to follow a network of indistinct station tracks like these. A man might as well get a job on a station and do the windmill run.

Satisfied that no useful tracks run north into the guts of country around Marymia Hill where I want to work, I returned eight mile to where the track on east side of the creek turns east to Pinyerinya Pool, then north up that creek, this time without the distraction of someone else's wheel marks. I'd prefer to make my own any day, station tracks seldom go where a dogger must go. Came to a big waterhole at three miles, and another even bigger at ten miles. At twenty nine miles I turned east and before long on that bearing, met my old wheel marks of a former east-west traverse. Those of the first trip done westward from the 470 Mile to Three Rivers Boundary in fact. Followed that route today for five or six miles east, and camped on the most eastern gum creek along it. Only one dog track seen all day, and clouds in the north this afternoon. One hundred and sixteen miles, with little to show for travel in station country, but some nice pools were found outside the boundary.

Thursday 26th - (10399) A mild night and clouds around this morning. Continued east along my former traverse line for seven miles then left it to follow a set of old wheel marks south, and was surprised to find the remains of a burnt out brush yard at one mile. The yard is located in open country, away outside the normal reach of Neds Creek cattle and was erected in a perfect secluded spot for duffers to take cleanskins and brand them undisturbed. I assume it is the yard Ken Hall is said to have discovered and put a match to some years ago, after he'd tracked strayed stock north of his boundary and found evidence in the form of a brush yard, that someone had been at his poddies. The Beyondie crowd were blamed at the time but nothing ever came of it apart from the burnt yard mentioned. From the yard, the track was followed west for one mile to the gum creek, and back along that creek to last night's camp. Then from there, east to the old track once more. A four mile circuit. Followed the track north again then for another six miles and came to a second brush yard, not burnt this time and not so old either. And a good pool in the creek nearby. Goodness me, it seems the country is dotted with poddy dodgers yards, this area must be a real robber's roost. I crossed the creek and turned east. Shot a turkey at one mile and went on to another pool down the creek to cook the bird for dinner and as I stepped out of the Landrover, noticed the petrol cap had once again been knocked off the auxiliary fuel tank so will have to go back over my tracks and find it.

The Clover Tabletop is quite visible from this pool about five miles distant to north-east. After the meat had been cooked and dinner eaten, I went back and found the petrol cap a good ten miles away. Just as had happened when lost before, it had twisted off the tank spout as the vehicle passed too close to a bush. Petrol cap retrieved, I took a straight course to the 477 Mile and found Roach's bough shed to be ten miles east of today's second brush yard at dinner camp. Plotted it on the map then travelled south down the fenceline to pick up the trailer and load it with old fence posts ready to take into Wiluna for firewood when I go to town next week. Left it beside the track when full and went back north to March Fly Creek at the 465 Mile to camp. Saw but one dog track all day. A lot of strong wind gusts and scattered storms around this afternoon. Ninety four miles.

Friday 27th - (10493) It was a pleasant cool change but the wind was too strong and blew a gale all night. Took a run up to the 467 Mile breakaways petrol dump this morning and refuelled. It was necessary to top up too, despite Fitzgerald' s insistence that extra fuel is not needed out bush. I do need it and I'm hanged if I'll follow his instructions to return the drums to town. Noticed evidence of recent dog activity nearby too and set a couple of traps before I left. Went north then to Roach's camp and from there travelled west to the last brush yard seen yesterday near dinner camp.

From the yard, travel was south for one and a half miles and west for eight at which point, I turned off the track and followed a set of old wheel marks south through spinifex country. The wheel marks crossed one of my former east-west traverse lines in the vicinity of what I have since named Dooley's Knob, an isolated black ironstone blow or perhaps bluff faced peak would be a more apt description. It is situated a few miles east of Three Rivers boundary, I just forget the exact distance, but to be more precise, I can quote it as thirty four miles west of the 473 Mile. Spinifex cut out altogether after only one mile and gave way to hard ground across which the old track became difficult to follow. I managed to trace it over the divide and down the southern fall whereon the topography consists of open flats and low rises all strewn with detrital white quartz and after travel over this for two miles, the head of a gum creek was met and followed down another mile to a small waterhole where a halt was made to boil a quart of tea for a midday spell. First thing after dinner travel was resumed along the south bound wheel marks and before long, yet another of my former east-west traverse lines was cut at right angles, I turned west along it until the first deep creek in that direction was reached and followed upstream for one and one half miles. Not one thing of interest attracted my attention along that upper section, not even an old dog track at which to gaze in awestruck wonder so, it was turn back and run the creek downstream instead and this proved to be a much more remunerative move when several small puddles of water appeared along its rocky bed. This string of small catchments led to a good little rock pool at five miles.

Near this rock water I was rather surprised to find some strange and quite fresh motor tracks, made within the past few days by someone, who like myself, has searched along this same creek for who knows what. My presence in the area is easy to explain for it is the dingo's lair, or the imprints of his paws upon the sand that I seek, but what the hell this other lot is after I do not have a clue. Seems to have been a large well equipped party too. Who was it I wonder! The first time in fact I have ever run into evidence of outsiders in any part of this open country during the three years I've worked hereabouts. Will stay tonight beside the rock pool.

Once a suitable campsite had been selected I left the vehicle at rest and took a walk downstream for about one quarter of a mile and found a series of little rock ponds at intervals all along the creekbed. Fifty three miles today.

Saturday 28th - (10546) Another cold night and no wind this time thank goodness. Broke camp early and set off down the creek wherein several good size waterholes were noticed and passed by. These extended at intervals the whole distance to where the creek junctions with another at eight and a half miles. The second creek comes in from the north-east.

Followed that north-east branch then, upstream along its west bank for two miles, where it was crossed to the east side and not long afterwards, wheel tracks of my last week's reconnaissance trip were met. Left the creek then and continued north-east across country for ten miles to a number of claypans and the gum creek which were found during an earlier east-west traverse run. The country covered this morning consists for the most part of white quartz strewn rises and knobs or quartz blows, with an overall vegetation cover of windgrass, herbage, and light mulga thickets.

Left that area behind at that point and travelled back via Roach's camp at the 477 mile to that grand rockhole west of the 485 Mile whereat I desired to enjoy an afternoon off beside the tranquil waters. Although not a football fan by any means, I had decided to listen in on the wireless to the Finals in Perth in order to get a few clues on what football is all about, as Wiluna men speak of little else when in the pub but I can't appreciate their conversation because I don't know the first thing about the game. Hence my belated decision to absorb a bit of its atmosphere today. Forty seven miles travelled and this must be the best rockhole in the country bar none. An exotic place to pull up and rest at, after the drab spinifex flats one has to cross in order to reach it.

Sunday 29th - (10593) Not a sign of dogs around this water despite an extensive inspection of the area on foot so returned to camp and stayed put all day. Washed clothes, had a personal cleanup, and cooked some tucker. On Monday 30th - I returned south to what I must henceforth identify as Claypan Creek because of the presence of those clay flats above and to one side of it. Once reached today it was followed south for all but nine miles at which point a noon halt was made for a spell beside a small pool in a little tributary branch that runs into the main channel.

On the move again afterwards, a beautiful and most unexpected sight greeted my eyes. A splendid big rockhole, or rather several of them, each lower than its neighbour, as the bare natural cement formation that contains them, descended in staircase fashion from the uppermost level over a series of low ledges. Beneath each step, rested a rockhole full of water.

Just below the last of these basins the channel resumed its sand filled character and was thereafter occupied by fine stands of eucalypts that continued downstream. This lovely place is a bit more than nine miles south of the claypans. No doubt the rockholes possess a suitable native name but I know not what that might be. From those waters, travel was east next towards the north side of a prominent white quartz hill with survey station on top. I calculate it must be the R 47 Trig marked on the map. I came abreast of the white hill on its north side at three and one half miles east of the stepped rockholes.

Continued east and was annoyed to get stuck for some time with yet another broken axle, whilst in the bed of a sharp little stormwater creek at twelve and a half miles. It was a heck of a job to get out of the deep narrow channel with only two wheel drive. The vehicle had to be rolled backwards and forwards several times before it would mount the steep bank, and even then I only just made it because the wheels skidded too much on the gravel at top. What useless things these Landrovers are when an axle snaps, but unlike the previous experience out in the desert sands, this time once the upper level of hard ground was attained, it was more or less normal travel thereafter eastward to the fenceline whereat, I came out right on the south bank of the 458 Mile Creek, seventeen miles east of the splendid rockholes described earlier.

Turned south along the fenceline from there and ran into Ken Hall with Johnny Brownrigg at Simpsons Mill both busy with wire strainers pliers and fence repairs. I told Ken about the strange vehicle tracks I'd seen west of the fence the other day and learned from him that they were made by a party of men who, with a Dalgety's Agent, had gone on an inspection trip of the open country out that way. Intent it seems on application for a new pastoral lease so, it looks like Johnny Roach might miss out on it yet if he does, then he will lose a lot of money as well as the hard work he's put into unauthorised improvements, and nowhere to take the mob of cattle he already has on hand either. If in fact they are still in the country, because neither Ken Hall nor myself have seen hair nor hide of Roach's cattle in ages. I wonder where they got to. Bill Green of Cunyu Station swears he saw some of them east of Windich Springs a while back, which I cannot substantiate because I haven't been in that area for a long time, but if Bill is correct, then Roach's stock have an extra wide spread on because Windich is miles away from his proposed Marymia lease. I left Ken and John Brownrigg to their task and travelled through the night to Wiluna with trailer load of firewood. Arrived in town right on the end of the month at the last stroke of midnight, after a one hundred and eighty five mile day or, one hundred and twenty five from Simpsons.

Figure 5 Windich Springs 1962

PREAMBLE

Edited extracts from the final chapter of a 1990 publication, the author's book:

"Dewdrop Fresh & Bitter Brine"

OCTOBER 1968

Tuesday 1st: This morning it was delightful to see Dooley, much happier than when I saw her last. We managed to have a brief chat but not in private as far too many black stickybeaks in the street. We could not talk too long. The Albion Downs car pulled up to take her back to the station and she had to go. We managed to do little more than arrange to meet again when she returns to town for the annual races on the 5th and 6th of this month. Once again frustrated, I could only watch as she sped off down the south road to disappear in the usual cloud of dust that has tormented me before. Dooley and I must run away together this month, there are no two ways about it. Dooley and I have waited too long already, we must elope. The exploration work is over and done with now and my incentive to stay on the job is not so strong, but a considered decision about future involvement with the APB is still in order and I should avoid being swayed by emotions, no matter how hot the inner fires might be.

Wednesday 2nd: Travelled to Meekatharra and put the government Landrover in for repairs then spent all day with Regional Vermin Control Officer Alex Campbell at his place. We went over the special report I'd written about the recent farcical trip we did to wind-up my 1965-68 three year period of explorations, known by head office as the "Savory Wild Dog Survey." APB supervisors had come from Perth for a final inspection tour only to display their complete ignorance of how to behave in the bush. Alex agreed with the contents of my supplementary report, but to my disappointment reneged on his former promise to sign it. He suggested it be submitted under my signature alone. Indeed, it will, although I feel certain the written complaint won't reach the Chief's desk. It is sure to disappear somewhere in the lower levels long before it can ever reach the top. On the same theme, Alex doesn't favour my direct approach, his ideal is to use more caution and his advice was: "It is better by far to hit an antagonist when he least expects it rather than attack head on. If you show your hand he can retaliate and do you harm, but if you use guerrilla tactics and conceal your actions, there is not much he can do."

These statements reminded me of others Alex has made in the past about retribution. He once told me: "I always like to pay my debts without delay, if I owe a person anything they get paid back at the first opportunity. Likewise, if someone does me a bad turn I repay the compliment in kind, at the earliest. It is foolish to store resentment and brood over things, get it over and done with, get it right out of the way." Well, that is

Alex Campbell's style not mine. I pay all financial debts on time yes, but those that involve personal injury or insult, I like to meet head on. That perhaps is why I never seem to get ahead like others do. They who use subterfuge, chicanery, and appeasement, tend to achieve their goals without any trouble. Old Wanda Ward was a former Matron at Wiluna hospital. She once told me after we had a small tiff: "Your trouble Peter is, you are much too direct and honest about things and thus let yourself open" I've often pondered over that advice and the more I do the more it seems she was right. One should never let the left hand know what the right hand is up to The latter is a worn out phrase but true.

Thursday 3rd: I had to camp at Campbell's place last night because the vehicle wasn't finished. It was ready by dinner time today though and I got on the road back to Wiluna with it right away.

Friday 4th: Purchased a load of stores and refuelled, then loaded the Landrover ready for the bush. That done, I took a run out to the racecourse to watch the horses and station people arrive for the weekend. Bob Adamson's team from Yakabindie were there in force, along with his two popular black housegirls Cecily and Gaye. I stayed at the yards for a while then came home and got my own private Landrover engine tuned up ready for the road at a moment's notice, just in case the need might arise. That done I adjourned to the pub for a few drinks with station visitors to town, whose company I always enjoy during this one great event of the year. One can't beat a good bush race meeting and the one at Wiluna of late is just as good as the famous Landor Races in that respect.

Saturday 5th: Race Day at last. Dooley was there, I hung around close to her most of the day, but to be together out bush would have been so much better, instead of merge with the crowd like we did. Despite Dooley's presence I did not enjoy the race meeting like I used to. The trouble was I had eyes only for the bright lights on her well groomed hair, and didn't mix with my stockmen mates in the usual boisterous way. Dooley and I had a good day though and finished up at the Race Ball, but only as onlookers. Dooley doesn't dance, and in anycase is too shy.

Sunday 6th: The gymkhana was better than a similar one held on Landor Station each year. Today Roy Linke compéred the Wiluna event with a megaphone. In a loud voice he kept the crowd enthralled with humorous quips and lots of encouragement. The day enhanced by a background of hillbilly songs played over a public address system.

A carnival atmosphere prevailed throughout the entire weekend. I took a full roll of 35mm colour slides for remembrance of the unique event but Dooley wouldn't pose for a special shot. I had to be content with a photo of Cecily and Gaye seated on a top rail beside the racetrack.

It is almost impossible to pin an Aboriginal person down to a specific date. They do not place the same values on time as white folk do. Dooley and I did however make definite plans to meet again within a fortnight and elope then. At long last I have a set goal to steer for. In the interim she will remain at Albion Downs for the next ten days or so.

Monday 7th: I was so busy over the weekend I failed to record one notable aspect of it, the weather. It was bitter cold for this time of the year and not only in Wiluna either. Snow fell in Perth last Friday night, but I only heard about it on the news this morning. A chill wind continues yet, and at present is right off the Antarctic. All I did today was get ready for the road tomorrow.

Thursday 10th: Left Wiluna early. Travelled north along Cunyu road to the Vermin Fence then followed it through Lake Nabberu north to the 477 Mile. Upon arrival I filled the tanks with good water and had dinner. Roach wasn't home so I went south again. and turned off at the 458 Mile Creek to follow last week's tracks. Travel one mile north at first, then seven miles west to another gum creek. Followed the latter creek down to a small waterhole that might last a few weeks yet. I camped beside the waterhole and went for a walk. Brumby tracks were numerous, along with those of dogs. This is a secluded spot and dingoes like quiet places. Kangaroos and emus were plentiful too, by the look of the tracks that is. One hundred and sixty-six miles all told today.

Friday 11th: I spent the entire day going backwards and forwards between Pinyerinya Rockhole and the 458 Mile, in order to run in a well-defined set of wheel tracks over the hard ground. Pinyerinya Pool will be a splendid base camp from which to work the Western Strip, either for myself while here, or whoever might take over this new 'control area' from me at a later date. Today was hot after the cool spell. One puncture to fix. Fresh dog tracks are absent and ants quite bad around camp here at Pinyerinya.

Saturday 12th: The Olympic Games commence in Mexico City tomorrow. America has sent a three-man team on an eleven day mission in the Apollo space capsule, in preparation for a trip to the Moon next December. While the astronauts are in orbit aboard their weightless craft I rode my ground vehicle under much more gravitational pull. I went downstream along the Pinyerinya Creek for ten miles, the last few through well-grassed flood country. Came upon a small open pool at four miles.

I think that network of flood channels confused me this morning. Somehow I got onto Yadgymurrin Creek. I reached the east-west graded track to Ned's Creek Station, then three miles west to reach Pinyerinya Creek and Pool. It was much further west than I calculated. There could of course be a wide flood loop that I followed around in mistaken belief it was the Pinyerinya. The latter creek might have swung away without my knowledge, hidden amongst the web of flood channels. Once at Pinyerinya again, I went further west to another creek in search of a spring marked on the map. It remains unnamed by the official cartographers but local whites and Aborigines call it Paltju. It

took me some time, but in the end I located Paltju under high sandstone banks within a channel choked by a thick stand of slender gum saplings. Like most permanent springs of this particular type, the outside surround consists of barren rock and bare gravel flats. This one however is different in that the spring itself has not a clump of reeds or rushes to mark it, whereas most others of similar type do. A most peculiar circumstance because Paltju is an alleged permanent spring and if so, should have at least a few reeds about the water, even if the outside area is bereft of vegetation.

A large bar of solid sandstone extends across the creek like a constructed dam wall, from one side to the other, the wall blocks off the creek below the spring. This rock bar would keep a large body of water banked up behind it even in a dry time. Paltju may or may not be an underground stream. Rain replenishes surface supplies however, and even without rain, soakage water should exist deep in the sand for a long time.

I found two ancient sheets of galvanised iron, each dish-shaped to hold water and no doubt used by an oldtime stockcamp to give horses a drink. Ken, and his late father Waddy Hall always used horses to muster cattle. They ran a proper stockcamp with five or six mounted ringers. Ken changed over to motorbike and vehicle only during the past few years, in conjunction with trap yards, to muster cattle.

Strong wind gusts blew a gale all morning and later brought a terrific downpour of rain at midday while I was still at dinner. The most severe and prolonged storm I've experienced in a long time. The rain was heavy and mixed with large hail stones. It continued to fall without a pause for almost four hours then stopped. The storm over I set off east across country to try the shortest route out of the area before I get bogged in and never get out. I'd only gone three miles when the Landrover encountered an unbroken sheet of moving water six inches deep so I had to turn back.

I knew the ground ahead around Grasscutter would be much worse. This is all flood country and no vehicle could ever get through after rain. I returned at once instead to Paltju Creek. The banks of the creek run for long stretches at a greater height than the outside flats that border them. I followed the creek down until it met the graded station track, then ran that road east to the 446 Mile where, It amazed me to find, not one drop of rain had fallen. It was then a dry run north to the 467 Mile breakaways. Once upon the elevated position above an escarpment, I at last felt safe from the floods of any deluge that might hit the country overnight, no matter how heavy the downpour might be. I have quite a complex about floods, ever since I saw the devastation caused by Cyclone Joan along the Yanneri Creek valley.

Went out before dark to hunt a kangaroo for meat and managed to get one. Rusty had fresh uncooked liver for supper, while I cooked the tail blackfella fashion in the ground. The violent storm this afternoon seems to have covered only a limited area a few square miles in extent. Heavy clouds still around at sundown and these persuaded me to rig the tarpaulin in anticipation of a wet night but as it turned out, no rain fell.

Sunday 13th: Went back south to the 458 Mile gum creek this morning and reset traps there. I returned to the 467 Mile on the same task, after which when completed, I went north to the 477 Mile. This time I found John Roach at home. Not long afterwards his neighbours Jack Gaston and Yipi George arrived, to be followed later in the day by their stockcamp and horses. Before sundown they went off down the creek a bit in search of horse feed for the night, while I stayed at John's camp to yarn into the early hours. Warm and clear today with cool winds. Thirty miles travelled.

Monday 14th: We all went down the 477 Mile wash to the east mill and yard this morning to spend the day there. John's cattle came in yesterday. He didn't say from where nor did I ask. Amongst the mob were two cleanskin bulls. Yipi claimed both and without delay decorated them with the Beyondie brand. John's branded his calves too. Today was quite hot and in complete contrast to the recent cold snap. A lot of clouds in the south. The most severe earth tremor ever recorded in Western Australian history occurred today. It caused some damage over thousands of square miles between Perth, Geraldton and Kalgoorlie. A small town called Meckering somewhere in the south-west, suffered severe damage says a news report. Nothing unusual felt here. Twelve miles today.

Tuesday 15th: Cool and clear last night. I had a beaut relaxed sleep for once. It is a wonderful sensation when lulled into dreamland by the constant ding-a-dong of Condamine bells on the still night air accompanied by a lighter jingle of hobble chains as horses grazed on good grass close to camp. The sound of horse bells is nostalgic music to my ears at anytime, but not to Jack Gaston. No sentiment at all in that fellow, he gets irritated by what he calls the hellish din. I'm sure Gaston hasn't spent a lifetime with horses. Most stockmen enjoy the sound of bells near camp.

The Beyondie crowd rode off early this morning to muster more cattle. I would love to have joined them but had other things to do. I set off instead up the fence and reached Kunmah at the 550 Mile for dinner. Refuelled with thirty-two gallons there, which gives a consumption over varied terrain of 13 mpg for the 409 miles travelled since I left Wiluna with full tanks. It seems that fuel dumps ARE an essential at strategic intervals in this area despite Fitzgerald's opinion to the contrary. I carried on north after dinner to Savory Creek to inspect Mick's expensive brisket baits along the track and around Burranbar Pool as instructed. Not one bait touched, nor any fresh evidence of dingoes seen.

The only life observed at Burranbar was a small flock of ducks and one solitary swan. I went on downstream nine miles past the old well at west end of the pool. Checked the area for tracks but saw none, so returned to Savory Well from where travel was north, right through to Jiggalong turnoff. I was to distribute commercial baits all the way in accordance with previous instructions and full Mission approval. That job took me twelve miles east through Jiggalong country to a gum creek where by this time it was almost dark. I camped there beside a small pool of fresh rainwater. Storm clouds about

and a hot humid day. More earth tremors reported to have struck the south-west again last night but this time no damage done. One hundred and seventy-one miles travelled today.

Wednesday 16th: Last night I had a strange dream about Dooley. She told me to make haste to Wiluna. This morning in the light of day the image was still vivid and clear. I wondered could it be that renowned Aboriginal ability to communicate over long distances, and the message be an urgent appeal from the one I love.

Whether my dream was real or fancied I wasted no more time, indeed I wondered what the hell I'd come so far north for anyway. Dooley and I had arranged to meet in Wiluna within two weeks. That time was up, yet here was I almost four hundred miles away when I should be in town ready to meet her. I moved off camp without breakfast and proceeded west to the Great Northern Highway. I fulfilled my obligations to the APB and chucked all the baits out along the road verge for twenty-eight miles to the first sheep fence. That job over and the last one gone, I sped on without further delay down the highway to Beyondie turnoff. Turned west along the

Beyondie track to the fenceline then south to the 477 Mile. Had a quick mug of tea with John and June. Bid them farewell then travelled on to Wiluna, a three hundred and seventy mile run. I inquired the moment I arrived, but Dooley was not yet in town.

Thursday 17th: Last night the dream was stronger than ever. Today I awoke with a sensation of apprehension. It was difficult to explain, but I held rein until time was right for the shops to open. At opening time I went off to the Garage to fill up with petrol. Next I went up the street to the Newsagent and saw the vision of my two dreams, Dooley with white teeth flashing across beautiful dark features, her face crinkled with the pleasure of obvious expectation, stood there with two other girls beside her.

She had arrived in the early morning hours while I dreamt of her and slept. Dooley came to town with the owners of Albion Downs, Jack and Seddon Howard, the latter were to travel overnight from their station to Meekatharra on business. Dooley asked if she could go along as far as Wiluna with them. Her thoughts had of late been about our tryst and she'd expected me to be in town to meet her as planned. So despite my distant position in the north, we had synchronised our individual movements and reached Wiluna at almost the same time. I am not psychic but if that is not telepathic communication then I don't know what is. She left her two mates and we went for a run out to a quiet creek seven miles north of town. In seclusion there, under the fragrance of a gidgea tree overladen with yellow wattle-like blossoms, we clung together in sheer joy at our good fortune. We breathed deep of the scented air around us for some time until almost intoxicated by the heavy sweet bouquet.

At long last our plan reached fruition. Tonight was to be THE night of our lives. We would follow a tradition most suited to our situation. A method often used by lovers in contrast to condoned tribal marriage. A sudden elopement was our plan. This action would shock close friends and relatives into recognition of our union much quicker than any firestick ceremony or give-away procedure could. The end result would be as permanent and true as any Registrar, church pastor, or tribal sanction could make it. To run away together without the tribes' knowledge, is the most adventurous form of marriage amongst Aborigines. Participants savour the thrill of escape and even enjoy the chase if one occurs. We knew the consequences. We knew not to dally in town too long at this stage. If others found out about our plan, they might harass us beyond endurance, even to the point of forced separation. We decided to leave under cover of darkness. Once away from the mob in a vehicle equipped with long range fuel tanks and with knowledge of the desert like I possess, there was no fear of being caught out bush by irate relatives. The initial getaway has to be swift and decisive. Our plan thus hatched to mutual satisfaction, I took Dooley back to town to arrange her small bundle of things. I went off alone to change the Landrover tyres. I fitted new rubber during the long afternoon wait, and sorted out what gear we might need for a prolonged stay away from fellow humans.

The weather today (as if it mattered) was hot and humid with thunder clouds on the move. The chance of a storm in my opinion would add an exotic touch to our romantic escapade.

We decided to meet after sunset in the main street. At that time of day in Wiluna the street is empty of people. Wiluna after all, is a ghost town. While still light enough to see, I drove past the old house where Dooley camped while she waited for me to appear in town. I caught her eye and gave a quick sign to tell her it was time to go, and was pleased to see that no one else had noticed the signal, or that something untoward might be afoot.

I drove on and turned into the deserted main street to wait. Dooley soon came around a corner to my north as twilight enveloped the shops, all long since shut and the owners gone to their homes elsewhere. I could just make out her small figure along with two others as she turned towards me. She had her tiny bundle of clothes in hand. Dooley didn't follow the Landrover and thus attract attention or arouse suspicions. She was astute enough to go around the block and come back from the opposite direction. It was now time for action. Three girls full of giggles crammed into the front seat beside me. Off we went to the northern outskirts of town, a quiet dark spot to say goodbye to the two conspirators who had come to see Dooley off. All lubras love a romantic plot. Intrigue is the essence of life to them. Lubras savour every aspect of a romance from start to finish, even if not active participants. The two girls, Gladys a tribal sister, and the other a niece named Veronica, alighted to strains of renewed merriment and thrilled chatter as the shared secret drew to a climax.

Dooley asked me to buy the girls a bottle of beer each as a token gift. Although not keen on the idea, I left them together in the dark and drove back to the pub. I bought a full carton of Swan Lager and a bottle of rum for myself. As half expected, the town being bereft of boisterous visitors, the publican asked, "What are you up to now Pete, are the Windidda ringers in town, where is the party?" I replied, "Oh no, Barney just gettin' in a bit of a supply for the road that's all." I saw an eyebrow rise in disbelief as I left, but no more said. The bar was empty of customers, so not much to worry about. With some haste I rejoined Dooley and broke the carton open. A bottle each for the two girls and without further delay Dooley got into the passenger seat beside me and we sped off into the night.

To say I was numb with joy would be an understatement. This was the real thing, not just a brief stolen interlude like our former secret trip out bush together. Tonight was the biggest and most important step of my entire life, the culmination of a long sought ambition to have Dooley as my own. I would fight to keep her and she vowed to stay with me no matter who might try to intervene, black white or brindle. We belong to one another. We travelled north to the Vermin Fence then north along it to Lake Nabberu. We spent the night near a ti-tree thicket on an island between the salt channels, a place where I've often camped before. Seventy-six miles travel and sweet dreams.

Friday 18th: We proceeded to Roach's place to say hello on the way past. John and June didn't seem surprised to see Dooley with me for the second time. I told them we had eloped. We joined them for a quick cup of tea then departed for a splendid rockhole. A romantic place oft described by me in these journals before. The rockhole lies about five miles due west of the 485 Mile Well on the RPF, north of Clover

Tabletop in a gum creek. The details of our sojourn are ours alone. Suffice it to say we spent two days in idyllic seclusion together and enjoyed our bush honeymoon undisturbed.

Sunday 20th: Yesterday was ours alone, and certainly not for the journals. The weather is hot and the skies are blue, sixty-nine miles from Nabberu. Time to leave our beautiful rockhole and move off up the creek to Beyondie homestead. We stopped there a while so I could show Dooley off to the George family. They none of them seemed too surprised, nor on the other hand were they overjoyed, just noncommittal and curious. Dooley is not a relative of theirs nor is she known to them. Perhaps they considered it none of their business. I did notice they were less talkative than usual though, so we didn't stay long, just had a brief chat then moved off north along the fenceline to Kunmah and camped. Sixty-nine miles again.

Monday 21st: We went on north to the Savory this morning then downstream east to Donkey Hole. This water was of extreme interest to Dooley, she has never seen an inland creek like this with such strange springwaters. Her Ngalia tribal country is unrelieved desert with few permanent waters. Her people relied for the most part on gnamma holes and other seasonal catchments. I saw where one dog had been at a bait but no sign of a carcase although we both searched for tracks. Back west next to Burranbar Pool but didn't stay long. Dooley was fearful to be in a strange land and

thought she might fall victim to a rainbow serpent when she saw a pool two miles long and quite deep. Burranbar is the largest body of water Dooley has seen in her life. No sign of dogs there anyway, so with nothing to hold me in the area, we returned east to Kimberley Well for dinner. Afterwards we went north to Robertson Range to introduce Dooley to Clarry Helyar. When Clarry saw my new marital state he was not prone to be as voluble as usual so I left him with his trauma and departed forthwith. We drove west to Old Jiggalong to camp the night. Tomorrow will show what sort of reception we might get at the Mission. One hundred and thirteen miles.

Tuesday 22nd: Dooley washed clothes before we left. The clothes dry, we continued north to Jiggalong proper. Upon arrival it was smoko time. The manager Trevor Levine and wife Peggy, disconcerted at first to see me with an Aboriginal female, seemed hospitable enough after introductions. To my amusement they refused to believe she was now my woman. They insisted she must be an unchaperoned passenger from Wiluna. Busy with tea, cakes, and biscuits, we stayed inside for an hour under the quizzical gaze of two native housegirls. They knew me as a single male before, but today because of Dooley's presence were full of giggles.

I gave the text of a telegram to Peggy for transmission to tell Alex Campbell the baiting drive was over. Then we said goodbye to our hosts and walked outside to the Landrover to discover that some black thief had pinched Dooley's cigarettes from the glovebox while we were inside.

Standing in line along the front fence of the Levines' house when we came out were several cheeky faced young bucks, with obvious scorn they stared at us in silent contempt. We felt certain they must be the culprits, but not a thing we could do about it.

"Walyku minyi tananya mulyatapayanu, warpuwa Peter, ngali wupawayi, ngaiyu tjalpu ngaanya." Dooley whispered in Ngalia lingo to me. A literal translation may not appear nice in print but it means: "The rotten thievin' lottta bastids, let's get to hell outa here, this place stinks." An admirable indication of what she thought of Jiggalong's inhabitants. I must say I agreed with her.

Tobacco is not available at the Jiggalong store and it is against mission policy to stock it so, I suppose the blacks think it okay to steal some if possible. We didn't favour their insolent attitude after they stole from us. Visitors deserve more respect than that.

Others of the black population began to ask why Dooley was with me. In the end they began to get cheeky and tense so we departed forthwith before they riot, with us the focal point. On the way out along the western road we had to cross a gum creek with blacks' camps in the sandy bed. One angry old buck tried to wave us down with unusual vigour. He rattled a handful of boomerangs at the passenger side window as we drove past. I didn't stop to pass the time of day, instead I accelerated up the opposite bank to skid the rear wheels and shower the old sod with gravel. In case he retaliate, we

then shot off down the track at full speed to get clear. Farewell Jiggalong. Once on the main road, more out of professional habit than anything, I took a look around some rugged ridge country near the turnoff for dog tracks but saw none. We continued from there north to camp at No 43 government well in order to confuse the Jiggalong mob in the event they chase us. They knew we came from Wiluna and would expect us to head south, not north. A strong south wind tonight and it looks like rain.

Wednesday 23rd: We set off south about mid morning down the main road to Savory Creek. We were not long at rest on the south bank when who should come along but Alex Campbell. He shot past in the proverbial cloud of dust, eyes fixed straight ahead like he always does when driving. Something made him turn his eyes in our direction. His surprise at sight of us beside the track was so great he jammed the brakes on too hard and almost tipped the vehicle over. The sudden stop allowed the dust cloud from behind to catch up and envelop his Landrover for several seconds before it settled. Once stationary Alex alighted to greet us in a serious and agitated tone. After gruff g'days all round he said he was on the way to Jiggalong to try and meet us there. He was happy to catch us, before we disappear into the bush and be hard to find. To cut a long story short he said someone from Wiluna had made a phone call and dobbed us in. Also he could not condone my changed circumstances, with Dooley's relatives upset and quite emotional about the whole business. Alex said the APB could not countenance such a situation at all. Dooley and me I thought, are the only ones jubilant about our being together. Anyway we boiled the billy and offered Alex a drink of tea to cool him down. I thought a bit more on the subject, then offered a fortnight's notice on the spot to ease the tension.

Alex accepted my decision with expressed regrets and will send it down to Perth. In the meantime he headed off south for Meekatharra again. We continued west down the Savory and back to the Rabbit Fence then south. Upon arrival at the 477 Mile we had a good yarn with John and June. I told them of my resignation and why, then afterwards moved on to the 467 Mile breakaways to camp.

Thursday 24th: The notation of one hundred and fifty-four miles yesterday is the last mileage record that will appear in this book. The discipline of daily journals is now over and I revel in such newfound freedom. Dooley and I decided last night that I should cut the fortnight's notice short and chuck the job in today. Incentive to continue is no longer there. I cannot work if my heart is not in it. We travelled into Wiluna under cover of darkness in order to avoid contact with irate black relatives who might spoil our plan.

I left Dooley in care of Constable Allen Phillips at the Police Station for safety while I went to my own camp to collect all the APB gear. I packed sufficient requirements from personal stock into my own private Landrover then drove it back to the Police Station for Dooley to settle in. Allen drove me back to get the government vehicle.

I put all the APB property into the APB Landrover. Constable Phillips signed a receipt for it and the gear is now no longer my concern. All is ready for Alex Campbell or whoever, to pick it up. I thought the constable's attitude a welcome change after the obvious resentment shown us by others. He seemed quite pleased to see us together and assisted in every way to make our departure swift and smooth.

Truth is indeed stranger than fiction, but of course I dare say he wanted to get rid of us so soon as he could and thus defuse the local situation. No lone police officer desires problems with an agitated Aboriginal population. He wished us well and shook hands, then Dooley and I set off immediately for Meekatharra. We were intent on a trip to faraway places like Marble Bar, Port Hedland, the Kimberleys, or perhaps maybe even Alice Springs.

For us Wiluna had become a dead issue and the sooner we got out of the place the better. With a seventy gallon auxiliary fuel tank in our Landrover, together with ample food and water supplies aboard, pursuit by others was right out of the question. No normal vehicle could match ours for long range travel. We laughed about this as we drove into the night.

With the above words, "we drove into the night." the 1968 narrative of a unique three year association with an untracked desert area north-east of Wiluna ended.

We, Dooley and me, and later the APB, now offer in chapters to follow, a comprehensive account of our subsequent colourful and adventurous life together during the past generation of years.

The Author
Leonora
December 1996

INTRODUCTION

I admit to more than a little pride in being a fifth or sixth generation Australian with at least one convict ancestor. The convict was my great-great grandfather William Hunt, who arrived in Van Diemens Land aboard the convict ship Elizabeth on 6 July 1832. He was transported for a period of fourteen years penal servitude for some minor offence. William Hunt obtained permission to marry a free immigrant of Irish descent, one Fanny Mason. Their union took place in Launceston on 14 July 1845. To them a child was born on 18 April 1846 and named William Hunt after his father.

William Hunt the younger, my distaff great grandfather, worked his way successfully through various government departments to eventually become Deputy Sheriff and Clerk of the Peace for what was by this time Tasmania. He was also connected with the defence force of that colony as a gunner in the Launceston Artillery. Much later in 1906 he was appointed Commissioner of Police, but unfortunately took ill soon after the appointment and died 17 May of that year just a fortnight before taking up his post.

Another of my Van Diemens Land distaff ancestors, great-great-great grandfather James Houghton, was a shipwright by trade. He was appointed superintendent of government boat builders by the authorities in Van Diemens Land and a notice to that effect appeared in the Hobart Town Gazette, issue of 6 July 1822. Research indicates that he came out to these shores possibly on a naval vessel, circa 1819. In later life he became a prosperous farmer.

A bit more genealogical research shows that my paternal great-great grandfather Robert Muir sailed from Plymouth aboard the barque Alfred. He arrived at the age of twenty-four years in Port Jackson after a voyage of one hundred and twenty-one days, on Wednesday 16 January 1839. The next morning he had his first view of what was then known as Sydney Town, which he described as a most disagreeable place. The most notable remark recorded in his diary being that George Street was about two miles long. Unimpressed by Sydney Town, he returned to the ship that night to dine on board. Next day he purchased horses, pack and riding saddles, stores, then left immediately for the bush where a partner named Campbell had a cattle station called Glenmore in the Hunter Valley. Great-great grandfather Robert, over the following few years had much experience with local bush natives, and on one rare occasion met a bushranger on the run from police troopers. He made a note in his diary to the effect that the said bushranger had riding alongside him on horseback, a young black gin dressed in boy's clothing, Robert Muir later took up a cattle selection of his own and called it Brezia, or Breezo for short. He married Isabella Ninian Lang my great-great grandmother. The couple settled on Dunmore the property of his Lang family in-laws, where Elizabeth died shortly after the birth of my paternal great grandfather in 1847, to be followed later by Robert Muir at the early age of thirty-six years in 1851. Along with other deceased members of the family both my great-great grand parents are buried in a vault or sarcophagus near Dunmore House.

The controversial character and would-be republican Dr John Dunmore Lang, whose statue now stands in Wynyard Park in Sydney, was my great-great grandmother Elizabeth Lang's uncle. The Lang family arrived in Van Diemens Land aboard the good ship Brixton in 1821. Dunmore House the Muir-Lang family home, still stands near Maitland in the Upper Hunter River district of NSW, but mow much reduced in size, is now occupied by other owners. After reading my great-great grandfather Robert Muir's diary I know I would have been quite at home with him, and in my former drinking days, would have been quite happy to share a bottle of rum with him beside some lonely campfire, even though I realise that could never be, considering the several generations that separate his time from mine.

I have gone to some lengths to provide the above details as a bit of background for my dearly beloved grandmother Florence Hunt who was born in Launceston Tasmania during February 1882. Florence Hunt was a daughter of William Hunt the younger, referred to in paragraph two of this text. She later moved to the mainland and married into the Rothwell family to produce two daughters and one son. The youngest daughter Bertha born in 1911 was my mother who later married John Muir. In 1929 I came along, although I don't recall all the circumstances of that illustrious event, being a bit young at the time. To cut a long story short as that overworked saying goes, my parents parted when I was still a toddler. My old grandmother became the woman of my life after that separation and I remained with her until the age of twelve.

There is no doubt in my mind that those first twelve fascinating years of my early youth laid the groundwork for even more interesting times ahead. I never knew my grandfather, he died long before I was born. My father didn't want anything to do with his first born, and my mother because of the separation had to work for a living. I only had fleeting glimpses of her, she played little part in my upbringing being always away somewhere else.

Grandma as I always called her, grew up in the atmosphere of what people these days refer to as the Victorian Era. She always sought work in far-off places of outback NSW. Pastoral properties, wheat farms, country towns, she went from one housekeeping job to another. We always travelled by train. And remember this was back in the 1930s when steam engines ruled the rails. Oh what nostalgic recollections I have of those journeys by train. The deep throated roar of the engine's whistle blasting the cold night air. Boyhood nose stuck to a frosty window pane as the train clicketty clacked over uneven rails, with carriages swaying to and fro all the while. We mostly travelled overnight. Sometimes we had to change trains in the we small hours. This nearly always meant a cold shivering delay at some wayside stop. The passenger waiting room would have a big open fireplace with back logs ablaze around which the adults would sit and chat, but I never seemed able to get close to the fireside. A porter or station attendant would come in every now and again to stoke the fire and keep the waiting adult passengers cosy and warm.

The expected transfer train would eventually herald its arrival at the lonely stop with yet another deep throated roar through the darkness outside. The train would huff and puff to a halt at the lonely station and blow off steam with an even greater roar than the whistle blast. Then with a bit more huffing and puffing we would soon be off again to yet another exotic destination.

Those train travelling days certainly did gladden the heart and provide fodder for fanciful boyhood dreams. Once arrived at our destination, the owner of whatever property we were bound for, would meet the train and transport us thence in a vintage vehicle of one kind or another. On rare occasions we were sometimes met by a horse drawn buggy and pair. Our eventual arrival at yet another strange and often decrepit well-weathered homestead, was a source of never ending adventure for me. The scented aroma of candlesticks, hurricane lamps, and woodfire stoves would waft on the early morning air as we took stock of our new abode in the pre-dawn light. Such lifestyle was the norm during my childhood out in the backblocks.

Hospitality to all travellers was obligatory in those days. The homestead dining tables would seldom seat less than eight or ten. All food was home cooked, and roast legs of mutton or beef followed by fresh hot scones, were a regular part of daily fare.

I enjoyed a quite diverse education. At age twelve I lay in bed one night and counted a total of thirty-two different country schools attended during those early years. Most of them were the single room variety staffed by only one teacher who had to handle several primary classes all day without assistance. I was never a scholar, and never aspired to be one. My only real ambition in life during childhood was to be with horses and cattle. I intended to be another Clancy of the overflow or man from Snowy River when I grew up. I often too had thoughts of one day going bush with a tribe of nomadic Aborigines. I would often make toy spears and boomerangs to play with when without the company of other kids, as I often was on some of the properties where grandma worked.

Grandma eventually decided to bundle me off to complete the last two years of elementary education at a high school. By this time it was 1941 and I surmise, that the 1939 War may have played some part in her unwelcome decision to pack me off. I also suspect that her twelve year old grandson might have become a bit too much for the old lady to handle. Anyway I did complete school, right up until the day I turned fourteen. School holidays were on at the time and I never went back after that break.

During that same end of term school break the smell of horse dung one day wafted across my nostrils and the bellow of bullocks in a nearby paddock hit my ears. Then a travelling horse dealer came along. The dealer had a mob of forty or more horses and was walking them all over the country, or droving if you like, from place to place in search of sales. He agreed to take me along as offsider at £1-0-0 a week and keep. A one pound note is the official oldtime equivalent of our current two dollars, but of course back then it was a huge sum of money. One pound then could buy a hundred times or maybe more, than what two dollars does now.

I spent twelve months with that horse dealer, riding in the saddle all over the country, and learned more form him in that one year than some so-called horsemen learn in a lifetime. The long and short of it is that I left the travelling dealer and headed for the cattle country out along the Birdsville Track north of Marree in South Australia. For the next twenty years I followed full time cattle and horse work, either on foot in a stockyard, or riding in the saddle all the time. In addition to South Australia, I roamed all over the Northern Territory and Western Queensland before coming across to WA in 1959 in search of the last vestiges of real horse and cattle work. Those twenty years of full time stockwork as a ringer, put me in regular contact with tough whites and tribal Aborigines. It may sound corny but I really did love the lifestyle of camping on the ground out under the stars each night. Exotic is too weak a word to describe the richness of regular life in the unfenced bush and whole days spent in the saddle.

As a youngster I never had much opportunity to enjoy female company and if the opportunity had arisen I must admit my first preference would have been for a fullblood Aboriginal girl. Someone I could relate to and who would be accustomed to life in the bush. Work on cattle stations or droving the stockroutes with bullocks on the hoof, does not provide much contact with female company of any kind. It is hard work with long hours and little time for rest.

As diesel road trains took over from the drovers and modern methods made inroads on the cattle properties, pure saddle work became increasingly hard to get, so that men like me began to seek those few places further out, the last frontiers where mechanisation did not yet prevail.

My search brought me to Western Australia and after a couple of years in the Gascoyne, I ended up in the little township of Wiluna. By this time the stations around Lake Carnegie east of Wiluna were also on the verge of displacing stockmen with vehicles. Drovers had already vanished, due to the advent of road trains not long prior to my arrival on the scene. I was by this time somewhat disheartened to see the end of a horse mounted era vanish in front of my eyes.

The only genuine bush work of any appeal to me after demise of the stockhorse, was to become a dogger with the Agriculture Protection Board, the APB. The only catch being that in those days of 1964, a prospective applicant to that august government department for a dogger's job, had first to produce a four wheel drive vehicle of his own. In other words a man had to outlay a considerable sum of money just to get the job.

Being fortunate in that I was never one to waste my meagre resources, I had sufficient in the bank to buy a second-hand Landrover, so hopped on the local mail plane which was at that time one of the last Douglas DC3's in regular flight. After a bumpy ride to Perth, I purchased the vehicle and set off that same day back to Wiluna. Because I was not accustomed to city traffic, the salesman had to drive me out to the Great Northern Highway and put me on the road, he then caught a Taxi back to town. That was my first ever trip to Perth.

The allocated dogging area was along the Ashburton Fall, in a stretch of rugged untracked and totally unoccupied country, behind the pastoral properties known as Mount Augustus, Dooley Downs, Elliott Creek (now called Wanna) at western end and southern side of the run, and Mount Vernon at the extreme eastern end. That was a most fascinating fifteen months. I eventually wrote a book based on comprehensive field notes kept during that 1964-65 period.

In the early part of 1965 I was offered the opportunity to literally explore a virgin wilderness of isolated desert breakaway systems, sandhills, and open spinifex beyond all station boundaries. This was called a wild dog survey. It covered pure desert country from a salt lake north of Wiluna known as Nabberu, north to the inland flowing channel of Savory Creek and on to Jiggalong.

The western side of this area was bounded by the long abandoned and quite derelict Rabbit Proof Fence. I was to extend the explorations and survey of wild dog movements east from that fenceline, to the then untracked Canning Stockroute. There wasn't even a bullock pad visible on the Canning then. As mentioned earlier in this Introduction, my childhood, and later teenage stockwork days of full time work in the bush, fitted me well for such a task. I wrote four books about that wondrous three year exploration phase. The books were based on detailed field notes recorded beside numerous smoky campfires at the end of each long interesting day, between the years 1965-68.

I said before that my one romantic ambition in life was to one day wed a fullblood Aboriginal girl. My ingrained psyche would never consider any other option. I was three full years on that exploration job and during that time met the desired fullblood woman of my dreams. In her own sphere she was as widely travelled in the bush as myself. Known far and wide as Dooley, she was and still is, highly respected by both black and white. Before we met, she was already a notable character in her own right. A real daughter of the Dreaming. As a child Dooley knew the nomadic desert life of her old people from personal experience, before settling down on the inside pastoral country. We were a perfect match when we first got together and still are. The following narrative describes only the first two of our wonderful thirty odd years together.

I dedicate this book to Dooley.

The author
February 2000

Figure 6 APB Supervisors inspect Rabbit Proof Fence 1968

Chapter One - CHERISHED REFLECTIONS

NOVEMBER 1968

The morning of Friday 25 October 1968 saw Dooley and me in Meekatharra where who should be the first person we saw other than Mick Fitzgerald my recent Agriculture Protection Board supervisor. Mick greeted me with the news that he was quite glad to have spotted me in town. He had a load of beef brisket on board for me to begin a baiting drive in the Savory Creek area. I'd saved him a trip to Jiggalong he said as he'd expected to meet me there.

I told him I'd resigned and he seemed perplexed at my leaving the APB, he seemed at a loss what to do next but soon regained composure. He expressed surprise that old Alex Campbell my immediate boss had not yet informed either him or the APB of the fact. We exchanged a bit of small talk then shook hands and he departed. I never saw Mick Fitzgerald again after that but did subsequently learn of his untimely death from cancer some years later, poor old Mick.

After Mick left, Dooley and I turned to see a fullblood bush lubra watching us intently. The woman looked out at us from under the verandah shade in front of Elder Smith's Store. Stony faced and without a word uttered, the lubra stared and stared. We reckoned our obvious close relationship puzzled this lone woman because mixed marriages between Aboriginal and white were by no means the socially accepted norm in those days.

The encounter with Mick had been out in the full glare of bright sunlight on the roadway. As eyes adjusted to the verandah shade, I focused on the individual watching us. This bush lubra wore nothing but a light cotton, low neck, sleeveless dress. This revealed in great detail a profusion of tribal welts or cicatrices on both her upper arms and between her breasts. In profile, daylight glinted through a hole in the woman's nose. Pierced nasal septums are common among tribal folk. After a brief perusal I recognised her as a recent arrival at Jiggalong, she was one of several natives from desert regions centred on the McKay Range and Rudall River country.

Those last desert nomads had roamed an area not far north of where I'd carried out exploration work for the APB along outer desert reaches of the Savory Creek. Our intent female observer remained silent and after curt nods of mutual recognition we left her to move on about our own devices.

There was not much for us to do in Meekatharra other than top up the seventy gallon fuel tank and replenish our stores for the proposed trip north. This done we moved on to the Post Office corner, opposite the Meekatharra Hotel, where we met one coloured lady named Bessie Wheelbarrow, an irate relative of Dooley. Bessie took her tribal niece to task for her unsanctioned elopement with me.

After a short initial tirade of mild abuse, Mrs Wheelbarrow caused me some amusement with her quaint brand of English. She sort of got her articulation back to front as she addressed Dooley, "What did you want to run off like that with a whitefella for. We don't know where you got to. **I'm not very popular with you my girl,** you shouldn't a done that, **I'm not very popular with you at all.**" Of course she meant we weren't very popular with her, but in her excitement got her expressions out of kilter. Her anger didn't last long and she was soon passing the time of day as though nothing untoward had occurred.

Soon after this little incident with Bessie Wheelbarrow we left the main street of Meekatharra behind to travel the so-called Great Northern Highway. A much too narrow stretch of bitumen, afforded reasonable travel for a few short miles. Then the sealed stretch ended with a sudden clatter and roar of disapproval from the Landrover. The unwelcome change occurred opposite a huge signboard that bore the most inappropriate legend imaginable: **WELCOME TO THE NORTH WEST.**

Once past Karalundi Mission I decided to give the UNWELCOME corrugations best for a while so left the main highway to head off at a tangent, north-west along the road to Mount Vernon. I wanted to show Dooley the Pingandy country where in 1964-65 I'd worked for the APB as Dogger along a rugged stretch of jumbled ridges and tangled gum creeks known as the Ashburton Fall. Our trip north would be quite a new experience for Dooley and a chance for me to revisit old campfires.

Captain Scott and his lifelong mate Ethel had established a new cattle station since I left the area on the 29th of August 1965. Whereas previously the country had been untracked and uninhabited, their new earlyday style little homestead now had a graded road right to the kitchen door. Nearby a small undulating switchback aerodrome ran the length of a cleared ridgetop above a gorge. The house and station buildings nestled within a tight gully below the airstrip, beside a springwater known by the most unimaginative name of Flat Rock.

I had obviously misjudged my expected reception. The Scotts were not their usual cheerful selves. They used to put out the welcome mat for all visitors no matter who, but today however, they seemed displeased and annoyed at our unannounced appearance on the scene

I soon realised it was my newfound marital status that upset them so. Our presence seemed to disturb them. There was an obvious note of rejection in the air. Eventually Ethel broke the silence. In well-remembered tone of voice Ethel said she had not expected me to turn up at her door with a fullblood lubra on my arm. Eventually though, Ethel thawed, as did her husband Captain Scott and they quickly regained their normal composure. We were then without further ado invited to have a cup of tea.

Afterwards I took Dooley with Landrover to an abrupt fall on other side of the airstrip ridge. In four-wheel drive we wended our way down the steep slope to the cliff-like banks of what Captain Scott calls with his usual lack of inspiration, Head Creek. I had wanted to travel several miles south downstream to show Dooley some of my former discoveries in that direction. Back in those days the country was still wild and uncluttered by homestead infrastructure, or switchback airstrips.

Fourteen miles away the spectacular "Not Riley's Gap" and at seven miles "Dingo Soak" with a short distance beyond the latter, a cliff face marked with strange inscriptions reminiscent of hieroglyphs. I wanted to show Dooley all these things, plus several other points of interest. However it was not to be, the day was by now much too hot for off-road work. We decided against the rough trip for fear we breakdown in the heat. Instead we went to a nearby hidden soak I knew. An unusual native water in the creek bed, concealed by a stone slab lid.

That done we returned to the homestead to bid the Scotts farewell then started back along our tracks for the notorious, but much too narrow bitumen strip, known officially as the Great Northern Highway. We pulled up and camped the night near Balloon Pool, native name Pilyuwan.

Pilyuwan is a small shallow well in the sandy bed of a gum creek. The little well is near the ruins of an old hotel once located on this headwater channel of the Murchison River. It is beautiful fresh clean water despite the presence of small fish. Dooley told me she saw the Balloon Pool Hotel in full swing some years ago. She was little more than a girl then, out this way for a short time with goat musterers from Wiluna.

On the road again, we arrived next day at the wayside pub Kumarina, in one piece despite the corrugations, and decided to have a few days spell. We had no other commitments and Kumarina seemed as good a place as any to linger awhile. The day was hot and the beer cold as we sat on the front verandah with a clear view to north and south along the famous so-called highway.

Unbeknownst to us there were two housegirls employed at the pub. They came out to join us on the verandah later in the afternoon. Ruth Kelly I knew from Jiggalong. She turned out to be one of Dooley's tribal cousins. Her friend the other girl, we didn't know before, but we soon did. Our little foursome then enjoyed an unexpected companionship over the next few days, before moving on once more.

Kumarina is not only a wayside pub, it is also the homestead hub of a cattle station. We watched from the verandah, the transport of an upright windmill tower, complete with head wheel, balanced precariously on back of a truck. Somehow the tower remained vertical as the truck passed by. A bore site near a creek two hundred yards north of the pub was the mill tower's destination. An upright tower on back of a truck was a remarkable sight to say the least. I still can't work out how they managed it without mishap.

My old Landrover was an open back utility type with single cab. I noticed out front of the station workshop at Kumarina, a similar model to my own with a hardtop canopy. A full length cab for our Landrover was just what I needed for an all weather camp vehicle. Although I expected a gruff rejection to the proposal, I offered to swap my single cab for the hardtop and got a most pleasant surprise. The owner agreed to the deal without hesitation and we made a straight swap, my single cab for his full length hardtop. There was no money involved. I couldn't believe my luck. They unbolted their hardtop, I unbolted my short cab, and the deal was complete.

It took me half a day to fit my hardtop acquisition to the vehicle, but was well worth the effort to have an open interior from front to rear. How pleasant to reach back for an object stored immediately behind the front seat, rifle, water or whatever, all within easy access.

We watched the housegirls make off along the highway on foot a few times. We thought it was for leisure until we noticed how truck drivers often followed them. The trucks managed to draw level with the girls for what seemed a planned tryst. This would be when the girls got about half a mile up the road. The antics of the girls and those who chased them was none of our business, but it was certainly a great source of amusement. After a few days at Kumarina we left the roadside lovers to their own devices and departed north once more.

Next stop was near Roy Hill Station and the Wittenoom turnoff. We pulled up early to make camp beneath an overcast sky. The sun was not visible. Dooley being in strange country by now was a bit disoriented and asked which way was north. She was slewed properly because she pointed east and when I put her right she disputed the fact.

In order to settle the argument I took her across to the Landrover and showed her the compass bearing on the instrument I had mounted at eye level above the driver side. She had never had experience with such things before so of course had no in-built faith in such. I tried to explain in basic English how a compass works but to no avail. "North is over there" she said, pointing east again.

No one could ever lose Dooley in her own country, I knew this, but the extended travel with its consequent twists and turns in a strange land unknown to her, had confused her sense of direction. I took pains to explain once more to Dooley how compass needles work and then continued to amuse her no end by pointing to magnetic north. So convinced was she that her sense of direction was unimpaired she just looked at me with a sort of pitiful expression on her face and responded with: **"You and your bloomin compass."**

Twilight came and the cloud cover fell away to a starlit night. Dooley soon regained her bearings when the familiar constellations appeared overhead. Some time elapsed however before she would believe a compass could point north. For a long time she could not understand her confusion.

The following morning we did some washing in a nearby claypan full of fresh water. Nullagine was the next goal in what turned out to be a gauntlet of deep corrugations that shook the Landrover almost to pieces. The exhaust pipe was loose on the manifold and the engine noise became worse as the miles passed. There were no mechanics or repair facilities in Nullagine so instead of continue north to Marble Bar, I thought to return over our tracks and have a look at Wittenoom instead. The scenery en route was spectacular, no argument about that, but the engine roar once the exhaust pipe parted company with the manifold was torture on the ear drums. Wittenoom was a welcome destination indeed. The one garage there agreed to do the job, but had other work to do first. He said we could pull up and camp out front to one side of his workshop. This was most convenient as otherwise it would have meant an unpleasant ear shattering trip out of town to camp.

Repairs to the exhaust took three days to complete. We met a local identity who was putting a plant of horses together, ready he said to go contract mustering. There were horses all over the town, on every lawn in every street. I can't recall now, but think his first name was Scotty. An apparent lover of stockwork and horses, he somehow knocked out a living in Wittenoom. Scotty worked for the local Shire and also owned a small pig farm. He wanted us to shift camp a couple of miles out to his farm paddock. We didn't know him well enough though, so declined. The garage owner said Scotty was a good bloke and quite popular in Wittenoom, except for when his horses ripped into the prized flower beds of local residents.

Our business in Wittenoom over, we returned east after dark along the Roy Hill road and pulled up to camp in a mulga thicket. It was a pitch black night. Dooley and I bought four bottles of beer in town. We rolled our swag out in back of the vehicle. The night air was still hot after a scorcher of a day. We thought to relax when all of a sudden, a piercing whine from the darkness startled us both out of our wits. The weird noise continued unabated for several minutes, enough to terrify the faint hearted it was. Dooley was sure it must be a spirit of the dead singing out, she hung onto my arm in apprehension. As for me, I thought at first we must be under attack from some lunatic camped in the scrub. I grabbed my handgun from under the pillow just in case. I tried to imagine some rational explanation for the noise. Then the reason came to me in a flash as the vehicle sank with a pronounced slope toward the driver side rear. It was sudden leakage of high pressure from a small stake hole in an overheated tyre. Hot compressed air released in a banshee wail. It scared the daylights out of us. What an anticlimax that was. There was me, alert with gun at the ready, anticipating attack at any moment by a madman, but no lunatic emerged, it was only a flat tyre.

We slept on the slanted bed without further incident. I repaired the tyre next morning then continued our journey to Nullagine. The recent introduction of free drinking rights for Aborigines in WA had swelled the population of the little wayside town. The nearby creekbed held at least a hundred fullblood people camped between the gumtree lined banks. A scene reminiscent of Alice Springs, it was just like that latter town's famous Todd Creek filled Aboriginal residents. Long before drinking rights were even contemplated, the Arunta tribal folk of Central Australia favoured sandy creek beds as campsites. However I had not expected such an influx of this nature in Nullagine. The place had been an all but deserted hamlet during my first visit in 1959.

We arrived about midmorning when the pub was quiet, with only a half dozen whitefellas breasting the bar. Dooley and I were the only customers in what we took to be the saloon or lounge. This was a large room with tables and chairs separated from the main bar by a wide service window.

As I ordered a couple of cold beers I recognised one of the white customers on the other side as a former station manager named Colin McDonald. He was at this time a Regional Vermin Control Officer with the APB. The last time I'd heard of him he'd been manager on Munarra Station north of Meekatharra, a bit south of Karalundi. He recognised me as a former dogger with the APB and nodded to me from across the bar. That was the only welcome we got out of the Nullagine Tavern.

The other drinkers merely stared in disdain. No doubt those bar flies took exception to our mixed race relationship. Such unions were not the accepted norm in those bygone racist days. Dooley and I ignored them anyway and enjoyed our half hour of solitude seated at a table with cold beers in hand. We found each other sufficient company for our needs. There were no other customers on our side of the service area and in view of the large Aboriginal population seen along the creekbed outside we wondered why.

Tommy Stream an old acquaintance of mine from my Marble Bar 1959 days, entered the room to buy a beer, then came across to seat himself at our table. Tom was an APB Group Dogger. We were about ready to have a spell during the midday heat when Mister Stream invited us to come have a shower at his place on the outskirts of town.

Being hot and sticky we jumped at the suggestion to cool off. Of course the accepted thing to do in that country of notorious "Bloody good drinkers" [sic] would be, to always take along at least one carton of good cheer. Dooley and I didn't want to get involved with any drinking sprees though, so we went along to the dogger's tin shack, minus any beer. Our lack of local courtesy resulted in no shower for us. Tom's wife told us her bathroom was out of order. We bid the couple a curt g'day and drove on up the gorge a bit to boil the billy for dinner under the shade of a river gum.

Upon return to town later in the afternoon we found the pub almost bursting at the seams with inebriated Aborigines. The most memorable of which was one drunken old lubra seated beneath the table we had occupied, when that same room was empty earlier in the day.

The drunken old lady held the floor with bottle of beer in hand, while other most voluble companions cavorted around her. She appeared quite oblivious to the crowded conditions above her head and continued to occupy her chosen floor space as though it was the normal way to drink in a pub. With that comical scene impressed on mind, we departed Nullagine and headed up the track toward Marble Bar.

The country north of Wittenoom and Nullagine was strange and new to Dooley. She revelled in the coloured landscape but seemed puzzled by the complete lack of mulga trees. I worked for several months in the Pilbara during 1959-60 so to me the region was more familiar. For one thing I knew it was difficult, if not impossible to find firewood in some parts. Dooley soon became acquainted with this fact. We pulled up to boil the billy beside a windmill located in open spinifex a few miles south of Marble Bar. We looked for firewood in vain. Not even the smallest stick could we find.

Gumtrees mark the course of most creeks in the Pilbara. A flock of cockatoos can tear the upper branches of a tree to shreds. Destructive birds nip and tear with beak and claw at all within reach. They scatter fallen twigs and leaves in great abandon under their perch.

Creeks are a common source of detrital firewood in Marble Bar country. We went on to the first creek in search of such fuel for a fire and collected a bundle of small sticks sufficient to boil the billy. We enjoyed a sparse meal of tinned meat and dry biscuits. A pair of lovers should need more than such hardtack to sustain their ardour but we did well on it. When scorched by the midday sun it is pleasant to rest awhile until the day cools. The air was hot and shade from scraggly gumtrees near our dinner camp almost absent. We had no desire to hang back in the heat so continued our journey to Marble Bar.

I digress for a short paragraph as follows: "In the 1960s, the pace of life was peaceful and slow. In the 1960s there was no great surge of mineral exploration or other frenzied mining activity as prevails now in the 1990s. Near the end of the 1960's Aborigines got Free Rights and the privilege to drink alcohol.

Free Rights for Aborigines to enter hotels and drink was a tragic mistake for government to make. The Free Rights factor alone completely altered the face of the bush. The legendary outback changed virtually overnight. Dooley and I had come to Marble Bar from Wiluna where those Free Rights had not at that time in 1968, yet been granted."

We arrived in town late in the afternoon. The main street seemed unchanged since 1960. The town population however had increased beyond belief. An influx of Aborigines with the legal right to drink now dominated the local pub in great numbers.

Marble Bar has one liquor outlet known as the Ironclad Hotel. This pub is an old style building made of corrugated iron. When Marble Bar gets one of its famous long runs of 100 degree temperature the pub is the hottest place in town. Being the oasis where drinkers congregate, the hottest days draw the most patrons.

We got into town near the end of a torrid day to find the public bar packed to capacity. We thought to be strangers in town but to the contrary, we ran into two of Dooley's Wiluna relatives when we entered the pub. Jean and her father Scotty Tullock came to breast the bar alongside us.

A throng of Aborigines packed the bar. The room held standing room only. A babble of talk in the crowded space was a sustained roar. The din just about lifted the roof. The crowded room made it difficult to get service at the bar. We were the proverbial strangers in town. Scotty being a regular, knew the run of the ropes and managed to order drinks.

A native to one side of us had eyes on me. As a teenage youngster I submitted to Aboriginal law. My nose has a hole to take a bone ornament. The intent observer bent his body to get a better look. It was apparent the nasal hole was his focus of attention. Confirmation of the fact came when he turned to friends and pointed at my face. The scrutineer and his mates began a corroboree stomp on the floor right there in the crowded bar. I was the unwitting central figure of a dance that fairly shook the building. It was so obvious they knew I was a tribal initiate. From their perspective the performance was to honour my status in their eyes. The tempo of the impromptu act increased. The whole thing was so ludicrous in such a public place.

Scotty Tullock saw my embarrassment. With a few curt words he brought the thing to an end. He said: "Hey! leave the poor bugger alone you fellas, can't you see you makin' him shame?" The action slowed, then ceased. Some of the dancers pressed closer to shake my hand. Formal introductions out of the way we downed our drinks then left the hotel.

From the pub we went some ten miles west of Marble Bar to Moolyella and Scotty's camp, a large bough shed built on top of a stony hill. A unique site it was, set amidst a barren scene of rocky sun-scorched ridges and a sparse growth of spinifex tussocks.

We went inside the bough shed where Daisy Tullock produced a bottle of hot plonk and offered us a drink. "No thanks" said we in unison, "We never drink the stuff." How anyone can drink wine in a hot country is beyond me. Drinking beer is bad enough on a person's constitution, but fortified wine, all I can say is "ugh."

Billy, a chap I'd known in 1959, came inside and joined us at the table. He showed me no recognition other than a polite g'day. He didn't share our qualms about the merits and demerits of wine in a hot climate either. Without hesitation he joined old Daisy at the table to help her finish the bottle.

I first met Billy in Marble Bar when he worked at Limestone Station a short distance from town. The owner cum butcher whose name I forget, delivered fresh meat once a week to local mine camps and the town itself. Billy was the butcher's slaughter yard assistant. Billy's marriage was plural, his partners being Minnie and Polly. The younger of the two was a real coquette if ever there was one. She had a "dog ticket" back then in 1959, or Citizenship Rights, to give the correct term, and was thus entitled to drink at the pub. She was a real tease, make no mistake. Any male who drank with her at the bar was due for a shock. Those who spent lots of money to buy her grog, and at the end of the session wanted in, she always kept out. She'd chop their wishing tree down with an unexpected crash. The story goes that this female teaser thought to snuff the flames of one such optimistic lover's urge out at the Two Mile one night, but on that occasion she made a slip. The frustrated male suitor, ablaze with inner fires of lust, forced himself upon her. She was at first reluctant to participate, but suddenly had a change of heart and relished the event, while her rightful spouse slept off a drunken stupor in the creek nearby.

Eight years after the events described I was curious as to Billy's present circumstances. I learned that he and Scotty now worked together on a nearby mine. After he and Daisy finished the bottle of wine, Billy left. Daisy told me then that both his two former wives were deceased, Billy now being a widower.

Dooley and I went off to have a look at a new store located between Scotty's camp and Marble Bar. The owner of the store was another 1959 acquaintance of mine named Jimmy Jeffreys. Jimmy and I had worked at the Comet Goldmine for the Stubbs family. I was a truck driver there at the time, on the ore run to Copper Hills.

Jimmy was the son of a Scottish couple who owned a small store in Marble Bar. He remembered me at first sight and took one of my cheques in payment, without hesitation, for some pretty dresses that caught Dooley's eye.
As mentioned before, cohabitation between lubras and whitemen was uncommon in 1968. Dooley and I were careful not to drink too much while in Marble Bar. After the initial experience at the pub we avoided it like the plague. We enjoyed instead to observe the daily behaviour of townsfolk. During the few days we were in and out of town we liked to park our vehicle across the street from the hotel.

The police did their best to intimidate us. They would park their vehicle close by and stare. No response from us, we ignored their presence. They did this so often it irritated me, but we never let on that we noticed them. We just stood our ground until they tired of their harassment and went away. On several occasions we saw them rough-handle drunken Aborigines. The police picked them up by legs and arms and literally threw them into the back of the monkey cage.

One day an Aboriginal family group came up to Dooley in the street and claimed her as a daughter. They were complete strangers to her, but they persisted. They asked for money but we refused for obvious reasons. Once given money they would be on the bite every time they saw us.

The Aboriginal family asked, but when informed of where we came from they appeared to have no knowledge of Wiluna or Meekatharra. Then they tried a different tactic. In reference to my presence they said it was all right their daughter had a whitefella. Their ruse being a prelude to try and milk me as a newfound son-in-law.

Ulcerated sores covered their arms and legs. They were not clean. Dooley sidled away from them in distaste until safe behind my back. I edged her into the cafe doorway at our rear and once inside, ordered glasses of soft drink to while away the time. The ulcerated family of obvious bush folk didn't follow us. The shop proprietor to our surprise, made us most welcome, in contrast to the rejection we anticipated at such time and place.

Jean Tullock was a town resident at the time of our visit. She invited us to a party that supplied our first taste of how Pilbara folk relax. We expected the party to provide a few cartons of beer.

Dooley and I are still bush folk at heart, but in 1968 our ignorance of how the other half lives was supreme, kegs of beer being unheard of outside a hotel. We knew only of bottled beer or cans in cartons, not full-blown kegs at private backyard parties. Jean's party produced two big kegs, Scotty Tullock her dad in charge. We wished to remain sober, so did not drink more than two glasses each.

We left early when the others became too merry. The only thing of interest to me at the gathering was the presence of two more acquaintances from the 1959 era. Present for the occasion were Jack and Doris Mitchell, now nine years down the track, Jack by now a bit frail but still an active drinker. Doris appeared unchanged by the years. They both worked on Warralong Station when I left that district in 1960. We left the party goers to their fun, our departure not noticed by anyone.

Marble Bar being too boisterous for us we spent each night camped a few miles out of town near the racecourse. The latter was likewise our campsite after we left the keg party. Next day I took Dooley to Chinaman Pool a notable scenic attraction in a large gum creek not far west of town. We boiled the billy there and took a few colour slides, then back to town and on toward the main highway. We were now off to Port Hedland and points along the way. In accord with our usual custom we bid nobody farewell. Being so in love with one another we cared not for anyone. The world was ours alone.

The Port Hedland road has lots of river crossings. South of the road lay distant views of pastel coloured ranges. Up the Coongan River at about three miles, a prominent gap looks just like gaps in the Alice Springs area. Remnants of the old long-since abandoned train line from Port Hedland to Marble Bar are still visible at the Coongan. We pulled up and walked along the riverbed to give Dooley a closer look at the scene.

An APB dogger came along in a battered old Landrover overloaded with camp gear and his entire family of six. We watched from a distance as he pulled up under a shade tree and got out to look the ground over for dingo tracks, while his kids took off helter skelter up the creek. Their goal was a stand of trees growing in the channel itself. We soon saw what they were up to when they started to collect edible seeds hanging from the branches. Dooley showed keen interest as the trees concerned do not exist in her Ngalia tribal country.

Wages for Pilbara doggers are part government money and that of pastoralists, so because it is a joint group scheme, the station owners play a more active role in the doggers' work. My experience with the APB was quite different. I enjoyed a unique lack of supervision. For me to see a boss more than twice a year was unusual. My position was one of trust. A written report to head office each month was the only check on my activities. I had known this local dogger before, but did not bother to go along and renew the acquaintance. We were some way further down the creek from where he pulled up anyway.

We later resumed our journey until level with Warralong Station Outcamp near the Shaw River. I worked on Warralong for John Hardie in 1960. We saw only a deserted outcamp today, and no sign of use in ages. My memories of it were those of bustling activity at shearing time. We stayed a short time to show Dooley where I once worked then left to continue on our way.

A few miles further along the road, on east bank of the Shaw River in 1960 was a market garden. The farmer commuted from Port Hedland each weekend. He employed an elderly Aboriginal couple as caretakers during his absence and came out at the end of each week to collect vegetables to sell in town.

There was no garden nor sign of recent activity during Dooly and my 1968 visit. The place was derelict and deserted. The old enterprise now marked by only a few rusty sheets of iron and two garden posts left standing by the last flood.

Wide open spinifex plains run from Warralong most of the way to Port Hedland, broken only by small rocky outcrops here and there. We pulled up beside one such ridge where native fig trees clung to crevices in the rocks.
Dooley had never seen native fig trees before, although she knew about them from her old folk, as similar trees exist in far-flung reaches of her tribal land. The Aboriginal name for native figs in Ngalia language is yili. My knowledge of these figs extends back many years to the Northern Territory.

Port Hedland's southern mangrove swamps, crossed by a long narrow causeway, gave in this year of 1968, an unwelcome entry into town. Further on, a new industrial area where, due to the upsurge in iron ore mining, were new buildings under construction. An artificial avenue of corrugated iron, steel girders, cement bricks, and concrete foundations, ran all the way to the outskirts of town.

The first open business we came to on the edge of town was a big petrol station and garage. I pulled in to refuel and got the shock of my life to find the owner was my old boss John Hardie of Warralong. So pleased he was to see me again, that he gave us personal service at the bowser, to the consternation of his numerous employees who stood and stared with mouths agape. He told me he no longer owned Warralong.

I don't think Dooley saw much that she liked about Port Hedland, and to be truthful neither did I. We had a few drinks at a couple of the hotels just for the heck of it, then went in search of a dress shop. Dooley had no decent clothes. We had no cash at all, our only means of support being my cheque book.

John Hardie had no worries about taking a cheque and to my surprise, neither did the dress shop proprietor. Dooley chose two bright coloured floral frocks and some other odds and ends of clothing to fill her needs. I wrote out a cheque and that was that.

Next stop was to the highest point in town overlooking the Indian Ocean. Dooley had never in her life seen an ocean of sea water before. Dooley got such a shock at the unexpected sight of so vast an expanse of water that she nearly swooned. She was silent for several minutes until she regained her composure then said: "That's the most water I ever seen in me life."

The weather at the time of our visit was a real scorcher. It had been my intention to continue north to the Kimberley and work our way right around to Alice Springs. My desire was to acquaint Dooley with all my old haunts so she could relate to my background, as well as I was able to relate to hers. The heat however was against my plans in that direction. Her face shone with a constant sheen of sweat from the unaccustomed humid climate. Dooley pleaded for us to return south. so, we took a final run north to the De Grey River, where was a large group of Aborigines camped in the sandy bed.

The De Grey is deep and wide at the crossing so we were not close to the people, but could see them away below our line of vision. The only other notable thing we saw here was a the longest train either Dooley or even I could imagine. We now saw for the first time in our lives, an iron ore train coming from Goldsworthy en route the Port. It might seem strange to some people to read that a whitefellow could be so ignorant of what was afoot in the world. The facts are that I am a product of horse and cattle camps, a former ringer and drover, and of later years, from 1964 to 1968, a dogger working in remote areas and desert country.
I saw a look of sheer relief light Dooley's features as I swung the Landrover around and headed back along our tracks through Port Hedland en route points south. We delayed for half an hour at the Coongan crossing, to cool off in a shallow pool. Dooley was in joyous mood frolicking in the water and I got some good colour slides of her. With pannikin she was splashing an arc of spray toward me to make action shots for the camera.

We bypassed Marble Bar and continued south to Roy Hill country. Once there we pulled up for the night at our former camp by the Wittenoom turnoff. The morrow would see us back in familiar surroundings with not a care in the world and only each other for company, Dooley and me.

Chapter Two - THE ELOPERS RETURN

NOVEMBER 1968 (continued)

Dooley and I broke camp early and left Roy Hill country behind with few regrets. We travelled south to the Fortescue River. We paused awhile beside the river channel to stretch our legs. While at the Fortescue I showed Dooley a type of bramble bush that I knew was unfamiliar to her. A bush that yields edible pods, similar in texture and taste to domestic passion fruit. The bush itself is a tangle of pliable stems adorned with thorns, identical in all respects to a similar species common in the Northern Territory. The only difference between the Fortescue plant and that of the NT being that the NT plant yields yellow fruit, whereas the WA variety is deep pink in colour. We don't know the plant's name in WA, but Arunta folk of Alice Springs call it "arortninga."

We continued south past the Jiggalong turnoff to Mundiwindi to refuel. Mundiwindi must be the most remote and lonely PMG telegraph station in WA. When with the APB I was a regular customer for petrol, purchased from one of the line workers who had a fuel franchise there that he was permitted to operate in his spare time. I was far from pleased when the Mundiwindi fuel supplier told me there was no petrol in the full drum I'd left in his care a month before. No need of a name for the petrol seller now, but I thought of plenty unprintable ones to call him at the time. He had no petrol to spare at all he said, not until more supplies arrive from Meekatharra on the mail truck, and that not due for a fortnight. The only other petrol franchise in the vicinity was Jiggalong, but after our previous unpleasant experience with tobacco thieves and hostile elders there, that so-called Rescue Mission was anathema to us. Jiggalong lies well off the beaten track, and we had no real need to go there anyway, so gave it a complete miss.

My old boss Alex Campbell used to say: "No use to dwell on things Peter." so, in accordance with his advice, we put the Mundiwindi episode behind. Certainly there was no petrol at the telegraph station for us, but why worry, I knew of alternative supplies such as part butts of petrol in drums at some of my old bush stockpiles, and all well within range of what was still in the Landrover tank. There were several such butts left over from my desert explorations. One such dump of part full drums lay concealed on the desert fringe, only seventy to eighty miles away.

Our mutual infatuation was enough to sustain us. I was however in a more mundane context, already nostalgic for old campfires and the carefree desert life we both enjoy so well. Also I had much of interest yet to show Dooley on the desert side. We did indeed leave Mundiwindi in disgust at being let down by the PMG bloke, but not for long. We soon regained our normal cheerful mood and swung southward to the Savory Creek, then headed east, downstream beside the ti-tree choked channel.

We reached Savory Well at forty miles without the sign of a fresh tyre track all the way. The abandoned Rabbit Proof Fence route also showed no sign of traffic, other than my own old tracks from when I was last out that way on the desert exploration job.

It was not so long ago in real time since I left the APB, yet a strange atmosphere of loneliness and abandonment struck me as we drove along. It was not a feeling felt by me before, despite the fact my former presence as a dogger cum explorer was one that saw few intruders during the three years I worked the area. Only on rare occasions did my erstwhile boss Alex Campbell pay me a visit in the bush.

In particular I recall one meeting with strangers that astonished me. A Toyota with three occupants met me on the track one day. They were in my area on behalf of the Lands Department, to assess the desert fringe along east side of the old fenceline for pastoral purposes. One of the three introduced himself as David Harrington. At a later date in Wiluna David called in to my town camp for a yarn. We broached a bottle of rum together and talked of the bush all night. It was daylight before Mister Harrington went back to his accommodation at the pub.

The odd person like myself, who lives and works alone for long periods in remote desert regions, is prone to be jealous of the personal solitude, and even of the country itself. I know for certain how I tend to resent the sudden appearance of intruders onto my solitary desert scene.

Dooley and I left Savory Well behind after breakfast and turned south toward Kunmah, twenty-five miles down the old fenceline. Kunmah being one of my old fuel dumps would supply us with the petrol we failed to get at Mundiwindi.

When we came level with where I met David Harrington last winter, midway between the Savory and Kunmah, near the 555 Mile Peg, I wondered whether I might ever return to this country. This land of pristine sandhills and spinifex always enthrals me. I remain spellbound by it even now, after three full years of exploration work.

Kunmah five miles further on from the 555 Mile Peg, had changed little since my last visit. The only vehicle tacks visible at Kunmah being those made by myself when last here. The shallow well was free of dead birds or animals. The water was fresh and clear. I filled the water tank on the way past the well then went across to the fuel dump a hundred paces further on, to drain the drum butts and refuel the Landrover. That done there was time to relax and enjoy, what could be a last look around Kunmah for a long, long time.

Over the previous three years the Kunmah lake has filled with water to capacity twice, but for the most part it was bone dry like it is today. The fuel dump and my old campsite, were situated on higher ground, atop a mulga clad limestone ridge that skirts the lake on three sides.

One of the old fence riders built a hut here out of limestone rocks in earlier times. The hut nowadays has long since fallen down and only the base of three walls remain. I'm not sure, but I think the rider in question was an oldtimer with the surname George. He pioneered Beyondie Station whilst employed as a fence rider. He and old Yipi, his Aboriginal wife, reared a family of three girls and three boys. Ron George the oldest son, I believe was born right here at Kunmah.

We camped at Kunmah and had a last look around the area in the morning then took off south for Mobadu. My main interest was Smoky Soaks, to which place we turned off east across the spinifex. I reckon Smoky Soaks was my most favoured camp in the whole country, when the basin rockholes on top of the ridge were full. This day however we found every basin dry, bone dry.

It is remarkable just how quick perceptions can change, if seasonal storms fail to replenish a natural water catchment that by all the odds should be full. Water is the fluid of life and when found in abundance close to a good campsite, offers a safe haven for a time. The elevated view from the ridgetop was still wide and clear, but the old campsite being now dry and devoid of water, was one of utter desolation.

A dry camp is not the place to linger long. We next moved on south to the Yanneri Creek (Ilgararie) where I knew water was certain in a hidden soak. AW Canning of stockroute fame was the first whiteman to discover it. I relocated the soak from directions given in his journals when he surveyed a line for the (then) proposed Rabbit Proof Fence in 1904. There are two permanent waters in the Yanneri Creek.

One soak, a cylindrical hole through solid bedrock and covered with brackish muck, has a copious supply of beautiful fresh water when bailed. This soak becomes lost under six inches of mud and sand after each creek flow if not kept open by regular use. A person has to probe with a bar to find it. The site is fifty paces east of the fenceline crossing, in the most northern channel.

A second well dug by Canning lies west, upstream of the fenceline a couple of miles. It is hard to find, but to some extent made apparent by numerous old campsites and rusty tins that surround its vicinity. This second one is a native soak of shallow depth, squared and timbered by whites. Years ago the well had a constructed cover to prevent wildlife from fouling the water. Yanneri Creek must be the saltiest in the country, parts of the channel are pure brine, yet within this salt impregnation are such beautiful fresh waters.

Dooley impressed by the strange existence of fresh water in a salt creek, and her interest aroused, told me of peculiar waters in her own country. She would one day reveal such treasures to me she said, if I ever get the chance first, to take her back to her tribal relatives in Leonora.

Our next destination was Beyondie Station, to see if the George family might be home and indeed, this time they were. Apart from the George clan of boys and girls, was their old mother Yipi, her man Jack Gaston, and two stockmen, Tony Ingebong and Johnny O'Grady. We knew all those present.

Jack Gaston asked my plans for the future, me being at a loose end and no longer a dogger. He and Yipi were establishing a new camp somewhere at the north end of Beyondie, near the Yanneri Creek, as he was not on good terms with Yipi's offspring. They resented the intrusion of a step-parent into their domain, since the death of their natural father some years ago, hence the proposed shift by Gaston and Yipi to a new campsite.

In jest I responded with the quip that a good shade tree to sit under and a long spell from work might be a good idea. Jack thought I meant it and said I was welcome to settle down at his new camp. I had no such intention of accepting that proposition. I reckoned Jack really wished to have me on hand just to use my knowledge of the sandhill country between Beyondie and Savory Creek. I felt his welcome gesture was more to do with wild bush cattle running along lower reaches of the Savory than with any newfound love for myself.

Leaving the Beyondie crowd behind to sort out their own problems we moved on south down the fenceline to visit John and June Roach at the 477 Mile but they were not home. There was no sign of recent tracks around their bough shed so we continued south to the 465 Mile rockhole to camp.

The 465 Mile breakaway is where I kept a regular fuel dump. A couple of hundred paces south of the rockhole is a small mesa, where I always camp when at this water. A gravel flat runs from the rockhole down a gradual slope that comes to an abrupt end atop a low escarpment. The scarp forms a natural siphon platform. I would offload petrol drums on top near the edge, then drive off a couple of miles to skirt the abrupt fall, and come back right below the drum sitting up high on the clifftop. I'd then back the vehicle up to the base of the natural wall and siphon petrol into the tank from the higher drum. This natural feature was an ideal setup.

During three years in this country I cannot recall seeing any travellers anywhere near the 465 Mile rockhole. We camped only a hundred paces or so from the clifftop drum. Next morning after breakfast I walked past the drum and clambered down to the saltbush flat below for the usual toilet requisites. I walked around a bit while down there and naturally left fresh footprints visible on the soft ground. After the morning constitutional, I returned to our camp on top and sat beside the fire with Dooley to finish a mug of tea while we discussed plans for the day.

We were alerted by a low drone like that of a motor engine close by, but saw nothing and silence reigned again. Then we were both startled by the sudden appearance of two figures on the clifftop beside the petrol drum. We recognised one immediately, it was Alex Campbell. We guessed that the other figure must be a new dogger come to take over my recently vacated control area. The two men walked around a bit near the drum then pushed it over the cliff to land with an audible thud below. The thing was a half butt I knew, and could have been siphoned out by myself, but I'd not bothered as my tanks were nearly full.

They were quite within their rights to collect the drum, no worries about that. It amused us though because neither man saw us at all, yet we were in full view of them only fifty paces or so back from the clifftop. Our vehicle was in plain sight too, but they gave no indication they might have spotted us, no sign at all. Perhaps so engrossed with their task they had no eyes for anything else, who knows, but their lack of observation puzzled us. I felt a tinge of resentment at sight of a new dogger in my former area, so soon after my resignation, maybe a natural reaction I do not know, but the feeling was there.

The two men drove off and although hidden by the escarpment to our south, we could hear their vehicles turn north once they reached the fenceline. No doubt they were off to Kumarina via Beyondie. When they were out of earshot we packed up ourselves and headed south to the Ilatji turnoff, then east to the latter spring. At Ilatji we pulled up for a while to examine some bower birds' playgrounds. Ilatji is a lovely place with its forest of gum trees and thick undergrowth of slender saplings. Ilatji Creek flows south into Lake Nabberu.

We put the tea billy on, had a bite to eat, then got on the track again to bump and skid our way across the sticky mud flats of Lake Nabberu. This crossing is at the east end of the large open body of water that lies further west. The crossing is compact enough, but is always damp and spongy, with a profuse growth of low samphire bushes and other saltlake succulents. Our route was a two hundred yard stretch that constitutes one of only two main crossings over Nabberu. The second is much further east below Canning's Gap, near the stockroute's useless and abandoned No 4 Well. This well was good water when first put down by the Canning well sinkers in 1908-10 but turned salt when deepened at a later date. These days it is almost pure brine.

From the lake we travelled west, at first to Cunyu, then south non stop all the way to Wiluna. This return to Wiluna was for us the first daytime visit to that town since our elopement some weeks before. Except for the one quick visit we made after dark last month to leave APB property at the police station. On the outskirts of town the figure of a lone lubra stood beside the road, her arms akimbo and mouth agape with surprise. The woman recognised us as we did her, it was Sunshine Anderson. In the rear vision mirror Dooley saw her stride off at a swift pace to an Aboriginal camp not far away. No doubt Sunshine wished to be first with news of our return. The sudden appearance of two runaway lovers after a long absence, was an unusual event to say the least. In a sleepy little ghost town like Wiluna our unannounced return would constitute the best bit of gossip in ages.

Dooley and I pulled up at the Club Hotel. We had no desire to see any of her relatives at this stage. No sooner had we parked the Landrover however, than Dusty Stevens and Hazel Beaman drove up in an old ute. Hazel and Dusty were just the relations we did not wish to see so soon.

Hazel got out on the street verge and immediately tackled Dooley with a tirade of abuse. "Oh yeah so you come back did yuh? What you wanta go runnin' off like that for without tellin' anyone. You bin run off with a whitefella ain't it? I oughta flog the daylights outa you!"

Dooley did not respond in like manner, she remained calm. In the meantime Dusty came across to have a go at me. "What you want to do that for? runnin' off with Dooley like that!" I answered: "Oh well its too late now Dusty, me and Dooley been together long enough to be married." Hazel heard me say the words "too late" and this rekindled her boiler. She blazed off into another outburst of abuse. This time Hazel directed her ire at Dooley and me both. An inquisitive audience gathered too, as several hotel patrons emerged onto the pub verandah to watch the event.

Dusty's show of displeasure was only pretence, his heart was not in it, he only participated to show some support for his wife Hazel, and she too calmed down after about ten minutes. The bystanders then drifted back into the pub. They probably thought it the liveliest show they'd seen in town for weeks and it certainly did give them some fuel for conversation at the bar.

In 1968 Wiluna had a small population, it was a ghost town. The residents had little to do for leisure other than drink at the pub. Our noisy row right outside the bar door was a welcome source of entertainment for them. Wiluna Aborigines seldom came to town in those days. When a whiteman and his native lover were the focal point, it was a unique and rare event, something to be savoured by sensation starved spectators.

Dusty and Hazel, becoming normal again after the row, defused the situation with tentative smiles, then invited us to stay at their town camp so we accepted. At the time we had no plans for the future and took every day as it came. We were at a loose end, with only romantic notions to occupy our time. They wanted to go south to Yakabindie Station for a spell and asked would we look after their camp until they return so, we had their place to ourselves.

Dusty and Hazel departed for Yakabindie next morning and then to our surprise, Cecily Harris moved in to stay with us. I knew Cecily but did not welcome the idea of extra company. Dooley and I preferred to be alone.

One day we lay down together on the bed for an afternoon nap. Dooley was asleep and I was at half a doze when I felt a sharp tug on my big toe. I looked up to see Cecily at foot of the bed. "Give us a smoke Pete" she asked. Of course I was not a smoker and she knew it, so I wondered what she was coming at. I took no notice of her and she sauntered off to another part of the house. When Dooley woke I mentioned the incident and she responded that Cecily was more likely looking for a poke. The deduction was a choice one I suppose, but I had no need of another woman, I was too absorbed with the one I had.

We knew Sunshine wasted no time telling the town blacks about our arrival. Now we wanted to give Dooley's relations a chance to "growl" as Aborigines say, so we went to meet them of our own accord. We knew we must face the music sooner or later. Ours' was an unsanctioned elopement so there was no real alternative. We must present ourselves for chastisement. Only thus can a couple gain proper recognition. Not to meet relatives subsequent to an elopement on the other hand, can result in outright condemnation. The advantage of facing up to the relatives being, that a tribal marriage if accepted by close kin, gets full support in the event of any objections by others.

The meeting was an anti climax in that the only person to growl for any length of time, was one of Dooley's tribal brothers, Alf Ashwin. Alf's sister Doris also had a few words to say but only sufficient to satisfy convention, in reality she seemed more in favour of our match than against it. After that brief show of opposition, I was welcome to join the family circle and told, that henceforth I am free to come and go at will.

By the time Hazel and Dusty came home, we had itchy feet again, Dooley and me. The chance for us to see fresh horizons came sooner than expected. A battered Toyota pulled up out front one day. The driver had a note from a contract surveyor named Dave Falge. The scrawled message said a geologist name of John Clark thought I might want a job. Hearing of my exploration survey work for the APB, he thought in the context of minerals and theodolites, failing to realise that a more exotic interpretation of the words, **survey** and **exploration**, applied to me. I am a bushman not a surveyor or miner.

Victorian Antimony Mines, or VAM for short, was the first company to explore for nickel around Wiluna in 1967. We saw our first helicopters in Wiluna at that time too, and we bush folk puzzled at the frenzied activity. This was also the first experience we had with survey cut lines, with wooden pegs and coloured flagging, it was all new to us. Both Dave Falge and John Clark worked for VAM and now Dave wanted us to join him on his first job, south of Wiluna at Mount Keith. He had a contract to put in a surveyed base line from the old Mount Keith townsite, south to Jones Creek on Yakabindie Station. Being naive about the destructive aspects of mineral exploration and surveys, we were eager to join the surveyor as it was a completely new experience for us both.

Chapter Three - EVEN LOVERS MUST WORK

DECEMBER 1968

We got the job with surveyor Dave Falge. On the first day we went south in a Toyota with him to have a look over the proposed route of survey. Dave I am sure would be the fastest driver it has ever been my misfortune to ride with. We had to hang on all the way. I thought the vehicle might tip over several times because of the reckless way he negotiated some of the dips on that gravel road. We decided there would be no more long rides with Mister Falge if we could help it, that's for sure.

We did however get to our destination in one piece and saw where the base line was to begin. It was to start near what locals call the old Mount Keith townsite. From there it would be a hard task through heavy mulga scrub, midway between the Mount Keith shearing shed and main road. The scrub country eventually being left behind at Mount Keith southern boundary fence. The final lap was to run through much easier terrain of open spinifex, south through Yakabindie country to the headwaters of Jones Creek.

Dave Falge had one whitefella offsider whose name I forget, and in addition to ourselves he employed one fullblood Aborigine named Frank Wongawol. Frank was Cecily's current boyfriend. Cecily was to stay behind in Wiluna while the rest of us camped out on the job. After the inspection trip we returned to town for the night. Next day Dooley and I packed up our own Landrover and took off for Mount Keith shearing shed. Falge was there long before us and settled into his camp by the time we arrived.

There was nothing exotic about our new surroundings. The pegging job was mundane and boring, but the pay was good so I stuck it out. Dooley came along with us each day to hunt the sidelines for bungarras and other bushes tucker while we worked. She kept parallel with us about fifty paces away in the scrub as we men pegged the line.

Where the line commenced is a line of old mine dumps, at the south end of which, are a windmill and water tank on top of one dump. The peg line at this juncture went right through the centre line of the water tank. Dave Falge for a moment perplexed, tugged at his chin, then got a brainwave, and tossed one peg into the tank, "problem solved" he said.

One of our employer's idiosyncrasies was a penchant for leaving the day's coating of dust and grime on exposed parts of his body, and clothes. The only explanation I could think of for this eccentric behaviour was his recent English origin. I feel certain he was acting out his idea of how an Australian bushman should act.

The highlight of this "survey" experience to me, was the day Dave Falge walked off a few paces into the dense scrub to relieve himself. He was away about five minutes when we heard one plaintive yell after another from the thicket. Poor lanky, dust coated, would-be bushman Dave, managed to lose himself only forty paces from his survey line. The whitefella assistant gave me and Frank a sort of quizzical sympathetic look and walked off into the scrub to rescue his forlorn boss.

I wasn't in any way enthralled with surveys in the context of mining industry terminology, not in any way at all. My concept of a survey is the type of exploration work I did for the APB. We must work in order to live, there is no argument on that score. However my ideas about work do not include the driving of pegs into the ground, nor the lopping of branches off trees to clear a cutline.

I like something out of the ordinary to occupy my time. I could see that my future was not with Dave Falge, so I pulled out before being sucked into a rut that might be hard to get out of.

With Mister Falge's cheque in shirt pocket we headed south to Yakabindie to see some more of Dooley's relatives. The homestead is not far off the Leonora road and it was dark by the time we pulled in opposite the blacks' camp. I turned the engine off and sat in the Landrover waiting for someone to come along.

A dark face came to the driver side window, peered at me for a few seconds, then in a contemptuous tone exclaimed "Oh that's you is it." The owner of the face was Harold Beaman, one of Dooley's uncles. He sauntered off into the darkness without another word. It was easy to see he wasn't going to make us welcome.

I found out later why. Dooley told me he had wanted her for a second wife before I ran off with her, but she was not the type to go with "wrong way ones" as she put it. It is strictly taboo for tribal Aborigines to participate in an incestuous relationship. Many do, but not Dooley, her moral principles are far too high for that.

Despite the initial lack of welcome by surly Uncle Harold, we got out of the vehicle and walked to the camp to visit his wife. Vera greeted us in a much more agreeable manner. Another tribal uncle, one Croydon Beaman, and his wife Maise, came to sit around the campfire with us.

The latter couple appeared quite happy to see Dooley and myself. Vera gave Dooley a couple of floral dresses. She said she'd kept the frocks especially for this occasion, after learning of our elopement. It seemed that not everyone was against our being together. From Yakabindie we travelled on through the night to within a few miles of Leonora to camp. I was not keen to visit Leonora but Dooley insisted, we must meet all her family of the Ngalia tribe she said. Dooley assured me her people would welcome me with open arms.

I had strong doubts about Dooley's promised warm welcome in Leonora, due to a previous unpleasant experience with that dirty little town. My first visit to Leonora was during the winter months of 1959, when I was stranded there for two weeks while waiting for a lift to Meekatharra. The weather at that time was miserable in the extreme. There were no suitable places to camp near the town, or outside it either for that matter, and the townsfolk! Those townsfolk were the most miserable lot of humans ever seen in my thirty years on this planet. The Leonora residents were the unfriendliest lot of people imaginable. The rain drizzled. The ice cold wind blew a gale. I tried both pubs for an overnight stay but got an emphatic no from each establishment. "We have no vacancies" the respective publicans said, although I knew otherwise. In revenge I helped myself to a mulga log from one publican's woodheap.

I managed to get a fire going under an umbrageous peppercorn tree standing alone in the midst of a wide open flat between town and railway line. I had a good canvas swag cover with me at the time, so I enjoyed a warm dry sleep despite the drizzle and wind. My opinions of Leonora and its sour puss white people still remain open to change, despite the intervening years.

So with that background portrayal of my feelings for Leonora, you can see why I was doubtful about Dooley's choice of destinations. The only good words I can enunciate are that her people once met were so friendly toward me they became a nuisance around our camp. The only person who showed any sign of displeasure was her brother Paddy Walker.

The real reason for my welcome by the Ngalia folk was their knowledge of my initiated status in Aboriginal law. To them I was a wati and thus a fit and proper partner for their female relative Dooley. Most of the men were tribal brothers of the karimara skin. I am purungu. In Ngalia tribal society a person's brothers-in-law must be friends and help one another. For some reason karimara women of Dooley's skin were not plentiful like the men, so I did not gain many sisters-in-law.

We camped on the Native Reserve fringe with Dooley's Ngalia people until I tired of inactivity. Also the stench of human excreta hung heavy on the air. The Reserve community itself had toilet closets, but these were too distant from the fringe camp for convenience. A nearby mulga thicket served the twenty or so campers for bodily functions. A person had to watch one's step as the thicket was a scattered mess of stinking stools, both recent and old. We asked Eric James the manager of Elder Smiths, the local stock and station agent, if he knew of any houses for sale in town. This Mr James sent us to Biggs Butcher Shop where, Father Biggs as everyone called him, said he had a stone cottage to sell for $200-00. The stone cottage was a relic of the distant past. It stood in the centre of a bare windswept two acre block, a Garden Lease under the Mines Department. The lease had expired years ago but I was able to re-peg it and apply for a new lease if I wished, they told me.

I bought the place that same day. I agreed to buy, but only if assured of vacant possession by Xmas day 1968. The cottage had tenants. Father Biggs promised to get them out by the due date so I exchanged one of my cheques for his receipt and that was that for the time being.

We departed Leonora immediately after the house purchase, to travel north-east along the Nambi road. Erlistoun Station was our destination this time, to meet Dooley's uncle, her mother's only brother Albert Jones. He was boss of Erlistoun mustering camp. It surprised me once we met, to receive yet another joyous welcome into the family circle. I must add that Dooley is a most popular member of her Ngalia family. They all love her, she is quite a favourite.

Albert enjoyed a plural marriage, his two wives Esther Jones and Nawi Weslake were a lot younger than their husband. Albert's first wife Maise left him years before. She married Croydon Beaman, whom we saw at Yakabindie homestead the night we passed through there.

As a little girl Dooley rode horses in the Erlistoun mustering camp. At that time old Maise was one of the riders too. Dooley claims her aunt was a hard woman to work with. One day Maise caught a porcupine and hung it on Dooley's saddle to carry back to camp. The older lady wished to continue mustering unencumbered by the porcupine. At the time Dooley was of such short stature she always had to find a stump in order to reach the stirrup irons. She found a suitable tree stump and mounted, then urged her horse into a trot so as to keep up with her aunt, but porcupine quills dug into the horse's flank, like spur rowels. The frightened animal took off at full gallop until Dooley managed to lean back and stop the quills from pricking the horse, only then did the frightened beast slow down.

Erlistoun is about twenty miles north-west of Laverton. The homestead is central to workers' small cottages, sheds, and outbuildings, all with white painted walls and red roofs. The place is rustic but quite attractive. The manager Bill Barrett had a peculiar mannerism that irritated me until I woke up to him. He always responded to any approach with a gruff "**WHAT**" in a voice so abrupt and unexpected it disconcerted me. In reality however Barrett was quite a likeable old chap. He just loved to startle people. When he knew I was up to his game he stopped doing it. I noticed he never let up on his blacks though, they were set back on their heels by the Barrett "WHAT" response every time they spoke to him.

One day Albert took his wife Esther for a day trip to Laverton. His second wife Nawi stayed behind. Albert was not back by sundown. When night fell, Papalo Richards a Wiluna native and tribal brother of Dooley, began to make a nuisance of himself with Nawi over at Albert's camp. We could tell by Nyawi's distress calls that Papalo was giving her a hiding. Soon afterward she ran across to our camp for protection, followed by an irrational Papalo. He asked me for point 22 bullets which of course I refused, and maintained his rage until Albert and Esther arrived back from town long after dark. We could not see subsequent events from our camp but could hear the commotion. We knew from the noise that Papalo had assaulted the aggrieved husband when the old man objected to Papalo's treatment of Nawi during his absence.

Albert went to the house to report his injury and soon afterward old Barrett came out with a shotgun in hand. Papalo gave him cheek from the darkness outside, so old Barrett pointed the gun in that direction and yelled: "Get out of here you bastard, GET OUT or I'll fuckin well shoot you. Go on get going while your luck's in." Papalo wasn't having any of Bill Barrett's shotgun, he took off at a run down the Laverton road. Old Barrett had full command of the situation and chased him up with the station Landrover. He brought Papalo back to the homestead, paid him off, then to my surprise, alone and now unarmed, drove Papalo into town and returned alone an hour or two later. I'm sure I wouldn't have gone off like that with an irate Aborigine, I wouldn't have taken him in at all, I would have made him walk.

Not long after this excitement old Bill Barrett and his wife went for a holiday. Albert and his two women also went off to town for a spell. We stayed on to work with Billy Barrett junior and a station hand called Brian Roberts. One day while in the workshop the two whitefellows had their backs to Dooley who stood at one end of the shed. I was facing her, and in the way that native women tease their men, she was poking her tongue out at me in a most provocative manner.

Dooley's antics had been going on for several minutes while the two men examined a piece of broken machinery. They noticed how intent I was on something behind their back and both turned to look at what was attracting my attention, at the instant they turned, Dooley's pink tongue emerged to tease me. Billy and Brian looked at each other, they looked at me, then had another look at Dooley. It embarrassed me, and Dooley as well I saw, because she gave me such a shameful look as she walked out of the shed.

Our camp was a couple of miles away from the homestead, at the shearing shed. The place was alive with snakes of all descriptions, large snakes, green ones, yellow ones, brown ones, the lot. There were so many you couldn't lift a sheet of iron or shift anything without a snake be revealed. Not the sort of place to roll one's swag out on the ground, we always slept in back of the Landrover to keep away from the things.

We had our vehicle parked close to the shearers' kitchen and mess room. We used the kitchen stove and ate our meals inside at the big table. Every night without fail the sound of an eerie croak from the rafters overhead disturbed us. We searched the upper gloom with torchlight, and hurricane lamp, but could not find the source of that uncanny sound, it didn't scare us, it was more of a puzzle than anything else. The idea of a barking lizard or a night bird came to mind, but no sign of any living creature to be found. The croak sounded just like someone being strangled. Dooley said it was a **korti** (spirit of the dead) so I accepted her word in the absence of any other explanation.

Another day Billy Barrett and Brian Roberts took us to see the site of a new nickel discovery they had an interest in. Some name like Poseidon I think it was. Well, along the way Billy shot a bungarra (goanna) and flung it in back with us, to cook later. We'd only gone a mile when the reptile came to life and got into the cab with driver and passenger. Billy slammed on the brakes. The bungarra clawed its way over him and Brian, then in a split second the front seat was empty of all occupants. They jumped clear, while bungarra raced past them and made for the nearest bush. We caught it again and killed it properly this time. The incident was good fun while it lasted, and certainly broke the ice between us newcomers and the permanent staff.

Xmas 1968 was just between the two of us at Erlistoun shearing shed. I asked Billy Barrett to bring us a carton of beer from Laverton. Our festive dinner comprised a leg of mutton and a tin of plum duff. We saw neither hide nor hair of Barrett and Roberts until New Year 1969. We didn't want their company anyway, just so long as we had each other. Our attachment was as fresh and romantic as ever and quite unmellowed by time.

There was nothing wrong with Billy and Brian, nothing wrong at all, they both had pleasant dispositions, but being of such different backgrounds we had little in common. They kept to themselves too much. We didn't like the job anyway, so when old Barrett came back from his holiday I got my cheque and departed Erlistoun without any regrets for Leonora, to take possession of our stone cottage.

The stone house was a wreck, a real renovator's dream. It stood in isolated misery in the middle of a bare unfenced two acre block. A property located at the north end of Tower Street, Leonora's main thoroughfare. The house being only a few paces away from where the latter bitumen strip loses its lofty title to become a 200 mile stretch of unsealed gravel known as the Wiluna Road.

Upon initial inspection, the first thing we noticed at one end of the front verandah was a quantity of scorched material. Someone had tried to light a fire, with the obvious intention of burning the house down. We knew we were not popular with the previous tenants because we'd bought the place over their heads. The former occupants were a large family of part Aborigines evicted by old Bill Biggs for non-payment of rent over a long period. Mr Biggs had used our recent purchase of the place as a lever to evict this family. He told us he took a policeman along with him when he served the eviction order. Of course we knew nothing of this when we agreed to buy the property. We were some distance away at Erlistoun Station when it all happened and only learned of the sorry procedures later, when we returned to Leonora to take possession.

Townsfolk in the know, told us later, that one of the former tenant's sons was the would-be arsonist, who wanted revenge on us as the cause of their enforced homeless state. If we'd known all this beforehand we would never have done a deal in the first place, but too late after the event to worry, so for better or worse we got stuck with it.

The most remarkable thing about our new [sic] house was the way the large gable roof rose up and down on its loose tie wires at every gust of wind. The entire structure above the stone walls filled with air and billowed out like a parachute. It made me wonder why the tie wires held the thing down at all, with only lime mortar holding the top wall stones in place. At the rear of the house was a detached ramshackle corrugated iron structure. It served as a kitchen at one end, and a spare room at the other. A breezeway separated this outer annexe from the main building.

A shortcut for motor vehicles ran right past the kitchen door, from Tower Street on the west or front boundary of our block, across to the next street on the east side back boundary. No doubt this shortcut was an asset put in place by visitors to the former residents, but to have motorcars flying past us with such careless abandon, and so close to our house, irritated me. Most of the car drivers were impudent sods who treated us with contempt I'm sure, because none of them stopped to say g'day, or call in to visit, they just shot past us in clouds of dust and scattered us with gravel. My first job was to put obstacles in place to block off the shortcut.

We settled in to the grease splattered grime coated dwelling as best we could, then I took time off to look for some sort of a job. I was not anxious to take on a town job but needed an income. We required money if we were to stay put long enough to clean up the stone house, not to mention the accumulated rubbish that surrounded it.

People told me to ask one Don Tonkin for work, he was manager of a government facility known as the Nabberu Hostel, an establishment that catered for school kids with parents out bush or away somewhere. Don was also secretary of the Leonora hospital. He gave me a job to pull down an old building at the rear of his shop-front office in Tower Street. This demolition task took a couple of weeks during which time I always had Dooley for company. She stayed with me no matter where. Dooley was not one to stop home alone or even go off to visit relatives or whoever.

All Dooley wanted was to be close alongside me all the time, even when I was working. Well, the demolition completed, I only had the floor boards to pull up to finish the job. This day we had two visitors on the work site. One was Dooley's aunt Pauline Edwards, the other was Nungi Phillips, daughter of Dooley's sister Kutjikari. We thought they had just decided to call in and visit while I worked. I pulled all the floor boards up, stacked them to one side, then Dooley and I went home to get a rake to clean up the area of ground previously hidden by the floor. We thought we might find some old coins or other relics as it had been a Nineteenth Century building. We were away for only ten minutes. When we came back with the rake, Nungi told us that Pauline had already searched the area we proposed to rake over, and found a lot of silver coins.

Pauline took the silver coin relics to shopkeeper Bert Polletti and sold them for decimal money, then shot through. Pauline thereafter avoided us like the proverbial plague. We didn't see her again. That deceitful predatory woman had beaten us to the treasure after me doing all the hard work to reveal it. I could have throttled the bitch.

Don Tonkin gave me another job after that, to put in a lawn at the hospital matron's residence. I made the work spin out for six weeks. The only thing of interest there was a brown snake on the lawn one morning when I went to work. I killed the snake and hung it across the fence where it served as a source of wonder to matron and staff until someone removed the thing.

This type of casual town work served its purpose. The shed demolition and lawn job provided us with an income for a couple of months. Now with cash in hand I was more than ready for the bush again, and hang the stone house renovations. Work on our own job could wait. I asked Bob Cable for work. Bob had a general store in Leonora and also owned Merolia Station to the east of Laverton. He took us out to have a look at the place. While we waited some distance away from the homestead in Bob Gable's vehicle, he sacked the resident manager.

Bob claimed the manager was robbing him blind by selling station property on the sly. The dismissal completed, Bob drove us back to Leonora again, and from there we packed up and set off for Merolia in our own vehicle.

Merolia homestead was a leftover from days when a town called Burtville occupied the site. The shearers' quarters were once the Burtville pub. The station Landrover was a relic of Charlie Cable's sandalwood camps. Charlie was Bob Cable's dad. The Landrover was fit for the scrap heap. A perpetual cloud of blue exhaust gas enveloped it as it moved along. How Dooley and I missed being suffocated is beyond comprehension. Loose body panels, and even engine parts, being held together with wire twitches, made the vehicle a jewel of improvisation. An even greater puzzle is how we managed to get back to the homestead each day after a fifty mile windmill run.

The most memorable thing about Merolia apart from the decrepit vehicle, was one well that must have been at least three hundred feet deep. Water in the shaft was visible as only a pin prick of light, when picked up from above with the help of a reflector mirror. Perhaps the only benefit we got from Merolia was a look at some new country. We only stayed there a few weeks then pulled out and returned to Leonora. Bob did not understand my reluctance to stay, but Merolia was not for me. I might add that his decrepit Landrover with its wire twitches and clouds of blue smoke was not my idea of tempting providence either.

I went next to see Eric James the Elders manager about work. Eric sent me off to have a look at Fraser Range Station to the east of Norseman. I'd not been that far south before so took the job just to have a look at the country. We travelled the back roads from Leonora via Malcolm, Kookynie, Yerilla, Edjudina, Pinjin, Yindi, and Yindi Rockhole, to Karonie on the Trans Line. I thought to take a short cut from Karonie south to the northern boundary of Fraser Range. The idea was novel, but a confusion of well-used wood cutters' tracks was too big a puzzle to solve with a limited petrol supply. The tracks fanned out every which way, without any indication of which might be the right one to follow, as they all ran in a southerly direction. I gave that attempt up in disgust and turned west along the Trans Line to Kalgoorlie, then south to Norseman and from thence east to Fraser Range. It was just as well we did turn back I found out later, because our proposed route south from Karonie would have taken us through treacherous lake country.

I'd asked for an outcamp job and the owner commented at the time, that I must be one of a dying breed. He did however settle us in on the north end of Fraser Range in a little one room stone hut called Yardilla Outcamp. We drove our own vehicle out there then got a ride back to the homestead with the boss to take delivery of two saddle horses. The management ran some horses into the yards and picked two horses out of the mob for us. Mine pig-rooted around the yard when I got on, but soon settled down. The manager told Dooley her mount was a quiet old stager that never bucked, but I didn't like the look in its eye so said I'd ride it first. For a horse never known to buck it certainly put on a good imitation of such equine contortions. The moment I put foot in the stirrup iron the horse ducked its block. It twisted and turned like a veteran rodeo bronco. The onlookers were all eyes. One of them had hoped to take a rise out of Dooley, that's for sure.

The manager had a peculiar habit. He stuttered, and at every pause before bringing the next word out, he'd click heels together like a Prussian military officer. The heel click was a frequent and regular part of his speech. The poor fellow put on the best heel clicking performance ever, when he tried to excuse his mistake about Dooley's horse. We rode off from the homestead late in the afternoon and reached Yardilla Outcamp about sundown.

Unlike some Aborigines who sit slumped in the saddle like a bag of flour, Dooley has a good seat on a horse. This was also the first time I'd ever seen her on one. She looked a perfect picture as we rode together through an open forest of gum trees to the outcamp. I couldn't keep my eyes off her I was so proud of her ability.

This was all strange country to us both. We only see red granite in our country, but down here on Fraser Range the granite is all grey. The most interesting thing we found there was a big rockhole near the top of a hill. This catchment called Yardilla, had an ancient concrete rim on the outlet side to improve its holding capacity. The remains of a stone wall and netting cover also indicated its importance in earlier days. No doubt the outcamp got its name from its proximity to this rockhole.

The weather was of real southern type while on Fraser Range and far too severe for those from hot northern climes like Dooley and myself. The little stone hut though, was cosy and warm with logs ablaze in the large open fireplace, that took up most of one wall. With our swag unrolled beside the fire, we certainly slept as snug as the proverbial "bug in a rug." It was cold, wet, and miserable outside, with a constant fine drizzle of rain reminiscent of Victoria, or any other southern parts of Australia. I got a bad dose of flu while there and could feel it deep in my chest so thought it best to pull stakes and head back to Leonora and a warmer climate.

Leonora was not my choice of places to live. I didn't like the town when I first passed through it in 1959 and didn't like it in 1968 either. It was Dooley's idea for us to come and be close to her tribal relatives. She said: "They will all like you Peter because you are my man, and because you are a wati and know the wangkayi lore." (Wati is an initiated man.)

Dooley was born in Skull Creek near Laverton in 1936. Laverton is her country in that respect, yet she does not like the place and will not live in Laverton. She has no real ties with Leonora either. Her Ngalia people only settled there in recent years. The Ngalia once lived a hundred miles away from Leonora at a place called Mulga Queen, where the presence of a government ration depot kept them in that area. The chap in charge of rations at Mulga Queen was Jack Shepherd who cared for the Ngalia people for many years until his death in the mid 1950s. After Shepherd died the people all moved to the outskirts of Leonora whereat, in the mid 1960s a reserve was set aside by the Department of Native Affairs for their exclusive use. Dooly was quite right about me getting a warm reception from her people. The welcome they gave however, did nothing to change my dislike of Leonora. There is just something intangible about the place that makes me detest it, and I make no bones about my dislike for the town. Wiluna on the other hand always appeals to me.

The time had come by now to find a proper job out bush. The type of work I'd been able to find to date did not suit me at all. I missed the open country and the free lifestyle experienced when employed by the APB. My next move was in that direction as described in the following chapter.

Chapter Four - CONTRACT DOGGER ON KALUWIRI

JUNE 1969

The foregoing chapters describe a fruitless quest for suitable work to maintain Dooley and myself during our first months together. It is writ from memory alone. When I left the APB toward the end of October 1968 I stopped keeping field notes. Not until June 1969 did I recommence a daily record and hereunder are the first pages of it. I now begin a detailed and comprehensive account of years filled with adventure. The following is about an exotic lifestyle, the thrill of new discovery, the joys of success, as well as the inescapable sorrows we must all sometimes endure.

We departed Leonora on a Friday for northern parts in search of yet another job. The first night out we camped at an alluvial area known as "Never Can Tell" where Dooley wanted to look for gold nuggets. Her eyesight is good and she can find the tiniest speck. I can't even see the stuff until she points it out, and even then I have to get down on hands and knees to see it.

Saturday 28 June 1969 - Speedo 59047 - Today is my first to recommence a daily written record. We left for Agnew this morning in search of Billy Cock the owner of Kaluwiri Station and several other pastoral properties further south. Agnew has the appearance of a cowboy town, just like a picture right out of the old West. There is only a pub and a few scattered houses. The pub has a long frontage of verandah posts and couple of rails to hitch horses. Not used for that purpose now, but in earlier days they were in regular use as hitching rails, while the owners sunk a bit of grog inside.

The Post Office and Store are all in the same long building. The hotel used to be further south at Lawlers, but that former establishment is now only a remnant pile of large stones, from the fallen walls. The old Police Station at Lawlers is the home of a private resident named Bill Trundle. The police no longer maintain a presence there. The alcohol licence is now at Agnew, seven miles north of Lawlers. Dooley tells me that the present Agnew Hotel is actually a converted butcher shop and general store, but you wouldn't know just by looking at it. Mrs Trundle and son Henry are the managers.

Mrs Trundle told us Billy Cock was out at the Emu Mine two miles west of Agnew. In addition to pastoral properties, Mr Cock owns most of the mines around Agnew as well. The Emu Mine will reopen soon I believe. We found Billy Cock at that mine and he gave me a job as contract dogger on his station Kaluwiri, a few miles out of town. Billy reckons he has a lot of trouble with dingoes and wants to control them. His neighbours claim Billy is breeding dogs on his open country.

Bill said to go out to Kaluwiri Station right away. The idea said Bill, was for me to pick up all the traps, poison, and petrol I might need, from Leo Bonney his station manager at the homestead, upon arrival there. I was to travel via Altona Outstation to the Kaluwiri open country, and commence work in the area that lies west from Altona boundary fence, to Bungarra Rockhole. The old fellow is a bit eccentric. He insists he will not pay a penny more or a penny less than government rates, plus an equivalent of the ruling APB vehicle allowance. Our working conditions settled to mutual satisfaction, Dooley and I left for Kaluwiri forthwith.

This was all new country to me. I've never been here before. Dooley has lived on Kaluwiri for years and knows the run like the back of her hand as the saying goes, so I followed her directions. We left Agnew and Billy Cock at 10 am in the morning. A north-west course at first, took us to some gnamma holes, then past an old slaughter yard. From the slaughter yard, travel was through Depot Springs country, to Kaluwiri boundary fence. Dooley chose to follow an old unused road, overgrown with small trees and shrubs in the wheel ruts. She said it was the way she always used to go to Kaluwiri, so who was I to argue.

Eventually we came to a boundary fence and had to lay it on the ground to get through as there was no gate. We had not long stood the fence up again when Leo Bonney came along and asked where we were going. I told him we were en route Kaluwiri homestead and he gave us a quizzical look of disbelief. "Funny way to go to Kaluwiri" he said. Leo did not know that our route was the original old track to Kaluwiri, and we didn't know that a new graded road existed only a short distance to our west.

Leo Bonney had no traps, poison, petrol, or food supplies. He maintains he only ever keeps one drum of fuel at the station and has all his traps set. He keeps only sufficient stores on hand for himself and wife Betty.

The only thing I could do was travel back to Leonora because the Agnew pub keeps only grog in stock. So I went back to Agnew and informed Billy Cock of the situation, then proceeded south to Leonora. We arrived at 7 pm with well over 160 miles to record for the first day on the job. 165 miles today all told.

Sunday 29 June - Speedo 59212 - This morning I loaded up with all essentials and purchased a 44 gallon drum of petrol on my own account, from Keith Biggs the BP Agent. I also bought a bag of flour and a quantity of tea from the local baker. With speedo reading 59212 on departure, we got underway to reach Lawlers for dinner.

I forgot to mention in yesterday's entry that on the way to Leonora we met Jack Kerr on his way north to a doggers' conference at Albion Downs. Jack is now Regional Officer for the Leonora and Laverton region. He gave me the good news that he'd had me in mind for some time as a potential dogger and was glad he'd run into me on the track. He says he will definitely place me on APB strength as a government dogger when the first vacancy arises. This is excellent news for me indeed.

Lionel Heath, manager of Depot Springs, passed by our dinner camp today. I saw some of his traps set yesterday whilst on our way to Kaluwiri. He builds a yard around them, as most novices do.

We went on after dinner by way of the slaughter yard track, north-west to the sandhill strip. I shot a kangaroo at the first sandhill and poisoned some of the carcase near a small sandy wash known as Dead Horse Creek. This is about 30 miles out from Agnew.

Saw two dog tracks in the creek and found an old trap buried in the sand. I presume it is one set by Lionel Heath. The dog tracks show how they gave the trap a wide berth. We got to Kaluwiri by 4 pm. Billy Cock and Leo Bonney were both there. Bill was happy to see us back again. He said he'd seen Jack Kerr the RVCO at Agnew last night where they discussed my proposed dogging operation.

Leo Bonney gave us some meat for ourselves, and camels hump for baits. He also gave us directions to the area of proposed operations. We turned north from the homestead along the fence for a mile, to camp. We dodged Altona by turning off a mile south of that place, to run the horse paddock fence around past two claypans. One pan was full of water. We got back onto the main track about a mile west of Altona. A small roo came right up to our camp before realising its predicament in time to make off at top speed. 154 miles today.

Monday 30 June - Speedo 59366 - We broke camp early and soon found the cutline that leads to a windmill called Redhanded. We disregarded Billy's jumbled directions and took a shortcut. We found the camp of a fencing contractor Mervyn Stubbs there. He was away, but we met him and his wife two miles further north at Galilee Mill. We yarned for an hour then carried on north until past the boundary fence, out into the open country.

This stretch of unfenced country is the area in which we are to operate. I followed the cutline north. Saw signs of one dog not far out so set one trap and left a mutton bait. This spot is about one mile north of Galilee. The speedo back there was 59381. We came to breakaways clothed with a sparse cover of mulga and other bushes, at two miles, and at this point the dog track disappeared. Further north at three miles, the breakaways ended where we topped the escarpment to reach high ground. Spinifex sandplain with far distant red sandhills then occupies the country to the seventeen mile point, where mulga scrub and a gravel rise mark a change of country.

At eighteen miles north of the boundary, we came to a cluster of twelve gnamma holes in an open gravel flat. Some contained clean water, others were dry. Two holes polluted with decayed animal flesh, the stench being terrific. Another larger hole in which the water though still clean, held the bodies of six emu chicks not long dead. The chicks no doubt fell in this morning, and were unable to climb out because of the polished perpendicular interior walls of the rockhole. With water level a foot below the surface, the chicks never had a chance.

I fished all the emu chick carcases out of the hole and apart from a few feathers the water remains fit to drink. Put the billy on and had dinner, then went for a walk in search of dog tracks. None evident at first, but closer inspection revealed two scratching places, and dog camps, to one side of the rockholes. I set two traps on one dog camp, under a shady bush. I then dragged a scent trail with a kangaroo leg in a wide circle around the rockhole area, and poisoned the still fresh emu chick carcases at intervals along the trail.

On the way out here this morning we saw no sign of dog tracks through the spinifex. The only signs of wildlife were emus, kangaroos, foxes, cats, and camels, but not many. The granite outcrops and gravel flats ended at nineteen miles from Galilee. Spinifex sandplain then, with Montague Range visible to the west. Two high points in the range are Mounts Townsend and Marion. The most prominent rounded one of these being known by the native name Malumampa, a part of the kangaroo dreaming or, malu tjukurrpa. Mount Marion is nganamarra or mallee hen Dreaming. *

Prominent granite cliffs and breakaways, lie about one mile east of our northern route along the cutline. Saw two fresh dog tracks. The sandplain ends here at twenty-three miles. A small limestone rubble rise marks the start of dense mulga scrub and wash country. This scrub stretch leads to a fence that runs east and west along a southern boundary section of Yeelirrie Station.

We passed through the fence to follow it west on the inside. All signs of dogs disappeared at the rise of limestone rubble two miles back. At thirty miles exactly, we hit the main Wiluna to Sandstone road at a stock grid. We ran the main road a few miles in either direction to get our bearings. It appears we hit the road somewhere north of a government well marked on the map in spinifex country, but we didn't see the well. It is alright though because I am not to do any dog control inside fenced country, only out in the open. Someone has been quite active with traps through this inside country. Whoever it is, has traps set right along the fence, with several dogs already caught, and one fox in a trap on the main road verge, all dead of course. Satisfied with our traverse so far, I turned back from the stock grid and ran the fence east about a mile to camp just before dark. It's been a long hard day, but I accomplished a lot. It is now up to the wild dogs back at the gnamma hole cluster, to go in and get caught. 51 miles travelled.

JULY 1969

Tuesday 1 July - Speedo 59417- I went back to the cutline and put out four lots of camel hump baits along the track, at places with old dog tracks apparent, north of the gnamma hole cluster. Upon arrival at the gnamma holes, I inspected the emu chick baits there. One chick carcase been shifted a few paces and another taken away by a fox. The fox tracks were too difficult to follow over the hard ground. I saw no sign of fresh dog tracks and none been near any of the six bait sites. The traps I set are all okay and undisturbed.

Walking around the area I found where natives once camped to the south-east of where the cutline is now, within a patch of bogota bushes on a clean sandy flat, with wandary grass tussocks. Several sets of seed grinder stones lay scattered around the area. This is the only evidence of former inhabitants seen to date in this country. The camp is so old the blacks who camped here, are no doubt long dead and gone.

I found a shallow rock catchment with good water. It being situated on top of a granite whaleback half a mile to the east. I also found a deep gnamma hole four feet in diameter, half a mile west of the cutline. There is also a native soak at foot of a some granite one mile west. The soak being but a shallow depression in sand, scratched out by kangaroos looking for a drink. There is an old brush yard on a saltbush flat not far away.

A decomposed kangaroo carcase near the big gnamma hole looks as though dogs killed it some time ago, and scavenging foxes been dragging the remains around since. I baited the carcase and distributed baits along the track to Galilee Mill in order to keep faith with the job in hand, but saw no sign of fresh dog tracks.

I topped up the water tank at Galilee then started west, with speedo on 59449. At two miles in that direction is a little gnamma hole, just south of the track in breakaway country. The gnamma hole was quite dry. Put out a bit of camel bait. At three miles on the same westward course we came to a rockhole with water in it. This hole is a couple of hundred paces south of the track and situated under a hanging ledge. It held about ten gallons of good clear water. A dingo left fresh tracks near the rockhole and I saw one old track. Close by was a kangaroo carcase that the dog may have killed, at anyrate he had been eating it. I poisoned the kangaroo carcase and also a fresh roo leg that I tied to a tree near the rockhole.

We left the breakaways behind shortly after that and entered spinifex with scattered sandhills. This class of country continued four miles further westward on our course. The sandhill country then gave way to mulga scrub, with an undergrowth of scraggly spinifex, until we hit the Gidgee Station boundary fence at nine miles west of Galilee.

There being no gate in the boundary fence we pulled a post loose to flatten the wires and drove through into Gidgee country. We kept going from the fence a further six miles west along the station fence and camped on west side of a deep creek. The creek appeared to come from breakaways to the north of our route. Before settling down on camp for the day we went to the top of a stony ridge a bit west of our campsite for a look around. The view from the ridgetop gave rise to little of interest so we returned to the deep creek for a restful camp on soft ground. Marked on the map, and situated about five miles north of our deep creek camp, is Bungarra Rockhole. There is no sign of a gate in the fence we followed to this point, or any sign of a track leading to the rockhole. I had a look along the creek in both directions before dark, for any sign of dog tracks, but saw none. Distance travelled today is 48 miles.

Wednesday 2 July - Speedo 59465 - This morning we headed west for a few miles, then south along a fence to a gate, and west again along a well-used track to the main Sandstone-Wiluna road. We followed the main road north, and at a distance of nine miles from last night's deep creek camp, we came to Montague Well. At Montague we left the main road to follow the <u>old</u> Wiluna road eastward to a sandfilled rockhole in breakaways at seven miles from the new road, and twenty miles from last night's camp. We saw little sign of dogs whatsoever today, not even an old track at the rockhole, only foxes and other game. Someone has a trap set here near the rockhole.

We went south from the rockhole next, then north around east end of the breakaways for about seven miles, and saw no sign of dogs in that direction either. I find it is twenty-five miles, from where the Bungarra Rockhole track returns to the main road, north to the stock grid we were at the other day. (I refer to the stock grid from which we returned along the fence, east to Billy Cock's country on the afternoon of Monday 30 June last.) We turned in off the main road at the stock grid, and made an eastern return to Billy's cutline. South then along it, to the cluster of gnamma holes where we camped. 75 miles for the day.

Thursday 3 July - Speedo 59540 - This morning we did some washing and cooking, then Dooley and I had a last look around the rockholes for dog tracks. There is absolutely no sign of dogs here now. The dog tracks we first saw upon arrival at this place, were of two dogs on the move. They were passing through and no evidence that either dog lived for any length of time around these rockholes. They only camped hereabouts for a few days then shifted. I am leaving the traps set though, just in case they happen to return, and there is plenty of bait material ready for them if they do come back.

The wind this morning was bitter and cold, with winter clouds coming in from the south-west. While travelling south along the cutline yesterday, the engine developed a bad knock and lost power. I don't know what the problem is as I'm not much of a mechanic. I thought it best to return to the station. If Leo Bonney can't fix it then we will go into Leonora for repairs. Around midday the knock ceased. I stopped to reconsider my decision to go to the station, or town. I'll wait and see if the knock comes on again. After dinner we went back to the sand country and the knock did start again so, we must go in and get it fixed.

Reached Kaluwiri where Leo Bonney says he can't fix it, so we went on to Agnew and see Billy Cock. He gave me a check for $75-00 to cover the week's work to date, and wants me back as soon as possible. Shades of a visit to the dentist, how a toothache disappears the moment you sit in the chair. The knock ceased the moment we hit the main road to Leonora. I am now sanguine that it may be something to do with the ignition and not the engine bearings after all, anyway we'll see what tomorrow brings. We arrived in town to find plenty of mail in the Post Box. All the mail was mostly negative as regards employment opportunities. Except for one that promised a dogging job with the APB in the event of a vacancy arising. This promise being from Jack Kerr the Kalgoorlie based APB Regional Vermin Control Officer. I only had his oral confirmation before, now I have his promise in writing, so that is something. Distance travelled today two hundred and eighteen miles.

Friday 4 July - Speedo 559758 - I took the Landrover to Sullivan's Garage and had the mechanical faults fixed. We then purchased stores and commenced the return trip to Agnew. Billy Cock was at Agnew when we got there and gave me instructions as to what he wants done out bush. Billy Cock's name to the blacks who work for him, is Kunanyingkan. They call him this because of his idiosyncratic nature. His strange instructions to me bore out the suitability of his nickname. We travelled on to Kaluwiri to camp nearby for the night. I found a puncture upon arrival at the homestead but left it for the morning to fix. We had some meat for supper as Leo Bonney gave us a quarter of fresh mutton. 149 miles for the day.

Saturday 5 July - Speedo 59907 - I got up at daylight to a cold frosty morning, and found I now had two flat tyres to fix. This early exertion did a lot to warm me up before breakfast. We afterward travelled west via windmill tracks to a place called "54 Well" where Leo Bonney says he saw signs of two dogs recently, but we found nothing there today. From there we went a couple of miles north-east to a new mill pumping into an earth tank, where we pulled up for dinner. In the afternoon we travelled by way of Altona boundary to Galilee.
We saw signs of one dog track. I baited a roo carcase near the top of the breakaways, just above the escarpment, where the upper spinifex sand plain begins.

We saw no sign of the fencing contractor, he must be on the grog. We continued north along the cutline and baited an emu carcase at one mile near a trap set there. We went on another mile to camp at foot of a stony rise where, I put out two sheep shanks baits nearby. Saw no sign of dog tracks anywhere else today. At one point I drove in close to one of Altona's boundary fences to look at some breakaways on the other side. Found a new bulldozed cutline inside the fenced country, it ended just short of the boundary. We saw Frank Narrier's boot tracks too, both on the new cutline, and near a big rockhole on top of a stony rise. Dooley recognised his tracks. Sixty-six miles travelled today.

Sunday 6 July - Speedo 59973 - We returned south to Galilee, then west through the breakaways out from the fenceline, but found no sign of rockholes or any indication of dog activity there. The little rockhole we found on a previous trip is now dry. A fox has eaten some of the bait I left near the rockhole last trip, but we couldn't find any sign of its carcase. The ground is too hard to follow tracks anyway. We went back to Galilee for dinner.

Mervyn Stubbs the fencer came along while we were still on camp. He was drunk, full of skite, and anxious for us to visit his camp. I declined the invitation and got rid of him in a diplomatic way. He opened a bottle of plonk while we were talking and offered us a drink, but I told him we didn't touch the stuff. The moment he was out of sight we shifted north to the gnamma holes and granite area. We thought it best to clear out just in case he gets more sparked up and come back to seek our company. 34 miles today.

Monday 7 July - Speedo 60007 - We made a windbreak last night and slept behind it cosy and warm from the reflected heat of a small campfire. By daylight there was frost on the ground. All the bushes around our camp wore a coat of white crystals. The water in our bucket was solid ice on top. We had to prise it out to get water for the billy. I then took a photo of Dooley standing by the fire with the disk of ice from the bucket held aloft in one hand. This camp is not a great distance from Yeelirrie, where Dooley says severe frosts are a common event in winter time. If Yeelirrie is so prone to harsh temperatures then they can keep the place. I am not partial to freezing conditions.

The soak near camp is dry now, yet it had water in plenty when we found it last Tuesday. We searched all around and over the granites for some distance this morning. About one mile west of our ice bound camp, we came across some upright native marker stones, and nearby, some shallow water basins on top of a granite whaleback. On the west side of this rounded feature is a dense ti-tree thicket. We found there, an excellent native well or soakage. At first glance but a circular depression, but we knew it must be a well.

To one side of the saucer-like depression lay an obvious pile of ancient diggings. In form this pile has weathered by time, into a shallow compact mound. Sure evidence to us that former native inhabitants dug material from the hole to reach water.
Dooley and I spent a couple of hours digging down into the depression to open the soak, for the first time in a generation as far as we could see. Our work produced a rush of fresh muddy water which when bailed, was clear and good to drink. What a beautiful soakage it is.

I found a flat slab of granite to cover the soak hole and keep it clean while away. We then commenced a traverse on a bearing of 275^0 through virgin spinifex to the Sandstone-Wiluna main road. This line of travel was a bit south of Mount Townsend (native name Malumampa) which rounded highpoint stood out in front of us all the way. Mount Marion also being prominent in front but a bit further south. This course led us over open spinifex sandplain, with a scatter of low sandhills here and there to either side. We cut into the main road at eight miles west of the granite soak. Not a sign of dogs all the way.

We turned back east into the spinifex to a spot just short of the first low sandhill, where we pulled up to boil the billy and have dinner. While on dinner camp a cheeky bull camel came too close so I fired a shot and wounded him. He stumbled and fell a couple of times but recovered and got beyond range of another shot. The Spinifex being too rough to give chase I had no alternative but let him go. We continued east to arrive back at what I will name Granite Soak to camp a 5 pm, after twenty-two miles travel for the day.

Tuesday 8 July - Speedo 60029 - Cold this morning but no frost. Got going early back east to the rockholes, to find the distance between them and Granite Soak is two miles, a little further than I thought. A fox has had a go at the roo bait but no sign of fresh dog tracks in the area. We left the cutline behind and continued east for three miles, to look at some prominent breakaways near Yeelirrie boundary, but no sign of dog tracks there either. We drove back to the cutline then along our western traverse again, to run the track in a bit. We got to the main road, and this time found the government well that escaped us before. This old well, No 32, is just off the west side of the main road. We missed it before because it is behind a small clump of bushes, and large tussocks of spinifex. Also, it is on my map as being on the east side of the road, which is where we looked for it in the first place. Our western traverse of yesterday would have hit the well spot on if it <u>had</u> been on the east side of the road and not the west. I think people can put too much faith in maps at times. Cartographers often misplace man-made features like windmills, homesteads, fences, and etc.

With Well No 32 established as a starting point, we travelled next for six miles south. We went after that along a well-beaten wheel track east, for three miles to a good clayhole full of water, in a mulga wash. Low rock ledges along its eastern side mark the clayhole. We stopped here for dinner and did some washing. After dinner we turned off onto the old original Wiluna road, and followed it through the heart of some scrub covered hills for three or four miles. We came out into the open, then travel was along the reddish brown eastern flank of the Montague Range for a distance of four miles. This range got lower and lower until it petered out altogether. Travel was then level with breakaways on our east side, this took us into Bungarra Rockhole from the north. The track in was quite rough but runs through good dog country, yet not a sign of dogs to be seen.

Just before we turned off the old road onto the bush track, we passed a square rig bell tent pitched right in the middle of the old roadway. A bit further on we came across two nickel men putting in pegs. From Bungarra Rockhole we went halfway back to the old road to camp on an open stony flat by some Gidgee trees. This camp was just clear of the hills. The nickel men passed by with a wave not long after we made camp. They didn't stop to talk or anything, just a wave and kept going back to their own camp in the middle of the old road. We clocked a total today of thirty-six miles.

Wednesday 9 July - Speedo 60065 - Return east to the Granite Soak camp. On the way in I poisoned a roo carcase about half a mile east of the granite. No sign of dogs. I don't like this poison business but have to do my job. My dislike of a gruesome task balanced somewhat by the pleasures of seeing new country and other things of interest. Earlier this morning I shot a fox still alive in someone's trap set near the No 32 government well. Saw one old dog track near there headed north.

Thursday 10 July - We stayed on camp all day. Cold wind with an overcast sky and some misty rain. The weather dispersed by sundown and gave way to a clear starry night. It is wonderful to relax beside a good soakage water in open country, alone just the two of us, without a care in the world.

Friday 11 July - On camp all day again. We walked around the outer edge of the granite dome and all over the top of it seeking anything of interest. In soft ground a bit out from the perimeter of the granite, in various places, we found old native campsites and stone flints. Ancient charcoal and ashes, beneath a thin cover of stained soil, show where former natives' campfires burned to coals after their departure, never to return. There is no recent sign of former inhabitants. No natives have been here for a generation at least, prior to our appearance on the scene. We felt like staying in this idyllic spot for ever.

Saturday 12 July - Speedo 60088 - All good things must come to an end. With reluctance we packed up and left for Booylgoo Spring (Anglicised version of Pulyku, native name for kangaroo sinew) thence Kaluwiri and Agnew. We saw one dog track at Deep Bore to the north of Rainbow. Kunanyingkan Billy Cock was not at Agnew. I'll give him a report on recent activities later. We went on to Leonora. Picked up the mail and a telegram from David Henwood, advising me of a government dogging job. He has a vacancy at Wittenoom. Telegram also says he wants to interview me in person. If I can make the appointment with RVCO Henwood in time, I might take the job. Goodbye Kunanyingkan!

The Kaluwiri story is not complete without some anecdotes told me by Dooley, from observations and knowledge gained during several years spent at the homestead. Kunanyingkan was an eccentric of the first water. He was one to give lubras at the station grog and pretty clothes, in return for favours. He was away most of the time, at one or another of his several station properties. Those blacks left working on Kaluwiri often had insufficient rations, and seldom got paid on time. Kunanyingkan always seemed to have some good excuse for not paying, like forgetting to bring his cheque book. Not that he ever cheated, to the contrary he always paid what he owed, but the recipient had to go into Agnew to get it.

Workers left at the station always awaited his every return with eager anticipation. They knew he would bring plenty of grog, rations, clothes, and sweets, even if he did forget his cheque book. Upon each return after a long absence, his long neglected workers with their wives and kids, would gather around him in great anticipation of the treat to come. Dooley was not in the band of grog participants. She was one apart who watched the goings on from, a discreet distance. The night of boss's return was often a dusk to dawn booze session for all concerned. When the husbands got drunk or fell asleep, the wily lubras would visit Kunanyingkan for more grog. Sometimes a jealous husband would come to rattle a bundle of spears or boomerangs and prance around the homestead in search of an errant wife.

Next morning hangovers would prevail, or post mortems be held on the previous night's escapades. Kunanyingkan always managed to avoid conflict. At the first sign of trouble he would run off into the darkness and camp elsewhere. Sometimes he got in his vehicle for a quick getaway, and no one would see him again until weeks or even months later. After such a prolonged absence he would return once again to be the popular old bearer of gifts and goodies as before.

Dooley was not a drinker but she was nevertheless, respected and liked by Kunanyingkan. He often gave her special gifts and treated her more like a daughter. I noticed myself how she was able to handle the old man when I had problems with him at Agnew trying to pin him down. Dooley only had to speak and he would stop dead in his tracks to hear what she had to say.

Most of Dooley's Kaluwiri yarns are too hot to handle. I could never write them down for fear of defamation. Dooley tells spicy anecdotes of an earlier era she observed in her youth, a back country lifestyle that no longer exists. I remember those good old days myself, but from a different clime a thousand miles away in the Northern Territory. There are no blacks' camps on stations now, more's the pity. It was the illicit casual love affairs between whiteman and lubra that added such exotic colour to the bush. Oh how lovely it would be for a repeat of that ambient atmosphere of yesteryear. It was an essential theme for authors like Tom Ronan. That old writer could never have produced such gems of bush literature like "Moleskin Midas" or "Vision Splendid "without the red flesh of those old days. Tom Ronan must have experienced that lifestyle firsthand himself, because his tales are spot on. In the same way as Dooley and I relate to it, and not without a little tinge of nostalgia I might add.

One night all the camp women congregated around the boss's quarters while Dooley watched from the darkness outside. One of the husbands tired of being the classic cuckold, took a bundle of spears in hand and challenged the boss to come out and fight. The boss appeared on the verandah with shirt tails flapping but no pants at all. He made a comical sight as he dashed for his vehicle, got in, and drove off at top speed into the darkness to camp elsewhere.

Another time the boss guzzled too much whisky and the alcoholic excess became too great to endure. It was a hot day and the old chap rolled on the ground in a fit of horrors under the sun. He rolled from sunlit heat, to mottled shade, and back again, to an accompaniment all the while of shouts and groans. He kept this up until effects of the grog wore off, then he lay still like a dead man. One of the station hands threw a bucket of cold water over the old man to revive him. At the first slosh, the old chap woke up with a start and exclaimed: "Hey what's going on?" The water thrower asked: "Are you alright oldman? We thought you was proper deadfella!" "No I'm alright, nothing wrong with me" said the boss. Thus life at Kaluwiri rolled on until well into the late 1950s. The old era ceased almost overnight when the Whitlam government introduced full wages and free rights for Aborigines and as a result, they all soon became town fringe dwellers.

WITTENOOM

JULY 1969

Sunday 13 July 1969 - Left Leonora en route Wittenoom with the clock on 60296. Called in at Agnew to see Billy Cock. He wants me to stay but I told him it was money under false pretences as there are no dogs out there chewing the legs of his sheep, although he reckons they are. He gave me a cheque and paid me right up for a fortnight's work at the agreed rate. He is a real eccentric is old Billy Cock. I had to chase him all around the hotel complex and the outbuilding workshops in order to pin him down. He just won't stop and talk. The moment you approach him he sidles off to one side. I eventually cornered him in a passageway and shouldered him into his office where he couldn't escape. At first he made out he couldn't find his cheque book, then it was his pen went missing. At last I coaxed him into writing it out, then with cheque in hand I bade him goodbye. We travelled north Dooley and me, to within fifty-five miles of Wiluna for dinner, then on to Meekatharra for supper. Later we travelled through the night to Kumarina, the wayside pub, to camp across the creek at 11-30 pm.

Monday 14 July - Speedo 60765 - North along the highway the corrugations are so deep and rough they almost shook the Landrover to pieces. We pulled up for dinner at a clay swamp about ninety miles east of Wittenoom to repair a flat tyre. We had a bath there and Dooley did some washing. Camped further along the road to fix another flat tyre. 262 miles for the day.

Tuesday 15 July - Speedo 61027 - Suffered yet another flat tyre during the night. Got up at daylight to fix it then on towards Wittenoom. It is a lot warmer up here than back at Leonora but still cool enough. We arrived Wittenoom at 10-30 am and left a message at both store and garage to tell David Henwood I was in town. He came along late and said he'd start me on the job tomorrow morning. Thirty-three miles travel today.

Wednesday 16 July - Speedo 61060 - I make it 764 miles from Leonora to Wittenoom. This trip was a bit of an anti climax. After the interview with Henwood it was clear he had far too many petty rules and regulations for my liking. I enjoy my independence. I declined the position on the spot, and walked off leaving Henwood standing perplexed with mouth agape. He seemed not to know how to handle the situation. We spent the rest of the morning at the garage waiting for repairs to the steering relay rod. It is a wonder the steering rods didn't fall right off after all those corrugations on the Great Northern Highway (sic). The fuel tank took fifty-two gallons. The Henwood sod wouldn't even contemplate filling the tank at APB expense. I had to pay out of my own pocket. We live and learn. From Wittenoom we travelled via Kumarina and Beyondie, through the night to the 485 Mile Well, on the old Rabbit Proof Fence to camp. I don't know what time we arrived but it was late. A total of three hundred and forty miles for the day.

Thursday 17 July - Speedo 61403 - We went down to Roach's 477 Mile camp. I used this trip as an opportunity to take the shortest route home from Wittenoom and revisit my old run north of Wiluna, along the Rabbit Proof Fence. The trip was uneventful from Beyondie and disappointing to find John not at his bough shed. He'd not been there in several weeks.

There was however sign of new wheel tracks some weeks old, heading off west of his camp. We followed them to some thick mulga wash country where the track split up into several less distinct tracks, some of which led to new bore sites. The driller seemed to have done his job and gone. There were three new boreholes, all unequipped as yet, but no sign of John. We returned to the fenceline. He appears to have gone further west so nothing else for it but to give up the chase. We travelled right through to Leonora to arrive at 11-30 pm. Left Wittenoom at 61610 arrive Leonora at 61755, that makes it 695 miles from Wittenoom to Leonora by the shorter route, as against 764 miles via Meekatharra.

Friday 18 July - We are now back in Leonora and out of work again for the present. Dooley cut her leg badly. We were playing chase and tag like a couple of kids, when she slipped and fell in the doorway of the old detached kitchen. She gashed her leg on a sharp end of exposed sheet iron that overlapped the door frame. I rushed her to hospital where they put in about twenty stitches and gave her a large dose of anti tetanus injection. An accumulation of cooking fat, grease, and grime from the passage of many years on the corrugated iron sheet, was in my opinion a recipe for blood poisoning. I wonder how she escaped such dire complications, the sharp iron sheet was so filthy. She is alright now, but the leg is still sore.

Monday 21 July - We stayed awake all night to hear a radio broadcast of the Luna landing. Mans' first landing on the Moon. At 4:18 am in the nodule Eagle, from the Command Ship Colombia in the Sea of Tranquillity. A mystery Russian spacecraft also reported in a 10 to 60 mile orbit above the Moon. The American astronauts on the surface are: Neil Armstrong and Buzz Orldren, with Michael Collins in Colombia. They walked about on the Lunar surface for several hours before returning to Eagle for a rest, prior to departure. They are due to depart for Earth tomorrow morning.

Tuesday 22 July - Today I put the Landrover into the Garage for a complete overhaul and recondition. That done I started renovations on our stone house. We plan to put in a lawn and fix the doors to give some security and privacy. I purchased some things for a bit of building work: a saw, claw hammer, tin snips, nails, a paint brush, and large can of red paint.

AUGUST 1969

The foregoing account, completes my written records for the month of July 1969. I spent several unwritten weeks fixing up the stone house and making it fit enough to live in. We had a few incidents with drunken Aborigines trying to invade us and make themselves at home, but I gave them all short shrift. I know this didn't reflect well on Dooley's standing with her mob, they were after all, her kith and kin, however I was adamant that none would sponge on me. I have lived an independent life too long for that. Her relatives were welcome to visit in daylight hours if sober, but I will not suffer drunks at any time, day or night. My possessions always include a bundle of spears, a couple of woomeras, a few boomerangs, and a pair of fighting sticks. There was one memorable occasion when I had to evict an unwelcome visitor at spear point, and another when I had to defend myself with a block of sawn timber directed at an assailant's forehead. The clobbered individual went to hospital for a few days while I enjoyed a respite of peace and quiet for several weeks. I am soft hearted by nature but will not suffer abuse in silence, or assault without retaliation.

During the five weeks spent on house renovations I saw Jack Kerr the Kalgoorlie RVCO a few times and asked him when the promised APB job was to be available. The promise still held he said, but as yet he had no vacancies. He assured me each time I asked, that the first vacant position was mine. In the meantime the Landrover overhaul was complete and we had the use of our vehicle again. It was just like new, despite being almost ten years old. During the first week in August I contacted a bad dose of flu deep down in the chest, with a painful cough like I've never suffered before. One night I drank a flask of rum to ease the pain but the stuff didn't even put me to sleep. I learned to cope with the ailment after the first couple of weeks but the damn thing wouldn't go away. One day during the last week of August 1969 we had an unexpected visitor. Graeme Hardy, manager of Yundamindra Station, called in to ask if I'd like to take on an outcamp job as windmill man and part-time dogger. No word from Jack Kerr about the long awaited APB position so I agreed to take the station job on trial.

Figure 7 Wittenoom 1968

Chapter Five - YUNDAMINDRA

AUGUST 1969 (continued)

Author's note: "My diary of outcamp events has detailed notes on the condition of each water point visited on the windmill run during our time on Yundamindra. I will not however bore the reader with such mundane things. There was not a lot in the way of excitement or undue interest while we were there either. However this period of employment fills an important gap between the foregoing account of our honeymoon travels or wanngitjarra as wangkayi people term an elopement, and what was yet to come. This chapter will not comprise many pages, and for that matter need not even be read, but as part of a continuous record it is essential to include it."

Tuesday 26 - I started work on Yundamindra Station at Larkins Outcamp where cleaning up around the little cottage took all day. The former occupants left this place in one hell of a mess and in a real filthy state. A team of surveyors are camping nearby in the shearers' quarters only fifty paces away from us. My bout of flu is still with me after several weeks and dust from the cleanup today did little to improve the ailment.

Wednesday 27 - We finished the cottage cleanup this morning. After dinner I went over the station's SWB Diesel Landrover. This vehicle was also in a dirty state.

Thursday 28 - There were two punctures to fix before I could start out on the mill run. That done, I took Dooley with me and we started out for the south-west. This is all new country to both of us therefore I record it in detail for future reference. The manager gave me a good map of the station so I knew where to go.

Travel was southerly from Larkins past Richies Bore and along an unfinished fenceline. I was to pick up a full drum of diesel near a new cement tank that has no mill on it. This new tank is filled by a windmill located two miles away from it to the west. The latter mill is Celebration Bore. We had dinner at the cement tank then went west past the said Celebration and south-west from there to a bore near a lake. This is Porcupine Bore and the earth tank is nearly dry!

From Porcupine, travel was west at first then north to Percy Well. We left the fence there and took a run through the middle of the paddock north-west to Davis Bore. South-west then two miles to Dead End Tank right on the boundary. Return to Davis Bore and continue north-west to Davis Well where I met a station hand from the homestead on a motorbike. We passed the time of day for a few minutes then left him to his chores.

We went on north-east to a water point called Marloo Well, then east along the fence and back to Larkins Outcamp. The mill run today covered 42 miles. The first thing upon arrival home was to find that a hose connecting two water pipes had come adrift. There was water everywhere. I fixed the leak then unloaded the drum of fuel then went out for some firewood.

Friday 29 - Today I did another section of the windmill run, south-east to Lower Box Well. We passed a good waterhole in a creek when about halfway. There are a number of soaks in a wide creek with bullrushes, just short of the mill. Also a shallow well near the soakage creek, with water only a few feet below the surface. I presume this is the original Box Well as it has a slab timber lining. From Lower Box Well, travel was four mils east along a fence that runs over red agate hills to Dolly Pots Bore. The float in one trough needed attention and took me some time to fix. From Dolly Pots we went four miles south-west to The Gap Bore. This bore has a brand new Southern Cross tower with eight foot fan. It pumps into two earth tanks. I don't know why it's called The Gap as there is nothing like a gap anywhere near it. Our course next was south across a wide and open saltbush plain. This plain was quite a surprise. I didn't expect to ever see such a beautiful feature in the Leonora area. At five miles we came to a huge earthen dam in the middle of the magnificent saltbush expanse. This earth tank called Reedy's Dam is reminiscent of similar structures that are so common in the Northern Territory on stations around Alice Springs.

Travel next was north-west to Stewart's Tank, this tank has no mill. Troughs there, are either side of a fence running from north-east to south-west. The water for this tank and troughs comes along a pipeline from the north-east. We followed the pipeline in that direction and came to Stewart's Well at three miles. From there we went east through the middle of the paddock four miles to Kangaroo Bore which is salty. The country en route has a pleasant aspect with sandy soil and wattles. We saw some old mine shafts on a stony ridge just west of the mill. Plenty of cattle tracks. North-west six miles next to Mount Howe Well. From the latter it was four miles to Hills Well, which has an overhead tank and stonework around the well dump. The stonework is of excellent quality, no doubt built by a qualified mason. In addition there is an ordinary concrete ground tank. Not far to the north-east of Hills, is a big government dam. This large catchment has a corrugated iron roof right over it and sits within a barb wire enclosure. The roof is a huge structure. The water is excellent, clean and fresh. A lot of old mine dumps four miles west of the tank. Linden Well is behind some low hills. Six miles further west is Middle Box Bore where the tank and troughs are dry and the mill has no column. Another six mile west is Perseverance Bore. Perseverance has a lot of sheep on north side of the fence and though the tank is nearly dry, both troughs are full. The mill seemed to be pumping okay and I thought maybe it was only short of wind. This proved not to be the case however, I climbed the tower and turned the fan for some time but no water came up, so it must be out of order. Return home to Larkins after an eighty-four mile run for the day.

Saturday 30 - I am responsible for a huge windmill run here and today we set of on the third section. I had a puncture to fix before departure, then it was off we go, this time to the north-west for three miles to Pearce's Bore where was six feet of water in the tank and mill pumping okay. North then to White Quartz Tank where was also six feet of water, then west to White Quartz Bore, that has no tank itself but pumps into its namesake along a pipeline. While there I ran the fenceline west to a dry corner, just to get the lay of the land, then return 12 mile to White Quartz Tank. From there we went 15 mile north to Bore Well. Then south-east to Top Box Well and east again to Linden Well. From Linden Well we followed the edge of the lake around north-east to Linden Bore and return from there via the mine dumps to Linden Well again. I found this route to be one mile shorter than the route via lake's edge.
South next to Mount Howe Well, Stewart's, then south-west past Dolly Pots to The Gap for a late dinner. Then home to Larkin's after another eighty-four mile day to write all this minor detail down for posterity and some future bored reader.

Sunday 31 - My severe bout of flu has gone at last, and not before time either. We went in to the homestead today for meat, stores, tools, and some parts for trough repairs. I need a couple of floats and a plug to block the outlet pipes while working on the floats.

We returned to the outcamp via Murphy's Well and Pearce's Bore where the tank was dry and a lot of rams waiting for a drink. One ram is dead, and two are down. We offloaded the meat into the fridge at Larkin's then took off east to have a look at Perseverance Bore. The mill has been pumping and I waited for some wind to come up while there to make sure it was still okay. The wind drought is the trouble, just like I thought the other day. The mill is quite okay but my manual turning of the wheel before wasn't enough to bring water up the column. We got back home for a late dinner and afterward I had a flat tyre to fix. Some wind came up in the late afternoon and a few thunder heads in the east, to entice nostalgic thoughts of the desert land that I miss so much. Only thirty-one miles today.

SEPTEMBER 1969

Monday 1 - We went out to check Perseverance Bore again this morning. It was pumping okay but not enough water in tank to fill troughs. Further on at Middle Box I had to unhook a ewe tangled in the fence, her anxious lamb nearby was obviously happy to see her released. Hardie's Weir okay. Top Box Well okay with tank three quarters full, wherefrom we went into a V shape holding paddock west of Linden, then north along a fence to Con's Lake to have a look for dog tracks but none there. From Con's Lake it was back along the fence south for a while, then two miles west to a soak located in the middle of a laterite gravel flat.

The laterite flat itself being surrounded by a much larger expanse of saltbush plain along the lake's shoreline. To me this is a new type of soak. I have not seen the likes of one before in such a situation. The existence of this soak makes me think of all the similar type of country I have explored during 1965-68 for the APB. If a soak exists here then I may have missed others like it in similar country elsewhere. This soak has an open aspect broken only by a few mulga trees and willows along the south side. A person could walk within thirty paces of it and not see the soak at all. Looks like one dog track here.

I shot a boomer about one mile west and returned with the carcase to drag a scent trail right around the soak. I also made sure to keep some distance back so as not to foul the water, then left the remains as bait. A few miles west of the soakage we came to Con's Lake Dam and from there it is five miles north and west to Camel Backs Dam. Both dams are picturesque, set as they are in the midst of saltbush flats, with a scenic backdrop of high peaks and rugged hills. There are lots of mineral exploration and survey lines with pegs and ribbons of coloured flagging right through this area, this activity is maybe a portent of things to come

From the picturesque dams it is six miles southerly to Bore Well and from there five miles west to Eucalyptus Bore, where a nearby earth tank is dry. Thirteen points in the Eucalyptus rain gauge. Five miles further south to No 1 Bore and from thence on to Murphy's Well, which is okay. White Quartz Bore that is pumping alright but has three troughs dry. Called in to Perseverance Bore and found it now with water in the troughs for a change. Pearce's Bore has water in troughs but water tank is low. I shot a goat near Con's Lake today and brought it home for meat. I put in two dummy posts today whilst on the mill run. Got home to Larkins at 5 pm. Eighty four miles travelled all told.

Tuesday 2 - We had four points of rain at Larkins last night. I did the standard mill run today. There is not much to report except that Dead End Tank is empty but troughs full. Five rungs of water in tank at Perseverance so it is catching up after the wind drought. I put in two dummies along fenceline between Percy Well and Porcupine. Eighty nine miles for the day.

Wednesday 3 - We enjoyed a day at home for a change. I cleaned up along the 'board' in the shearing shed then put in a new gate post and a couple of dummies one mile along a fence west of the outcamp. In the afternoon I cleaned up around the yard first, then put in a couple more dummies east toward Perseverance Bore. I wished to see how the mill was pumping, it has pumped nearly a sheet of water since yesterday. Home then to clean out six troughs at Larkins. Only eleven miles on the clock today.

Thursday 4 - There are now five rungs of water in Perseverance. The interesting soakage we found on Monday, we now know as Green Hills. There are three foxes, one eagle, and one crow beside the bait, but no sign of any dogs been anywhere near it. We arrived at Murphy's Well to find an abandoned Mini Moke vehicle standing there. Pearce's Bore tank is dry and troughs are all empty. I put in several dummies along the fence to Middle Box Bore and shot three goats. The manager worries about the number of goats on his property. They are classified as vermin. Eighty miles travel today.

Friday 5 - Dead End tank now has a little water in it and both troughs are brimful. All the other water points are okay. We found a soak in saltbush country along a sandy water channel, between Celebration Tank and Lower Box, about one mile south of the fence. We went in to Mount Celia homestead to visit the owner Jim Norton, then home to Larkins after an eighty three mile day.

Saturday 6 - Mr Aubrey Hardie gave us a surprise visit at the outcamp with half a sheep for our meat ration. I worked for him on his Pilbara property Warralong in 1960 and last saw him in 1968 when I was still with the APB. I certainly did not expect to ever meet up with him on his southern station Yundamindra. After he left, Dooley and I went along the fence to pick up a drum of dieseline. On the way back I topped the load off with firewood for the camp and burnt some stumps out along the cutline to make it better for future travel. When we got back to the outcamp I cleaned the station Landrover as well as our own, then polished both vehicles until they shone. I knocked off at 3 pm to clean up for the picture show at the homestead tonight. The vehicle did twenty five miles today and the weather is cold again.

Monday 8 - We had a day off on camp all day Sunday. This morning we went west along the road from Linden and found some dry gnamma holes just south of a few low hills on the way to Green Hill Soak. From there we went around past Green Hill and found one more fox on the roo bait and an eagle on the poisoned goat carcase further on. We went on to Con's Lake Dam and inspected some breakaway country east of the dam. The breakaways are colourful and interesting but no sign of dogs or rockholes there.

Travel next was south to the old Linden to Murrin Murrin road then west to the Eucalyptus windmill run and back via Murphy's Well and Pearce's Bore home after ninety six miles for the day. We met old Aubrey Hardie and son Graeme working sheep in the yards at Murphy's. We also saw where the old man shot twelve goats along the fenceline, the carcases all in sight of the track and just through the fence.

Wednesday 10 - Yesterday was just a humdrum "run o' the mill" windmill run of eighty one miles, with little to report. Today I went out and put in twelve dummies. Straightened the fence north from Middle Box to Top Box, then back south-west through middle of the paddock to pinpoint Gardiner's Find, an alluvial gold patch. We picked up a load of firewood for the camp along the way. Only twenty six miles today.

Friday 12 to **Monday 15** - We did seventy seven miles on Thursday, and had a look along a lot of branch tracks at various places, but not much else to report. Today was similar in that respect with a total of ninety three miles. We came back home before sundown then packed up for a three day spell in town.

On Monday morning I got a telegram from Jack Kerr the Kalgoorlie APB Regional to inform me that a dogger's job is now available in the Laverton area. I am to start work for the APB again in about three weeks. Good news at last. Went back to the station.

Tuesday 16 -Wednesday 17 - Thursday 18 - Were humdrum days in all respects.

Today I went into the homestead for leather and gutter bolts to repair leaking troughs and obtained a new glass for the outcamp fridge. I gave Graeme three weeks notice. Graeme Hardie doesn't want me to leave and offers a higher wage to stay. I told him thanks but think I am far more use to him and other pastoralists as an APB dogger than as a part time one on the station. He is a good boss but my love of the desert is too strong to remain here.

I feel Graeme is not partial toward my potential new boss Jack Kerr for giving me a job, but that's how it is. I'm afraid the poor fellow has little option but accept my decision with good grace. We came back to Larkins to fit the fridge glass then travel south-east to Stewart Tank and bolt eighteen leather patches to holes in the tank. Not enough water in the tank to fill the trough yet, as the outlet pipe at the trough float is higher than the water level in the tank. On next to Reedy's and fit four leather patches to the trough there. After dinner we went south along fence to southern boundary, where I made a new cocky gate. While in that area we saw some low shrubs that look for all the world like the northern gidgea tree, that does not grow in the Leonora region at all. We don't know what species they are and doubt they are gidgea, but we wonder nevertheless. A gidgea tree in this country would be an interesting find indeed.
I finished constructing the cocky gate then we went for a drive away off the beaten tracks to look at country not yet seen by us. This trip took us through twenty miles of sandhills and lake country, west all the way to where I thought Celebration Mill should be, due north of our route. I next cut through the paddock over limestone and quartzose undulations to reach the mill right spot on target, as anticipated. Home then to Larkins via Richie's Bore. We suffered only one flat tyre all day despite the amount of off-road travel. The weather is still cold with a chill east wind. A seventy two mile run today.

Friday 19 - I rang Graeme Hardie the manager last night for the usual daily report and he said to go out north to Camel Backs today in search of cattle tracks. This morning I did just that. First I had a look around both dams there, then went to Box Well and Top Box, but saw no sign of cattle tracks at all. I criss-crossed the country after that preliminary look around the perimeter of the area, but could find no evidence of cattle at all. Later I went further east into the Linden paddock and there found fresh signs of cattle all over, but after following the tracks a ways, I saw that horse riders had got the lot. I gave the area a thorough search regardless, but feel sure the boys left nothing behind. They did a good muster in Linden paddock, although there is always a chance that one or two cunning beasts might be still in there. That job done we returned through Pearce's paddock from Top Box, south-west through the guts of it to Larkins without seeing any evidence of cattle, either old or new.

Saturday 20 - I haven't mentioned before that Dooley always comes with me. I never leave her behind anytime. We enjoy each other's company and work well together. This morning we set off early to continue looking for any sign of cattle missed by the riders. We looked all over Richie's but the riders left nothing behind, so all we had to do was check. We went next through the guts of Mount Howe paddock to the mill and found the boys there, with fifty seven head of cattle in the yards. Johnny Phillips brought in another fifteen head while we were there. Lenny Grey came in without any a short time later. One other man Lumi Nelson yet to come in. I did a count of how many beasts in hand. There should be at least another twelve head of cattle to get yet, maybe in Reedy's or Stewart's paddocks. The riders' camp is close to the yards. We saw Lenny's wife Irene there with little daughter Andrea. These are all Dooley's people. We left the boys to do their job and went south to Stewart's Tank to inspect the repairs I did to the trough last trip. It was full, but still leaking a little, so I threw some sand in to take up the leak, then home to Larkins to clean up for the picture show tonight at the homestead. Today also, we found several fresh soakage waters along Box Creek and an ancient well, all washed in. Seventy two miles all told.

Sunday 21 - We heard news on the radio this evening that Laverton Police shot and killed one man during a clash between five officers and thirty blacks on the Native Reserve. We stayed on camp all day. A quiet pigeon with a broken leg came along from somewhere. It hung around all day but was too shy to catch. The bird wore a leg band with lettering on it.

Monday 22 - We inspected Marloo and Davis wells, then from Dead End tank we tried a track as yet new to us. We followed the boundary fence west at first, then north to Marloo fence. Travel east then to Marloo, and south from there to an old gate, and back to the usual mill run track. Once on the track it was north-east back to the Larkins shed. We then took off again on the usual track to Percy Well and Pearce's Bore. From the latter it was south to the boundary, and along it east, to a big bald sandhill about one mile east of the Porcupine Hills. We found a small native grinding stone right on top of the sandhill. By the time we got through the rest of the mill run and home the clock had one hundred and two miles up. There was one Laverton native shot and killed today during a clash between thirty blacks and five police.

Tuesday 23 - We were all ears this morning as the ABC News gave more details of tragic events near Laverton Native Reserve at two o'clock on Sunday afternoon. Two police are in hospital. One who got speared during the fracas has a collapsed lung. The other has three broken teeth. Both police had ribs fractured by blows from iron bars. One native, a Raymond Watson I gather, got shot dead.

The fight escalated from routine inquiries about a stolen vehicle. Five police went to the reserve supported by a few leading white citizens from town. All the whites carried firearms. The police party itself comprised a Kalgoorlie Inspector, two Leonora constables, and two local officers from Laverton. We heard on the seven o'clock news last night how police arrested one native on Monday the 22nd for assault, and three others for illegal use of a motor vehicle. There will no doubt be public outrage and maybe even a Royal Commission. Unless the government decides to hush it up. They usually do when anything dealing with mistreatment of Aborigines occurs. Too much politics these days with the United Nations and all that. I feel that this latest smash should see the light of day so all can judge the rights or wrongs of it. We went out on the mill run again and covered a lot of country in the Camel Backs area today. We followed the embedded wheel ruts of old horse and cart tracks and enjoyed a most interesting day of eighty nine miles.

Wednesday 24 - We went to look at some new country again today and completely covered the diorite hills near Mount Percy. The only thing of interest we found was an old bore hole and a post cutter's campsite on the east side. Dooley thought it was a good prospect for alluvial gold but we saw no evidence of old dry blower workings. Next we had a look around Richie's and Pearce's for cattle tracks but found none. We got home early to find the surveyors packing up ready to depart. We had a good yarn with them. Mike the boss finds the Canning Stock Route of great interest, I gave him a photo of AW Canning, and one of myself. He seemed happy to accept the gift. We did fifty three miles today.

Thursday 25 - The surveyors all set to go this morning so we said goodbye to them and went off on our mill run. Nothing unusual to report for a day of eighty three miles. Friday 26 was a similar experience for a total of eighty eight miles back to the camp. After supper we left Larkins for Leonora in our own vehicle to stay the weekend in town. Monday 29 - We came back to Larkins and did a mill run of eighty miles, and the same routine again on Tuesday 30 September, with eighty nine miles to finish the month off.

OCTOBER 1969

Wednesday 1 - We went out to White Quartz. I fixed the trough there then spent the rest of the day putting in dummies around the perimeter fence of Pearce's paddock. Later at home, shortly after arrival, we got an unexpected surprise when a large party of nickel prospectors appeared and set up camp. They parked several big caravans to one side of the shed. Our run today was only thirty four miles.

Saturday 4 - We spent the last couple of days on the mill runs. Not much to report other than cattle at Kangaroo Bore and, I cleaned out every trough on the two runs. Today I mustered one hundred and thirty sheep from Richie's Well which is almost dry, and took them to Perseverance. Total of thirty seven miles.

Sunday 5 - We on camp all day. I did some transcription of my 1965-68 handwritten exploration journals for the State Library in Perth. This is going to be a long and tedious job but I cannot part with the originals for fear they go astray. They are irreplaceable.

Monday 6 - I did the south-west section today. All okay except Richie's Bore. It still has only six feet of water in the tank. Davis Bore is down to one sheet of water at the bottom. All the others are okay. Did ninety three miles.

Tuesday 7 - Everything is okay on the north run. One sheep bogged in Camel Backs Dam and a lamb hooked up in the fence at Eucalyptus. One hundred and seven miles.

Wednesday 8 - We went and had a look at Richie's waterhole. It still has water enough for a couple of days but looks like most of the sheep I shifted away from here last Saturday are back again. They must like the place, wet or dry. It is no wonder sheep perish. They are so stupid. They may as well stay here now until the waterhole dries up.

I found a bore hole that Graeme told me of, near Richie's Waterhole. It is a good mile or more to the west of Graeme's directions and in thick scrub country. Only the bore casing, no mill or anything. The hole has water in it about ten feet from the surface.

We went across to Camel Backs dam to find one lamb bogged in the mud. I pulled the lamb out then we went back to Larkins, where is an extra three caravans with more men and vehicles, to add to the lot that came along last week. This makes a total of eighteen Kelmscott Exploration employees working out from here altogether now. The place is getting overcrowded and far too much traffic for my liking.

On a more pleasant note, we had a surprise gate opener on hand to greet us as we drove in to our camp. He was visible well before we got close, and even from a distance we saw on his head a big sombrero, like the one I always wear. Not many people wear ten gallon hats in this neck of the woods, so we wondered who he might be. There never was such an exuberant man. He waved us down with arm fully extended in a most amiable and eager-to-meet- you fashion.

The moment we pulled up at the gate he introduced himself as Rick Edwards the new Yundamindra overseer. Rick began to swap reminiscences when told how I originally came to WA from Alice Springs in 1959. It soon became apparent that our paths crossed on numerous occasions in one part of the Northern Territory or another, but we never met. This was a puzzle to me in a way, but I had no reason to doubt his veracity because he spoke of oldtimers known well to me back in those old days.

Thursday 9 - We did our second last windmill run for Yundamindra and nothing wrong anywhere for a change. I reckon that is a good way to finish a job. We saw our exuberant visitor of yesterday, Rick Edwards again today, on his way back from Richie's Bore. To my surprise he now informs me he is leaving Yundamindra next week. I do hope our nostalgic journey through the past last night was not the cause of his sudden decision to pull out. He says he is not long down from the Kimberley cattle country, and as I know full well from personal experience, you just cannot make a sheep man out of a stockman. I wouldn't be in this blasted sheep country myself except for the government dogging that kept me here so long, and soon will again, as from October 13 next. The wide open desert country for me and bugger the mutton. I don't blame Rick Edwards at all. We did eighty three miles today. This evening we packed up all our gear in readiness for departure tomorrow, just so soon as our last windmill run for the station is over.

Friday 10 1969 - We enjoyed our last trip around the windmill run and found everything in order. We packed up everything on our own Landrover yesterday soon as we got back to Larkins. We started for the homestead immediately to get my cheque. By the look on Graeme's face when he paid me off I could see he didn't want me to go. If I name my own price I'm sure he'll say yes I thought. We parted with a strong handshake on the office verandah. I went over next to see Rick and look at his two ponies in the yard near the overseer's quarters. He has a wife and couple of kids and floats the ponies behind his car when on the move. We yarned for a little while and I asked him why he was leaving. He just doesn't like the work system on this station he said, and with that snippet of information on board, we waved goodbye, and set off for Leonora to await the arrival of Jack Kerr. Jack is to sign me on as the Laverton Region dogger next week.

Figure 8 Our Old Stone House "Hometead Palms" Leonora 1969

Some Afterthoughts

I took pains at the beginning of this Chapter Five about our time on Yundamindra to warn of possible mundane issues that might bore my readers to death. However as the reader may by now have discovered, I had in fact forgotten that there was a lot of interest and one notable historic event that did occur during our stay at Larkins Outcamp. This makes me glad I included the full diary account after all. I now commend following chapters dealing with the APB and desert environs to all who care to follow my tracks out that way.

"Look out APB here we come."

Chapter Six - BACK IN THE SADDLE AGAIN

OCTOBER 1969 continued.

Wednesday 15 - I was right on time for the Monday appointment with Jack Kerr but he didn't turn up until today. Not to worry though because he signed me onto the APB soon after his arrival and handed me a government vehicle, together with APB stores such as traps, etc. Most important of all, I got an LPO book (Local Purchase Order) for fuel, maintenance, repairs, and other official expenditures. By the look of the battered old Landrover, the repairs part of the equation might come much sooner than later. I counted four bald tyres with visible stake holes, and fracture splits on the side walls of each. To top it off the two spare wheels were as flat as the proverbial pancake. I suggested to Jack Kerr that I might be better off using my own vehicle but he wouldn't even contemplate it. "You can't use your own vehicle at anytime Peter." Jack said, "That is just not an option, the APB wont wear it."

The run I'm to take over is the biggest in WA. It has the number **G6** but locals call it the Laverton Dogging Area. Another dogger, one Happy (Alex) Absalom, is to meet me tomorrow to show me around. I met Happy Absalom two years ago at a doggers' conference, held at the shearing shed on Albion Downs station in June 1967.

When I left the APB last year I was happy to see the end of daily journals. I do admit I enjoyed writing notes on exploration activities, but disliked the official requirement to do so. My independent nature does not align well with such disciplines. This is the rebel within, and my ancestral Irish dislike of anything to do with authority. Now however, I must begin again the daily chore of recorded mileage and activities.

Thursday 16 - (34250) We left Leonora early Dooley and me, to arrive in Laverton at 9 am after a trip of sixty-seven miles. We met Happy Absalom at 10 am and left town for Cosmo Newberry right away. I had no call to visit anyone at the mission so let Happy go there himself to say a quick hello. We then headed north into new country for me, but well known to Dooley, she walked all over these parts on foot as a child with her tribal people.

At thirty miles north of Cosmo, now well into open unfenced country, we came on first signs of the former dogger and his work. We saw a desiccated fox carcase in one trap and a bit further on an exposed trap with nothing in it. We stopped to reset both traps and while stationary, I wrote my first notes on activities to date.

We passed over, or perhaps I should say through, a range of dark coloured hills. The map I had with me calls these rolling humps the Ullrich Range, with one high peak named Mount Strawbridge. The local name however is Gregory Hills. The latter nomenclature being borne out by the headstone on a grave we came to at a distance of about fifty miles north of Cosmo Newberry.

The grave is close to the motor track just a few feet north of the road verge. It has a neat iron fence surround and the somewhat peculiar situation of two headstones, each at variance to the other. One is a natural stone slab from the nearby hills, the other an orthodox marble headstone. The natural slab bears a simple legend gouged into the stone's red patina, and leans against the fence surround outside the enclosure at foot end of the grave. It reads:

The natural slab bears a simple inscription while the marble headstone portrays a more elaborate message.

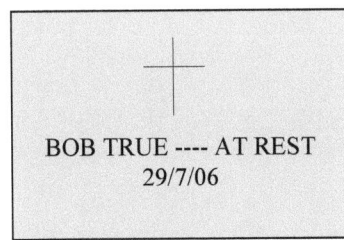

BOB TRUE ---- AT REST
29/7/06

Robert Irve's prospector mates of 1906 spelt his name as True. The headstone mason inscribed the name as Irve. I take it the earlier version was a mistake and the deceased was really Irve. From this lonely grave we went west for a few miles then left that road and followed wheel tracks north through lake country, to a shallow bore hole with windmill called Earli Earli. There is no stock out here. This is all unfenced open country at Lake Wells. Peter Hill the part owner and manager of Bandya Station, intends to settle out this way at some time in the future. He has three

IN
Loving Memory
OF
ROBERT IRVE

WHO DIED AT GREGORY HILLS
JULY 29   1906
AGED 43 YEARS
ERECTED BY HIS COMRADES

waters equipped with windmills in readiness. Odd dog tracks all the way out here from Cosmo, with plenty of kangaroos and rabbits. A total of 176 miles travelled today.

Friday 17 - (34426) This seems a small mileage for such a decrepit rattler of a Landrover, but that is what the speedo says. The Earli Earli windmill pumps out onto the ground. There is no tank or troughs. Happy says the mill is here for the dogger's benefit. The water is beautiful fresh fluid and delightful to drink. Someone thought to plant a date palm here. It is only a small one but should do well as it sits close to where the ground is moist with water pumping from the windmill. We drove two miles north to Earli Earli waterhole. This catchment lies in a stony creek that runs south out of a tangle of dark scrubby hills. The hills constitute a low range, running at this point from east to west across the northern horizon. The pool is up a tight little gully hemmed in on either side by unattractive rough stony hills.

Old Happy says it is twenty years since he was out this way, and some of the tracks out here now are new to him. The narrow graded road we followed north from Cosmo was a gift put in by Laverton Shire Council for Peter Hill. It will give him easy access to his proposed new cattle station when the time comes to begin operations. So far he has the three mills already mentioned, together with a pile of paraphernalia to the east of Irve's Grave. Around a windmill at northern extremity of the graded track from Cosmo Newberry, he has a fenced enclosure. Inside this enclosure are piles and piles of corrugated iron sheets, stacks of timber, and all manner of other things. Prominent to one side is a small, but tall shed. A relic of the long since defunct Laverton railway line.

There are a few signs of dogs around Earli Earli that I will have to investigate later when this guided tour is over and we are by ourselves on the job. In the meantime we went two miles further west and came to another windmill on a well, this is Escreet. It is not pumping and the well is much deeper than the bore back at Earli Earli. I took a look down the shaft and saw neat timberwork all the way. Whoever put this well down was a good craftsman.

Three miles further west of Escreet we turned north along wheel tracks that skirt the Earli Earli range of hills where they turn north-west. Three miles north along this old track we came to a dry rockhole. Another two mile on from the rockhole was a sprung trap, on a bend where the track takes a turn to the south-west. We went west a further two miles from the sprung trap to cut a brand new, wide graded road, running north and south.

This grandiose new graded by-way is a designated beef road, a project of Laverton Shire Council. The road will service new cattle country around Lake Carnegie. The beef road will cut out a four hundred mile trip west to Meekatharra via Wiluna. The proposal is for cattle to travel in road trains, south via Laverton to Kalgoorlie, instead of the much longer journey over rough roads west via Wiluna. This so-called beef road bears no signs of recent use at all. The only evidence of large beasts on it, being a host of fresh camel tracks stringing along up and down its length.

From where we hit the bovine road, travel is level with, and west of a southern extension of the Von Treur Tableland. There is a magnificent white bluff to be seen as the road nears Warren's Well. The bluff is on west side of the road and faces east, set at the end of a line of orange red escarpments, coming in to meet the road from west side. The Von Treur Range forms a backdrop to the east, still running parallel with the road, as both run north and south. We passed a survey party with vehicles in convoy at one stage but they didn't stop so we kept going. We came to Warren's Well at twenty miles north of where we hit the beef road earlier. The first signs of cattle are present here. There are two more windmills north of Warren's Well. The first bears the unlikely name "Rock And Roll" and is met at ten miles north-east of Warren's Well near Bonython Creek. The second is called "The Jump Up" which lays three miles north of Rock And Roll and as the name suggests, Jump Up sits at the southern foot of Von Treur Tableland where that range trends toward the west. We turned back from here. I wanted to see Windidda Spring but old Happy Alex Absalom was setting the agenda this trip, and he wanted to turn back. I was a ringer in the stockcamp on Windidda Station in 1963 and rode on horseback over that country. Never mind I'll see that end of the run later when me and Dooley are alone on the job.

We came back to Warren's Well, then went two miles west to Kurumin Claypan. This is a fairly large circular claypan surrounded by a low sandy bank. The pan itself supports a dense growth of edible bush tucker, an annual called kurumin. The plant consists of a main stalk about two feet high, with side stems growing out from the main trunk like branches on a pine tree. We saw no sign of seeds on the plants today. Maybe the season is too dry. From Kurumin we travelled along a winding set of wheel tracks, about eighteen miles south-west, for some fifteen miles through scrub wash country, then south for three miles to Deleta.

Deleta was an oft mentioned place when I was in the Windidda stockcamp six years ago. I found the name most fascinating. It seemed one of those unattainable desert spots that one would love to visit but seldom gets the chance. Deleta's location is in the midst of trackless desolation. The manager put a mill on the old well there, in defiance of his female boss Margo Doman, who told him not to put horses on it. She considered the place much too distant from station control, but her manager disregarded her instructions, he took all the saddle horses to Deleta and left them there.

The manager thought the abundance of grass around the far distant well was too good to miss. His intention being to leave the horses out there until the drought broke on the station, but he didn't foresee the smash to follow. The windmill broke down and most of the horses perished. They didn't get regular checks on their welfare, as it is about a hundred miles from Windidda homestead along a roundabout southern route to Deleta.

These thoughts went through my mind this afternoon as we paused at Deleta. The controversial windmill of horse perish fame is no longer present, and no sign that one ever was. The well is now a mere circular depression in the ground, washed in by storm waters years ago. The obvious subject of flood inundations. Deleta Well, the idyllic Shangri-la of my imagination, no longer exists. It is not even a good place to camp. Deleta must be the perfect example of anticlimax if ever there was.

We continued our journey of education, and at five miles south of Deleta came to a well with windlass, beside the track. This well is in good condition and about fifty feet deep. We let the rusty bucket down on the ricketty old windlass to sample the water. It is fresh and good to drink. We have plenty of water with us in the vehicles, but it is good to know where to obtain other supplies in an emergency. This place is known as Jerry's Well. From here we tuned off the north-south track and drove west along an old long-abandoned fenceline. We camped at half a mile in mulga country, with low stony hills to our north. We saw quite a few dog tracks during our trip from Earli Earli this morning to Jerry's Well. The vehicle distance totals eighty-seven miles all told today. It feels as though we did a lot more than that. Maybe the new country makes it seem longer.

Saturday 18 - This decrepit fenceline we camped beside last night appears to me to be at least forty years old. Maybe some oldtimer took a fancy to this little patch of isolated pastoral country, in the hopes of making a station out of it. He sank a couple of wells, erected a few miles of fencing, then abandoned the place. There is no sign that the property ever carried stock. In anycase it is much too small an area, and too far from settled country to be a success for anyone, except perhaps for a would-be claypan squatter. I asked Happy if he knows the history of the place but he doesn't. Nobody on Windidda knew anything about its origins either when I was there. All they knew was the yarn about the perished horses. The track we followed to Deleta and Jerry's Well continues south to the northern boundary of Bandya pastoral lease. The track we followed in to the night camp here, continues west. Happy continued along this western track today. He is the official guide, so that's the way we go. I'm glad I have a map with me, even if it is in tatters and short on detail. I don't have a lot of faith in old Happy as a guide. I'd be a lot happier without him. However the boss sent him to show me the G6 dogging area, so there is little option but humour the old fellow and let him take the lead, to wherever. I'll enter mileages and compass bearings all the way today so I can plot pertinent positions on a good map later. The map I have is the one given back to the boss by the former dogger when he quit. At first travel was west, then a gradual turn to south-west for twenty-four miles to a turnoff. Happy followed the right hand fork west for half a mile. We came to a dead end at a low breakaway escarpment with a small cave, above where the track terminates. We returned to the turnoff. South next for eleven or twelve miles to where more breakaways appear to the east. These cliffs cause the track to take a big swing around to the west at first, then south, then east, as the track skirts the escarpments. A big horseshoe bend it is, with saltbush flats running out from the base of cliffs all the way. At about six miles from where the bend began, to where it turns south again, we came to another junction. One track goes east the other continues south.

The track going east looked like a good proposition for water catchments, but Happy wanted to go south, so south we went. Four miles further on we came to yet another junction. This time the turnoff has a rough bush signpost. A small sheet of galvanised tin with lettering indented by hammer and punch. The sign on southern track read Mulga Queen. We turned west with old Happy in the lead. At half a mile is a small dry gnamma hole on south side of the track. We continued west at first for a short distance then the track heads north-west, through open spinifex sandplain, with sandhills here and there in the distance. At about twenty miles a lone system of breakaways, gave us a hairpin bend for the second time. This one is a lot sharper than the other bend that we went around earlier. Just west of where we cleared this last lot of breakaways is an open gravel or laterite flat with five little gnamma holes. This spot is the Seven Sisters says Happy. In that case there must be a couple more holes yet to find. I will search them out later when we are by ourselves, Dooley and me.

We left all sign of breakaways behind west of the gnamma holes. At five miles to the north-west and well into the spinifex, we pulled up for dinner near a cluster of desert gums. After the meal we continued on a north-west course for twelve miles, where we came upon two gnamma holes, both quite dry. Travel was then more westerly for seven miles to where we hit the eastern boundary of Wonganoo Station. At one mile south along the boundary fence we came to a mill on a bore hole with excellent water. I filled our water cans here. I still carry my old packhorse canteens. They are a bit heavy and awkward to fill but sentiment for the old days gets the better of me at times. I don't like the twelve-gallon galvanised drum the APB supplies. Happy didn't bother to top his drum up, he reckons he has plenty.

From the boundary mill travel is southerly for nine miles, to where a big well-used kangaroo pad crosses the motor track. Not far ahead we came to some more dry rockholes. I think the roo pad must go to a station mill west of the boundary fence. Four miles on, are some shallow clayholes in a little creek running west, from some cliffs eastward of the track.

This should be part of the Scholl Range. It is, because at five miles further south we came to a big rockhole. This hole is situate within the bosom of high spectacular white cliffs. This is the Scholl Range for sure. The water is Karli Rockhole. Dooley knows it well, she has been here before from the west, years ago as a young girl on foot walkabout with her people.
With the high range running along eastward of the track all the way, we continued south to Bandya boundary, reaching it at ten miles. This marks the start of thick mulga country. The Scholl Range takes a big swing away to the east, then disappears from view behind mulga scrub. There is another dry rockhole a bit east of the track in a small scrub enclosed clearing. It is not a good place to camp, being too rough and stony all around, even if the rockhole was full of water it is still an unpleasant place. Its name is Kulitjanu says Dooley. Kulitjanu means 'hot place' and because of its confined situation I can quite imagine this to be the case in mid summer. Dooley says her people seldom if ever camped at Kulitjanu, they only called in for a brief respite when on the way to Karli Rockhole or elsewhere. We came south past a mill with good water in spinifex country, well inside Bandya pastoral lease, then turned east to camp at eight miles from where we passed the boundary. I wrote a lot of notes as we came along today to keep check of the mileages and bearings. Now for a few more notes while on camp: "The G6 Area to date has not shown much sign of dogs at all. For the most part what we have seen consists of spinifex sandplain and scattered sandhills. This class of country includes some small, mostly isolated, breakaways. The Scholl range is the largest system of escarpments and cliffs encountered on this western side of the country. Von Treur Tableland and its southern spur south of Warren's Well, being the largest range to the east.

There is plenty of scope for minor explorations in the area covered to date. Most of the tracks we've been on so far serve only to provide APB doggers with easier access. Formerly this was all untracked virgin country. The tracks are but one single cut of a grader blade, the meandering handiwork of a contractor employed by the APB a few years ago. I heard about these tracks when I was with the APB before (1965-68 Survey) I wondered at the time what they'd be like. Now I can see them at firsthand. They are quite good, although they seem unplanned and haphazard, as though the grader driver didn't have a clue where he was gong, or where he might end. The hickledy pickledy nature of the tracks is what leaves me room to work. There is plenty of country that looks good, off the beaten track. All the rockholes seen so far were small and dry, the only big one being Karli in the Scholl Range. I forgot to mention that Karli was bone dry when we called in there, and to make it worse, contained a stinking dead goat carcase right in the middle of the water catchment. The days so far seem long and tiring, but then that maybe because we took no rest. We travel from daylight through till dark. Happy reckons his speedo is out twenty miles. The speedo on this old bomb they gave me is probably out as well, but we'll get there. We came one hundred and twenty-two miles today, faulty or true.

Sunday 19 - I thought old Happy Absalom knew this area. After all, he came out to show me the run, but I'm afraid he doesn't seem to have a clue really. I could do as well or even better by myself. He is good company in the bush though, and an oldtimer as well, he says he is a Crow Eater too. He talks a lot of South Australia. He reckons he was on the Birdsville Track years ago. I was too, back in the 1940s. I can't get old Happy to talk about his experiences much. He won't even talk about his dogging area on the Nullarbor Plain. I don't know why he is so reticent. When he has a few drinks in, he is the biggest skite going. He is a good old chap really but tends to get slewed. I had to advise him which way to go several times yesterday. Tattered and torn as it is, I knew from my map that he was off on the wrong track. A bit of diplomatic advice to keep the right direction did the trick though.

That is enough about old Happy for now, better to concentrate on the job in hand. From night camp we went south-east along a paddock fence, and came to a mill in a corner at one mile. Next stop was a station outcamp and woolshed at seven miles. Milyirri is the name of the outcamp. Milyirri is twenty miles from Bandya homestead and from the latter, it is twenty miles to the station's north-east corner. From this extreme north-eastern boundary gate, the road enters outside-country again to run through an extremely wide expanse of clear and open spinifex, upward along a gradual rise. We topped this long rise at five miles, where it enters hard gravel laterite flats clothed with mulga. A small dry gnamma hole near the track on north side has an ancient survey peg close to it. The road runs next, through patches of open spinifex, and low breakaways, for twelve miles to Miltji Rockhole. Miltji has a surround of high cliffs and peculiar rock forms. Old Happy got his camera out here to take photos of what he calls Elephant Rock. It did resemble an elephant, but I prefer to equate such things with animals of this country, not exotica from overseas. I fear I'm a lone voice in that respect. Few people even Australians born, are really at home in the bush. Most are full of foreign culture from their childhood upbringing. I remember my own grandmother in this respect. My gran was a third generation Australian. She was, born and bred in Van Diemens Land, in the days when it still bore that colourful Dutch name, yet she always referred to England as home, or the Old Country. Poor old Gran.

I hate to dwell on a person's idiosyncrasies but sometimes can't help it. On the cliff face above Miltji Rockhole, several old explorers, prospectors, or whoever, recorded their initials and dates of visitation. The earliest being the year 1894, others were the early 1900s. I drew Happy's attention to these inscriptions, but he reckons these oldtimers put their birth dates on the rock. "None of them were out in this country that early in the piece." Happy said. I insisted that the dates indicated the years they came to Miltji, but old Happy was contemptuous of such an idea. Happy "humph humphed" with contempt, all the way back to his vehicle. I gave him up as a bad job after that. In future I'll keep such logic to myself.

Happy was anxious to reach what he terms "Cairo Soak" six miles beyond Miltji. We flew past it at speed before Happy knew it. He jammed the brakes on and turned back. Dooley told me the real name for the soak is Karu. Once again Happy favours overseas equations. The native word **karu**, in Happy's mind, conjured up thoughts of Egypt and Cairo. The word karu means creek. The soak is in a small insignificant creek that cuts south across the road. The De La Poer Range is the creek's watershed. Escarpments of the De La Poer are visible a couple of miles back to the north. Happy missed the creek because it is only a shallow depression in the road. I could easily make the same slip, the creek is so hard to see when travelling. There is nothing to distinguish it other than the sudden dip in the road. No trees line the banks. The creek at this juncture has a wide spread on it, as it begins to flood out into the spinifex. The area is a veritable field of high grass. The ongoing road takes a sharp turn to the east from Karu. Ahead is more spinifex country all the way to an outlying section of Lake Wells, thence back to the Ulrich Range that we passed through the other day. Plenty of dog tracks around Karu.

We hit the beef road again at thirteen miles east of Karu. The lake crossing is a bit slippery but not a bog. We came to a fork in the track after crossing the lake. One leads north-east to Earli Earli. The other track goes east, to that conglomeration of Peter Hill's junk, stacked within the fenced enclosure we saw the other day. There are two windmills therein, not just the one, that I first mentioned. This enclosure and two windmills terminate the road that comes north from Cosmo Newberry. When we reach Cosmo, our trip of the past few days will complete a long circuit, around the western portion of country I'm to work.

From the two windmills and junk heap, we turned south toward Cosmo Newberry. Gibson Hill is a prominent feature about midway along this track. I took note of two old dog tracks there. To date we have been able to find only two of Bob Geradi's traps during the whole trip, and are sure there are no more on the run. I forgot to mention before that Geradi was the former dogger. I am sure I will do a much better job than he. We pulled up to camp near some broken granite country, marked on the map as Point Pater, with one hundred and sixteen miles for the day.

Monday 20 - (34751) - This morning we passed Cosmo without calling in. The place is a mission, and visitors seem unwelcome. We arrived at Laverton to fill the tanks with a total of forty-four gallons, at mileage of 34810. The speedo was on 34250 when we left Leonora on Wednesday, October 15, so that makes fuel consumption twelve miles per gallon over five hundred and sixty miles. We said goodbye to Alex Absalom. He reckons he showed us the country, poor old chap. I reckon to do much better alone. I had to humour the boss however, as his intentions were good.

Dooley and I did not delay in town, we left immediately along the Warburton Road, to pull up for dinner just past the first rockhole named Deepa, in the Adam Range. This gnamma hole has a good lid fitted, to keep it clean, and stop animals fouling the water. Lots of tribal Aborigines use this road on a regular basis, to commute between Warburton and Laverton. The entire area easterly of Laverton is still tribal country, in every respect. We saw numerous heaps of campfire ashes around the Deepa area, old and fresh. The sky is heavy and overcast today, with a promise of rain in the air. We bypassed Cosmo yet again, and headed north. I shot a fat kangaroo near Gibson Hill, then on to Gregory Hills to camp and cook the roo in the ground blackfella fashion for supper. We'll have meat leftover for tomorrow too. A good shower of rain fell as we came along the road. We saw not a sign of dogs anywhere. One hundred and fifty miles today.

Tuesday 21 - There was a live kangaroo tangled in loose fence wires two miles south of the range this morning, and we saw one fresh dog track. I took the usual control measures. I forgot to mention last trip, the presence of a windmill tower on the ground not far north of the Earli Earli turnoff, a nearby borehole is no doubt it's intended location. It will make a good reference point until we gather more place names. I'll call it "Mill On The Ground."

At Earli Earli we counted fifteen fresh dog tracks since the shower of rain. I carried out control measures. There are plenty emus and kangaroos watering at this mill. We filled our tanks to capacity here as this is such good water. We went on past the Escreet Well and turned north to a place called Nyiruru. Dooley often spoke of Nyiruru before I got this job. She described it as a springwater. As a little girl, she remembers scraping away surface sand in the bed of a little creek, to reveal a copious supply of fresh clear water. Being a child and so fascinated, she spent hours there enjoying the experience of water so readily available by a mere scrape of the hand. Her vivid descriptions gave me visions of a similar type of soak in the Northern Territory, known as Raggart Spring. A few miles west of Alice Springs, and north a few hundred paces of the road to Jay Creek, stands one large corkwood tree. At the base of this tree, a hidden water supply exists in a flat sandy wash, with nothing to show it is there other than the cork tree. One can obtain water only inches beneath the surface there. Just scrape the sand to one side with cupped hand, and water appears. Raggart Spring fits Dooley's description of Nyiruru to perfection. Today she was to show me her childhood treasure.

It is more than twenty-five years now, since Dooley was at Nyiruru last, but she found it again today spot on target. No mistake about it she said, but what a disappointment. The water catchment was dust dry. The sand was there alright, deep sand in a small narrow gutter of a creek, but even as I got the shovel to dig, I knew it for wasted effort. Dooley's face was sadness typified. I felt deeply for her, and experienced a let down feeling myself, because of our mutual expectations of beautiful spring water in an otherwise barren land. The place she saw all those many years ago, is a rockhole filled with sand. The creek runs down from nearby stony hills after rain, to fill the rockhole. This creates a waterlogged body of sand so, the experience she had as a child is possible anytime after the creek flows, but is only seasonal. To the north of Nyiruru is a secret red ochre deposit, up a gorge in the dark scrubby range, It is taboo to all women. The name of the red ochre site is Taral Kutjarra. Only initiated men ever visit Taral Kutjarra. I wanted to leave Dooley with the vehicle outside the gorge, and walk in to look, but she refused to stay alone for fear some men might come along from Cosmo.

We saw four fresh dog tracks along the road as we travelled west to another of Dooley's childhood memories, our destination being Tui Claypans. These lie hidden from view on the eastern side of a wide and dense thicket of ti-tree scrub, that is higher than the Landrover. I had a hard time getting through it in places, but at last we came out into the open, to see a big claypan appear in the windscreen. It was dry, but this time we expected it to be so. Just south of the first claypan, beyond a low sandbank supporting a few mulga trees, is a second pan. They are dry now but when both are full the claypans must be a delightful sight. Dooley says the north pan is always clear and fresh while the southern one is always muddy, although fresh and good to drink. This variance factor is the result of a Dreamtime incident that took place in this area. The claypans represent the campsites of two women, one was jealous of the other. Each had their own camp. The lady on the north side where the clear water rests, got angry with the lady on the south side, and came to fight her. As a result of the violent fight between these two women, the southern claypan now always contains muddy water. The women were Mauwan and Mawi. Mauwan is the Dreamtime kaparli of old Willy Hill, Dooley's tribal dad, and Mawi the Dreamtime kaparli of Nawi Westlake, Dooley's niece. There is a lot more to the story, but that will have to suffice for this particular narrative. Kaparli means grandmother.

I counted plenty of old dog tracks around the claypans but saw nothing fresh. This morning was cold but after dinner it became quite hot. I had a hard day's work and feel quite knocked up. Our camp is near the dry claypans. It is a pleasant place even if there is no water. I did a lot of walking today. The vehicle only did thirty-two miles.

Wednesday 22 - (34933) We left Tui claypans and made south-east to a surveyors' temporary trig station or whatever they call the things. This one is a circle of deal boards from packing cases, located on western edge of the greasy lake crossing we passed over the other day, when in company with old Happy Absalom. We went next, south and west to Karu Soak, where I scalped the dry carcase of a male dog found near a kangaroo bait. To take control measures is my job so I set two traps after dinner. The channel with soakage known as Karu, goes by a different name, it is marked on the map as Moxon Creek. Two miles downstream of the road, the creek spreads out to a considerable width, and supports an abundance of swamp grass, several acres of it. Upstream, the creek is narrow and more defined, with banks about three feet high. Some parts of the channel have a natural cement bed, while other sections, like where the soak is, are full of deep sand. Karu is about fifty paces north of the road. The creek eventually disappears into spinifex flats a few miles south of the road.

The inspection of Moxon Creek being complete for the present, I made south for Miltji. Travel at first is across open spinifex sandplain, then changes when near Miltji to a jumble of crumbled granite ridges. Short sections of cliff undershot by caves, appear at intervals. This class of country leads onto a wide saltbush flat bounded by low cliffs south of the flat. North of the road the cliffs are high and sheer. Miltji lies at base of eighty feet high cliffs that form a scenic backdrop to the rockhole.

A pronounced fold in the cliffs encloses Miltji, to conceal it from outside view. Entry to the rockhole's confined enclosure is only possible after a kick and stumble over fallen rocks and boulders. The catchment is at present dry, with only a little soakage water at bottom. It is difficult to understand how such a shaded water can go dry, because the sun's rays seldom reach it, but dry it is.

I sought a way to reach the clifftop and see what that might reveal. A short distance away to one side of Miltji, is a steep slope, I clambered up this slope to reach the escarpment rim. There, in a basin rockhole, I found the desiccated carcase of a long-dead dingo, but not a sign of water. All the catchments are dry. After having a look around the Miltji area for a little while longer, we went four miles south-west to a place marked on the map as Dumbung.

Dooley disputes this and says the proper native name is Tjampan. This at present is a dry rockhole full of sand, but I'm sure water is available at depth. Later I may dig it out to see what potential it has. There are numerous old campsites all around the stony saltbush studded flats near Tjampan, so there must be water here sometimes at least. After the Nyiruru experience, we both hesitate to claim any place as certain. The road here runs parallel with a line of low cliffs on the north side, with peculiar rock formations here and there.

Dumbung, or Tjampan, to give the native name, is situate about half a mile from the road. It is up a little creek that runs south and east over the road. The creek rises from within a unique enclosed gully with a narrow entrance, or should I say exit, where the creek emerges. Within this natural gateway, the soak rests midway between two buttress rocks, one either side of the creek. A lone willow tree just a little upstream, marks the spot.

Our next stop was Patapuka gnamma holes. This place is distinguishable by an unusual species of mulga tree known to natives as wirinyimiri. The tiny needle-like leaves are so sparse they throw no shade, and grow on a skeletal umbrella type branch structure. The ground is stony and bare. We followed a set of indistinct wheel tracks from Patapuka north for six miles. The wheel marks led at first through scraggly spinifex, and sorry looking mulga thickets, to end near a small area of breakaway country. An inspection of this area led to a dry trough-type rockhole on top of a brownstone ledge, half a mile east of the track we came in on. This natural trough is at the eastern end of a narrow saltbush flat. What a lovely place it might be if full, but so dismal when dry, its name Narrkal, is the native word for concealed.

We left the Narrkal trough behind and travelled another five mile to the site of what is obviously a large rockhole, but it is full of sand right to surface level, with a clay crust. This rockhole is Pilki, native name for mud. A heap of sandalwood chips nearby, show where one of Dooley's tribal brothers Murphy, once camped. Her people came out this way on walkabout in earlier days, from the ration depot at Mulga Queen. I hear a lot about this Mulga Queen settlement from Dooley. She was there from time to time as a child, and as a young woman, but the place is long since uninhabited. We saw banks of thunder heads behind us while at Pilki but saw no rain falling anywhere. We got quite a surprise upon return west, to find that a heavy storm had caused water to run for several miles along the track while we were at the rockholes. We decided to go north-east to Tjampan and camp, although the ground there is not a pleasant campsite, and wood is in short supply. Flat surface areas at Tjampan are all pebbles and small rocks of decomposed granite, with rasp like qualities. I like a campsite suitable for bare feet, but this type of terrain is like walking on a rasp, where every kick of a misplaced foot peels the skin off in slices.

Thursday 23 - There were heavy thunderstorms and lots of lightning north of us last night but not much fell here. I got to work with shovel on the soak this morning. Dooley was a great help with the bucket as the hole became too deep to throw dirt out with shovel alone. I should say spade not shovel. I cleaned the soak out to a depth of eight feet before striking water, then pushed an iron bar down through the remaining sand, to strike bedrock at ten feet. The water is of excellent quality, but slow to make. Most likely this soak is only a rockhole filled with sand to the surface level every time the creek runs, as it is right in the channel, although a bit to one side. I came across an old pannikin at a depth of five feet, so someone has certainly been down here before me. There is quite a large mound of greyish colour soil on the downstream side of the soak. This no doubt being an accumulation of excavated material from centuries of digging for water by former native inhabitants of these parts. At this date however, there is no sign that the soak has seen the light of day for many, many years. The rusty pannikin I found at depth, was like a fossil embedded in compact long undisturbed soil.

Dumbung is marked on the map. I asked about it before I ever took this job, but none of the whites I spoke to knew its exact location. Some told me of others who searched for the soak's whereabouts in vain. I can understand this because before I dug it out you could walk or drive right over it and not be aware that water existed under the ground. The surface area was bone dry before I commenced to dig, and I was down a couple of feet before reaching damp soil. I felt like giving the dig up as a hopeless job several times as the hole got ever deeper, but I persisted, and got the reward of beautiful fresh water in good supply, as described above. This experience today makes me ponder on the hard job the old natives had, to reach water with digging sticks and coolamons alone. No shovels. No crowbars.

We took off for the north-east to see the results of last night's storms. Miltji is still dry. No rain at all. Karu Soak was a much better proposition with the waterhole being brimful. There was a terrific hail storm here last night, with lots of hailstones washed down from the bordering flats toward the creek channel. There is a veritable windrow of hail stones here this morning, at least a foot in height. Some of the hail is still the size of marbles, so was no doubt much bigger when it fell. Makes us feel glad we didn't camp here last night. No dogs been back since we were last here, but all traps got sprung by the deluge. I reset them. Frogs are numerous in the replenished waterhole and full of joyful noise at their good fortune.

Being optimistic of more widespread rain further afield, we set off for Nyiruru and Earli Earli, but found only disappointment there to greet us. No sign of rain at either place. The sky however looks as though we might be in for some big rain tonight. I might be too optimistic, but thought a return to Nyiruru might be a good idea. A chance to see that dry catchment full like Dooley's recollection of it. That is if rain does come tonight, so off we went to camp there. Strong gusty winds all day. It being still early enough to look around, I went for a walk and found a little gnamma hole on east side of the wheel track, just south of the creek. This hole is the shape of a woman's vagina so now I know where Nyiruru got its name. The native word for vagina in this area is nyira. I asked Dooley and she confirms my deduction. The rain cleared off in the late afternoon, so decided to travel on again, via the beef road while the air is cool. Got over the slippery lake crossing before dark. We camped near a clump of gidgea trees, about midway between the lake and the Gregory Hills road to Cosmo Newberry. Seventy-five miles for the day.

Friday 24 - No rain last night. The storms were all bluff and bluster. We cooked a damper this morning and listened to the Kalgoorlie RFDS for a while. Later we went past the head of the Cosmo road, east for about twelve miles, along a dragged sandalwood track. It is nearly as good as a graded road. You can't see it from the Cosmo road. You have to follow around the outside perimeter of Peter Hill's two windmills and junk heap enclosure, to find the sandalwood track. The track begins its eastern run from other side of the said enclosure. I believe a sandalwood puller name of Johnny Griffith was after sandalwood out this way a few years ago and it was he who put the drag track in place. At twelve miles we came to the first signs of rainfall from the recent storms. A saltbush flat that runs across the track being too boggy to continue, so we had to turn back.

South of Gregory Hills about two and a half mile from the two mills and yard full of junk, was one male dog in a trap. Reset the trap and hung the carcase in a tree beside the road. I started east along south side of the range, over untracked terrain in search of a soak marked on the map. I found it at four miles, alongside an old wooden survey peg, marked only with a broad arrow. No numbers or initials. I dug the soak out but found it dry. There is only wet sand at bottom and appears to be merely a small rockhole full of sand, and not deep. From the survey peg rockhole, we continued east and north, along a line of detached hills, in search of Peter's Pool. We found it dry, near the northern tip of the detached range of hills. It is about twelve miles by the zig zag route the terrain forced us to take. Plenty of old dog sign all around, but no fresh tracks. On the return trip I left our outward track and drove nine miles due west, in a straight line, back to the Cosmo road.

We next went about four miles south of Gibson Hill, on the Cosmo Newberry road, then westward along a set of old wheel tracks, two miles to Kuta rockhole. Kuta had nothing in it except a couple of euro carcases. Some shallow basins along the creek had a few inches of water, most of it unfit to drink on account of washed-in camel and euro dung. Only one clean puddle near the creek's lower end. The creek itself didn't run. The water is only rain wash from the rocky creek banks. I must mention that the gully in which Kuta rockhole lies hidden, is the most dismal place I ever saw. The whole gully consists of extremely rough, decomposed granite rubble, with not one clear place big enough to sit down, let alone roll a swag out and make a camp. The side ridges support a tangle of low bramble-like bushes, while the rockhole, being so dry and polluted, does nothing to enhance the place. The whole area reeks of menace, with a pronounced funereal aspect. Dooley agrees with my opinion and tells me it is an abode of mamu creatures. I believe her. I doubt I will visit the kuta place again. No sign of dogs. We did seventy-five miles today.

Saturday 25 - Went in to Laverton to fill the petrol tanks. Twenty-three gallons with speedo at 35239. We purchased a handful of stores at a cost of ten dollars, an exorbitant price. Travel back north-east, past Cosmo Newberry, this time en route Lake Throssel. We camped approximately sixty miles east of the mission. Wild turkey, native name nganuti, for supper. No sign of dogs. One hundred and seventy miles all told.

Sunday 26 - Bitter cold morning, with typical winter clouds coming from the south and east. Continue along the Warburton Road north-east and came at eight miles to a rockhole in rubble breakaways. There are lots of native paintings in a cave here under a low cliff. This place is Eurotharra Rockhole on the map. It is close to the southern end of Lake Throssel. Only a little water in the hole, and no sign of dogs. Lake Throssel came into view for a short distance. Later we came to a little tin signboard with the hand painted name Wort, and an arrow. The arrow pointing to where, at a short distance off the main road is a limestone blowhole, at a distance of one hundred and forty-four miles out from Laverton. The name Wort is a mispronunciation of the native name Worr, with a double RR trill at the end, rather than a letter T. I often make this mistake myself with similar words. I went back to the visible portion of lake and followed along it's north side for a few miles. We saw no sign of dogs so returned to the main road.

Continued travel north-east to Paltju Soak where was a big mob of natives, all after tobacco. We gave them none. We did not delay at Paltju in case they begin to pester us for our meagre supply of stores. What makes it worse is that most of them class Dooley for a relative. In Aboriginal law all must share everything they have. If we complied with such custom, they would continue to live off the land as a viable group, or live on rations back at Cosmo. We on the other hand, if we complied the request for stores, must battle along with depleted stocks in a country almost devoid of bush tucker at present. Even kangaroos are absent from most of the dogging run to date.

On the way back from Paltju we bypassed Wort, or Worr, and returned to Eurotharra. This latter seems to be another of those misspelt Aboriginal words. Eurotharra should actually be Yuratjarra, a term that describes a goanna's seasonal practice of blocking off the entrance to a burrow. Goannas always seal themselves off from the outside world prior to winter hibernation. Leaving the vehicle at foot of the escarpment, we went for a walkabout over the rough upper level plateau. We found an unnamed rockhole up there, with a survey peg marked PB55. Down below near the cave with paintings, is another peg with PB49 on it. Then we came upon yet a third survey peg marked PB41, near an old Holden wreck not far from the main road. I picked up two dog scalps on top of the escarpment, both from old carcases. Further on were two more dead dogs in the spinifex. No doubt these animals succumbed to aerial baits some time ago. I wanted to go in and look at Jutson Soak but saw from fresh tracks, that some other natives were in that way, so we gave it a miss for this trip. Instead we deviated from the main road to follow the old road for about four miles. I found a soak amongst some granite outcrops in the midst of spinifex sandplain. The first three miles were saltbush flats and mulga, spinifex over the last mile to the granites. This place is Ardagh Rocks, it has a number of initials and names hammered into a flat face of granite near the soak. It looks like a quiet place with no fresh car tracks, so we took the risk of possible intruders and made camp, after a one hundred and twenty-six mile day. I hope no unwelcome visitors come along. I had enough wangkayi cadgers for a while. The trouble is, these missions won't sell tobacco, it is against their religion. I love traditional native culture, but cannot wear a mob of bludgers. The old bush people were a different uncontaminated breed. A cool day with south-east winds and no fresh sign of dogs anywhere.

Monday 27 - Left Ardagh Rocks and went back east five miles to a windmill beside the track. This might be Jutson Well, I'm not yet sure. Followed wheel tracks south from the windmill about four miles, to an old mud brick ruin. Turned back to the Warburton road from the ruins, and travel west through open spinifex sandplains. Next we came to limestone rises with sheoak trees, native name djinkarra. At this point we turned south-east along an old track, and at six miles came to an old well with mill tower, but no head or tank. From there I made a turn back to the Warburton road again, then west along it for two miles. North-west along a set of wheel tracks for half a mile, then to yet another mill on an old well, not pumping. From there I followed an old track six miles west to a big kurrajong tree, and an old dry government well, with a rusty bucket lying discarded under the kurrajong tree. Six miles along the same course we came to a small gnamma hole on north side of the motor track. We then went in to Cosmo to refuel, and continue north along the beef road for dinner at a spot, between Point Pater and Gibson Hill. Saw tracks of two vehicles as we drove along. One fresh dog track visible along the roadway for some distance. Signs were that the dog smelt at several baits as it walked along, but ate none of them and bypassed a trap set at the Gregory Hills. It was here at Gregory Hills that one of the two strange vehicles left the road. Maybe they are company prospectors.

Earl Earli has no sign of dogs at all. A rabbit was in one trap and a fox in the other. We went on around west side of the lake. The two strange vehicles came in past Nyiruru. At the lake crossing was one dog in the trap I set before near the improvised survey station. I reset the trap, and set an additional one, although by now it was well after dark. Tracks show where several dogs were here, and appears like they savaged the dog caught in the trap. We camped a few miles further south. I found out at the mission today that Jutson Soak and Well, is further north than where I thought, and the old mud brick ruin goes by the name Shenton. One hundred and thirty miles all told.

Tuesday 28 - I set one dog trap a mile south along the Bandya road. Dogs been around traps at Karu but none caught. Set two additional traps, then continue south and west to Bandya boundary then proceed south along west side of the fence. At fifteen miles on this course, we left the fence to travel outside the boundary in open country for two miles to a place that the whites call Lulu rockhole. Dooley says the native name is Liuliu, so Lulu is an obvious corruption of a good native word. Dooley has told me a lot about Liuliu, same as she did about Nyiruru. Today disappointment was once again the sight in store. We found the large rockhole as dry as the proverbial bone. It would be a splendid rockhole if full. It is deep and well protected.

One thing of interest there, was a circular mark on the ground some distance north of the rockhole. Dooley describes how as children, she and her mates played ring a ring a rosy around a desert poplar tree that used to grow there. The play went on each day, on a regular basis, for hours at a time. After a while a deep pad wore into the ground around the tree. She told me all this in graphic detail long before we ever came out to this country. Well, believe it or not, today she took me to the site, and there in the ground was the deep pad. Lying across the pad, was the dead remnant trunk of the once living tree. I estimate a passage of some twenty-five years, since she was a child at play around this tree circle.

We left the dry rockhole and the nearby playground circle with its forlorn dead tree trunk, on a course of 120^0 with the speedo at 35655. We were in search of a suitable route through untracked country south-east to Cosmo Newberry. For a start we only went one mile to the top of the breakaways past the dry rockhole, and pulled up for dinner. Far too much dense scrub for my liking. The tyres on this vehicle are fodder for the rubbish tip. They need replacing at the earliest opportunity, but I doubt they will. The APB is not as generous with tyres on this job as they were during the 1965-68 Survey north of Wiluna. We turned back. The weather is much too hot for these perishing tyres. I may make another attempt at a later date, after rain replenishes the rockhole. On the other hand, it may not even be necessary to push a track through that way. I still have a lot of country to investigate south of here, and another track may already exist. There were dogs here a while back but none now.

Returning back inside the boundary fence again, travel was south to a mill with good water, located along a fence running east, back to the boundary again at nine miles. Travel from there tended west instead of south in the way I wanted to go. We came out on the Laverton to Bandya road, at a distance from Liuliu or Lulu Rockhole, of about twenty-one miles. This old map is no damn good. Reached Mackenzie Well at three miles. The natives call it Mikintji. We took a turn to the south-east and came to a dry well at seven miles. From there it was north-east six miles to Christmas Well. Dooley's tribal sister Nunguta was born here. Both Corner Well and Christmas Well were dry. Continued south-east four miles to an old well with no mill. Then it was nine miles through dense mulga scrub at first, then open spinifex and sandhills, with no sign of a wheel track. We camped well after dark. Ninety-eight miles today. Storms are a spectacular sight right around the horizon, with lots of lightning.

Wednesday 29 - (35705) - We were on the road early this morning, and came at ten miles to some granite hills, followed by saltbush flats, then dense mulga thickets to the fifteen mile point. We were travelling almost south. At twenty miles, an old track crossed our path at right angles, heading just a shade north of east. We left our untracked course through virgin country, in favour of the wheel marks, and reached a small rockhole at four miles from the point where we first hit this track. The hills near Cosmo Newberry are visible to the east. The storms of last night dissipated and we now have a clear blue sky, but this pleasant picture somewhat spoilt, by a bitter cold south-east wind coming off rain that fell elsewhere.

I called in to Kalgoorlie RFDS Base to give our position as west of Cosmo, and coming in to that settlement. We had breakfast at this little rockhole. Dooley knows the rockhole, but not its name. It is not on the map, so we will refer to it in future as Breakfast Rockhole. It was just daylight when we started off this morning. We being anxious to get out of the tangled scrub, we thought it best to continue travel while the weather is cool, rather than waste time with breakfast before starting.

I don't fancy this part of the world for cross country traverse at all. The mulga thickets are far too numerous and dense. So dense in parts that axe work is necessary to get through, and how our radiator escaped stake holes on this last trip is beyond comprehension. I had my heart in my mouth all the way through one thicket. There was scarce enough room to allow a vehicle between the trees. It was horrific. My handwritten diary notes say it was like a solid wall of scrub. I just bulldozed my way through, as that was the only option other than turn back, and I didn't want to do that. We already turned back once at Liuliu.

The granite hills we skirted at ten miles after entering the open country, looked interesting enough for later examination. We saw lots of big roo pads there. I feel certain that those scrub-bound granites, contain a rockhole or soakage water. Dooley's uncle Albert Jones back at Erlistoun Station, told us once of a rockhole out this way he calls Pine Soak. While at our breakfast rockhole, we did some washing, and cleaned ourselves up a bit as well. After that we set off again in a south-east direction to hit the Warburton road at four miles. A distance of eight miles from where we first struck the old disused wheel track that led us to our breakfast stopover. Being somewhat fascinated by the find of such a long unused set of wheel tracks, we decided to backtrack and follow it right through, to see where it goes. At fourteen miles on a general north-west course, we came to a native soak, marked by a termite-ridden survey peg standing to one side, and just a bit south of the soak. The only evidence that a soak exists here, is the circular patch of white ground in and around a shallow dry depression. The hole has a cover of heavy timber on one side, but no water is visible, nor has anyone been here in a long time. The track turns more west from this soakage and at six miles reaches a shallow dry well. The well sits on an open clay flat, in the midst of scrub country. Driving on north-west of this, we came to yet another well, ten miles from the clay flat. Went on another mile, then turned back to the breakfast rockhole, this time we had dinner here. After dinner we went on to the Warburton road and reached Cosmo at four miles. It seems strange that we saw no sign of natives' recent travels along the old track this morning, yet it is so close to where they live at the mission. Even our breakfast stopover shows no sign of recent visitations.

I'm getting used to the Mission staff now, after a couple of visits. I refuelled there at mileage 35777. We went next, back along the Warburton road twelve miles, and located Bullrush Rockhole, a good one, with plenty of water from the last rain that fell a few days ago. I don't think it will last long as it is not deep enough. It would be a pretty place with its small waterfall, red rock surround, and contrast of green rushes, in a good season. At present however the rushes are brown and dead. This shows that the water here now is the first in a long time, and has not been in the catchment long enough to rejuvenate the dead rushes.

From the Bullrush catchment, at one mile south-west along the Warburton road is a claypan, near which a track turns off to the north-west, and follows the winding claypan creek along for several miles. It comes back to the main road again near Claypan Mill. I followed this deviation all the way. Next we went down through Laverton Downs boundary to camp near Bubbles Rockhole. Ninety-four miles and not a sign of dogs anywhere today. Not even old dung. Dooley now remembers the name of our breakfast rockhole. Is Purrkanu.

Thursday 30 - Bubbles' native name is Papul. Papul means a basin or rock catchment. It is too stinking to drink at present, so I went two and a half mile north-west to a windmill with good water and filled the cans there. We returned to the main road, and at one and a half miles followed a turnoff track heading south-east. At five miles along this track, we came to a derelict windmill and an old cattle yard. Ten mils further along the same track, we came to a tank and trough, with water coming from a pipeline running in from the west side. We continued south along the track and hit the old original road to Warburton. There is a rockhole close to the road, located in low granite breakaway country. At five miles north-east of the rockhole, is a windmill with no column, right on the White Cliffs Station boundary fence. Some new timberwork around the trough's ball-tap, indicates that the new owner is making progress with improvements to his acquisition. This property became derelict after the former owners, Graeme Canning and his wife the present Leonora Hospital Matron Sadie, abandoned the place. Four miles further east is a large granite outcrop or whaleback called Ivor Rocks, and the turnoff to White Cliffs homestead.

Ivor Rocks is a magnificent place, with numerous shallow basin or saucer type water catchments all over the top of it. Today they are all full of fresh clear rain water. There is a soak at the base on north-east side. On top of the whaleback at its highest point, stands a large Trig Station with iron sails, that quite spoils the otherwise aesthetic beauty of the place. Ten miles further along the road we came to yet another derelict windmill and troughs. We saw nothing, either on or off the road, during the next forty miles of travel. The Yamarna Station boundary fence cuts across the road and blocks it.

There is no gate. We found a way around the obstacle via a short detour that took us along a station track to a tiny shearing shed, where we pulled up for dinner. Afterward we came to Yamarna homestead, about one mile north of the miniature shearing shed. Dooley recognises the homestead as the old Police Station from a former town called Mount Ida, a town that once existed west of Leonora. Most of the outbuildings are also from there. How they got these old weatherboard buildings over the narrow and rough roads that lead to Yamarna is a puzzle to me.

Anne, the lady of the house, made us most welcome, and asked us inside to have a cup of tea. Quite a nice friendly person she was. Anne gave us directions to Thatcher Soak, Rutter Soak, and Minnie Creek. We departed next, eastward along a good road for Minnie Creek, and reached the old homestead there at sixteen miles. The old building is derelict, but good enough to use during inclement weather, if we ever get caught out this way by a storm or big rain. No water available from the old well, but there is soakage in the nearby gum creek. A wooden survey peg above the creek bank reads: PB16, and I found a dead dog not far away. Minnie Creek is an important Aboriginal site named Pilpirr a part of the kangaroo Dreaming.

Returning to the last gate, we followed a graded road north, until it met the proper old original road to Warburton. We turned west then to Thatcher Soak. This is a deep rockhole, with improvements put in by the authorities. It has a fence around it, a corrugated iron roof, and secure lids fitted, to protect the water from pollution by native game or birds. At present it has only three feet of water in the bottom, and this is not easy to get at. Thatcher Soak has featured in several books about this area. "Hell's Airport" by Errol Coote, and "Untold Miles" by Michael Terry, are two that come to mind. There are indications that natives performed ceremonies here not long ago. As witness to the fact, there is a circle of dried bushes a short distance to one side, and a lot of wood shavings from the manufacture of sacred artefacts.

Thatcher Soak marks the north-western extremity of a fairly high red granite range, composed of a piled jumble of round boulders. Travel west along the north side of this range, leads at seven miles beyond Thatcher, to Rutter Soak and a grave. The soak at Rutter has similar improvements to those at Thatcher. The grave and soak lie at the head of an open inlet, running north into the granites. The inlet supports a few corkwood trees, and soft soil quite devoid of stones.

The granite headstone reads:

> W. RUTTER
> DIED
> 9 - 7 - 94

From Rutter, a track goes around a corner at the south end of the inlet, the track then turns north, and at a distance of five miles passes Lang Rocks. This is a flat granite face of some width, covered with a veritable honour roll of early day travellers, and explorers, who sought water at this spot. At the northern base of Lang Rock, is a dry soak. A variance occurs here, in that the granite outcrop is Lang Rock, and the now dry water catchment at the base is Shenton Soak. The variance is, that this soakage is several miles east of the dark scrub covered visage of Mount Shenton, from which the soak derives its name.

Four miles further north of Lang Rock, after passing through low rolling hills, the winding track reaches the old mud brick ruins we saw the other day. Mission staff tell me this place is Brown's, others say it is Shenton Hut. We saw not a sign of dogs today. The location of both Thatcher and Rutter Soaks is close to the outside perimeter of a picturesque red granite ridge. This ridge is some seven miles in length and five to six in width. Composed for the most part of round red boulders or tors, piled one atop the other to a good height, this ridge is unique because of its unusual extent. Vegetation amongst the boulder piles is sparse in the extreme, and what vegetation there is, offers no shade for wildlife. The conglomeration of red tors however, offers plenty of well-shaded nooks and crannies, and appears to be a favourite daytime retreat for literally hundreds of euros.

A large mineral exploration crew was camped near Thatcher Soak not long ago. Although it is a deep squared cistern with large storage, they depleted the supply to a depth of twelve or fourteen feet by excessive use of water for daily showers. They had a shower tripod rigged near their camp. Inconsiderate lot of bastards they are.

After our extensive tour of the past week or two, I now feel as though the bulk of this **G6** dogging area is familiar territory, with only a few connecting tracks left to investigate. It is a large area to cover that's for sure. A few days more than two weeks on the job, at an average in excess of one hundred miles per day. It is interesting country too. This job is nothing like the exploration work I did north of Wiluna. On that Survey I had to traverse virgin country, and put in my own wheel tracks. This job down here is a different proposition altogether. This **G6** Area is a veritable network of roads and tracks. Some faint and indistinct, others plain to see, but all good travelling. What I've done so far is the extreme outside boundary of the area, then filled in the major gaps by running the existing access tracks. Later, if all goes well, I will do some (unofficial) exploration, to cover blank spaces on the maps, between these tracks. Later still I hope to go further afield, but need to be careful I don't overstep my authority, else the boss might step in and restrict my movements. After all, it is he who must sanction the purchase of tyres, and payment for repairs and fuel. One hundred and twenty-seven miles today.

Friday 31 - An old boss of mine named Maitland John Quartermaine, died yesterday age eighty years. Quartermaine of Earaheedy Station was the most exacting man I ever worked for, but I held the greatest respect for him despite his idiosyncrasies. I did not always see eye to eye with his strange logic, nevertheless he left a great impression on me.

I filled the water canteen, then travelled twelve miles north to Jutson Soak. There is plenty of shallow water under the surface, but I didn't bother to dig it out. Just so long as I know where water is. The whole area is a mass of shallow soakage holes exposed by kangaroos and euros. It seems so strange to find such a large number of dead kangaroos lying everywhere. There are old desiccated carcases as well as more recent fresh ones all around this soak, yet not a sign of dogs anywhere.

We went back to Rutter Soak and took the old Warburton back-road south-west. We came to a creek and dry soak at about ten miles, and three miles further up the creek another dry soak. One mile further west again is a third soak, under a ledge or bar across the creek. This one has a little water present, but not enough to get a good drink. At about forty-two miles from Rutter Soak we hit the main track we were on earlier. The one that runs between Ivor Rocks and Yamarna. Five or six miles west along this road, brought us back to Ivor Rocks for dinner. We had a bit of a bath here with the wash dish, and did some laundry. We later followed a road north from Ivor Rock to Cosmo Newberry, where I refuelled, then north a few miles to camp. One hundred and fourteen miles to finish the last day of October 1969. We've enjoyed an interesting start to the job and seen a hell of a lot of country. We now have a good broad picture of this new jurisdiction and time now to wonder what November will bring?

Figure 9 Rutter Soak

Chapter Seven - MOTORISED RIDERS OF THE OPEN RANGE

NOVEMBER 1969

Saturday 1 - Last night was quite cold for this time of the year. Strong gusty winds rocked the Landrover like a boat in choppy seas. We always unroll our swag in back of the vehicle if too late to look for a campsite free of things like scorpions, centipedes, and other pests.

Dooley likes to find the scorpion holes and dig them out. She is pretty good at it too. If at the end of a long day we pull up after dark, the only practical thing to do is sleep in the Landrover. This country is the worst I have ever seen for scorpions and centipedes, almost every place that looks like a good campsite is usually infested with them.

West of Ullrich Range today, we saw tracks of a dingo with missing toes. The animal no doubt escaped from a trap set by an amateur. That is how cunning dingoes get their education. Back near Lake Wells crossing, we found a trap sprung by another wily dog. It exposed the paper that keeps dirt off the spring plate, by pawing at it in a most tentative and cautious way. Once the paper came into view and the dog saw it, we could see from tracks, how the dog took off at full lope to get away from the revealed danger

Our indigenous dog the dingo has a deserved reputation for intelligence and cunning. I reset this trap, and also carried out the usual control measures elsewhere, from time to time as we moved along. We did a big circuit today, via Karu Soak and south through Bandya. We camped inside the Erlistoun run, after a long day of one hundred and eighty miles.

Sunday 2 - We back in town. The radiator has given a lot of trouble since I started this job. The top tank has nearly boiled dry of water several times out bush. We could find ourselves in a bad predicament if the tank blows out or the motor overheats and seizes, miles from anywhere. A telegram arrived from RVCO Jack Kerr to advise he will be in Leonora to see me on the 9th.

Monday 3 - In my opinion there was no option but put the Landrover into Sullivan's Garage for routine service and repairs to the radiator. There is no sense at all in waiting for official authority to fix a problem like that. I did however contact Jack Kerr in Kalgoorlie by telephone about the radiator, in order to inform him about my decision. He is one of those people who like to be the boss. He said I should always let him give the okay first for such major repair jobs, as there are things like alternative quotes to consider. He now expects to be here in the morning at 9-30 am, a week earlier than expected. I spent the rest of the day doing the APB Journals for last month.

Tuesday 4 - to Saturday 8 - The vehicle was in the garage all week for repairs, and waiting for authority from Jack Kerr. Jack didn't turn up here on Tuesday after all. This morning, Saturday, I took delivery of the repaired Landrover from Sullivans, and loaded up with stores ready for a quick departure, after the RVCO arrives tomorrow.

The LPO list at mileage 36874:

1 gallon motor oil
10 pints motor oil
1 pint gear oil
Change oils and general service
Repairs to engine head and front wheel hub

Sunday 9 - Jack Kerr came back from the north and called in to see me. He says APB bosses are happy to learn I am back with the department again. In particular he said that Des Gooding, the one and only APB Research Officer, was sorry that Fitzgerald my former supervisor made things so difficult for me toward the end of my previous term of employment. He also informs me that Sandstone will not now have a Group Dogger like the Pilbara has with their group system. Sandstone squatters don't consider the situation warrants the expense of a special dogger.

Jack had a look at the supplementary report I wrote at the end of the 1965-68 Savory Survey. This report makes special reference to Fitzgerald's behaviour during the final trip in 1968. The finale that wound up the wild dog Savory Survey I was on for three years. The one I did north of Wiluna between the Rabbit Proof Fence and Canning Stockroute. Jack grasped the document with obvious interest. He appeared somewhat enlightened after reading it.

It is unfortunate, that although I served almost five years with the APB before, I must start from scratch again now, since rejoining that department. Jack says I must now serve twelve months on probation, before being entitled to increased margins for skill and expertise as a dogger. This is the penalty for broken service. No worries about that though because it feels good to be back on the old job. I can't think of anything better.

I was like a duck out of water when away from the APB. Twelve months spent on the outside proved one thing. I will never settle down to any other kind of employment again. Once a government dogger, always a government dogger. A man has freedom of movement and almost complete independence on this job. It is true though, that a dogger must not leave his designated area without permission, but even with that restriction, there is still ample room to move around. There is plenty of new country to explore in all the APB desert areas. This time I appear to have the largest control region in the State. I got all the packing up and loading done today in preparation for departure tomorrow.

Monday 10 - We made an early start for Laverton this morning, and reached that town okay, but the radiator boiled all the way. I bought a bottle of BARSLEAK and put it in the top tank with the engine running. The substance took up the leak, and got us back to Leonora about 6-30 pm after a slow stop and start run. A regular halt to let the engine cool was necessary at ten mile intervals.

I saw the garage and arranged to have repairs effected first thing in the morning. They said it was okay last week when I took delivery. They had the vehicle in the workshop all that time. One hundred and thirty-two miles.

Tuesday 11 - The garage had another go at the radiator and got us on the road again by 10-30 am. We arrived in Laverton at 1 pm and refuelled with thirty gallons. We then had a spell in town for a couple of hours. We started for Cosmo Newberry with ten cases of commercial baits.

I detest the things, but it is all part of my job so I have to wear it. The APB and their useless baiting drive! In all the years of poison baiting drives I've yet to see evidence of their worth in the destruction of dingoes. The whole idea is political, meant only to appease the pastoralists. I am certain baits kill more native wildlife than they do dingoes. Not even foxes seem attracted to a bait of commercial manufacture. Now I have ten cases of the blasted things to get rid of. I topped up with fuel from a drum at Cosmo, then travelled north to camp in the spinifex a bit south of Gibson Hill. One hundred and thirty-nine miles.

Wednesday 12 - I dumped half the cases of baits under the shade of a mulga tree, to pick up later for the Thatcher Soak run. We saw only a few dog tracks on the way to Earli Earli whereat we stopped for dinner. I can't get over what beautiful water this is. The sun is a scorcher today. I got four scalps from dogs in traps, and carried out control work via Lake Wells. We travelled to the west at first, then north via the roundabout Nyiruru track that took us back to the Beef Road. Once on the big road it was northerly all the way to Warren's Well. This well is near the unfenced southern boundary of Windidda. By the look of tracks here the stockcamp is working the area. The stockmen were all away, but we saw Alf Ashwin's wife Tjipingka on camp near the well with two kids. Alf Ashwin is one of Dooley's tribal brothers. Tjipingka is one of the big Wongawol family. She told us that the boys are all out tailing cattle. We had a bit of a talk with her for a while, then continued north past Bonython Creek, to camp near Rock and Roll. Ninety-one miles.

Thursday 13 - A mob of camels with a pure white calf amongst them came in to drink at the mill this morning. I went north to the jump-up below Von Treur Tableland, and found two traps set beside the road there. Maybe it is the Wiluna dogger encroaching south into my area, or maybe the traps belong to Bob Geradi the former dogger. Returned to Rock and Roll, then travel was west, parallel with Von Treur cliffs to our north, to reach Panton Bluff at six miles. A turn south-west from Panton then, to hit the Bonython Creek three miles from the Bluff. This brought us to Joey Jarra Pool where several feeder channels meet on their downstream path. No water in the pool at present, only soakage. It is good water. From Joey Jarra we went north about five miles to look for dog tracks but saw none, we did however meet the stockmen on their way back to Warren's Well.

After a yarn with the riders, we went ahead of them to Warren's Well, and from there took the Deleta track south-west past Kurumin claypan at three miles, and Kuntapapa claypan six miles further along. This claypan is south of Collurabbie Hills and known as Collurabbie Claypan to those unaware of the native name. The Aboriginal words kunta and papa in combination, mean an embarrassed dingo. A bit north of the claypan a small black knob depicts the metamorphosed remains of a Dreamtime dog. One mile past Kuntapapa I saw the first sign of fresh dog tracks. We pulled up for dinner then carried on afterward south to Deleta at twenty-five miles. On next past Jerry Well to Tjilpitjara, a little gnamma hole beside the track on west side, twelve miles south of Deleta. Dingo tracks down here before the rain, but the rockhole is dry and no fresh tracks now. Three miles south of Tjilpitjara is another little gnamma hole also dry, and this time on east side of the road in the middle of a small gravel flat. This gnamma hole has a stone plug lid. It's native name is Djutunu. The word djutunu simply means covered up, eg. the stone plug.

Five miles south of the plug gnamma hole we came to a sprung trap and a dead fox. From that point we saw dog tracks all the way along the road to Urarey boundary. Urarey was once a small selection taken up by an oldtimer named Peter McNee whom Dooley in her young days knew as Pirriti or bandy legs. We saw a live dingo on top of some low breakaways at one stage but he took off too fast to get a shot. He was resting in the cool shade of a small cave under the cliff rim. We reached Urarey to find only derelict remnants of the old abandoned homestead, brush shearing shed, and stock yards. The oldtimer who owned this place had a fullblood lubra name of Fanny. She later had another white man called Wack Lloyd and they lived together on Windidda Station. She had the reputation of being a good horsewoman who sometimes rode a hundred miles or more across country to meet with relatives on stations further west. Despite the nearby dereliction, Urarey now boasts a new windmill and tank. It is excellent water so we pulled up to camp. Ninety-two miles.

Friday 14 - A lone dingo came in to the trough for a drink at daylight this morning, but like the one we saw yesterday, made off before I could fire a shot. First job today was to take a run south into Bandya country in order to ascertain just how far the station track to Karu Soak is from our present position. This is our first trip out this way, and we not yet familiar with all the tracks. The Karu track we sought, by the way, is twelve miles south of Urarey at a windmill marked on the map as Wallbroo, near a road junction. Natives call it Walaru says Dooley. I asked why, so in explanation she took me a mile or so west of the mill to a dense thicket of low bushes. There in the midst of this scrub is a part-open mine stope at ground level. Rain storms fill the stope in the same way as rain fills a natural rockhole. The stope contains beautiful fresh, cold water, thousands of gallons of it. This catchment has a dense surround of bogota, other acacias, and mulga trees, making it an ideal place to camp. It was a main campsite for bush blacks who roamed the station country around these parts back in the 1940s. They call it Walaru, and because the windmill is not far away they use the same name for both places.

Four roads meet at the Walaru junction. The one we came south from Urarey on, continues south to the site of an old mining town called Duketon. This north-south track crosses a bigger graded track that comes from Bandya homestead. (The homestead lies away to the south-west.) This road coming from Bandya, continues north-east past Walaru to Red Well. From Red Well it carries on through a gate in the station's extreme north-east boundary fence. From the boundary gate there, the road continues in the same direction out into open country. It passes several points we already know, such as native waters Patapuka, Tjampan, Miltji, and Karu Soak. From Karu the road turns almost due east. It terminates eventually near Ulrich Range, Mount Strawbridge, and Gregory Hills, they are all in close proximity to one another so the reader can take a pick.

Satisfied with this acquired knowledge of the Bandya road network, we returned along our outward tracks, twenty-five miles north to the sandalwood camp we saw earlier, to look around that area. There being no indication of native waters near this old sandalwood campsite, we went on a bit further north to a junction, where a wheel track turns west. We followed the faint wheel track and came to a little creek running out of decomposed granite ridges, with low and quite rough cliffs. Swarms of finches flying in and out of a narrow chimney type crevice in one cliff, led me to a water catchment. It looks just like a little trough, located well above ground level, and halfway up the cliff. Too small to be of much use for human domestic requirements, yet it can hold several gallons of water. I failed to get at it from below, so climbed the cliff to one side, and had a look down into the chimney crevice from up top. No water visible, only wet mud at bottom. The birds most likely drank the last drops only a short time prior to our arrival, that is why they are still on the go and anxious to get a drink. For now however they are out of luck and will have to wait for the next rain to fill the trough again. The best description I can think of is a natural bird bath. Dooley offers two alternative names for this place so we must ask some of her people the correct one when next in town. The older generation knew this country well, but this is Dooley's first return visit since childhood. She is a bit hazy about some details, which is only natural. The name might be either Yantakanngang or Tharukati she is not sure which.

After some contemplation, I feel further comment on this subject is in order. There are lots of fresh dog tracks at this place. It is a strange sort of rockhole, concealed as it is within a narrow fissure or chimney. From top of the cliff, the fissure descends about ten feet to the rocky trough, then beyond that, slopes down out of sight. From my high vantage point above, I could see the wet mud in bottom of the trough, as clear as anything it was, but no way for me to descend and get a closer look. It is difficult to imagine how dingoes could jump down there, crawl underneath to water, then climb out again, but their tracks are right there in the mud to prove it. There is no doubt that dogs have access to that trough. It is too deep for a human, and too deep for a kangaroo, but despite the access problem must be a good rockhole when full.

We left the rockhole puzzle behind. South next to the Bandya northern boundary. West then along the fence for about fifteen miles. Then north-west four miles to where a road cuts the fence from north to south. We left the fence here and turned south along the track for eight miles, to find it led to Mulga Queen. Dazzling white cyanide tailings' dumps are most prominent here, on top of a low open rise covered with wandary grass. This open grass swath provides a pleasant change from the normal dreary scrubs that cover most of this country. It is not a natural grassland but rather the result of extensive tree cutting by miners earlier this Century. Dooley has graphic memories of Mulga Queen. Her Ngalia people lived around here when it was a ration depot. Jack Shepherd and his wife were official Protectors of Aborigines at the time. The people loved them. Dooley says Jack was a huge barrel of a man, who had to sew blankets together to make his own trousers, as he was so big he could buy none to fit. The settlement of Mulga Queen is no more. The only indications of former habitation now are the remnant sticks of numerous native brush shelters. Puri is the Ngalia name for such shelters. Dooley remembers how she once played here with other kids when the nearby mine was still working, thirty years ago.

No water at Mulga Queen now, but a couple of miles south of here, a windmill with good water pumps into an earth tank. We went there to do our laundry and clean up a bit. After that we shifted east to the old Mulga Queen townsite to camp. Only mud brick rubble, broken glass, rusty food cans, and a couple of cellars to see now. It is easy to trace the outlines of old buildings, the main street, and a few side streets. Even the pub verandah site is still visible as compacted earthen pavement. Not far away a low pile of rubble indicates the remaining bricks of a baker's oven. Old native campsites are visible every which way, scores and scores of them. This place was once alive with Aborigines. Mulga Queen and it's outside area being their most favourite camp and hunting ground.

The ration depot ended when Jack Shepherd died about 1957. Then the Ngalia people began to drift in to Leonora to camp as fringe dwellers along the creek just north of town. Mulga Queen mob were for the most part unsophisticated Ngalia people from Mangkili, away out east in country nowadays bisected by Len Beadell's Gunbarrel Highway. Mangkili is a hundred miles east of Carnegie Station. These days most whites think these people belong to Leonora but in reality they are Ngalia elders from the Gibson Desert, along with their descendants. Today was hot with no cloud. Tonight we can see the glow of a big bushfire burning in the north. Seventy-seven miles.

Saturday 15 - We retraced our route of yesterday to the Urarey track where it comes through the Bandya boundary gate. From the gate we continued east along the boundary fence to look at some more country not yet seen by ourselves. This route brought us to the Karu Soak road, and the eastern boundary gate. We turned then north-east through the gate and travelled to Lake Wells. From there we continued north-east to Earli Earli where, I siphoned all the fuel out of a twelve gallon drum into the tanks. Then it was south-east to the two mills and junk yard just north of the Ullrich Range. Plenty indication of dog activity all the way. It is too repetitious to record every action of control work performed. Suffice it to say that I performed the requisite duties, well enough to keep faith with the APB.

We made a half circuit of the junk yard to where the dragged sandalwood track starts and ran it along for twenty miles, at which point is a turnoff going north. I took note of the turnoff mileage, and continued east then north-east. The road takes a wide swing around the southern end of Lake Wells to head north. Having ascertained the road's probable main direction, I turned back at that stage. There is insufficient fuel in the tanks to continue on a long trip. We saw three fresh dog tracks in the lake country.

We camped beside the two mills and junk yard enclosure fence on it's east side, where is a good stand of mulga for shade and shelter. This APB vehicle is a real bomb. The gear box is sticky now. It looks like rain in the south somewhere, but I doubt it will come here. We can see smoke billowing up from a fire in the vicinity of Earli Earli to our north-west. I wonder how that started. There is no sign of travellers anywhere in the country that we know. There are no thunder storms or any other obvious reason for a fire to start, and we certainly didn't light any. It is a bit of a mystery.

The second Moon Mission is well underway. The Apollo spacecraft is now 100,000 miles from Earth. A fantastic achievement by any standard. Here am I running around this way and that, looking for the destinations of various bush tracks. Later I hope to traverse large tracts of virgin country in a phase of literal exploration, yet there they go on the second expedition to the Moon. This Earth is a big place with much to find out about it yet. One hundred and fifty-four miles.

Sunday 16 - A cool south-east wind this morning, no doubt from rain out of the storms we saw to the south last night. I went west to Irve's grave and found several dogs' scratching places, so did some control work there then travelled south to Cosmo and emptied the APB drum into the vehicle tanks. I have no petrol on hand at Cosmo now until I bring some more out from Laverton. We then went north-east along the Warburton road to Jutson Soak, where two dingo pups appeared from nowhere just as the Landrover had a flat tyre.

I fitted the spare while Dooley took off with her rifle and stalked the pups. She had a shot at both of them, wounding one in the hip and killing the other with one shot. She then shot a third pup in the hip as it appeared on top of the granites, but it got away in the crevices amongst the boulders and was impossible to get out. Anyway she did a good job killing one outright. My eyes are not the best for shooting these days with open sights, but I still have a go, even if I do miss a lot. Dooley is the best. Only ninety-five miles today.

Monday 17 - Early this morning we both had a good look around for the wounded pups but saw no sign or indication of where they might be. The perimeter area around Jutson Soak abounds with dead euros, there are carcases everywhere, dozens of them. I collected all of them together in a large pile and burnt the lot. After that job we went in search of a euro or kangaroo to shoot. We got one about two miles north. We came back with this and left some of it as fresh bait material for the pups or any other dogs that might come along. I hate to leave animals wounded at any time, but there is no room for sentiment, it is all-part of the game.

Lang Rocks was our next destination. I took photos of the names and dates recorded on the rock face. The oldest appears to be 1895. Frank Hann and his offsider Talbot placed their names here too, but no date beside them. That done we travelled south to Rutter Soak for dinner and while there had a good look for names on flat granites behind the soak. The only one I could find was that of ARDAGH MLC but no date. Now I know how Ardagh Rocks got the name. Ardagh I believe was a politician travelling the backblocks. From there we travelled eastward to Thatcher Soak to camp. Two dead dingoes there, both poisoned. The only mark I can find on the rocks at Thatcher Soak is a broad arrow with a capital T and the figure 9 depicted in a vertical arrangement. I don't have a clue who the author might be. It might be a surveyor from the Water Supply or a Lands Department, who knows? I forgot to record that the two dogs were both males. The APB insists on all such details. Only a short run of eighteen miles today for a change.

Thursday 18 - After breakfast I had a look around to the west of Thatcher Soak and found two more dead dogs, both poisoned. We went north to Ardagh Rocks where I took photos to complement those taken of Ardagh's name at Rutter Soak. We can see no sign of any dogs coming near the bait at Jutson Rocks. It appears that they fled from this area after the shooting the other day. I don't blame them but they might come back later. Michael Terry's book "Untold Miles" refers to a couple of miners at work near this soak when he came past here in 1930. Terry claims he took the first ever motor vehicle to Warburton Ranges along Sam Hazlett's waggon tracks of 1929. I found the old mine a bit east of the soaks. The frame of an old bough shed still stands there, derelict and abandoned years ago.

We got on the road again, this time west toward Laverton and pulled up for dinner at Deepa Rockhole. Dooley did some cooking while I made a new billycan from an empty Sunshine Milk tin. We continued to Laverton. I purchased a full drum of petrol to fill all the tanks, left the butt on the ramp at the fuel depot for next trip, then we carried on west to Leonora. One hundred and sixty-six miles.

Wednesday 19 - I am due for official time off in town for the next few days. We went to the police station and got a full Driver's Licence for Dooley this morning. She did an oral version of the written test, because she can't read or write. Bill Pense is a good cop. He is good with us that is, but I can't speak for others. Dooley is the first fullblood woman in Leonora to obtain a proper licence. Not even the part coloured people around here have unrestricted licences. They all have conditional ones, good only for the local area, and an odd trip to Kalgoorlie.

I also initiated proceedings to have my firearms license restored. It is six years now since the police revoked it, due to a shooting incident in Wiluna. I had to hand in all my guns and an automatic pistol at the time.

Charles Conrad and Allan Bean in the spacecraft Intrepid, are on the Moon. They are due to commence a moonwalk in about half an hour at 7-30 pm. They enjoyed a perfect touchdown earlier this afternoon, and we Earth people can hear them talking on the radio, as clear as the proverbial bell. Oh yes, and the news says that Poseidon Nickel shares are at a high of $55.00. I put nineteen dog scalps in at the Shire Council today, but have to wait for the bonus as they have no money to pay me, so I'll pick it up later. The bonus is only two dollars a scalp anyway.

Monday 25 - A week off in town can sometimes be bit of a bore. It is always good to get out bush again. Out bush is where we are now, on the beef road, and three miles in along the turnoff to Tui claypans. This trip, the idea is to connect up some as yet untravelled tracks, and with this in mind we left Tui behind to travel north five and a half mile, to find an old dry well. The track turns west just past the dry well. Two miles on, it passes a big claypan for which we have no name. Then it is north-west for about thirty miles to Kurumin claypan near Warren's Well.

Our next destination was Deleta where to our surprise, were two nickel men with a Toyota and trailer. One was beside the old well fixing a flat tyre, the other doing something a bit further away. This pair seemed the most uncommunicative men it has ever been my displeasure to encounter. I wasted no time with them at all. I walked off right after ascertaining their problem was not a major break down. Their information in this respect was no more than a gruff "We're alright mate, we don't need no help." A strange reaction I thought, to meet anyone in the bush and not even pass the time of day. When I got back to our Landrover, Dooley told me that as I walked away from the two men, the more distant one of the pair raced over to his mate behind the vehicle. He appeared to point at, and talk about me as I walked away. We both began to feel apprehensive about the pair so wasted no more time on the scene. There are far too many strange people in the bush lately, it seems isolated no more. At Jerry's Well we turned west, intent on camping off the track in a concealed place, twelve or fifteen miles in, behind a prominent knob with a hidden flat on it's north side. One hundred and twelve miles.

Wednesday 26 - The weather is quite hot now with bushfires ablaze in the east, their smoke was a pungent scent on the air all night. This morning we found two small rockholes near camp. It seems old sandalwood pullers were everywhere throughout the **G6** dogging area. We found yet another heap of old sandalwood chips here. Further on about thirty-five miles from last night's camp, we came to breakaways with numerous rock catchments, all dry. A corkwood tree in a blind gully has a blaze with the letter **M** but no other information. It stands a short distance from a shallow rockhole at head of the gully. A low water shute cuts down the cliff to fill the catchment whenever it rains. Dooley says the rockhole's name is Paiyari. The blaze I think, is that of an explorer called Mason. We had a shot at two dingoes as they ran out of the gully but missed. We then came on south to Mulga Queen for dinner, a washing day, general cleanup, and do some cooking. We shot a bird this morning so as to enjoy a welcome change from tinned meat. There are not many motor tracks left to trace now, but still enough to keep me busy for another month. From the travels done to date, I have a good picture of the land over a wide area. Once a person knows the run, it is like an actual map in the mind, that is my experience anyway. Of rockholes with water out this way, there are none. There are one or two with water on the Warburton road, but they have government covers or lids to prevent evaporation and depletion by animals drinking. This entire country is drought stricken now. The native word paiyari is not of great significance, it is merely a term for wash-dirt or creek gravel. An apt description for the dry water catchment Dooley calls by that name.

After the cleanup we returned north to Bandya boundary for a bit more looking around. We followed the boundary west for five miles inside the fence, then turned north through a gate into open country. We followed a faint track for a short distance outside the fence and at three miles came to a large dry rockhole situated in a gully, with indigenous pine trees all around. At top end of the rockhole, I saw an old dog trap hanging from a tree. We returned one mile back along the track, and found a series of dry rockholes in a deep gorge. Six dingoes raced out of this defile as we approached, of these we shot two, and one got away. We then went back to the fence and resumed our former western course inside the boundary fence, to camp the night on some granite country, after a long day, but only seventy-five miles.

Thursday 27 - We came to a fence going south so followed it to a mill pumping into a creek. No tank or trough. Three dog tracks there. We next got through a gate and went west again past a gum creek, then turn north through another gate, to follow the creek along it's western side. One dog track at the gate. At two miles along the creek, we came to a dry soak, Tjutuwara, but no sign of dog tracks so returned to the fenceline to continue our western course. This brought us eventually to a gate that leads out to open country again, out to the Scholl Range. Came to a few dry rockholes half a mile off the track on east side, at three miles due north of the gate. At about fourteen miles we came to what Dooley says is Karli rockhole proper, as distinct from a smaller one to the west that we visited when in company with Happy Absalom. This hidden one is a most unusual rockhole, held within a fold of the big high crescent cliffs. From our vantage point above it, we could see down into the fold. The range wraps around a big rockhole full of water that rests halfway between ground level and the clifftop. It appears quite inaccessible, with a high sheer wall rising twenty feet or more above it, a drop of equal height below, and not a foothold anywhere to climb up or down. I never saw a rockhole quite like it anywhere. It seems unique in it's seclusion, and impossible-to-get-at situation. A lone manan tree or black wattle on the plateau above, marks the location of this strange rockhole. I saw only one dog track here.

We left Karli to follow a cutline west to reach Wonganoo boundary fence at five miles. A dry borehole marks the turnoff into Karli. The distance from Karli to the boundary ascertained, we went back to the Scholl Range track, then travel south led us to a second dry borehole, west along a mulga wash, a few miles on. From there we went back south to Bandya north boundary, and through the gate to a windmill in spinifex country. This was good water so we pulled up for dinner. Not much sign of dogs at this end of the run at all, there seem to be more where we went yesterday. From Spinifex Bore we went after dinner, west to Tharukati, or is it Yantakanngang rockhole, and from there south past the old Duketon townsite to Coxes Find and camp. One hundred and twenty-seven miles.

Friday 28 - Today while scouting along some of the old tracks north of Coxes Find, we ran into Dooley's uncle Albert of Erlistoun, with two wives, and other family members. They are putting in a new fence. We had a bit of yarn, then Dooley and I went off to look at where old prospector Stan Bridgeman used to camp in the early days, before moving to Laverton. Stan is quite a character. I ran into him near Karnka rockhole out in the Warburton Ranges. That was back in 1967. At the time I was on my way back to the West from Alice Springs. He had with him a number of tribal men. He was bringing them back after an extended trip to look at cultural areas south-east of Warburton in untracked country. He was so happy to see a traveller like me come along at the time, because both his starter motor and generator were out of order.

Dooley told me a number of yarns about Stan Bridgeman. One is worth relating now. Years ago Stan was sinking a new well near his camp. His offsider was Dooley's brother-in-law Rorn MacArthur. Stan was down the well, setting a fuse to blow a charge of gelignite. Rorn was the windlass man. Before going on, it might be best to mention that Rorn was an unsophisticated bush native, not long in from the desert. He was a real munjong with little understanding of English.

Well, so the story goes, Stan lit the fuse and yelled out for Rorn to wind him up quick and bloody lively. "Yah" from Rorn, "What's that boss?" The fuse by now spluttering and hissing away at a furious rate, Stan was quite anxious to get out of the shaft. He gave another loud yell back at Rorn: "Go for you're bloody life you stupid bastard, get the bloody bucket out of here. Go for your life" Rorn it seems, took the angry shouted order the wrong way. He mistook the word bucket for an oath and ran off back to his camp to tell his wife, Dooley's sister Kutjikari. "C'mon quickfella, boss bin growl alonga me properly, tellum get to bloody fuckit outa here." So Rorn and his wife rolled their swag and took off on foot, in great haste for the nearest scrub, leaving Stan down the shaft with his spluttering fuse. Alarmed by total silence from windlass man above, Stan managed to pull the fuse in time to stop being blown up. He was down the shaft for some time until another native named Ned Elliott stuck his head over the edge and shouted "Hey! anyone down there." So that is how Stan came back to the surface to ask where his offsider Rorn had got to. Ned told him "Oh, Rorn, last time I seen him he took off down the track with Kutjikari, he reckon you tell him to get goin, so that's what he did."

From Bridgeman's camp, and mine dump in the creek there, we followed an old track going east, and came to some dry soak holes in another creek near granite outcrops at five miles. The vehicle ran out of petrol in the big tank at 37747 so switched over to the other tank.

We reached a place called Christmas Well at six miles east of Bridgeman's gully. Dooley's tribal sister Nunguta, was born here. We saw this well on our trip to westward of Breakfast Rockhole on Wednesday 29th of October last. We know all the country from here on east, and today we went east to Pilki Soak again, only to find it still dry. Then further east to Yantatjipi Soak, which to our pleasant surprise is full of good clean water, now covering the timberwork at top. No sign of dogs there, so we had dinner, then return west to Pilki, and from there north through spinifex to mileage 37767. We saw nothing but spinifex beyond the five mile point of return. After that minor bit of exploration, we proceeded west to the main road to travel south, and camped a few miles north of Laverton after shooting a fat kangaroo for supper. Eighty-two miles today.

Saturday 29 - After breakfast we went on south to Stone Soak to clean up and fill the vehicle water tanks. This old government soak is full of sand, and has a kortan tree or minga bush growing out from the stonework around the top of the sand filled old shaft. The nearby water trough is also full of sand. The well lies in the bed of a quite narrow sandy creek, bordered by sand flats to either side. By digging down through the sand we obtained good quality water at shallow depth. Stone Soak is north-east of Laverton Downs station. We went in later to Laverton to fill the fuel tanks. A total of forty-four gallons of petrol, and a quart of motor oil. Invoice No 804440. Tanks now full at mileage 37833.

Travel was north-east next, along the old Warburton track to look for a couple of big rockholes, at mileage 37883 or fifty miles out from Laverton. Nanairie and Boolallie the map says, but the way I spell the native names is Nanari and Pulali. Also a place here known as Hunter's Waterfall, where a wooden survey block bears the legend FM 13 but I don't know who FM was.

FM 13

Those we saw are splendid rockholes full of water. The best seen to date. They are in a tangle of rough broken granite country, a mile or two north of Red Hill. Hunter was a Laverton policeman of earlier times, who left his name on the map whilst out on camel patrol in the tribal lands. We didn't locate Boolallie this trip but will look for it another time.

From these lovely rockholes, travel was north-east past Uhr Rocks, south of Point Charlie, then Dadgun, native name Tatjan, and Nord Rockhole, that should be Norr. Further along the track we suffered a flat tyre at Rutter Soak and after changing it, reached Thatcher Soak at 37913 or one hundred and three miles for the day.

Sunday 30 - (November) I fixed the flat spare this morning. It looked like rain for a while but soon cleared, and a bitter cold south-east wind makes for a miserable day. Most unusual weather for this time of the year. Century temperatures one day, thunder storms with lightning the next, followed by typical winter clouds with icy winds, and here it is nearly the end of another year. If this unusual weather keeps up we might see snow for a white Xmas yet.

I found another dog poisoned at Minnie Creek, and a couple more rockholes. One is a shallow open pool beneath a picturesque low waterfall, or rock bar, that crosses the creek. It might hold water for a few weeks after the creek runs. It would make a fine picture when full, but right now all the holes in this part of the country are dry, except for some small sand soakage in Pilpirr.

Mileage at Minnie Creek 37928 when I left to follow a road north, to the new Warburton road at 37938, and return south to Minnie Creek at 37952. We then followed the creek west for one mile, where is small waterhole with six dead euro carcases. It seems obvious that eagles killed the euros as there are no dog tracks anywhere near them. I poisoned all the carcases for the APB. Next I examined several old motor tracks leading off in various directions, but found nothing of interest. Later we saw a mob of ten camels with two calves. I got around the mob and held them for a while to take some colour slides, then left them to their own devices. I'd love to get a string of camels in hand, for old time's sake.

We went off to Jutson Soak for dinner and found one dead dog from the baited carcases I left here last trip. It looks like the mother of the pups Dooley shot. Three dead foxes and a couple of dead crows were the only other results, and no fresh sign of dogs since. The others left here for good. We reached the Harris Hills ten miles north of Jutson, where is an old asbestos prospect with an unfinished shaft eight feet deep. The asbestos is of green and brown colour. Return from there to Jutson, filled the tank with water, then proceed south to Rutter Soak. From there I followed a track north four miles to a windmill with good water, then east to Lang Rock and camp. Saw two fresh dog tracks running from Lang Rock south to Rutter Soak. One hundred and ten miles today to end of the month of November with much more accomplished than expected. It has been a most interesting thirty days for both of us.

Figure 10 Camels on Road

Figure 11 A Doggers Bounty

Chapter Eight - THOSE GREEN EYES

DECEMBER 1969

Monday 1 - Cold wind all last night. It was still blowing an icy gale this morning. From Lang Rock we took a drive around to the eastward toward Mount Shenton. We saw two dog tracks going into the windmill below the Mount, so set a trap on west side of the water point. We then returned south to the old Warburton track. We came to a "T. Murr" water, at eleven miles. I turned off here at mileage 38039 to follow a set of wheel tracks north-west through spinifex country. At one point (for which I neglected to check the mileage) several other tracks turn west. I followed the most southerly of these, and after a short distance came to a cluster of dry soaks at 38053, or fourteen miles from the old Warburton track. A few hundred yards past these dry soaks are some granite hills whereat, I found a good soak with water available. Native campsites, both old and fresh, are everywhere around here. This place appears to be a favourite campsite for blacks, but none here at present, and no sign of dingoes.

We returned to the Warburton track and followed it south-west to Nord Rockhole, in Mulgabiddy Creek. The name Mulgabiddy on the map is a misnomer, or rather an English corruption of the native word Palkapiti. The word palkapiti in dialect means, tail groove or the tail track of a kangaroo. There is still soakage water present in the sand at Nord (Norr) below the rock bar that crosses the creek. I was walking in to take a photo of the wet sand from atop that ledge of rock behind the soak, when a giant ngintaka (perentie) came out of a crevice straight at me. The reptile had its neck puffed up in anger ready to fight. It certainly frightened the daylights out of me anyway, with its sudden unexpected appearance. From a safe distance I put a couple of stones across the reptilian hide, to pay back for his bad manners. We left ngintaka and his precious soak to their own devices. I journeyed on south-west to Uhr Rocks for dinner. Afterwards to dry rockholes with survey peg marked FY113, then south past Red Hill, with survey peg FY114 and followed a mulga wash for three miles, but saw no sign of dogs. Returned again to the beaten track and found some soakage water half a mile north-east of Red Hill. Travelled through the night to Leonora for official time off.

Tuesday 2 - We spent the next six days in town enjoying time off. Jack Kerr came along to see me on Wednesday. He gave me some APB supplies. I filled him in on progress to date and in turn, he gave me instructions for the job. On Monday the 8th I rang him regarding the government vehicle, before leaving town. We finally departed late in the afternoon, bound for Stone Soak to camp. Before we left Leonora, I took Dooley along for peace' sake, to see one of her tribal sisters. This girl made eager eyes at me the other night. After imbibing a few drinks of beer, my normal defenses were down. As the night wore on, tribal sis' became tired and went to sleep in our bed. Dooley and I did not disturb her. Later, after more drinks together, Dooley and I went to bed too. Sometime around midnight, tribal sis' moved close to me and cuddled. Of course Dooley took exception to her proximity, and got even more angry when I didn't push my recumbent new bedmate away. This lack of conjugal fidelity on my part, resulted in cuddlesome sis' suffering a bottle blow to the head. At almost the same instant I got long, deep, fingernail scratches down my backbone. Recumbent sis' woke up with quite a start. She took off like the proverbial cat on hot bricks, and departed for who knows where. She did not return. Of course I suffered a constant reprimand for the rest of the night. This monotonous scolding continued at intervals over the next few days and following nights. Slighted Aboriginal women customarily like to wake a sleeping husband in the wee small hours, just to remind him of his errant ways. This method works too, because it is most unpleasant to have one's sleep disturbed at an unwelcome hour. Well as I said earlier, I took Dooley to see the other girl before we left town for the bush. Dooley belted the daylights out of her. I did not interfere because that is the Aboriginal way. Women must settle disputes in their own fashion. Men must not intervene. So much for green, green eyes. On the way through Laverton, I picked up two drums of petrol. It was still daylight and too early to camp, so we bypassed our intended stopping place and continued north along the Bandya road for Baneygo to camp.

Tuesday 9 - Got going early via Duketon, north-east past Tjampan, and Miltji, to Karu Soak, where we found several interesting developments since last out this way. One dog trap had in it the remains of a baby camel. Two other traps sprung on purpose, by some useless mongrels who camped here not long ago. Their campsite was right alongside the waterhole. Since the creek flowed, a pool of water now covers the soak. There is plenty of evidence to show how they did their washing in the waterhole, and probably had a swim in it as well. To top off that bit of bad news, a kangaroo died in the water after they left, now as a result, the water is putrid and green. Nevertheless the two campers were the first to despoil one of the few surface waters left in this drought stricken country. It really gets in my neck when strange travellers come along and make a nuisance of themselves. How they let such people loose in the bush beats me. I also found one dead dog poisoned near a kangaroo bait left here some time back. Disgusted with the Karu Soak pollution, we went on to the beef road junction to camp. Fresh tracks of one dog running along the road.

Wednesday 10 - Just for a change of routine, we went around the southern side of Gregory Hills, and afterwards on to the north side. By the look of fresh tyre tracks someone drove in there with an extra large four wheel drive vehicle. I saw this bloke in town, a Canadian name of Cam Cooper. He is a speculator. He goes out bush to peg blocks then sells them to mining companies for a big profit. We followed his tracks in amongst the hills and found they led to some old mines hidden away in a gully. I heard about these mines a few times, but this is the first time for us to see them. There are pegs bedecked with red, yellow and blue flagging all over the place. With all our time taken up following access tracks, we have no time left for jobs like pegging blocks. We miss out on opportunities to enrich ourselves, while strangers come into our country and get all the spoils. The whole country is going mad on mineral exploration lately. This Canadian fellow had Aboriginal guides with him.

We came down from the hills again and across north to Irve's Grave, where was a cat in one trap. While there, I this time went for a look around, and found Irve's old campsite not far away. It is three hundred yards north-east of the grave. He had a shaft about eight or nine feet deep with a drive at bottom running east. I don't know if it was a mine prospect or a water well. If a water well then it either fell in, or went dry, because it has no water now. Earli Earli was the next stop after leaving Irve's. Nothing in the traps except a kangaroo. The baits remain untouched as well. Drove south along west side of the lake, then back north to Nyiruru, where the traps had two dogs, one male, and one female. From Nyiruru we travelled west to the beef road and camped.

I had a change of plans after we set up camp. The muffler is hanging loose and one of the wheel bearings leaks a lot of oil. Repairs being essential I decided to get closer to Leonora for this purpose. So we set off again to Karu Soak, and got a surprise to see a fresh caught dingo jumping around in a trap. A female not long caught. I shot her and reset the trap, then carried on for another thirty-eight mile to camp.

We got to Leonora on the 12th. I put the vehicle in the garage for repairs. This took until Monday the 15th. I had to put the thing back into the garage for further attention next day on the 16th because the mechanic did such a bad job. I rang Jack Kerr about it. He said to take it down to Kalgoorlie on the 29th and I'll get a brand new one. Dooley has not let up on her opponent of the 8th since coming back to town. She had three separate fights with her this week. Finally they shook hands and made friends. They are alright now thank goodness, but I do hope no other girls pay too much attention to me in future. This last trip out bush, Dooley woke me up on a regular basis all night long, every night to remind me of my aforementioned indiscretion.

Wednesday 17 - With great reluctance, for fear the vehicle might breakdown again, we proceeded east to Laverton. Once there I decided to return to Leonora via Erlistoun and the Nambi back-road. The speedometer broke at mileage 38735. Not long after that the exhaust pipe fell off. The tyres being all bald and the engine erratic, this Landrover is now quite unfit for bush work. On Thursday the 18th once back in Leonora, I unloaded everything off the vehicle in preparation for the trip to Kalgoorlie. No vehicle parts arrived on the train, so now there is little I can do but wait. Wait for Xmas. Wait for the 29th. Wait for a new Landrover. Wait, wait, wait.

Wednesday 24 - Xmas Eve. I rang Jack Kerr about repairs to the WAG vehicle. The garage refuses to do the repair job due to some imagined slight with regard to LPOs or Local Purchase Orders. Sullivan says there is too much delay in payment of accounts rendered to the APB. The promised parts came on the train at last, so I also sent Jack a telegram today, to tell him I can effect the repairs myself. I did so anyway, otherwise it will not make the trip to Kalgoorlie.

We enjoyed a good break during the festive weekend, and got away from Leonora on Sunday afternoon for Kalgoorlie. We had tyre trouble all the way. I had a hard job to find out where Jack Kerr lives but found him eventually after getting his address from a halfcaste name of Jessup Sullivan, a Vermin Board dogger. I surprised Jack near his back porch. He was sitting down with head in hands. He looked miserable at first, but brightened up when he saw me. He says there will be a further delay of three weeks for the new vehicle as it broke down this side of Perth and had to go back for repairs. Not a good omen for the future by the sound of that. If the new one breaks down before delivery, what will it be like after a month in the bush.

Monday 29 - A Kalgoorlie garage did some repairs to the old bomb and it now seems good enough for another trip or two. I went to see the boss at his office. He gave me a requisition order for two new tyres and tubes. He is a bit mean with tyres is old Jack. Official duties finished, I next attended to my own business. I borrowed $500.00 from Custom Credit to put with two thousand bucks I have in the bank, to purchase a luxurious caravan. It bears the legend Travel Home on a plate fixed to the front panel and has two rooms. It is not really worth the money, but I want something substantial for a good camp out bush. A base, so we can stay away from town for longer periods. There are twelve easy instalments to pay at $45.00 per month, on the $500.00 loan, but I hope to clear it up quicker than that.

We returned from Kalgoorlie to Leonora with caravan in tow, then spent the rest of the month loading the caravan and vehicle ready for the bush. I completed the month's journals and reports, repaired two spare tyres and that was that. The twelve months of 1969 are now behind us and oh, what a year it was.

Chapter Nine - SEARCH PARTIES & EVENTS AT THE PUB

JANUARY 1970

We are off to a good cool and quiet start for the New Year, if current weather patterns hold, and other circumstances continue unabated. I am now, thanks to the caravan purchase, in debt for the first time since 1960 - to the tune of $500-00. During the past decade my bank accounts have always held a few thousand dollars on deposit. It was obligatory to open a cheque account for the first time in my life, in order to receive salary payments from the APB, before beginning work with that department in 1964. Cheque accounts are okay, I don't have any worries with them at all, a person only has to keep the records straight, be careful not to overdraw, and you can't go wrong. That is my experience anyway. In retrospect I am certain it was the possession of a well-run cheque account that put me ahead savings wise, but alas, those savings are rock bottom at the moment. I should soon pick up again though, as APB wages will continue to roll in each month.

Thursday 1 - We now have no money, but with a valuable asset on wheels in tow, we left Leonora for McKenzie Well south of Bandya. I shot a small kangaroo and a bird along the way for a New Year feast of fresh meat, instead of our usual fare of tinned tack. Canned meat rubbish is our mainstay when out bush. The road was almost devoid of traffic. We only passed one vehicle north of Laverton, it looked like the former dogger Bob Geradi in his decrepit old Landrover, but he didn't stop. There was only one vehicle parked outside the Laverton pub too when we came through, and we caught sight of the local cop sitting at the bar as we drove past. One hundred and fourteen miles for day one of a new decade.

Friday 2 - We left McKenzie Well at mileage 38958 to reach Mulga Queen at 39004. After unloading all the stores, we set off back to Laverton to get fuel for our proposed supply base. With the fuel on board we made an immediate return to Bandya. where we dropped in at the homestead to see Peter Hill and stayed to have a meal there, accompanied by a long interesting yarn about the desert. We spoke at length about Lake Wells, Empress Spring, and the man who named those places in 1896, the noted Scottish explorer David Carnegie. From Bandya it was on to our new caravan base at Mulga Queen, where we arrived well after dark. We travelled today, one hundred and ninety-four miles at 39152.

Saturday 3 - Last night and this morning were nice and cool, until about mid morning when it began to warm up a bit. I repaired a tyre or rather should say, I fitted a new tyre and tube. After that it was load the Landrover ready for the bush. Our vehicle loading when on the move, will be much less henceforth, as we will leave the bulk of our gear behind at the caravan. That was the purpose of the new caravan in the first place, to set it up as a base camp to store supplies, so the Landrover can travel light. I filled all the water drums, topped the fuel tanks, and had one last look around camp to make it secure. We are now ready to travel with only basic rations on board for the first time ever. Previously we had to cart everything with us all over the country. We had no base camp to leave anything at. Now with the suspension up instead of weighed down, we are off for a "flying trip" as the oldtime explorers used to put it.

We now find that this thicket at Mulga Queen where the caravan stands, is an old ceremonial area. All the singing sticks that men used to thump the ground with while sitting around in a circle, still lie scattered about here. As a result, Dooley is not keen on my choice of campsites. She is afraid of the old law. She was happy enough though, after I picked up every stick in sight, and removed them all to another thicket. I carried them to another place where lots of similar sticks lay scattered about. I respect the old law myself, being a fully initiated man, but have only contempt for the present day town blacks in Leonora, who no longer follow the law. The Leonora mob is the one that years ago left these ceremonial sticks lying around here at Mulga Queen. These days however, having abandoned their ceremonies for good, they are no more than a bludging lot of pub crawling alcoholics.

With that bit of reflection notated and out of the way, we broke camp and proceeded to my north-east work area. We came past Red Well to the Bandya boundary fence, then on and out into the open country past Patapuka, Tjampan, Miltji, and Karu. Not a sign of dogs until one mile from Moxon Creek where lots of fresh tracks are running up and down the road to drink at the soak.

Karu Soak gained prominence again this trip. First item: There was another dingo still alive in a trap by the creek crossing when we came along today. She was difficult to kill. This is the second live dingo in a trap here, the other was on Thursday the 10th of December last year. Dingoes seem as tough as a kangaroo to dispose of when wounded. Second item: We found more evidence of interference with traps by white prospectors or whoever. Their boot tracks are still easy to see all along the road here in both directions. There are seldom any travellers out this way to obliterate tracks on the motor road. Also being open desert it is devoid of stock, which in station country would erase all sign of such tracks in a day, or overnight, while walking into water and returning to feed.

When we stopped off at Bandya homestead on the way back from Laverton last Friday, I forgot to record in the diary that Peter Hill told us the reason for last month's interference with our traps. The people concerned were two white prospectors who broke down fifteen miles away on the shore of Lake Wells. They walked to Karu Soak, the closest water they knew, to await help. They told Peter Hill they made use of my traps to catch a kangaroo to keep themselves alive. When I learned these facts, my immediate response was to take back all my hard words said on Tuesday the 9th of December last year. At that time I cursed those who fouled the precious water at Karu. I forgave them after Peter explained the circumstances, that is until we came along today and found traps deliberately sprung again. This time we found evidence that the same two, or maybe some other two, had broken down and walked into Karu again.

The pair of visitors at Karu whom we saw signs of on December 9 last, camped on the other side of the waterhole that they fouled with their washing and bathing. This time it looks like another couple of individuals. We found quite a neat little native style puri, or brush shelter, close to the creek crossing. It was on the downstream side of the road. Numerous sandalwood nuts lay scattered around the campsite, showing how the two individuals ate nuts to sustain themselves. On the ground nearby was a broken shangai or rubber slingshot, whatever it is they call those things these days.

We used to call them catapults when I was a kid, but that was a different era. The two marooned individuals at Karu used the slingshot to kill birds for food. They also fashioned a rough sort of digging stick, possibly to dig witchetty grubs or bardies.

It was evident also how they burned the traps in the flames of a fire, an obvious attempt to rid the iron jaws of strychnine and dead carcase contamination. Also, with a couple of wire strands from trap tethers, they fashioned a rough wire grill to cook meat. Some remnants of kangaroo flesh still lay about the camp, half cooked and near raw. This showed how they merely singed raw flesh in the flames. It is obvious they had no knowledge of how to cook meat in the ground under a cover of coals and ashes. Nevertheless all personal umbrage aside, I still take my hat off to their ingenuity.

They did a damned good job to keep themselves alive at all. These latest two castaways and those of last December had no chance of rescue by me. I was away from Karu for weeks, both prior to the 9th of December and after that. We did one flying trip past Karu on Saturday the 15th of November, but for the rest of the month we were east of Laverton.

After that we did make another flying trip past Karu on Tuesday the 9th of December. We did see old evidence of campers, and fouled water as already described, but we never went near Bandya homestead at all. We learned nothing from that source at that time. Then for the most of part of December we suffered vehicle troubles ourselves. We didn't learn anything of the Karu Soak drama until we called in to have a meal with Peter Hill the other day.

This is a bit of a mystery. The signs of two people at Karu today do not tally with those we saw on December 9. There is no sign of vehicle tracks on the road before we came along, so these two must be still out here in the bush walking somewhere, poor bastards. A pair of good improvisers who just lacked that little bit of bush knowledge, that distinguishes a novice from an experienced bushman. I hope we run into them if they are still out here on foot so we can help them along. Looks like I'll have to hang extra traps in the trees around Karu from now on so stranded travellers can catch kangaroos when broken down. That way they might leave my set traps alone.

The whole issue of different unfortunates is confusing to say the least. One lot accounted for, the other not. What a conundrum. Two sets of boot tracks we studied today in front of the little brush shelter indicate two people, but whether it be a man and woman or two men is difficult to say. Boot tracks do not always indicate the sex of a wearer.

After dinner at Karu we went along the road east toward lake Wells. At the lake I caught the glint of a shining object about half a mile south of us on top of a rise composed of white kopi and studded with sheoak trees. This kopi undulation borders the lake proper. I engaged 4WD then drove in closer to have a look. The sun was reflecting from the window glass of a half buried utility. A hopelessly bogged utility, no mistake about that. This kopi bulldust has the consistency of talcum powder. I was apprehensive as I drove in, and pulled up some distance back from the submerged vehicle in case I get bogged myself.

The former occupants of the stricken vehicle left everything strewn around all over the flat. jacks, shovel, axe, empty petrol cans, spare tyres, a full drum of petrol, and most ominous of all, an empty water can.

No country for a Holden Ute this. Even a Landrover can bog down in this kopi dust. It is treacherous stuff. In the cab was a scrawled note that read:

A big message HELP inscribed in the white bulldust ground surface nearby as well. We had already come across a similar message reading HELP, together with an arrow pointing to Karu Soak, back west of here when we were following the footprints east, this afternoon, it was right in the middle of the beef road near the junction. These must be the unfortunate pair Peter Hill told us about on Friday the 2nd last. We also

> HELP
>
> Mark Sinclair (Field assistant) Falconbridge Aust Pty Ltd Louis Bell (Geologist) 190 Hay St East Perth.
>
> BOGGED in bulldust 10 am Tues 16th Dec 1969 Leaving car 5-30 pm same day to walk to KARO SOAK
> 14 miles west along road in order to obtain water. May try to travel overland to Urarey Well tomorrow night,
> where our caravan is parked.

saw patches of burnt spinifex along south side of the track as we came along, no doubt lit as signal smokes. At that point though, we knew nothing of the bogged utility.

I called in to the RFDS Base in Kalgoorlie with a message about the stranded vehicle. John Flowers the operator told me that Peter Hill drove out from Bandya and rescued two people on Xmas Day after he failed to find them at their caravan camp near Urarey. It seems strange that Peter failed to give us all the details. He certainly told us nothing about a Xmas Day rescue. Nothing at all. I wonder why.

There was no way those two men could dig themselves out of that treacherous kopi powder. No way at all. They drained all the drinking water during the strenuous shovel work. If they had kept on going under the blaze of midsummer heat, the result could only be a tragic perish from thirst of two young men. A walk of fourteen miles to Karu was a notable feat in itself. But after the exhaustion of so much shovel work, to continue on across country to their caravan at Urarey during such heat! I hesitate to think of the consequences. Two desiccated cadavers being the only possible outcome.

It annoys me that we were not on hand to effect the rescue, but recriminations against us are not in order. The APB insists that all holidays be taken as time off, in particular the Xmas - New Year break. This is the one time of the year when a dogger is not active out on his run, so in that respect the breakdown occurred at a most unfavourable time for the characters involved. Our prolonged absence from the scene both before and after the event, became even longer as a result of official business that required my presence in Kalgoorlie, and vehicle troubles of our own.

That is enough of that episode for now. Work calls, and duty bound, I found the carcases of two dogs along west side of the lakes as we proceeded north from the abandoned Holden. One male and one female. Nothing at Nyiruru, and nothing north along the beef road until near Warren's Well, where two fresh dog tracks appeared. I must set some traps there tomorrow. By this time it was getting late so we camped at the well. It is cloudy this evening and could rain. Ninety-four miles, 39246.

Sunday 4 - We went north past "Rock and Roll" windmill to where Ricky Houston the Wiluna dogger had traps set in my area. His traps are still there. Returning to Warren's I set three traps, then set off to Deleta. Got two more dogs along the way, another male and a female. Set two more traps before getting to Deleta, then went on south to a trap set a little north of Tharukati, a gnamma hole in a granite outcrop beside the Deleta track. Fresh dog tracks up and down past the trap but none went near it. I placed some fresh lure there to encourage a bit more canine curiosity next time they pass by. It is a stinking hot today, and the lure I use to attract dogs to the traps, stinks.

Blasted prospectors' tracks everywhere all through my dogging run. The country is crawling with bloody nickel men as we call them. The native girls in Leonora and Laverton call them tickle men. We located a shallow old well about thirty feet deep, in a thicket on east side of the track today. It is hard to see any indication of the well when driving along and easy to understand how we missed it before. Water is only about twenty feet from the surface. It is about midway between Tharukati and what is known as Jumbo Claypan. Peter Hill told me about the well last Friday night. There is a faint track into it, but that is too is difficult to see.

The Falconbridge caravan, the one mentioned in the distress note at Lake Wells, is still at Urarey. No sign that the occupants ever returned to it. It seems funny to me. It makes me wonder now, if they are the same pair that Peter Hill rescued, or another lot. I'll have to ask him and make sure. No hurry though, because if there is another lot missing then it is too late for them now. It is more than three weeks. If they walked across country to Urarey as the distress note suggested they might, then they must be dead for sure.

Dog tracks all along the road between Tjilpitjara and Urarey. I'll have to go back and set more traps there. I topped up with water at a mill four miles east of Mulga Queen, and we both had a bath under the overflow pipe. The water is a bit hard for washing, but good to drink. We went back to our caravan at Mulga Queen to call it a day. A real scorcher with clear blue skies. I'd like to know where those dogs are watering. One hundred and sixteen miles. 39362.

Monday 5 - We passed an alluvial gold prospect east of here called Patch yesterday. I forgot to record that we left a butcher knife behind. We stopped off to let Dooley do some eyesight specking while I cleared bushes away from beside the track over a distance of several miles, in order to allow clear passage for the caravan. I intended to shift camp today to another windmill in that area, but now, the more I think about it, the less attractive the idea seems. The same objection applies to seven other windmill waters I had a look at as possible campsites. The only exception being Hootanui, a windmill with good water near a gum creek to the north-west of Mulga Queen. Hootanui however, is much too close to the main road for my liking. I think I'll stay here at Mulga Queen for the time being.

We decided to go north and have a look at Yultu, a rockhole outside the boundary. Yultu is the rockhole where six dingoes came out of a gorge on Wednesday the 26th of November last year. Another rockhole north of there is Kutjurrkapi. An inspection of the area shows that none of those dogs ever came back since we shot one on the first trip. Today we approached the hidden rockhole on foot. This time not dogs, but at least forty disturbed euros came out of the narrow gorge in leaps and bounds when I threw a stone down from the clifftop. The place is a shelter from the heat, used by native animals because of the almost permanent shade thrown by cliffs on both sides of the narrow cutting. It is really summer weather now, hence the large number of euros seeking shelter from the excessive heat. The dogs that were here before must know a better place.

There is a windmill pumping into a little creek on south side of the boundary fence. Peter Hill calls it Wilson's. It is beautiful fresh water to drink. Just like rain water. I saw one dog track near the pool, and a station trap with a dead fox in it. I also noted that the trap had no poison applied to the jaws. I must tell Peter Hill about that before we get a dog with three legs running around the country. If the jaws have no poison, a dog will chew its own leg off to get out of the trap. If you wrap strychnine in a hessian strip around one jaw of a trap, then the dog chews the hessian instead of its own leg, and the poison kills the animal in a short time. On the other hand if the dog gets away, it becomes cunning, and will seldom if ever go near a trap again. One has to be an expert to catch a cunning dingo. A real expert.

There is some of what they call brain stone, about three miles east of Mulga Queen. I believe it indicates nickel bearing country. So far there are no pegs or flagging near it either. The prospectors haven't found it yet. This heat is going to make dogging hard and tiresome work for me henceforth. The only advantage of this uncomfortable weather is it will force dogs into water more often, then they'll leave fresh tracks for me to follow.

We saw a Landrover full of young natives going past Walaru this morning, headed toward the Karu track. I hope they leave my traps alone. They are strangers to us, although Dooley most likely knows their families. I used to love the old tribal people. I'd take my shirt off and give it to them if they asked, but as for this younger generation, you can have them. They are just town parasites. Good for nothing bludgers. Eighty-two miles 39444.

Tuesday 6 - We went back north to Wilson's again this morning, to where we saw the dog tracks before. I set one trap each side of the windmill. Because Yultu is not far away, I fancy that these tracks here are those of the dogs we frightened away from the rockhole when shooting at them a while ago. Along the way we saw, about seven miles east of Mulga Queen, where a dingo got caught in one of the Bandya station traps. We tracked it up for a considerable distance before locating both dead dog and the trap that caught it. Like the trap we saw at Wilson's before, this one too had no poison on the jaws. The poor dog died from heat exhaustion after a frenzied struggle with the trap. When we found it, the trapped leg was hanging by only one sinew. Just another half hour of life needed for that animal to escape with three legs, and a trap shy mentality. It was a female, so I can imagine the hue and cry that would ensue in a year or two, with a cunning bitch on the loose. And all the result of pure ignorance.

Today at last we found the best camp in the country. They call it the Ten Mile. The windmill is right alongside the main road to Bandya homestead, but it has an almost impenetrable mulga thicket behind it. We chose a tiny clearing in the thicket about half a mile off the road. I had to cut a way for the caravan to make headway. Our chosen site and caravan are not visible at all from the road.

This is just what I wanted. Good water, good shade, and concealment from passing traffic. We shifted camp without delay and settled in to our new abode.

A plane flew over while we were still in the thicket. Later at the station, Peter Hill told us the plane was looking for three men lost up the north end of my run somewhere. While still at the homestead enjoying a mug of tea, the aircraft returned to Bandya and landed in front of the house. They located the trio near Trig Station B56 wherever that is. They gave us a bearing of 292^0 north of Deleta. A message written on the ground by the missing party read: IGNITION TROUBLE plus other writing that the aircraft crew could not read as it was too small. The stranded people lit a smoke and the plane crew spotted it straight away, so it was a successful search to that point.

My drums being still at the Mulga Queen petrol dump, we went back there and refuelled, then proceeded immediately via Urarey to the Deleta track, in case I might assist with the rescue. By this time it was late, so we camped at Jumbo Claypan, about thirty-five miles north-east of Mulga Queen. Oh yes, and I nearly forgot to mention that I asked Peter Hill about his alleged rescue of Mark Sinclair and Louis Bell. He says it was indeed the ones he brought out of their predicament, but he never did see their vehicle. What happened was: Peter knew they had a base camp at Urarey. When they failed to come near Bandya for several weeks he drove out that way to see if they were at the caravan. The pair were not at their camp so, acting on a hunch, he took a run out to Karu Soak just to have a look. Of course as we now know, he found them there and brought them back to the homestead for Xmas. We did eighty-six miles today.

There seems to be a plethora of stranded bush travellers and rescues lately. The Laverton police party came along past our night camp on Jumbo Claypan, about two o'clock this morning. One of them, a constable everyone calls Banjo, made a gruff approach when he woke us. He asked: "Hey what's going on here." I told him this country is our work area and we have a perfect right to be here. He changed his attitude then and said: "It's alright mate, don't take any notice of me, that is just an expression of mine, to ask what's going on." That settled, they departed again, so we rolled our swag and followed behind, wanting to be in on the action if possible.

We pulled up to camp again until daylight, near Jerry's Well. When it was light we went on to Deleta for breakfast to see where the police were, but it appeared they had no intention of stopping anywhere and kept travelling through the night.

We returned south to the fenceline and followed reasonably fresh tyre tracks west, as we thought that to be the direction in which the people in trouble last went. Speedo 39554 when we left the main track. We went in for five miles and felt more certain then, that this route led in the direction of the missing people.

The longer we followed fresh tyre tracks, the more certain we felt that these tracks led to the people in need of rescue, how far ahead though, we knew not. I was a bit concerned too about possible interference with the official police rescue mission, although certain we could reach the distress scene much sooner than the police. My better judgement said to give it a rest for a while. We don't wish to make a fool of the police. If they want to cut through virgin bush on a compass bearing that is their prerogative.

If they fail, then we have a good idea which way to go by way of this new well-beaten track, no doubt made by the broken down party. We turned around and went back to Jerry Well to cook some meat and wait to see what might transpire. To fill in time I set one dog trap nearby. The search aircraft came along and flew low over us, obviously they wished to identify our vehicle, and satisfied we are not the police, they climbed to a higher altitude and flew on. One hour and a half later, while I am still writing this account in the diary, we can hear the aircraft engine flying around north of us. They are circling around, so must have the police vehicle in sight, and are flying around the distressed vehicle party so the police can home-in. I am glad now I didn't take a leaf out of their book. When I offered my services last night they declined, so the best of luck to them now.

We went in west along the old long abandoned fenceline again. This time we followed the tyre tracks for nine miles, but they seemed to be trending much too far west. I reckoned those in need of rescue were more to the north. I gave it away again and returned to the main track at Jerry Well. We took a run up the road and found where the police camped last night, about ten miles north-east of Deleta. It is no wonder the plane was looking for them. They were to start their search from Deleta, but went right past there without stopping. Looks like they lost themselves in the dark. I gave it up in disgust, although their tracks were easy to follow if I wished. Instead I continued east to Warren's Well resetting traps along the way. Had dinner at Warren's then turned south-east to Earli Earli. We had a bath there in the overflow pool. Beautiful fresh water this.

The windmill needs oil. The bearings need seals too. I pulled up all the traps here. The dogs are not getting caught at Earli Earli, yet the same dogs seem to get in traps, or take baits, further away at such places like Nyiruru and the lake. They must be the same dogs, because this is the only surface water in the country at present. On the way past I took the traps away from Irve's grave too. They only attract foxes and cats. I won't bother to inspect Gregory Hills or Point Pater traps, not worth it this hot weather. We are now getting intense furnace heat and cloudless blue skies. It is well over the century mark every day. The sand reflects the heat like an oven, and the ground is much too hot for setting traps.

We took the Karu track south-west. No dog tracks at the soak itself, however there are fresh tracks all the way along the road to Miltji. The rockhole at Miltji is still dry. I set some traps to that point. On then past Tjampan where we got a surprise to meet Mark Sinclair and Louis Bell on their way out to collect their bogged vehicle, the cause of their pre Xmas troubles. This time they had a Landrover that will assist them to pull the Holden out of the bog. We had a short chat to pass the time of day then left them and came home to the Ten Mile camp via the old Mulga Queen back road.

Thursday 8 - We stayed on camp cleaning up all day, like raking leaves and sticks from around the caravan in case of fire, and all that sort of thing. That done we rigged the annexe on the van and it looks real good. It keeps the sun off the eastern side in the mornings, while thicket trees shade it on west side in the afternoon. When our strenuous activity ceased, some pretty little blue wrens and small finches came along to visit. Dooley and I don't know this species at all. It is quite hot today, even in the shade. Thunder heads are rising in the north. I know that Jiggalong natives are holding rain ceremonies this month, but the rain is a long time coming. I counted a total of nineteen dog scalps on hand this month to date.

Friday 9 - Peter Hill called into our camp this morning and gave us a bit of information on the search trip the other day. He said the cross-country traverse to reach the stranded party was rough-going through thick scrub, all the way from where they turned off ten miles to the north-east of Deleta. They staked two tyres, and had a bit of bother with the aircraft not cooperating correctly. Finally they reached the B56 point, and the men with Landrover ignition trouble. From the breakdown site they followed the other party's motor tracks east. They came out between Deleta and Jerry's Well. That was the same track Dooley and I followed on two occasions that same day, but we didn't want to interfere. We could have been first on the scene, by continuing along the fresh motor tracks we followed for nine miles earlier that day. We could have been waiting with the stranded lot for the police to arrive from the east, after their traverse over untracked country. We turned back though, because we didn't want to be unpopular with the Laverton party. In retrospect I think it just as well we did keep out of the way and mind our own business.

After Peter went, we travelled north and got one black and white male pup from a trap south of Wilson's Bore. From there we came back via Hootanui to Mulga Queen to pick up the two drums of fuel I left behind when we shifted camp. Later we did some washing and filled our water cans. Thirty-six miles today.

I wrote out a telegram to:

AGPROTECT
Perth

Both rear springs main leaf broken. Stop Please advise whether to repair at Leonora or not.

Peter Muir

When I tried to send it the radio was on the blink so the telegram is now CANCELLED.

Saturday 10 - I went into Leonora via Nambi, the shortest route, to take delivery of two new tyres and tubes. The government has to replace one of my tubes. Also picked up a load of personal gear, including books, to take out to the caravan. Came back by way of Laverton. We pulled off for a while, and totally out of character for me, we had a few drinks with some of the Laverton police. It seems they found out a bit about my background since the search party episode. They now have knowledge of my 1965-68 exploration work in the desert north-east of Wiluna. The main spokesman says they now regret they didn't take advantage of my expertise, and my offer to assist them in the search last week. Henceforth, said the spokesman, they will be after my services. I retorted that next time I may not be available as they neglected me before, but they just laughed at this response.

After the cops left, a Leonora resident noted for his dependence on guns in an argument, came into the pub and we had a few drinks with him. This man irritated me. He was dropping clear hints in my direction that if anyone ever tried to get around with his lubra he would, in his words: "Shoot the bastard and her with it." I took exception to this blatant threat, because she is not only one of Dooley's nieces, but I am not after her, nor will I be. I always take strong exception to anyone who threatens me with firearms. In direct response to his veiled accusation I said: "Look here old fella if you wanta talk about shooting people then it's best you come outside right now. We can have it out. I've got a.303 in the Landrover, you get your gun, and we'll see who wins." That rough-neck went to jelly. He laughed it off; but I wasn't going to drink with him anymore. I would not make friends. No one is ever going to bluff me out, not with guns they're not.

Another fellow name of George Owens came along and we drank with him until the pub shut at 11 pm. Just prior to closing time, Banjo the Laverton cop came in and bought some bottles, then invited me and Dooley to join him outside for drinks. Laverton in this year of 1970 is still a frontier town. The hotel has a wide open frontage of about two normal town streets in width. Wyatt Earp or Wild Bill Hickock type of thing. A wide dusty street with not a person in sight. Well, we drove the Landrover away from the pub and pulled up a bit to one side to settle down with Constable Banjo and drink some beer. The three of us crammed in the front seat. Dooley in the middle. The would-be gunman of earlier in the night probably told the police that I threatened *him* with a gun, so as to get one back on me for calling his bluff. Banjo asked in a diplomatic way: "You wouldn't use a gun in an argument would you Pete?" To reassure him I replied: "No, only in self defence." He continued: "Yeah, that's what I thought, you look like you can use yourself a bit, you've got the build of a fighter. I didn't think you the type to threaten people with guns for no reason." He had no more to say on that subject and let the matter drop.

During this conversation, Dooley appeared to be on edge sitting in the middle, and asked would I let her out on my side, I did and she walked off into the dark for a few minutes. She returned, then told me to shift over into the middle seat, so I did. Banjo handed me an opened bottle of beer. He said he had to go on duty for a while, but would come back later; and asked us to camp nearby. I said: "We can't camp in the main street even if it is empty." "Oh that's alright." Said Banjo. "I'm the only policeman on duty tonight, and I say you can camp here. Just move the bus a bit over that way where the shadows are, and I'll come along later." He then left Dooley and me to ourselves. Dooley expressed some qualms about the policeman's suggestion to camp just off the main street, although she didn't elaborate. "Don't camp here Peter, get going out bush and camp off the road somewhere." So, that is just what we did do, we drove about a mile or a bit more north of town then went in along a fence, well out of sight from the main road.

Sunday 11 - Slept like the proverbial log I did, or was it a hairy dog. I felt more like a dog this morning. Dooley was shaking me awake when I opened bleary eyes to a dazzle of sunlight from an orb much higher in the sky than at my normal time to rise. "Come on Peter get up. Someone will come along soon. We not far from the road." Oh goodness my head was thick. I feel certain someone slipped me one of those things they call a Micky Finn last night. Probably in that last opened bottle our policeman companion handed me, just before he left us, with directions as to where he wanted us to camp. The reason seems obvious. He wanted to have me out to it so as to make love with Dooley. She will never do that. Dooley is true blue if ever a woman was. She is the best. Dooley already had the Landrover packed up and ready to roll this morning, so I got up on groggy feet and she threw the swag on while I clambered up into the passenger seat. I asked Dooley to drive. It took us all day to get back to our camp at the Ten Mile.

I was so sick today I thought to die. Dooley frightened and uneasy too. We made frequent halts every ten mile or so along the road. I only started to get better by 7 pm tonight. Dooley tells me that the cop was fondling her knee when she was sitting in the middle seat, that is why she got out and asked me to change places. The only good thing to report today is that we accomplished the sixty-nine mile journey home to camp without any untoward incidents. I know I'll be extra careful about whom we drink with in future.

Chapter Ten - CHILDHOOD RECOLLECTIONS REVISITED

JANUARY 1970 (continued)

Monday 12 - Hot today with thunder heads around the west and south-west horizon. I'm okay myself, but I don't like going out anywhere with this government bus, not in its present state. Even the transceiver is on the blink now. The tyres are threadbare, no tread at all on some, and canvas showing through on others. Only one headlight is working, and one tail light. The steering is crook and all over the road. The brakes don't work. The engine is guzzling large amounts of oil. There is no glass in one rear side window. The canvas hood is in shreds. The only sensible thing I can do is stay close to camp until Jack Kerr comes back from holidays. I feel good today. The Micky Finn effects have worn off. No more drinking in company for me.

Tuesday 13 - I wrote a letter to Michael Terry today, to supply details of hieroglyph inscriptions I found on a cliff face over on the Ashburton Fall, south of Pingandy Creek in 1964. Michael feels Canberra might like to record the site, to fill a gap in Australian history. In his letter he relayed information from a Professor Rona of Ottawa University in Canada. Rona feels sure the hieroglyphs are an ancient Javanese script, and claims to recognise several characters. Oh well, that's his opinion. To me the hieroglyphs look like dendritic markings made by some mineral leaching out of the chalk-like cliff face that supports them. We will see what the experts decide when they view the actual site, that is if they ever decide to make a move in that direction. One thing is certain, they will need me to guide them to the spot. It is in an inaccessible place. Today was hot, humid, and sticky. It could rain. We went south-east to try the water in a station well two miles away. It is beautiful soft fresh water but tasted dead. We shone a mirror down the shaft and no wonder it stinks, it had a decomposed snake of about seven feet in length, floating on the water.

Wednesday 14 - Quite humid last night with one or two spots of rain. Just a damp tease nothing more. I usually feel sleepy when the weather is humid but this morning I rose early and wrote another long letter. This time to Miss Mollie Lukis of the Battye Library in Perth. She wishes to know can I submit some of my field journals for the 1965-68 Desert Survey for the library to copy. I quite like the idea of my writings being recorded for posterity. No tickets on myself though. I just wish to share some of my experiences with others. At least two vehicles passed by here on the main road last night. One turned around at the windmill and went off along the north-east track. I wonder what they are up to. I fixed three tyres and tubes today, then packed up and came into Leonora. Killed a snake in the town house toilet when we arrived, after a one hundred and fifty-nine mile trip via Darlot.

Thursday 15 - I got up from bed to find another flat tyre this morning. This vehicle has really had the bomb. I took the tyre to the garage for repairs this time. They do a good job of tyre repairs. I posted off my 1965-68 diaries to Mollie Lukis at the Battye Library. She assures me the books will return without fail, once they copy the contents. I do believe this material is important to preserve, the whole job being a waste of time, if the information is not available for others to read and study. I made a great effort to write down everything of interest when on that job. The weather is still hot and humid. The few spots of rain that fell last night did little to benefit anything. I sent a telegram off to Jack Kerr advising him of the numerous vehicle defects, so he'll know all about them when he returns from leave.

Friday 16 - Sent another telegram, this time to AGPROTECT advising them of the Leonora Garage quote for vehicle repair is $35.00. They replied in the affirmative and to have the repairs done. The garage booked the vehicle in for Monday morning. We saw Billy Cock of Kaluwiri in town tonight. He is happy to know I am the Laverton dogger and working out from Bandya. He has a half share in Bandya. He says he has excellent reports on my work out that way.

We had the weekend off in town, then put the Landrover in for repairs on Monday. I took delivery of it again in the afternoon. On Tuesday the 20th I purchased fuel for the bush and loaded up for departure. It was hot all day with temperature around 114^0 Fahrenheit, exacerbated by a scorching wind. Too hot to travel, so postponed departure until after dark when it was still hot, but we proceeded east to Laverton to camp just out of town. No drinking in company this time thanks.

Wednesday 21 - Handed in twelve scalps to the Laverton Vermin Board this morning. They gave me a receipt as they had no money, but will post a cheque later. The cheque has to bear the signatures of two Board members. We didn't delay in Laverton this time, not so soon after the last episode. We returned to our Ten Mile camp. Everything is in order, and no sign of visitors anywhere near the caravan during our six day absence in Leonora. A lot of traffic on the Bandya road though, and more today.

On the way out from Laverton we came via the old Duketon townsite of earlier this century. Dooley's brother Patjata was born somewhere near Duketon. It is another scorcher today. The ABC News says Cyclone Ada is responsible for the death of seven people so far. No sign of rain here yet, but a lot reported in the Kimberley. Also a big storm with 100 mph winds hit Kununurra township yesterday causing much damage. Today around 3 pm when it cooled off a bit, we took a run north to Wilson's Bore. Got one dog scalp from the first trap, a male. Reset the trap again. On the way out we met two prospectors, one of whom we knew, it was Percy Rumble. We reached camp with speedo on one hundred and fifty-four miles for the day.

Saturday 24 - I was going to record the vehicle mileage but what is the use, the speedo breaks down on a regular basis. Three times to date as I recall. Clouds came over last night with more of those rare rain spots that are no good for anything. We went north-east to the old north boundary of Urarey, and followed the fenceline west. The track came to a dead end at half a mile, so I gave that one away, to go west next along another fenceline further south.

This one proved a better proposition. We came to some small dry gnamma holes in hill country at about three miles, then another dead end corner where the fence turns south. This north-south fence brought us out on the northern boundary of Bandya. We then followed the Bandya fence west back to Wilson's Bore, where I inspected traps, then continued south through the paddock. We were looking for a childhood memory of Dooley's and found it hidden in a thicket just east of the track. It is shallow old shaft where she and the old people camped years ago, when she was a young girl. The well is actually in a watercourse that runs through thick mulga scrub. It has no water now. Numerous old campsites around the well testify to the former presence of natives out this way.

We pulled up north of Mulga Queen at a dryblower patch for dinner, then moved on west afterwards to Hootanui where we got a shock to see prospectors rigging tents. This unwelcome influx of strangers into our country brought on a tinge of resentment. Doggers who control remote areas tend to react that way against any intrusion of outsiders into their run. Well, at any rate I do. However personal feelings aside, I do admit the campsite we saw today was a historical portrait. A colourful background of red ridges with a contrast of green gum trees along the foreground creek framing a pleasant scene of tents and activity, reminiscent of earlier times. Busy men were securing tents against the weather, while others were cooking over smoky campfires outside in the rain, their bodies wet by a steady drizzle falling at the time. The olden days must have presented a similar picture, except for 4WD vehicles being the current mode of transport, rather than the horses and camels of last century. We did not go to visit the newcomers. Hospitality is not the order of the day in the 1970s as it may have been a hundred years ago.

We bypassed those tents all a glistening with moisture under a dull blanket of grey sky and continued west along north side of the gum creek in search of a rockhole. Our route enhanced by the presence of numerous old native campsites, set back from the creek all the way along. Dooley has childhood memories of a place around here known to her people as Nganpa, and in English as Waterfall. This year is her first return visit to this area in the twenty-five years or more since she was a girl. She only has faded recollections of its location. All she knows at present is that the rockhole rests under a waterfall ledge, or rock bar across one of the numerous feeder channels running into the main creek. The main creek by the way bears the name Erlistoun, and that is confusing because it is nowhere near the sheep station of that name. This Erlistoun Creek runs through Bandya station country all the way. L A Wells named the creek in 1892 whilst on the Elder Exploring Expedition. We failed to locate Nganpa in the time available. It was by now late in the day and rain on the windscreen, although not heavy was obscuring vision, so we came back to camp and got a surprise to find no rain there. I wish we could get a good general rain. Our search for the waterfall rockhole Nganpa will continue later. No sign of dogs today at all. Ninety-four miles.

Sunday 25 - We awoke to find hot clear blue skies this morning and not even a scent of rain on the air. The drenched Hootanui atmosphere of yesterday has dispersed. Today we went along the Bandya road to Mulga Queen turnoff and from the grid there, followed a track west along a fenceline. This track took us six miles into a confined blind gully, wherein two springs named Wurnpu and Warnpu, are situate inside a natural pound on west side of the Neckersgat Range. High precipitous cliffs enclose the gully on three sides and mark the head of a small gum creek running down from the gully. Warnpu at head of the gully, is a secret place where only initiated tribal men can go. The other one called Wurnpu says Dooley, is open to all, and constitutes the domestic water supply for natives who camp in the vicinity. Wurnpu in line with its open status, is likewise in the open, about midway down the gully in a limestone bed, shaded by a clump of eucalypts. I walked alone to see the hidden spring and noted its dank obscure situation. No tribal woman would ever dare to go there. A tribal woman would faint from fear the moment she saw it I am sure. The reservoir that contains Warnpu water, appears to be always full, and the cliff wall behind it has a patina of jet black. There is not a ripple on the water's surface to indicate any constant flow, however there must be permanent seepage from the rocks to replenish the supply.

Some oldtimer wrote on the cliff wall behind the top spring. The inscription is hard to read but looks like POME 1891. There are also a number of more recent names hammered into the cliff. One being scrawled across the cliff face by Cyril Barnes, a Leonora resident of part Aboriginal blood. The lower or outside spring is larger than its secret counterpart. Supposed to be secret I should say, but the appended names of uninitiated Aborigines belie its former status. These two springs are stagnant and putrid now, both from the excrement of domestic stock, and the decayed flesh of dead animals. This is a sad but true circumstance that always seems to follow the departure of Aboriginal inhabitants from any bush area. Within a short time of any native water being abandoned by the original inhabitants, it seems to go downhill fast, and never return to its former pristine state. Such is the case here. Dooley recalls how as a young girl, she saw these spring waters flowing all the time. Even when polluted by cattle, she says the constant flow of water kept the springs clean. Now the waters are still, and require a big rain to wash out the accumulated filth before they can ever run again.

Dooley has no trouble with her sense of location in this area. Leaving the springs behind, we turned south to follow the range four or five miles to another old campsite where she stayed as a girl. This being a soakage known as Tjilkatjara. At first sight I thought the soak to be just another rockhole full of sand, like the one I dug out back at Tjampan away to the north-east a while back. My supposition upon arrival at Tjilkatjara was a bit premature though, because Dooley put my thoughts into words and told me it is a rockhole. She says it was always open in her young days. Sad to say it is now full of sand, flood debris, and no doubt the bones of animals. Soakage is present in the sand at shallow depth but the water is putrid.

We continued south along the range. At ten miles we came to a large open rockhole in a gum creek, with a granite bar across the top end. This water is Puntin. It is in Vicker's Creek. From Puntin we made a ten mile trip in search of yet another of Dooley's long-unseen sites, a place known to her as Mulga Well in the Erlistoun Creek. We found it after a bit of trouble, concealed by an almost impenetrable thicket of gum saplings. I found it difficult to get the Landrover in close, so we had to get out and search around on foot.

Dooley was looking for a windmill and the puzzle was that she could see no sign of a mill tower where she supposed one to be. We found the well shaft, but the tower was no longer there, only the old well. This find was close to the road that runs between Bandya and Banjawarn stations, so we soon came out into the open again. The next stop was at the original site of the one-time Mulga Station homestead.

Dooley says Mulga was once a thriving cattle station. Foundations of the homestead are still there on the west side, back a bit from the road. The remaining posts of a big bush timber cattle yard bear witness to the former presence here of an oldtime cattle run.

We spent a morning full of interest and got back to Hootanui in time for dinner. More clouds rising at midday. Had a feed beside the junction, then followed a smaller creek upstream from the main channel. This small creek rises in the extreme north-east corner of the Neckersgat Range and runs north to meet Erlistoun Creek at the junction of our dinner camp.

This little water channel is Minga Creek. I walked most of its length on foot to locate numerous dry soak holes in the sandy bed and a small rockhole near the creek's head, where the first gum trees begin. From that point upstream the creek is of the typical dry breakaway type, with mallee gums and stark white chalky flats to either side of a parched channel. No promise of water upstream. From where the first gums start, there are numerous old native campsites along both sides of the creek, all the way downstream to Hootanui.

I shot a fat bungarra for our supper, then we returned to our camp at the Ten Mile. During our absence today someone has been drinking plonk beside the windmill. I can't understand how they can drink the stuff this hot weather, especially in the morning as this lot did. We know what time they stayed here, because they pulled up under the morning shade side of a tree. We have no idea who it was. I would like to know though, because I am wary of drunks tracking me up. I had enough of that from the drunken fencer over at Kaluwiri, when we were contract dogging there. We saw a lot of things today, but only did seventy-three miles.

Monday 26 - I find this morning, that the Landrover speedo cable is broke again. We returned over some of yesterday's tracks via Warnpu and Puntin, south along a Banjawarn station fence to Barney's Well on Erlistoun country. Then north-east to the Erlistoun-Bandya boundary. I followed it west at first, then north for about six miles through a jumble of rugged ridges and hills, that I think must be an eastern extension of the Neckersgat Range. The fenceline we followed, came out onto a tableland above the breakaways, in a dead north-south line. I had to engage low range gear to negotiate the gradient leading up to the tableland. It was stiff climb.

With that bit of extra knowledge in hand, we returned to the main north-east track leading to Bandya and had dinner at Risden Well, also a bath under the overflow pipe. Risden has good shade trees near the mill, and no ants to bother us for a change. We carried on past Bandya, then north-west back to our Ten Mile camp. No sign of dogs anywhere today. Before the day was out we took a tour around the Bandya windmill run to the west of camp, so as to get familiar with that side of the country. We got a flat tyre, and after repairing the puncture out bush, we came back to camp, arriving about sundown. A long interesting day of one hundred miles around the Neckersgat Range.

Tuesday 27 - First thing this morning early, before the flies got too sticky, I wrote up the January journals until yesterday, getting them ready for submission to head office at the end of month. Later we went out north-east to inspect a trap near what is known as the old Public Battery. The carcase of one female dog in trap, I reset it and came back to camp. A heavy overcast all day with promise of rain. A promise supported somewhat by the pestering bush flies.

Too hot to travel until late afternoon. When it cooled down we went across to a feature known as Mason Hill, native name Ingitjingi, and set two additional traps in the vicinity of this morning's scratch place. Also set one at the windmill on the old Battery site. I'll have to ascertain the name of this mill from Peter Hill. Dooley herself, and her old relatives who once lived around here, have their own brand of English for places like Public Battery. They enunciate the name as Papuli Pitri. This quaint rendition of words applies to many places in the country.

Another instance of name variation between natives and whites is an old gold mine a bit east of Mulga Queen called Famous Blue. Dooley and her lot call it Paimat Plu. Also McKenzie Well south of Bandya, they pronounce this as Mikintji Well, and so the list goes on. I love it. I hesitate to insist on the usual way to say English words. Last time I did so, Dooley gave me a puzzled look and appeared let down by the new information, after a lifetime of saying the names in her own way and that of her people. I seldom correct her anymore. I merely tell her the English way so she knows, that is all, because I feel it is not right to shatter a person's perspective of things known to them as something else for a lifetime. I go along with the native rendition of words these days and by doing so, have been the victim of some embarrassment myself, tinged with a spot of amusement I might add. One day when on Erlistoun Station I was talking to old Bill Barrett the manager about a well on the Nambi road. I said: "You know that well Bill, that Kimberless." I reeled back on my high heel boots when old Bill barked back at me in his usual gruff manner. "WHAT" Said Barrett. I repeated: "Kimberless, you know, that well in the limestone." Bill thought for a moment then said: "Oh, I know which one you mean now, that's Gambier Lass." That was my turn to look perplexed. I only knew the name from Dooley's telling of it and in my ignorance of the proper name, used Dooley's version all the time. Such is some of the fun we get from life. I could not get a kangaroo today so we have no meat and only hot dry damper for supper. It continues to look like rain this evening. The air is humid and still, a typical lull before the storm sort of thing. Lots of insects around too.

Wednesday 28 - I set two more traps near New Bella Well, then inspected traps north along fence. No dogs in the traps, only one fresh track on the road. Reset a sprung trap, then west to Wilson's Bore but found no sign of dogs there. Those duties attended to, we set off to have another look for Dooley's waterfall rockhole in the Hootanui area. This time we located it without any trouble. It is at the head of the same creek we followed for a short distance the other day in the rain, but turned back because of poor visibility through the wet windscreen. Nganpa or Waterfall Rockhole, is a few miles north-west of Hootanui. It is a picturesque place. The creek channel above the ledge, or waterfall cliff, cuts across the creek from bank to bank. Gum trees begin below the fall, and stand all the way from there downstream, to where this creek joins the Erlistoun below Hootanui.

Above the waterfall cliff the creek changes character completely. Above is a wide pavement of solid red rock that stretches upstream for about a hundred paces or more. From this rock massif, the creek upstream of there is an insignificant looking mulga lined channel. Out on the stony flats to either side, are scattered low outcrops of rounded granite boulders. Dooley told me how she and her people used to come out here in good seasons. They had to get away from tormenting myriads of mosquitoes that infested the usual campsites lower down along the main creek, the Erlistoun.

From Nganpa waterfall site, we continued west along faint wheel tracks to locate another soakage Dooley calls Tjutuwarra, some six or seven miles west of Nganpa waterfall. A cairn marked GM1 on a granite knob, that must be Mount Arthur, on north side. We kept following the faint track. It led us at about four miles north-west, to Dooley's Wingkurra. This is yet another rockhole type soakage, marked on the map as Wingora. Dooley is fearful of this place, she says it is an abode of Yarr Yarr females, that she can only describe as red devils. They live beneath the dark granite ridges that encircle Wingkurra, in underground caverns. Dooley says they are always up to mischief. They have no men of their own, so yearn for the men who pass through this area. One of their antics is to change into the physical resemblance of some man's wife, and try to seduce him. For some reason however they seldom succeed, and in anger at their failure, tease the real human women in all manner of awful ways. Dooley told me of one Yarr Yarr victim she has first-hand knowledge of. They tipped Dooley's mother out of a horse-drawn cart. I felt qualms about Wingkurra myself. The granite formations are identical to many similar scenic attractions, yet there is a clammy atmosphere of foreboding about the place. I even felt the cold chill of apprehension. Wingkurra the soak, is near a granite outcrop in a little creek gutter, water was visible in the sand, but we didn't stop to dig as we had no need.

From Wingkurra we carried on west by north to Turnback Well on Banjawarn country. No sign of dogs all the way today. The country around the granite hills we came through, is similar in many respects to that south-east of Cosmo Newberry, and that further east around Jutson Soak, off the Warburton road.

I heard on a radio news bulletin today that the share price of a small mining company named TASMAN X jumped from $3.00 to $90.00 on the Stock Exchange. The rise due to reports of nickel sulphides in a water drill hole at Mount Venn, one hundred miles east of Laverton. Mount Venn is south of Rutter's grave. Another News item also said, that a mining company has purchased the Palace Hotel in Laverton for reasons unknown. A spokesman for the company only forecast a great future for nickel prospects in the Laverton area. Western Mining also it is said, has made a rich strike at Mount Clifford north of Leonora. I missed the name of the mineral but it would be gold I suppose.

From Turnback, we carried on west to Emu Bore, then followed the boundary south until we came to an old track leading east to Biddy's Patch, native name Milkupurru. Milkupurru was a big native campsite at one time. The Ngalia people stopped off here for a while after they abandoned Mulga Queen.

Those who didn't want to go into Leonora stayed at Biddy's Patch, so it became a de facto native reserve in practice, but was never gazetted as an official one. No native residents there now, they all shifted to a new place further south somewhere, Flower Well I think. The old people call it Blouse Well, but the maps say Flower so that's what I'll record. Milkupurru is a beautiful campsite. The well is shallow and the water within easy reach, with the aid of billycan and a length of fencing wire, dog chain, or light rope. It is has a hand pump fitted, but that is not working now, the leather buckets being worn out ages ago. I lowered a billycan and sampled the water, it is lovely and fresh. The little well rests in a sort of hollow, at the foot of a low sand hummock, I hesitate to call it a sandhill as it is too small.

Behind and to the north, the hollow rises to a stretch of wide spinifex sandplain, with a clear and open aspect. It is the kind of place I could set up camp and live for the rest of my life. This makes me wonder why former native inhabitants ever left it.

From Milkupurru or Biddy's Patch, we returned to the Ten Mile camp via Hootanui, then set off again immediately to cut a traverse south. This led through dense mulga scrub, to hit a fence running east to Bandya from Thomson Well. After a lot of rip and tear through the thickets, we reached the fence okay, but away off course, so missed the well by at least a couple of miles. The scrub pushed me too far east. I hate driving through scrub country. Continued east along the fence to Stella Mill, then cut through the paddock again, this time north, to reach the track running past our Ten Mile camp. This last course was much more open and I intend to use it, in order to bypass Bandya homestead in future. We had a long busy day, and clocked up about ninety miles, but don't know the exact figure for sure, because the speedo is broke.

Thursday 29 - We enjoyed a good soaking rain nearly all night, I reckon there might have been fifty points or thereabouts. Cyclone Gladys is somewhere off the north-west coast and reported to be building up. I suppose this country will miss out on any rain off the cyclone. We are a lot further south than Wiluna, which region always seems to be the limit of southern penetration by cyclonic rain offshoots. I did however hear of one big cyclone that went south, right through to the Bight some years ago, before I ever came over to WA.

We started early, by the shortest way for Leonora, to reach Nambi after only two hours running, despite the number of gates along the way. It is a god road apart from the gates. We kept going until noon, then pulled up for dinner. On again after dinner to reach Leonora by 2 pm. A one hundred and fifteen mile trip via Nambi, the shortest route.

I was wild when we got home, to find signs of kids all through the house during our absence out bush. They shifted the garden seat. Scattered our heap of asbestos samples from Harris Hills east of Laverton and left a mess on the front verandah. The kids made good use of our bathroom too, leaving it in a most deplorable state. They also left evidence such as Story Lids or Milpinti Wires all over the place. The story lids gave a good indication that native kids were the culprits. If they sat down on the ground telling stories with milpinti wires to draw illustrations, then they certainly felt relaxed at the time, and not expectant of us returning out of the blue. Little mongrels. I gave Wulapa the four dollars I owe her husband Ken Miller, when she came along to tell us more about the kids who were here. Once we settled in to the camp again and cleaned up the mess, I completed the January journals, time sheets, and month's report, but too early to post them yet. Sent off $90.00 to Custom Credit, making three payments to date, with the $45.00 cheque I paid before, off the $500.00 I owe them. No more time payment jobs for me, they are a pain in the neck. No rain in Leonora.

Friday 30 - Put the government Landrover in for service and repair. Bought two drums of petrol. Returned two empties. Got everything ready for departure next month. Then, with all duties attended to, Dooley and I proceeded to have a wet weekend that terminated on Monday 2/2/70 feeling most sorry for ourselves.

Figure 12 APB Landrover

Chapter Eleven - CYCLONE INGRID

FEBRUARY 1970

Tuesday 3 - We left Leonora sick, tired, and hungry. Not hungry for ordinary food that is, but starving for fresh roo meat. I shot a kangaroo about dinner time so that solved the meat problem. We don't favour butcher's meat because there is far too much fat on it. We live on game most of the time when out bush, but of course do have to fall back on tinned stuff when game is in short supply. We ran into a most refreshing fall of rain after shooting the kangaroo. The storm lasted all the way along Barney's Flat while travelling north through Erlistoun country. A hub-depth torrent of water ran along the road and turned it into a creek. This area of rainfall referred to along Barney's Flat, is a section of flood country notorious for its treacherous boggy patches. There is no way to dodge anything through there because dense mulga scrub comes right up to the road verge on either side. Bog was not a problem today however as rain had not long started to fall. It takes some time for water to soak in and put the road out. The pleasure of a good downpour did not last long and all sign of rain vanished at Monday Gap where the boundary fence marked an abrupt change from wet to dry. Monday Gap, near southern end of the Neckersgat Range, is of course an elevated area. The rain was all down in the lower flood country. Monday Gap is another English corruption of native language. The name should be Manti, a native word that means male. In this case the gap called Manti, denotes the passage of a Dreamtime boomer kangaroo being chased by Tjiinkuna, the same dragon fly who stalked three carpet snakes much further west in the Barr-Smith Range. We reached our Ten Mile camp late in the afternoon with a flat tyre, after a one hundred and twenty mile trip from Leonora.

Wednesday 4 - Last night was humid in the early part, then some light rain fell and cooled the air down a bit, but the ground is not even damp this morning. I completed the January time sheets and decided today, to begin the full month's journals and other reports early. In future I'll try and keep them up to date in line with my written field notes. Otherwise it means a full day at the end of each month researching the daily written record. The sky and clouds threatened rain all day but none fell. All the clouds went away soon after sundown.

Thursday 5 - I inspected traps between Wilson's and the old Public Battery. All the dogs appear to have cleared out. I pulled up three sprung traps as it is not worth setting them again. After dinner we set off via Duketon, south through Bandya and Erlistoun country, along the Laverton road. This great influx of nickel prospectors lately, is not doing the country any good at all. They cut the road up something awful. We notice that bulldozer blades have cut swaths along some of the peg lines and this ruins the country too. They must have some good mineral prospects to justify all this activity. No sign of dogs. Not many kangaroos. We camped on north bank of the last gum creek on the Laverton road before reaching Stone Soak. Eighty miles travel and a mild day, but still humid and uncomfortable with millions of bush flies.

Friday 6 - Laverton saw us arrive early. I posted the January reports away, then purchased fuel and oil, before driving out east a few miles in search of a kangaroo. I shot one and returned with it to the government dam to cook in the ashes and eat it.

I should say ate some of it, as we took a good parcel along with us for the next couple of meals. The steering is wobbly and a front spring shackle-bolt broken. The brass bushing also gone. We decided to return to Leonora and get the vehicle faults fixed. A telegram in the post box with a request to ring Jack Kerr on Thursday 5 and that of course was yesterday when I wasn't in town, so couldn't ring.

Saturday 7 - Sent a telegram to Kerr over the RFDS stating I would ring him Monday morning next at 9 am and on the hour thereafter until I get him. Later in the day I saw Karl Srb the Czech dogger. He told me that Jack will be here in Leonora before 9 am Monday anyway, so everything should now be okay. We visited Karl at his home. He showed us colour slides of his recent holiday trip in the South West and along the coast to Esperance. Some of his shots are quite good. Dooley and I went to the "Drive In" this evening to see the pictures. The programme was a good one. We not drinking this trip. Alcohol is for fools and idiots.

Sunday 8 - There was a big fight amongst the wangkayi mob living at Gwalia, and another fight on the Leonora Native Reserve. This didn't effect us in any way though. Today I did a lot of work around the house and garden. A snake startled me as Dooley was cutting my hair. It made her jump too. The snake got away under the house so looks like we sleep on the bed tonight.

Monday 9 - Jack Kerr arrived later than expected around 11-30 am. I handed over the transceiver unit for him to take back to Kalgoorlie for repair. The rest of the day I spent at Sullivan's Garage waiting for a quote on the cost of repairs to the WAG Landrover. Got the quote, and the repairs done, then wrote out an LPO or Local Purchase Order in payment thereof and took the vehicle home.

Jack gave me final instructions before he left, to go and attend a Field Day near Sandstone. While I was at the garage waiting for the Landrover to get fixed, Karl and Jack were in the pub on the grog all day. Good luck to them both. I don't want any. Nice cool weather for a change.

Tuesday 10 - Cyclone Ingrid is active off Broome. We got away from Leonora by mid morning and shot a bungarra when about halfway to Laverton, so pulled up in the lake country to cook it for dinner. We carried on after dinner to Laverton, where I topped up with petrol, then took twelve dog scalps to the Vermin Board for a return of $24.00 bonus. We spent one dollar on a bag of oranges and apples, then left town for the north. I shot another bungarra and a kangaroo before reaching Duketon. We drove on to have a look at traps past Papuli Pitri and got a wether sheep out of one trap, so pulled it up. There are far too many sheep about this area for traps. No dogs in that area now anyway. We got home to the Ten Mile and caravan about sundown, to find everything okay. One hundred and fifty-five miles.

Wednesday 11 - We set off early this morning on a long trap run. We did a complete round via Karu, Nyiruru, and Warren's Well on the east side, then south-west via the Deleta track. This took us past Tjilpitjara, Yantakanngang, Paiyari, Mulga Queen, and back to the Ten Mile camp. There was one dog in trap on west side of the lake country, one in trap north of Warren's Well, and one in the last trap just north of Yantakanngang.

We saw little sign of rainfall anywhere around the run until we reached Tjilpitjara, the rockhole soak. This had a little water above the sand. Around to this point there was no sign of dog activity at all. From Tjilpitjara, fresh tracks of dogs were evident all the way south, to within two miles of Yantakanngang, where all sign of dogs ceased. I set one extra trap near Tjilpitjara, but removed a number of traps from other areas in the northern section. The stretch between Warren's and Deleta in particular, has no dog sign present. I have twenty dog traps set at the current count.

We came right back to the Ten Mile to camp, as not much point in stopping out in the bush when things are slack and the weather hot. It was a long hard scorcher of a day with some cloud cover, but no real sign of rain. The vehicle fan belt broke when only one mile from camp. I continued on without it and arrived home after a two hundred mile circuit.

Thursday 12 - We enjoyed a reasonable sort of night for sleeping although it was still quite warm. I awoke this morning to the wondrous sight of a flat tyre. Still, as the old saying goes, it was only flat on the bottom, the top and sides looked quite normal. Cyclone Ingrid is still off Broome somewhere and widespread rains are falling in the Kimberley. No sign of rain here yet. A light aircraft was flying around over our camp this morning. An ABC News report says that Japan launched her first satellite into orbit.

I had to shift our caravan out from under the trees into an open clearing. There were far too many ants dropping down from the trees onto the roof and getting at our tucker in the van. I also removed the annexe as it is too hot. Jack Kerr chatted me about excessive petrol consumption last time I spoke to him on the radio, so I wrote him a letter today in explanation. The aeroplane flew over us all day, doing a grid pattern with some newfangled scientific instrument trailing from a cable behind. Gawd knows what they'll get up to next. Everything is getting far too technical for me. Had a hot day on camp and that is something I do understand.

Friday 13 - Last night was muggy, and today is too hot to go anywhere, with this worn out Landrover. Great banks of storm clouds come up late every afternoon, but rain never seems to eventuate. Cyclone Ingrid is still stationary out from Broome. That is about all I have to record today. I may get going somewhere tomorrow.

Saturday 14 - Awoke early and up before daylight. Had breakfast by 6 am and away, to follow the Bandya west boundary south. We carried on south through Erlistoun country past Mount Porter windmill and another mill south-east of there called Simeon. From Simeon Well, the track carries on south-east to Lizard Soak, native name Nyami. Saw no fresh sign of dogs anywhere to this point, but I did find an old dog trap near the soak.

The Nyami trap was sprung, and by the look of it was in the ground unattended for years. I left it undisturbed as it was an oldtime Delamy brand and much too big in size for me. I shot a bungarra and turned back with it to Mount Porter to cook before the day get too hot for comfort. It was a fat one, the bungarra that is. We cooked a kangaroo tail at the same time.

Like most so-called soaks in this country, Nyami or Lizard Soak is really a rockhole full of sand, it rests at the base of a large granite outcrop. Soakage water is visible near the surface. We went back north after the feed, to the southern Bandya boundary and followed the fence east past Torondo Waterhole, native name Kurunta. This Kurunta pool is in a small gum creek called the Borodale. The waterhole is a good catchment but is at present dry. The creek runs from north-west through the boundary fence and eventually floods out near Namendarra claypan, six or seven miles north of Erlistoun homestead. Namendarra is the English version of native name Nyamantjarra. Kurunta has to do with a kangaroo whose eye burst, in the Dreamtime.

From Torondo or Kurunta, we continued east to hit the Laverton road, and travel north along it to Swanson's government well for dinner. Later we followed an old cutline heading south-east from the Duketon track. The line starts just south of the first fence north of Swanson's, and leads past two old wells, not equipped with windmills and of unknown names. The same cutline brought us to Moolart Well, native name Ngulart, from where the line turns north to German Well, the site of numerous old native campsites. Dooley remembers German Well and the surrounding area as a great hunting ground, when her Ngalia people lived in the bush out here twenty odd years ago. These old cutlines on this eastern side of Bandya, Dooley says, are the result of hard yakka and axe work by her people. The cutlines first being cleared of scrub, the stumps then fired and burned out to ground level, or if too big, grubbed out and shifted off the line by hand. The original owner of Bandya had big plans for fencing and access lanes, all of them through the densest scrub so characteristic of Bandya country.

The most notable thing about German Well is the abundant evidence of old Aboriginal campsites, they are everywhere. The frames of brush shelters, native name puri and flattened rows of long-dead bushes still in place on the ground, show the former position of windbreaks and old ash heaps, where campfires once blazed. Broken artefacts and wood shavings still lie on the ground, exactly where last dropped or thrown. Even remnant scraps of fabric from dress material and other clothing, are still there, either rotting on the ground, or hanging in faded tetters from the frames of old shelters. This was a big camp. It was an obvious source of nostalgic memories for Dooley.

German Well was also in the news lately as being a rich new nickel find. We expected to see the place a hive of activity with a big camp of prospectors. There is however no sign of nickel men, other than a few coloured ribbons of flagging hung at random it seems, from bushes here and there. There is not even a diamond drill or bore hole here. We saw not a sign of dogs all day. Thunder storms hovered all around the horizon for hours, but they were all small and no rain for us. We got back to the caravan at 4 pm. after a one hundred and sixty miles round trip.

Sunday 15 - I stayed on camp today. It was hot and muggy. The frustrating afternoon storm clouds, today brought a few spits of rain. Cyclone Ingrid is now off Onslow and North West Cape. I wish it was right here. I read extracts from Carnegie's book Spinifex & Sand and deduce that he passed through the Neckersgat Range in 1896. He also crossed somewhere along the De La Poer Range. I can't be positive because the information is too sketchy to plot his exact route. I would like to have a copy of his original diaries and field notes, if they still exist.

If the track to Warburton Range be included, then this G6 Wild Dog Control Area is just as interesting from a historical perspective as was my former exploration area north of Wiluna. The only major difference being the preponderance of access tracks here, in contrast to the total lack of them up there. However even down here there is a great deal of untraversed country off the beaten track. The rewards may not be as great, but the interest of new things to discover remains the same. Not much chance of finding permanent springs in the G6 area, but plenty of dry rockholes, dry soaks and initials of explorers engraved on rocks in various parts. Gee if only it would rain.

Monday 16 - What a pleasure it was to hear a sprinkle of rain all night, but not enough to wet the ground. The only benefit being some cool air and that beautiful scent of wet mulga. Ingrid is now off Carnarvon. Widespread rain for the State today is the radio forecast. We packed up and off to Leonora via Laverton. One hundred and sixty miles travel.

Tuesday 17 - Cyclone Ingrid came right through Leonora last night, but brought not a drop of rain. The town only got a terrific dust storm and cyclonic winds. We decided to abandon our house to the storm when we saw the outside detached bathroom shed lift up off the ground and fly through the air. We took the Landrover with swag and tucker box, three miles out of town to a sheltered thicket off Laverton road to camp. We sheltered in the back. The vehicle rocked and swayed like a boat on rough seas. I had to start the motor on and off all night at regular intervals, to face the bonnet into the wind so the storm wouldn't hit the vehicle side-on. The wind howled and howled. We had a sleepless night. By daylight the storm had blown itself out.

We went back to Leonora to find a scene of devastation with some houses blown flat. The Church of England was completely demolished. Awnings all along the main street were either blown away or hanging askew. Apart from the flying bathroom, our place was unscathed. Once before in this narrative I mentioned the loose roof of our old stone house. I wrote how the roof is prone to lift inches above the top walls with every gust of wind, to strain against the loose tie wires supposed to hold it in place. The loose roof was the reason we left town, yet upon return this morning, the whole structure was still in place. Not even out of alignment. Miracles never cease, I believe a prophet once said. Our only problem apart from airborne bathrooms, was a burst water pipe spraying water like a fountain into the air. The meter was okay so I was able to turn it off and solve the problem until fixed.

Yes indeed, it was quite a sight this morning, was Leonora town. As for us, we packed all my valuable possessions like books on exploration, manuscript copies, colour slides and photos, ready for transport out bush to the caravan. Not safe to leave them in town anymore. We stay away and leave the place unattended far too long for safety. We left Leonora at midday, refuelled at Laverton, then on to our caravan base camp. No damage here.

Wednesday 18 - It was a good cool night for sleeping, but a bad dose of flu kept me awake. I can't stop coughing. The cough was so bad on one occasion I thought I might choke. I'm not so bad this morning though. Stowed all our belongings from Leonora in the caravan cupboards. Then we returned to Leonora via Laverton. One hundred and fifty-five miles.

Thursday 19 - A letter in my post box this morning from Kalgoorlie APB office, wanting clarification on excessive expenses for service to WAG 4895, the government Landrover. They also consider I use too much petrol for mileages done. They suggest I cut down on daily running. Cutting mileage is something I just cannot do if they want the job done properly. This is the bloody government all over. Some departments like National Mapping, have a free go, with expenses being no object. Others like my APB lot, won't cooperate with their men in the bush. They have no idea what conditions are like and are as mean as anything. They keep a tight rein on both finance and equipment. Witness my allocated worn out bomb of a vehicle. It was due for the scrap heap months ago. Hundreds of dollars go to keep this government heap of trash called WAG 4895 on the road, but it was all money down the drain because the thing is not worth the repair bill. I've worked a total of five years with the APB to date. During that time, I spent hundreds of dollars of **my own money** for extras essential to the job, yet never as much as token appreciation from the APB for such personal expenditure.

This is the only type of work I can get in the desert country. It gives me a great deal of independence and free movement around the country, but I would prefer a return to the old system, whereby doggers had to buy their own vehicle. When a dogger has his own vehicle on the job there is no niggling about expenses.

What's the good of growling anyway? I sorted out the controversial LPOs and dockets covering vehicle repairs with Joe Sullivan at the garage. After that I wrote an explanatory note to Jack Kerr and posted the lot away. There I hope the matter will rest. I don't want to hear any more of it. Mollie Lukis of JS Battye Library wrote a letter thanking me for the loan of my old diaries. She now wishes to borrow negatives of photos for copying too, so she can put them in the archives with the copied diaries. Included with her letter was a complimentary copy of the Surveyor's House magazine. It contains an article by Russ Wenholz & David Chudleigh, about their trip along the entire length of the Canning Stockroute. I first met the pair with crew, when they caught up to me near No 15 Well in 1968. I wrote Wenholz a letter today too, congratulating him on his notable achievement. In it I also expressed regret that he gave me no recognition for the foot work I did, or the vehicle tracks I put in by myself prior to his advent on the scene. Tracks that he took advantage of I might add. Just for the hell of it I wrote a letter with similar sentiments to Mollie Lukis, to put my displeasure on record about this failure to give me credit due.

Friday 20 - I put several innovations on the WAG vehicle to make things more comfortable and accessible whilst out bush. In the evening we went visiting and showed some slides to Karl Srb's wife. Saturday I cleaned out the spare room to use for a town office. Cleared everything from the outside storeroom too. We now have the place cleaner and more comfortable to live in than before. Sunday saw us removing all APB stuff from the aforementioned office space, and putting it outside in the storeroom. There is a lean-to garage built on north side of the house, that has a rough and ready storeroom behind it. Most paraphernalia supplied by the APB seldom sees use. Apart from extra dog traps and strychnine that is. They give us galvanised drums that leak after one rough trip and tattered worn-out tarpaulins that are good for nothing but discard. That is the type of gear the APB calls official stores. In the evening we went out spotting for a kangaroo but had no luck.

Pinkari Tom Williams a tribal brother of Dooley's, gave us some interesting information today about a trip he did out bush with a whitefellow name of Hanlon. Pinkari says he took Hanlon to a rockhole called Wakulyakutjarra along the Deleta track. He told us where to find it. I took him to task for showing the whitefellow, but Pinkari said he'd please himself about such things, so I said no more about it. He also mentioned stopping the man from scalping a dog from one of my traps.

Monday 23 - We travelled from Leonora to Kalgoorlie to see Jack Kerr about the transceiver and make preparations for a proposed bush trip, in company with other doggers during the last week of February. This all came out of the blue. It was quite unexpected. I also wish to ask him when if ever, we might hope to get a new Landrover. We did the one hundred and fifty miles to Kalgoorlie in the old bomb without incident. Thanks to Providence more than good management I reckon, as I expected the vehicle to fall apart any minute along the bitumen. It is a pity I didn't let Cyclone Ingrid's wind gusts hit the thing side-on and demolish it in Leonora that night of the 17th.

Chapter Twelve - APB CONVOY - KARONIE TO LAVERTON

FEBRUARY (continued) & March

Tuesday 24 - Jack Kerr has no definite information about the promised new vehicle, or the proposed long desert trip in convoy with other doggers that is due to take place soon. The transceiver I put in for repairs has nothing wrong with it says the RFDS operator, but when I rigged it up to try it out it still won't work. When switched on it won't switch off again. The pilot light stays on and the set kicks up a lot of noise. Later I went to see the caravan people to pick up the promised tyre lever and a handle for the rear jacking stands. Also filled the fuel tanks with thirty-three gallons.

Wednesday 25 - Tried to get the transceiver fixed again today. I had it operating for a while but it still won't switch off when the mike is in its body bracket. There is a bad short in the set somewhere. Kerr found out about the proposed trip at last. We are to set off east for Karonie on the Trans Line, but none of the expected six other doggers are here yet. Not even Alex Absalom whose area it is. This is my life all over. Always waiting for someone or something.

It was late afternoon before the absent doggers began to drift in. First to arrive were Bill Brown and his wife. Next old Alex Absalom came along, followed soon afterward by Karl Srb. Dooley and I got quite a surprise to see at Karonie, the fellow who wanted us to drink plonk with him on Kaluwiri Station last year, Mervyn Stubbs the fencing contractor. He is now pulling sandalwood around Karonie. We doggers had a good yarn for several hours then split up to camp in different directions for the first night. Seventy-five miles from Kalgoorlie.

Thursday 26 - We found it delightful to be actually present to see the India Pacific train make its inaugural run through Karonie around midnight. Nothing spectacular about it, just the same ordinary old train with a change of name. It was a busy night, as several goods trains also sped past not long after the India Pacific went through, then the Tea & Sugar train came along last of all. This is the first time I ever saw the renowned Tea & Sugar but have over the years, heard a lot about it.

This portable transceiver is still playing up. It most definitely has something wrong with it. All the other doggers have good reception on their radios, this set has none. Bernie O'Driscoll the APB training officer arrived unaccompanied. Jack Kerr came along late in the afternoon about 5-15 pm. Jack was the last to arrive. The whole party now in attendance, we all proceeded in convoy east along north side of the railway line for five miles then camped.

Friday 27 - The weather was cloudy and cold this morning. It is quite a pleasant change from the heatwave conditions of late. Everyone was up around 5-30 am and ready for the road by 6-30, but remained on camp some time for more conversation. We eventually got going and reached a dry water catchment called Dingo Dam, said to be an abandoned cattle station. To my and Dooley's great amusement, one lone dog track near the dam, was the subject of close scrutiny by all present, in particular by Bernie O'Driscoll the expert dog trap trainer. At the risk of seeming cynical, I must say that this undue attention shown toward something in no way unusual, reminded me of eager school kids on a nature study excursion. I thought we were all professional doggers. We passed a granite outcrop, where a dry rockhole on north side has a constructed lid for protection. A nearby kurrajong tree marks the spot.

Our next stop was a large granite outcrop with some big rockholes but all were dry. The best of these rockholes being covered with rail sleepers. No more dog tracks cropped up after the first lot that became the subject of such intense observation earlier, so the supervisors decided to continue north.

This northern course took us after several miles travel to an open saltbush flat, where numerous dog tracks became evident in a small gutter that the locals call a creek. The bosses with obvious elation at the prospect, asked Bernie O'Driscoll to give a trap setting demonstration. Old Bill Brown also gave an exhibition of his expertise. A few miles further on we came to a big but quite dry catchment called Bronco Dam, marked by a derelict windmill tower. This place is twenty miles east of Karonie. We pulled off here for dinner.

On the move once more, it was south-east a few miles, then north to Anketell, a miniature dry dam about twenty feet in diameter, located across a small gutter creek in gumtree forest country. The name Anketell for some reason fascinates me. It seems out of place in this desert region. I felt sorry the dam was dry. To me a place with such a nice name should be full of water. Foolish thoughts I know, but that is how it affected me at the time. After a brief stop to look around Anketell we carried on north to Emu Rocks where is a rockhole, long dry, on a small flat area of granite pavement. We also saw a smaller rockhole half a mile south of Emu Rocks.

The gum forest continued north. As the miles rolled back, low ti-tree bushes and tussocks of spinifex began to appear beneath the taller eucalypts. An unexpected surprise also, to see a few scattered mulga trees in a hollow. I thought the mulga belt was still further north. Dooley and I always miss the sight of mulga trees and tend to dislike country that has none.

Before sundown, our convoy pulled up to camp in a wide open flat adorned with scattered gumtrees. This particular lot of trees being of much greater height than any we saw back along the track between here and Karonie. So far the only break in this monotonous desert forest is the occasional tiny clearing with a granite outcrop. The pleasure of these odd breaks though, is always subdued by the ubiquitous dry rockholes found to date.

This overnight campsite is a couple of miles south of a place with two official names. Some maps say it is Goddard Creek, others say Ponton Creek. I prefer the Ponton version, it sounds better. We are due to pass it tomorrow. The dogger whose area this is, says the Ponton is always full of water, which I am sure will be a pleasant change from everything seen so far, however he also says it is salt. and if that be the case then the water will only serve to alleviate our eyesight rather than our thirst.

So far I failed to put down the names of those present in this convoy of six APB vehicles. This is the first camp. The expedition members are:

Happy Alex Absalom	Dogger
Bill Brown and wife	Dogger
Karl Srb	Dogger
Dooley & Me	Dogger
Bernie O' Driscoll	Instructor
Jack Kerr	Regional Vermin Control Officer

Today was lovely and cool with good cloud cover and a south wind. Such a dull day though, was not the best for taking photos, but I used a lot of film just the same. Who knows, I may never see this country again, so must use the chance to make a photographic record of it. Not that I would ever come back here of my own choice. It is not my type of country. At this juncture we are fifty-four miles from last night's camp and about twenty miles due north of the Trans Line.

Saturday 28 - Jack Kerr peeled off today for Kalgoorlie. I reckon he's had enough of this country and found a good reason to excuse himself. He is to call in and see Mervyn Stubbs at Karonie and offer him a dogger's job at either Norseman or Southern Cross. Goddard or Ponton Creek made a quite attractive picture when we arrived on the southern bank. It is a deep, quite narrow salt channel, winding through open country, with lots of low samphire bush and other saline succulents all around. Nothing in the way of trees. The high salt encrusted banks are a prominent feature and brine pools lie either side of the crossing. The creek seems to come in from the north and west and continues south. Some of us walked over the crossing to test it, then back to the vehicles for a slip and slide trip across. It is solid enough but slippery.

The next stop was a rockhole soak called the Twelve Mile. The first drinkable water this trip. Only a little in wet sand, but the fluid is there in sufficient quantity to dig down and get a drink. This soak gets a lot of use by natives from Cundeelee Mission only twelve miles away. Its name on the map is Jumania and that in our opinion indicates the native word tjamu or tjamunya meaning grandparent. Some good open mulga country around the rockhole and numerous native campsites, both fresh and old. I always wanted to visit Cundeelee but no chance to do so this trip. There is a deep valley north of the rockhole with high ground beyond it on the horizon. This rockhole is eight miles from last night's camp.

Twenty-seven miles from last night's camp we reached a junction, where one road continues north three miles to a rockhole, while our road turns west. The place in question is Mavis Rockhole named by dogger John Carlisle after his daughter. We didn't go in to see it. The western track we followed, soon veers north again and at about five or six miles ahead, we came to a place known as Flat Rock, with a big rusted square tank nearby. The rockhole is full of dirt and at present is bone dry, like so many others back along the track.

Fifty-six miles from last night's camp, another turnoff on our righthand side, leads two and a half mile south to John's Rockhole. Further on at the sixty-six mile point, Mulga Rockholes. are on a wide open stony flat, with mulga trees around its perimeter.
One rockhole has a cover of corrugated iron and is full of water. The others are all dry. The carcases of several dead emus pollute one of the dry catchments. The convoy stayed here for a late afternoon spell and to camp the night. We got three buckets of water from the rockhole to wash some clothes, have a sponge down ourselves, and fill the tea billy. The granite around the rockholes here has a cover of dry green moss. From a distance as we approached, it looked like patches of green grass, but we soon saw the error of our vision. It does however mark a change in the country as we come ever closer to our own bailiwick. Sixty-six miles today and not much sign of dogs. The initial excitement exhibited by the supervisors is now at a low ebb. Our night camp is a pleasant place. All the doggers took time to cook a decent meal for the first time this trip.

Bill Brown does all the cooking for his wife. He was busy peeling vegetables for a stew. We had our supper finished early so waited for the Browns to finish their meal before paying them a visit. Mrs Brown it seems has personal knowledge of Linden, an oldtime mining town south of Laverton. Dooley and I saw remnants of the place when we worked on Yundamindra. We often wondered at the time, what life was like at Linden in earlier days. Now to our delight we have some of this information from a former resident. Mrs Brown was a boarding house cook when the town was alive and well. She told us she loved listening to Aboriginal women singing corroboree songs. To encourage them she would offer a billycan of tea with cakes or other food, if her native visitors would agree to sing. This old lady even remembered the words of some songs that Dooley could recognise. One song being descriptive of trains approaching along the Trans Line. It told of bright headlight beams getting closer in the night, along with the clicketty clack of wheels on iron rails, and the shrill warning of whistle blowing as the siding drew near. They didn't use the English clicketty clack words though, but rather the native expression kaka-rra-rra kaka-rra-rra. The trilled rr's indicating the roll of train wheels over points along the track. This particular lot of singers, although camping near Linden at the time, came from further south around Cundeelee, and of course were quite familiar with such aspects of trains in the night.

Mrs Bill Brown also confided in Dooley how when on trips out bush, she would hide items of tinned food under other loading in back of their vehicle. This idea she said, was a safeguard against possible breakdown. She always had a reserve supply of essentials on hand, but never lets her husband know. Bill being the cook in charge of rations when out bush, would of course try to solve the puzzle of missing stores. He knew what should be there because it was his tucker supply. This cooking business was a moral issue with Bill Brown. He maintains that he is the dogger not his wife. It is his job, so he should be the cook. Mrs Brown he says, can resume normal domestic duties when they live in town.

Mrs Brown also suffers from arthritis and to alleviate pain, wears a broad band of pure copper on one wrist. Her skin bears a large stain of green verdigris from constant contact with the bangle. I was curious about this and asked if it was an effective remedy. She was emphatic in her affirmation. Personally though I do not like the idea of verdigris stain on the skin, yet she swears it soaks into the body with beneficial results.

MARCH 1970

Sunday 1 - It was a warm humid night. Today just as anticipated, the country opened out a bit around dinnertime, in the vicinity of what old Happy says is Lake Sheppard. I couldn't see any lake though, only open country covered with dwarf ti-tree bushes about one foot in height. Maybe it is a swamp in good seasons. We came to Lake Minigwal a bit before midday.

There are two dry rockholes in a granite outcrop near the lake shore, just east of the track and thirty-five miles from Mulga Rockholes of last night. We went on another five mile for dinner near a stand of mulgas. It always amuses me the way these doggers eat standing up. They get a handful of food and stroll up and down while eating. I never knew bushmen to act like this lot does. Some of them carry chairs around to sit on too. Dooley and I always sit on the ground, cross legged native style. On the other hand, old Absalom makes himself quite comfortable when eating. Happy puts his Landrover's tailgate down to use as a table and with four gallon drum for a chair, sits in style like a gentleman.

Reached the eastern end of Lake Minigwal soon after dinner. Our route then wound along through wide open flats covered with low saltbushes growing thick and luxuriant. This is now Karl Srb's dogging area. Bernie O'Driscoll gave some more demonstrations with Karl's traps as we came to the setting sites. Thunder heads began to rise in the north so we kept travelling until late. It was 7 pm before we cleared the lake area. This type of lake country is all prone to flooding and bogs after rain, and not a nice place to get floodbound at all. A hot humid seventy mile day.

Monday 2 - Framed in our windscreens at fourteen miles along the road this morning, Lake Lightfoot was a pleasant sight, with one dry rockhole in granite on west side. Eloa Rocks, about five miles further north has a dry rockhole, after which we entered spinifex sandplain. We felt more at ease now, being in country more familiar to Dooley and me. The sandplains along here support an open forest of white boled desert gums, known to us by the native name para. This class of country continued to the dinner camp at noon. At this point we met a track coming from a place known as Karara, to the south-east, and Cogla Well to the north-west. This is Karl Srb's dogging area. Karl expressed a desire to inspect some traps while passing through his jurisdiction, so we all joined him in a run of fifteen miles to Camel Rockhole, then Karara Rockhole at twenty miles.

Our convoy returned then from Karara to the dinner camp to continue north-west. This route led us along a graded sandalwood track that passes over extensive burnt spinifex country with undulating sand rises. Because of the widespread burn, this made an interesting picture. The ripples of drifting sand along the road being a complete contrast, to the black limbs and trunks of burnt gumtrees just starting to sprout fresh green shoots again. We pulled up to camp after a ninety-five mile day.

Tuesday 3 - Light rain fell all night but not enough to wet the ground, just intermittent spots. Our convoy of doggers got a late start this morning. Although Dooley and I were ready to travel by sunrise as we always are, the others delayed our departure until 9 am. That is the worst aspect of travelling with superior officers, they always hold things up. We reached Cogla Mill and Outcamp.

This now defunct water point has been dry and derelict for years. The windmill has not seen repairs since I was managing Burtville Station for Bob Cable in 1969. The only reason I didn't fix it then was because I couldn't get the owner to supply necessary parts and equipment. The property has since changed hands and still nothing done by the new owners.

Mister Happy Absalom is still playing guide to the party as he has all the way from Karonie. Others know the country too, but let Happy have his way just to humour him. I know we had to put him right several times, when Jack Kerr sent him out to show us around the G6 area last October. Bernie O'Driscoll is the senior officer on this trip and I can't make out why he didn't pull the old know-all back in line after we passed Happy's official boundary. We have been in Karl Srb's area for the past two days now, yet Happy is still in the lead-vehicle usurping Karl's rightful position. Karl is too much the gentleman to assert himself.

"Blah blah blah, yap yap yap." brags Happy Absalom: "I made all these tracks. I opened up the country. I caught all the dogs." So it goes on the whole day long, yet we can all see that the tracks he says he made, existed before the old windbag was born. Sandalwood pullers' horse and camel waggon ruts, are still evident under the present day motor vehicle tracks. Old campsites and iron tyred dray and waggon tracks are everywhere around here, they criss cross the entire country. I hope he doesn't get sent out with me anymore. I can't stand bullshit. I'll follow anyone if they are capable and know what they're about, but I can't stand a skite. Especially an old one.

Mrs Brown met her dreaded nemesis today. Husband Bill's Landrover broke down only a few miles from Burtville. Karl Srb took him in tow. I can imagine the poor old lady's ears attuned to every rattle from her hidden cache of tinned foods in the back as they bumped and jerked along behind the vehicle towing them to Laverton. No doubt old Happy was already there, breasting the bar at the only pub. I say this because the minute we hit the main graded road to town, Happy abandoned his role as self appointed leader and shot off in a cloud of dust without telling anyone, Laverton bound.

Dooley and I let the others go ahead. We pulled up at the Burtville government well for dinner and a clean up. By the time we got to Laverton all the doggers were at the pub except Bernie O'Driscoll. He, like us, has given up drinking for the time being. None of us can vouch for the future, but alcohol is not on our respective agendas for the time being. The expedition is now over. The convoy is due to disperse. Bernie O'Driscoll took more than three hours to get through to Kalgoorlie office on the phone. There is a considerable delay because of the large number of mineral people in town using all available phone lines. When he did finally get through, his instructions were to disband the expedition, at least until after the Doggers Conference on the 9th and 10th of this month. After the conference he may do a trip through our G6 Area.

Our friendly old lady of the bush trip, had a complete change of personality once she reached town. We almost ran into her as she and Bill came out the hotel door, yet she ignored our cheery hello. She gave the impression she didn't want to know us at all. Dooley and I both felt deflated. Those two, along with the other doggers, were on the way to their respective vehicles, parked along the street outside. Happy Absalom was to tow Bill Brown and wife to Kalgoorlie. Mrs Brown was in the passenger seat ready to go, but husband Bill was still outside on the roadway, when Happy took up the tow rope slack with a jerk. Happy didn't even look back, he just took up the slack and moved off. He was towing a driverless vehicle with Mrs Brown helpless and alarmed in the passenger seat. Bill Brown took umbrage. He gave a surprising show of agility for one of his age.

With leaps and bounds and loud shouts of anger directed at the towing vehicle, Bill Brown sprang at Happy's driver side window swinging a fist through it, to hit Happy on the body somewhere. Bill Brown then abused Happy something cruel. It was a bad blue on Happy's part because the old lady could easily have suffered injury.

We watched the conclusion of this unhappy incident. After a few more terse words it was handshakes all round. We saw it finish, then we took off for Leonora to get some gear and our mail. About half way along the road we came to a caravan tipped up on its rear. It had a broken axle, and six men gathered around it waiting for their vehicle to return with a new one. Later when returning from Leonora to Laverton, we found the six men gone but the caravan still there.

Not long after passing the caravan for the second time, we ran into a terrific thunderstorm. It ran water all along the road for miles. The storm passed and a bit further on we made dust, it was so dry. There were still storms all around in the distance though, and lightning everywhere. There was no sign of the other doggers when we got back to Laverton, they obviously went right through to Kalgoorlie while we were still in Leonora. We stayed a while to have supper in Laverton before departing north to our own caravan. A long day of two hundred and eighty miles. No wonder the office brass question our mileage.

Chapter Thirteen - A NEW LANDROVER AT LAST

MARCH 1970 (Continued)

Wednesday 4 - The doggers' convoy from Karonie to Laverton is over. We are alone once more. I did a lot of work on the old APB Landrover wreck today. I cleaned spark plugs and engine first, then I unloaded everything to sort things out and discard all non-essentials before packing up again. While I was busy at this job Dooley did our washing. We also tidied up around the camp and did some cooking.

Some good rain fell here while we were away on the expedition and by the look of things there is more brewing. Bernie O'Driscoll demonstrated a rather tidy and effective way to poison trap jaws, as opposed to the older methods used by us doggers. Once our camp was in good order we went into Bandya to get a few empty chaff bags from Peter Hill. Bernie's latest innovation requires narrow strips of hessian to wrap around a single trap jaw only. Previously most doggers padded both jaws but that idea is now out of date.

Peter Hill gave us the hessian. We proceeded next to Mulga Queen to look for heavy scraps of iron that I want to use as trap drags. The old idea of tethering trap chains to a tree is no good. A struggling dog held by dual padded jaws, takes advantage of a solid tie to strain against the pull, thus often getting out of a trap. There is no give in a tree, it is a solid anchor. The new method requires a heavy weight, but one a dog can still drag away. The drag mark is easy to follow and offers little resistance, so there is no counterweight to assist the dog getting out of a trap. We arrived back on camp at 4-30 pm. I caught up with some book work. We are both knocked up from the recent long trip. Thirty-five miles.

Thursday 5 - We got away for the north end of our run this morning via Public Battery, where one trap had a kangaroo in it. I removed the trap and took it along to reset near Tharukati, a gnamma hole at a large granite outcrop near the road north of Yantakanngang. A bit north of this granite outcrop is a faint set of extremely old wheel tracks heading east through the spinifex. We followed the tracks for five miles until I deduced they were making in the direction of Tjampan on the Karu Soak road, much further east. I wanted to keep going but the blasted starter motor packed up at the granites before we left there and I felt it unwise to travel too far off the beaten track. When we saw Peter Hill at Bandya yesterday I told him how bad this vehicle is. I assured him and also the APB per RFDS radio, that for safety's sake I wouldn't go off the roads anywhere while on this northern run. From Urarey we go north past Deleta to Warren's Well, then return by way of Karu, Miltji, Tjampan, and Patapuka, to Bandya. We are due to call in at Bandya by Sunday next, if not, then they can expect to find us in trouble somewhere out along the track and raise the alarm.

One dog in a trap near Tjilpitjara, and one of former dogger Geradi's traps with a kangaroo leg in it a bit south of Jerry's Well. Funny we never saw it before. Further on near the dense ti-tree thickets north-east of Deleta I got two dogs. Tracks there also showed how a couple of nickel men not only interfered with one trap but took it with them. They untied the tether and left the wire behind, taking only the trap. It seems they wanted the trap for a souvenir because they didn't scalp the dog. Dooley recognises a set of footprints here as those of a tribal brother named Pinkari. He was with these whitefellas. Pinkari told me in Leonora a fortnight ago he was out this way with Ernie Hanlon and at that time gave us the name Wakulyakutjarra for a rockhole they visited. He also said Hanlon wanted to scalp a dog in one of my traps, but he, Pinkari, stopped him. Something funny going on all the time in this area. I'd like to catch some of the mongrels in the act.

One more dog in trap further north-west, where the ti-tree thicket opens out into spinifex. I reset all the traps visited today, using Bernie O'Driscoll's new method. He is an expert and I am not too proud to try anything out. His innovation seems a good one. I wish he could work out a good way to stop interfering bloody nickel men messing around with my traps though.

When we got to Warren's Well it was time for the evening meal so we pulled up to have one. There are dog tracks everywhere around here and all the way north of Deleta. I can't do a damned thing about it now either, because I'm due in Kalgoorlie by Sunday for the Doggers Annual Conference on the 9th. We have not only that appointment to keep, but the perils of this most unreliable vehicle to consider. It gets worse every day. No starter motor, it is firing on three cylinders, and has bad oil leaks from engine and wheel bearings.

At Warren's Well we saw foot tracks left by Alf Ashwin the Windidda head stockman, who is another of Dooley's tribal brothers, it appears he was looking around for dog tracks. I suppose he wants to find a dog or two in my traps too, so he can scalp them. That is not paranoia on my part either, despite the evidence of a stolen trap earlier today. John Roach the former Wiluna dogger, caught Alf Ashwin red-handed scalping dogs from his traps on more than one occasion. The excuse when caught is predictable, the scalper always maintains he did it out of good will, with the intention of handing the scalp over at the first opportunity. We had an overcast warm and humid day with no wind. We got four dogs out of traps, two males and two females. After supper we took advantage of cooler conditions and travelled through the night to our Ten Mile camp. Two hundred miles for the round trip.

Friday 6 - We enjoyed a good light rain this morning. It lasted a couple of hours. When the rain eased we got going for town. All sign of rain ended near the Bandya boundary, then dry all the way through Erlistoun and Laverton to Leonora, where we ran into a thunderstorm at 4 pm. One hundred and sixty miles.

Saturday 7 - Our private vehicle that we put into the garage for repair some time ago, was ready to go. We decided to use our own Landrover for the Kalgoorlie trip instead of risk a breakdown with the government wreck. I don't know why I left so early. A weekend in Kalgoorlie is not my idea of fun at anytime, however we didn't go into the city at all. The Doggers Conference is at a Rifle Range on the outskirts and we set up camp there in the hope one or two other doggers might turn up early to help pass the time on Sunday but none did.

DOGGERS ANNUAL CONFERENCE

Monday 9 - Two familiar faces amongst early arrivals were Mick Fitzgerald my erstwhile recalcitrant supervisor of 1968, accompanied by kangaroo research scientist Des Gooding. Mick seemed pleased to see me again. Both he and Des welcomed me back into the fold. Other notables were Mr Tozer and Peter Downes, both of who were previously unknown to me. A Norseman resident and the Nullarbor dogger, one Wally Scudds was another familiar acquaintance. It was a good day with interesting discussions and some trap setting demonstrations by Bernie O'Driscoll.

Later in the afternoon when the meeting finished for the day, we went to town and while there, ran into a couple of women in Hannan Street, namely Tjamukalu and Kutjikari. Tjamukalu is a tribal sister, and Kutjikari is Dooley's real sister. Tjamukalu is mother of Wulapa, the wangkayi girl living with a whitefellow in Leonora. I had an argument involving his threat to use firearms, whilst drinking together at the Laverton Hotel sometime back. Two women by themselves were okay, but when others came out of the woodwork soon after, we left. We don't like a crowd at anytime Dooley and me, especially drunks, so we came back to camp at the rifle range. Only one dogger stayed the night, the others having dispersed until tomorrow. The chap that stayed was not one of our type so we kept to ourselves.

Tuesday 10 - A trap setting competition took all morning. Olin Dimer won the event. I was only one point behind in second place. After the competition we spent the rest of the morning with late discussions and knocked off for dinner at 12-45 pm. While the impromptu meals were underway, there was a bit of excitement when someone nearly trod on a dugite snake inside the rough bush toilet.

We all adjourned to the rifle range in the afternoon. Karl Srb took the double on 22 and 303 rifle shoot. I thought it not too bad coming second in both events. but old Bill Brown was not of like mind. Bill it seems, lost a carton of beer and some money when I got second instead of first place in the rifle shoot. He backed me to win. Bill got his share of beer in the end anyway, because Jack Kerr and Bernie O'Driscoll put on a couple of cartons for the boys. I'm still not drinking so joined Bernie O'Driscoll and Peter Downes in cans of coke. The party was no fun for non drinkers. We left when the others got sparked up.

Mrs Brown was more talkative than she was when we last saw her after the Karonie expedition. I've already written an account of that incident earlier in this narrative. Today she gave us her version of the row between Bill Brown and old Happy in Laverton last week so, at the risk of repetition, here it is: "It appears that old Happy was drunk when he drove off with the Brown couple's vehicle in tow, without dogger Bill Brown being behind the steering wheel. Mrs Brown was in the passenger seat, but Bill was still standing outside on the road when Alex started off. After the fight they made friends and went off together to Mount Weld Station where Happy's brother is manager.

Mrs Brown says the station blacks were all drunk and fighting when she, Bill and Happy arrived there to camp the night. She says the blacks kept to themselves though, and left the whites alone. From Mount Weld they went on to Leonora next day via Mount Margaret Mission. She has no idea why they called in at the mission. One other item of interest she mentioned was how the towed vehicle had its windscreen broken when their tandem passed another vehicle." The conference finished today, but we decided to camp at the rifle range until tomorrow. Before we left, Jack Kerr told me to expect a new Landrover next week.

Wednesday 11 - We started off a bit late. As mentioned before we drove to Kalgoorlie in our own Landrover. From Broadarrow north today, a strange squeaking sound came from underneath the vehicle. I got out several times but couldn't trace the source. The noise grew worse as we got closer to home. Just south of Lake Raeside, with Mount Leonora in full view only fifteen miles ahead, the squeak increased to a high pitch squeal and we cut a front wheel bearing. This was the last thing I expected. The vehicle was not long out of the garage after extensive renovations that included new seals and front wheel bearings.

I tried to flag down at least a score of passing motorists before a Good Samaritan, one Don Tonkin, the manager of Leonora's Nabberu Hostel, stopped to see what was wrong. Not one of the others even slowed down. I wished them all well as they sped past. The mongrel lotta bastards.

Don agreed to take a message to town and it was not long before Sullivan's best mechanic Bob Ward came along, complete with new wheel bearing. Bob couldn't get it to fit so had to go back to town for more tools and come back again. He got us mobile, but only just. The front wheel hub had no oil in it he said. We had to crawl all the way to Leonora at slow speed. Bob told us to bring it in to the garage in the morning and he'll fix it properly.

Thursday 12 - I took our Landrover to the garage for repair and had a difference of opinion with Sullivan's business partner Dean Detez, over whose fault the wheel hub problem was. He tried to put the blame on me, but I wasn't having any. It was only a couple of days since Sullivan had our Landrover in his charge. It was he or one of his mechanics who forgot to fill the wheel hub with oil after the renovation job. In the end I managed to convince Dean who is right and who was wrong. He finally agreed with great reluctance to cover the complete cost of today's repairs. It is going to be an expensive refit too, with a complete hub assembly shot, and a brand new replacement. Maybe next time they'll take more care.

While our vehicle was in the sick bay, I spent the rest of the day cleaning out the government Landrover and removing all accessories. Most of the innovations were those I'd put on at my own expense, for personal convenience, and to make the job easier. By day's end I had it ready for handover when the new vehicle arrives next week. Friday the 13th I spent compiling journals and reports. I also made out a cheque to Custom Credit for $270.00 **in final payment of the caravan.** I paid this loan out as quick as I could. No more time payment deals for me, they are just a rope around the neck.

Saturday 14 - This morning I posted the journals away and sent the cheque off to Custom Credit. Our Landrover is still in the garage and won't be out for a while yet. It is hotter today than yesterday with some thunderstorms over the lake west of town. On Sunday we stayed home all day. The weather is still hot with a bit of light wind.

Monday 16 - Today I sent away for some "4 mile to the inch" maps. These are now available to the public. I want those that cover the G6 Dogging Area and the Karonie to Laverton trip. Later I took Dooley to hospital for maternity examination. She is okay says the doctor. Tonight it looked like police were busy with spotlights at the native reserve. The lights were sweeping around for a long time, so must be something seriously wrong. We took a walk up the street to find out, but the only information available was "They are looking for a man." (Most informative, I must say) No word today from Jack Kerr about the promised new Landrover either.

Tuesday 17 - Still no word from Kerr about the new Landrover. Our colour slides of the Karonie trip were in the mail this morning. The slides came out much better than expected, considering the sky was cloudy most of the trip, but nothing spectacular about the scenery. That country is drab and uninteresting really.

We found out today that it wasn't police at the reserve last night after all. It was male residents of the reserve themselves with spotlights and vehicle head lamps, sweeping the darkness in search of alleged tjinakapi killers, or feather foots as they say in English. They claim that at least twenty tjinakapi were sneaking around the reserve perimeter for hours. Personally I think it was a put-up job by the native men. They probably organised a scare to stop their women from running around on the loose every night, giving their pubic cheque books away. Dooley agrees with my assumption too. The women have been playing up a lot lately, since the nickel boom brought so many itinerant strangers into the district. Most of them are sex mad, white and black. On another note, we saw Paddy Sommers the Irish publican full of booze today. He must be celebrating something.

Wednesday 18 - A telegram from Jack Kerr on the RFDS session this morning. He wants me to ring him so I did, and got through after a long delay due to busy lines. He may advise me on the afternoon session today between 4 and 5 about the new Landrover. If not today then I am to listen in on the radio again tomorrow.

Thursday 19 - Telegram on this morning's RFDS session to say the new vehicle will arrive Leonora late tomorrow, or if not then it will get here on Saturday the 21st. What a long winded process this new vehicle business has become. In anticipation of its arrival this time, we purchased stores sufficient for the bush, ready to get away this weekend as we hope.

For some time now we have thought to have a new roof put on the town house. I got a quote from Eddie Bush the builder today. He says he'll replace the existing hip roof with a flat one for $120.00 so I told him to go ahead and do the job while we are out bush. He was also keen about some nickel samples we showed him. He appeared excited about one particular piece of greenish stone.

Friday 20 - I have a bad cold this morning. Jack Kerr and the truck driver came along with the new Landrover this afternoon. They left the new one with me and took the old one away. Good riddance. The new vehicle has a weather proof hard top with roll up canvas sides. It is real neat and well worth the long wait. I'm quite happy with it. The only miles on the speedo are a bit of Perth running. Mileage clocked so far is only sixty-seven.

Saturday 21 - Mileage 67. Loading up for the bush most of today. We departed about 3 pm. Topped up the fuel tanks at Laverton on the way past. Called in to Bandya for a few minutes then on again and get to our caravan just after sundown. The new Landrover appears to be doing about 20 mpg after the one hundred and fifty-eight mile run from Leonora. Peter Hill came along to visit us at 8 pm. We had a good yarn and directed mutual curses toward all nickel men and kangaroo shooters too for that matter. Also we discussed at length our common interest in Western Australian exploration.

Sunday 22 - The Landrover needed going over to tighten a few loose nuts and bolts. Sorted out the loading and departed for the dogging run at 11 am. We met a party of prospectors at Urarey on the way past. One was the Ernie Hanlon fellow Pinkari told us about, the others were Eric Thomas, a halfcaste from Leonora, along with a couple of strangers. Hanlon mentioned a rockhole (He says he discovered it?) situated near Mount Gerard. His directions were most confusing to me. He mentioned windmills with names, amongst a number of other ambiguous points. This makes me think he must have been roaming around on Windidda station country, rather than off the beaten track as he claims.

We left the Hanlon party and went on. I got a female dog from a trap twenty miles north of Urarey. Later at fourteen and a half mile north of Deleta, where some of my traps are, I walked into the dense ti-tree thicket and located the elusive rockhole Wakulyakutjarra. This is the native water that Pinkari informed us of, in connection with the man Hanlon. It is a beaut hole, about eight feet deep in solid limestone, situated in centre of a clear space surrounded by ti-tree. The site is not visible from the main track. Around the hole are several vertical indicator slabs. These placed in position by former native inhabitants of this area. Of course like those seen beside most native waters, the indicator stones are right alongside the place they point to. It has been my experience in the past, to find a natural water before I saw the indicator slabs. There is a sort of depression just north of the limestone hole. Shallow water is visible below. It appears clean and devoid of pollution. I can't see any bones or other rubbish in or near the water at all. This could possibly be a spring, since water is present in a dry season like this. In appearance the place brings to mind visions of Carnegie's illustration and description of Empress Spring. The one he found in 1896 about one hundred miles east of here. He wrote a chapter about it in his classic exploration book "Spinifex & Sand" published in 1898.

I can't see any sign of vehicles other than Ernie Hanlon's the other day. He had Pinkari Tom Williams with him as we know, and Pinkari showed Hanlon the rockhole. It is quite certain those two were together, because Pinkari says he stopped Hanlon from scalping one of my dogs. Pinkari also gave me and Dooley the name of the rockhole he took Hanlon to. Yet when I asked Hanlon if he'd been out here with Pinkari, Hanlon said no. He said he flew over in a plane, but knew the rockhole in 1943 when he was a stockman on Windidda. On that occasion said Hanlon, he'd been here on a camel. I asked Hanlon did he know the name Wakulyakutjara. He said no, and couldn't repeat it either. Like most whitefellows who don't talk native lingo, he found too many syllables to enunciate. It seems to me that someone is telling lies. I don't know who, but have a pretty good idea.

We saw one dog track along the road but no more in traps. On to Warren's Well to camp. We had to shoot three kangaroos before finding one good enough to eat. No cattle here this time. Warm clear day. Flies a bit sticky. Ninety-six miles from our Ten Mile camp.

Monday 23 - After a nice cool night it was up early to travel north. We bypassed Bonython Creek and Von Treur Tableland. This time we continued on through the Wiluna dogger's area to have a look at Prenti Downs. This being a new cattle station twenty-five miles north of Warren's Well. It came into existence when two large holdings owned by Margo Doman had suffered an enforced reduction in size. It is government policy that no one property be bigger than a million acres. I like to picture that measurement as a bit more than fifteen hundred square miles. Station sizes are easier to picture in square miles, as in the Northern Territory scale that I grew up with. Prenti Downs is close to Windidda Spring, a native water at the extreme eastern end of the former Windidda Station run. I was there on horseback in 1963, the last year of using horses and riders in the stockcamp.

Beautiful water at Prenti Downs homestead. Nobody home there so I filled our water tank and came back immediately to Warren's Well. We saw no sign of dogs up that way whatsoever. The cattle are all in poor condition. From Warren's we came south along Linke's beef road and turned off to Nyiruru for dinner. This time I took a walk up the gully for half a mile and found two shallow rock catchments, both dry. The gully is a tight pinch with sheer but low walls along some sections. It might be a pretty place when the rock basins are full and surrounded by green vegetation in good season.

Saw tracks of one dog scratching around near the lower rockhole after the last shower. After dinner we inspected the lake further south where was a male dog in one trap and the other sprung. I reset both then came north-east to Earli Earli to camp for the day. No sign of dogs here at all except for bones of a dead one in the waterhole, no doubt a victim of baits put out here before. I feel convinced there is a natural water close to the lake traps somewhere. I've caught nine dogs at that spot so far, yet no sign of dogs at any of the surrounding waters. One hundred and nine miles. The new Landrover speedo now reads 321 and we got a flat tyre soon after arrival on camp.

Tuesday 24 - Found the bones of a second dog in the waterhole this morning. I fixed the puncture and reckon these new Firestone tyres are a lot worse than the Hardie brand we had on the other vehicle. This Firestone brand is extremely hard to fit on the rim and the bead on the new tyre is buggered already. Dooley shot a kangaroo near the waterhole just before sunrise so we had fresh meat for breakfast. A fat one too. Dooley did the washing and we both had a bath, then left for Gregory Hills.

An item on ABC News this morning that Native Welfare officers made contact with a group of ten nomads living at a permanent soak near Mount Madley. The munjongs elected to stay put. They refused passage to Warburton Mission. This is the mob I wanted to meet up with during 1965-68 but lost the chance to do so when the APB called off all exploration work. Mark de Graaf and Stan Gratte of Geraldton tried to make contact in 1968 too, but failed in the attempt. I knew years ago about these nomads. Town-based Wiluna relatives of the bush mob, told me about them. I was not wealthy enough to finance a private expedition to go look for the nomads so, it was just not possible to go and find them. Now it is too late. One thing is certain though, they won't be in the desert much longer. Another government party will go out and encourage them to come in or, they will walk in of their own accord out of sheer curiosity. I'll lay a bet they will be in before this year ends. My expectation in this regard being based on the fact they sent a boy back for initiation at Warburton, on condition he be returned to his family at Mount Madley. When the boy goes back is the time they will decide to abandon their tribal land. The boy, or rather initiated man as he will be by then, will tell of all the wonderful things he saw at Warburton, then away they'll all go to have a look for themselves. End of nomads.

I nearly got my foot caught in a trap at Irve's Grave today so removed it. The trap that is, not my foot. Far too many travellers through this country of late. Someone might get caught when they pull up to look at the headstone. From Irve's, we went southward bound for Karu Soak, to find five dogs poisoned from baits left there some time ago.

Still a number of dog tracks here and lots of dead kangaroos around the soak. I can't make out what they died of as still plenty of surface water present. It is a bit of a puzzle really because there are lots of live kangaroos as well. I shot one to bait the carcase, along with that of a dead one I pulled out of the soak hole. That done I had another look around for more dead dogs but found none. We decided to stay the night and camped on top of a sandy rise south-west of the soak. Old native campsites are numerous around here. Also the camp left by those two unfortunate prospectors who broke down and got stranded for nine days at Karu before rescue by Peter Hill on Xmas Day.

I forgot to mention that Peter Hill was out at his (junk yard) enclosure not long ago to erect a notice board. The notice warns pilferers, robbers, or anyone else interfering with his property, that he will prosecute without further ado.

Fixed to the entrance gate Peter has a large sign painted with the legend opposite:

> THIS PROPERTY HAS NOT BEEN ABANDONED
> TRESPASSERS WILL BE PROSECUTED

It may be just as well he placed it there because I never saw such a perfect depiction of dereliction in my life. The man must be a real bowerbird. The enclosure has in it two broken down windmills, Stacks of old roofing iron and piles of bore casing. Heaps of cast-off household effects and other rubbish too varied to record. These things lie all over the flat in reckless abandon.

The notice I am sure was for the benefit of delinquent nickel prospectors, who by the look of numerous tracks left all around Peter Hill's fenced enclosure, must number in the dozens. I know they annoy me. Gregory Hills or Ulrich Range if you prefer, has their wheel tracks all over.

Personally I doubt Peter Hill will ever develop this place, yet it might be good cattle country in good season if he ever stocks it. To me though, the ecology out here is much too fragile to withstand the pressure of cattle, and if stocked with sheep, damage to the environment would be more severe

So far I see no evidence that the place ever had stock of any description, yet there are six windmills ready to go if fixed. Also a couple of fenced paddocks going to waste. Today was hot and clear with forty-five miles on the clock.

Wednesday 25 - Pulled all traps out of the ground at Karu this morning to reset in better sites less attractive to kangaroos, foxes and cats. No dogs came to water last night, only kangaroos and camels. Later we went down to Miltji. No water there now, no dogs and no kangaroos, so carried on south-west to Tjampan for dinner. One fresh dog track there so set a trap. After dinner we gathered some samples from an unusual outcrop of honey colour gemstone. We camped after another hot and clear, sixty mile day.

Thursday 26 - There are 525 miles on the clock now and today looks like being another scorcher. We had an easy morning, then on down through Bandya to remove all traps between Bella and Wilson's bore. Back south next to Hootanui and from there north-west to Waterfall, native name Nganpa, now quite dry, and no sign of dogs.

The nickel prospectors at Hootanui cleaned out a shallow well just north of Erlistoun Creek. They put up a small overhead tank to reticulate water and built a little shed nearby. It is now a picturesque campsite, with colourful red background hills and a frontage of green gumtrees along the creek. Nobody home. They must be all away for the Easter break.

When we got back to our Ten Mile camp, I saw where someone left a siphon hose hanging over the water tank. Looks like they washed clothes in a dish and had a shower bath. The hose left behind like this, could indicate they might be camping nearby and intend coming back for water, or more likely they forgot to take the thing when they left. I hope to hell they are not staying close to us. We've had a gutsful of strangers lately. Forty-two miles today.

Good Friday 27 - A gazetted public holiday. The APB likes us not to work, so we obliged their wish and stayed on camp all day. I stuck masking tape around the edges of all my new map sheets to strengthen them. Nothing worse in my opinion than tattered and torn maps. Dooley did the washing while I prepared to leave for Laverton tomorrow. Hot again today. It is a long, long summer with no change in sight.

Saturday 28 - I read some of Carnegie's book Spinifex & Sand yesterday and noticed reference to the names Swincer and Haden, prospectors of around 1896. These two could be the authors of initials on rocks at Waterfall and Miltji Rockhole. I'll have to check both places. Other references made by Carnegie were: Point Robert east of Lake Wells, Mount Lancelet, Mount Courtney, Point Katherine, Mount Dora, Mount Elizabeth, Lyell Brown Bluff, Parsons Bluff and Bonython Creek. The last ones we already know.

A visitor at Bandya today was Keith Comer of the Laverton fuel depot. He looking over Bandya cattle to buy some for Burtville Station that he bought not long ago. I wish him luck with those two hundred feet deep wells on that place. We had a cup of tea with Comer and Peter Hill, then carried on to Laverton where we topped up with petrol, before heading east along the old Warburton track. The mileage on new Landrover with full tanks being 650 on the clock. Travel was by way of Ivor Rock then leave Yamarna main road in favour of the bush track to Hunter's Waterfall. The rockholes there are all dry now and dead kangaroos everywhere. Still some fresh tracks though, so they didn't all die. Also one fresh dog track and those of a few camels.

Must be water somewhere. Hunter's Waterfall is fifty-seven miles from Laverton. We came out of there back to the main track, to camp above the breakaway in open spinifex. Whether it be bone dry, or brimful of water, Boolallie Rockhole is somewhere in this vicinity. I'll seek it out tomorrow. A lot of prospector traffic been through here, no doubt headed for Mount Venn. Warm clear day of one hundred and thirty-three miles.

Sunday 29 - Cold east winds this morning marked my forty first birthday. That is a bit too long in the tooth for my liking, but I've seen lots of country beyond the station boundaries in my lifetime and hope to see lots more yet. I located Boolallie, or Pulali as I like to spell it, on top of the escarpment about one mile back along the track from Hunter's waterfall. It is quite close to the track that leads to Hunter's actually, on the south side, but is hidden and easy to miss.

There are numerous old campsites of both whites and blacks, on an open mulga and spinifex flat above the rockhole. I took mileages: Pulali to Dadyun (Tatjan) rockhole is seven miles. To Nord (Norr) is nine miles. Travel then is north-east along Mulgabiddy Creek (Palkapiti) for ten miles across spinifex sandplain to Lang Bore (dry) and reach Rutter's Grave at twenty-seven miles from Pulali.

Prospectors' new roads and wheel tracks everywhere and three caravans parked near Rutter's. Just before we reached the hills, a new trench two feet deep, cut across our usual set of wheel tracks. We had to go around to dodge it. Why they let such bastards loose in this beautiful country is beyond me. They did the damage with some sort of a trenching machine by the look of it and no good reason for a trench there either that I can see. If they want samples they should drill, not cut the country to pieces. Sure must be a lot of good prospects for nickel around here.

We went over to Thatcher's Soak and found one caravan there too. Next we followed an old set of wheel tracks south from Thatcher's. These led to Yamarna boundary. We came back to Thatcher's via the main road as the bush track is much too scrubby and crooked. This time we drove around south side of the granite range and came to a drilling site about half way along. At extreme western end of the range, we came to a big well established mining camp, with tents, sheds and caravans. They have their own private bore and reticulated water supply. Sprinklers going on a green lawn and garden area central to the various living and work quarters. We could see a diamond drill in operation not far away. A few miles further north we came to a new aerodrome. This set-up belongs to TASMANEX of Mount Venn nickel-find fame, with shares rising on the stock market. We next followed their new road north and north-east back to Rutter's Soak. From Rutter's we went via Lang Rock to Jutson Soak and camped, after another warm clear day of one hundred and five miles. Saw the first sign of dogs in any numbers, at Jutson.

Monday 30 - Mileage on the speedo is now 805. This morning we travelled north from Jutson to Mount Cumming and found two prospectors there pegging a grid pattern over a three hundred acre lease. They pulled a caravan into the area and like us, wished to locate an Uhr Soak marked on the map somewhere to the north-west of Mount Cumming. Their problem like mine, is the presence along this range of seven or eight almost identical high peaks, any of one of which could be Mount Cumming. The map shows Uhr Soak on north side of the range. The range however is too rough to cross by vehicle and the weather is much too hot for walking. Later I might get more precise information as to the soak's whereabouts. In the meantime we returned to Jutson, thence to vicinity of Rutter's, where I shot a fat kangaroo for dinner. During the afternoon we went south-west twenty miles to camp near Uhr Rocks. The same Uhr, but a different feature. The speedo indicates Mulgabiddy Creek is about six miles long. We travelled eighty-eight miles today.

Tuesday 31 - Last night was warm. We got an early start and found some dry soaks and waterholes one mile east. Old native campsites are numerous. We also found the iron frame of an old camel saddle. The ironwork is in excellent condition, only the padding gone. This is the only perfect iron frame I ever found. Most of those I've seen before were broken or bent out of shape.

Not far from the camel saddle we came across an old cutline. We followed the cutline to where it ends at four miles. Some unknown claypan squatter intended to build a fence along here by the look of it. Faint wheel tracks led on from where the cutline finished. We continued along the faint tracks and at three and a half mile further, came to a place shown on the map as Punjadda Soak. This soak is east of a Punjadda Hill. It is a good one with water visible at the surface and located near some small granite outcrops in grey soil. It must be good to have water in such a dry season. Emu tracks all around here and plenty of euros looking at us from amongst the rocks. One dingo was drinking at the soak when we arrived, but made off before I could get a shot. A lot of dog tracks. No one has been here in ages. The wheel tracks I followed are so faint I had to get out and walk to find them at times. I shot a euro and baited the carcase, then we returned to Ivor Rocks on the main road. From Ivor we drove north in search of Cutterblood Rockhole. It is a bit hard to find, but was well worth the effort when we did locate it, as it is a big rockhole with undershot cavern-like walls, and deep. The hole is deep I mean, but no water in it. How a big shaded rockhole like this can be so empty of water is strange, despite current drought conditions. Rockholes of this size usually have a bit of soakage water in sand at the bottom, or under a ledge to one side. Cutterblood is near the top rim of a breakaway escarpment.

From Cutterblood, old wheel marks led north atop a long line of breakaways, until they converged with a new graded road running parallel, only a short distance west of the wheel tracks. Both old track, and new road, run north to Cosmo Newberry. The roads cross over one another at Cosmo Newberry's south boundary windmill. We had no idea the new graded road was so close to our just-travelled wheel-track route. From the convergence point, we ran the new road twenty miles south to Ivor Rocks, thence two miles east to a new windmill along the Laverton road to camp. One hundred and twelve miles.

Figure 13 APB Trap Setting Demonstration

Chapter Fourteen - WIDESPREAD TRAVELS & A SHIFT OF CAMP

APRIL 1970

Wednesday 1 - We travelled to Laverton today for a drum of petrol. The new Landrover is giving good mileage. The clock now reads 1002 miles and the last refuel was at 650. On the way home I called in to have a yarn with Peter Hill at Bandya then back to the caravan and listen to the RFDS schedule. A telegram from Jack Kerr to say Bernie O'Driscoll not available yet and for me to carry on as usual. On Thursday I did the journals and reports for month of March plus an extra copy to deposit with the esteemed JS Battye Library. On Friday I annotated some features on the maps and read a bit of the Spencer & Gillen Diary 1901-02, of an anthropological expedition through the Northern Territory.

Saturday 4 - Time to do some work again. Mileage now 1103, with full tanks and a late start via Mulga Queen to Bandya north boundary and through the gate into open country. I wish to take mileages along the back way, via the dogger's graded access track to Wonganoo east boundary. This unplanned road has lots of twists and turns and is not good for accurate bearings. It is not on any maps yet, so for what it's worth I want to put a compass on it and plot the route for myself. Starting at boundary gate due north of Mulga Queen, the bearings read as follows:

ENE	1 mile	
NE	2 miles	reach hard flats and turn north
N	3.8 miles	reach breakaways start of graded track
N	0.2 mile	reach spinifex
NW	1.8 miles	granite rubble and road junction

Turn north-west at junction eight miles north of boundary. Pass gnamma hole and turn:

WNW	1.4 miles	leave hard country and enter spinifex
NW	5 miles	reach quartz rubble

Fifteen miles north-west of the junction, road turns north, not far past a little swamp in the spinifex. Reach mulga country and a couple more swamps at sixteen miles. Then the first little creek with a small dry waterhole at eighteen and a half mile, or three and a half mile NNE of where the track turns north. Reach the second creek at nineteen miles and follow it up about one mile north. Follow breakaways north-east then for two miles. Pass over them at the north end. Road turns west through spinifex running on top of the escarpment at twenty-one miles from junction.

W	2 miles	
SW	2 miles	reach breakaways again and run four mile along south side of same
W	2 miles	to Seven Sister rockholes (Kungkarrungkurru) on gravel flats
SW	2 miles	through spinifex
W	8 miles	reach scrubby quartz hill at sixteen miles
WNW	8.7 miles	road turns north after reaching dense scrub
N	200 yards	to a gnamma hole then west again
W	9.5 miles	

At the last bearing we came to Wonganoo east boundary fence, after first travelling for five or six miles through scrub covered stony flats. Lot of deep cattle pads in this area. The graded access track terminates right at the boundary fence, then a rough track runs south one mile along the fence to a windmill with cattle yards. We saw fresh tracks of two dogs on top of a sandhill thirty-five miles east of the windmill, but couldn't get a shot at them. Lot of dog tracks along the road at a point twenty-five miles east and from there, west to the gnamma hole at ten miles east of Wonganoo boundary. The dog tracks disappeared near the dry gnamma hole, to cut across country for a drink at the windmill, whereas the vehicle took the longer route by way of the wheel track. That ended this bush traverse from a point north of Mulga Queen, and gives me a rough plot to trace on a map.

Next are some bearings and mileages taken from the boundary windmill and cattle yards. Start along fenceline north four miles, then west a half mile to the main Shire road. Follow the main road fourteen miles north to Irwin Bore. At nineteen miles north, the road runs over a high rise. From the top of this rise a windmill is visible off the road in scrub country to the east, about one mile away in a hollow at foot of the rise. At twenty-four miles north is a creek, wherein lays Doyle's Soak. Three miles north of the soak, this road meets the Wiluna road from Carnegie at Doyle's Well, about thirty-one miles from the starting point at windmill on Wonganoo east boundary. Reverse mileages on return south, read as follows:

Doyle's Well at road junction south to Doyle's Soak is	3.3 miles
Doyle's Well to windmill in scrub at foot of rise to the east	8.2 miles
Doyle's Well to Irwin Windmill and cattle yards	13.2 miles
Doyle's Well to Mount Fisher and old mines	20.7 miles
Doyle's Well to Wonganoo north boundary fence	27 miles
North boundary gate to mill on Wonganoo east boundary	4.4 miles

Shot a fat young kangaroo for supper. Pulled up at dusk to cook it and camp near the last mentioned windmill. Total travel since this morning, one hundred and forty-nine miles. I find all these rough notes confusing myself, and hereby offer sympathy to some possible reader who might scrutinise them at some distant date in the future.

Sunday 5 - There are more notes to come. We got out of the scrub soon after leaving camp. Still travelling in a SSE direction we passed over nine miles of spinifex with a scatter of low sandhills. Came at ten miles to a deep kangaroo pad crossing the wheel track at an angle, from NE to SW. I assume there must be a station windmill west of the boundary fence or, soakage water available in open country to the east. I consider the latter unlikely. Reach hard country at eleven miles.

SSE	11.3 miles	rockhole
SE	13 miles	road turns
NE	14 miles	turnoff to bore hole with cement base marked water 90ft
	1.4 miles	return from bore to main track
SW	15.7 miles	reach Scholl Range and continue in southerly direction to:

Dry waterhole in mulga creek	7.8 miles
Karli Rockhole	23.8 miles
Turnoff NE of track	27.2 miles
Reach dry rockhole	28.2 miles
Return to SW to main track	29.2 miles
Gnamma hole N side of road	37.3 miles minus two miles dead running
Turn off to rockhole east side	37.6 miles

Rockhole	38.1 miles
Return to main track	38.2 miles
Bandya NW boundary corner	40.7 miles
Spinifex Bore in Bandya	45.4 miles
Waterfall Rockhole (Nganpa)	58.7 miles

We met old Jim Hooper the manager of Peter Hill's Milyirri Outcamp. He and son were hand-feeding quiet cattle with hay at one of the windmills, the name of the windmill is Limestone Well. We stopped to yarn for a while. He is a friendly old chap. Dooley knows him from years ago but for some reason he kept calling her Mary. She told me later that he mistook her for Kutjikari her older sister, who goes by the whitefellow name of Mary. We left Jim and son for Waterfall, where Dooley spent some time digging for bardies or witchetty grubs as I prefer to call them. On home then back to the Ten Mile, to complete a two day circuit. Eighty-eight miles today.

Monday 6 - We went into Leonora via Nambi. One hundred and twenty-two miles this way, the shortest route to town from Bandya. There was a lot of APB mail in the box. On Tuesday I put the new Landrover UQD-634 into Sullivan's Garage at mileage 1452, a bit overdue for its first 1000 mile free service. The mechanic also has my private Landrover nearly completed, but is still waiting for parts to finish the job.

Wednesday 8 - I don't leave our Landrover in the garage all the time. It is still mobile enough to take home, but it had to go in again today. Some of the expected parts arrived and they hope to complete the job soon. Old Anne Walker was in police custody today. She has a house right behind our block, across a street to the east. Keith Biggs the butcher has the corner block next door to her, and has builders at work there doing extensive renovations. They have a lot of building material stored in a small garage jammed between the two houses mentioned. We saw old Anne Walker busy one night carrying lots of this material away from the garage to her house. She isn't the sort of person one would expect to steal things like that, so we presume that a bit too much beer must be the reason for her fall from grace. She was out free and walking around again this afternoon, as we watched the builders cart the stolen property back to their own side of the fence. Quite humorous really and no one suffered in the end.

I got our repaired Landrover from the garage at no cost to us. Sullivan did the job free of charge as it was his fault for not filling the wheel hub with oil in the first place. I still rankle at Dean Detez though, for trying to put the blame on me. That was adding insult to injury.

Late afternoon I loaded up again and departed for Laverton, where I refuelled at mileage 1532 with all tanks full. It is essential to keep the mileages now, so I can calculate safe margins for long bush trips. The BP Agent owes me (The APB that is) in excess of twenty gallons. They are selling out and want $30,000.00 for the business. We had to travel as far north as Swanson's before getting a kangaroo for supper, then carried on to the Ten Mile to camp. One hundred and fifty-nine miles by way of Laverton. Gusty winds all day.

Friday 10 - Stayed on camp all of yesterday, annotating last weekend's bearings and mileages along the dogger's access road. The end result puts that route into much better perspective. Some bends were confusing before, but much easier to visualise now, once plotted on the map. I've been planning for some time past, to look around the country eastward of Lake Wells. There is a sandalwood track running out that way from Peter Hill's two windmills and junk yard. I believe the track was the work of our friend Johnny Griffith. He did it with a length of railway line dragged behind his truck last year. An excellent job he made of it too. It looks more like a graded road than a drag track.

There is no fun in wild dog control. To me this job is only a means to an end. It allows me freedom of movement, within certain bounds of course, but freedom and independence nevertheless. I set traps to catch dingoes, that is my job. I carry it out to the best of my ability, as I would never break faith with an employer. I am on trust as are all other doggers, and am proud of the faith shown in them and myself by the APB. I kill kangaroos and put strychnine on carcases in order to kill vermin, to whit dingoes, foxes, and cats. I really do hate this part of the job and find it abhorrent, but if I don't do it someone else will. I set traps, catch dogs, and scalp the carcases. In reference to carcases and scalps I might mention that it is seldom a fresh carcase that greets the dogger doing his rounds of the trap run. The size of the control jurisdiction is hundreds of square miles in area. It takes months to visit all parts of the run. To date I have not seen even half of the country under my control. A dogger may not see a particular trap run, more than once in six months, or even longer. So it is, that a dog caught in a trap is often only a desiccated carcase when the dogger revisits the site of the kill. Perhaps the only sign of a dog is a heap of bones by the time a dogger gets back that way to inspect the traps he set months before. Not much to become sentimental about. The methods used improve all the time, and the aim is always to be as humane as possible.

The foregoing paragraph is the nasty side of the equation, the other side of a dogger's duty is much more pleasant. A dogger should have an intimate knowledge of his country. That is where exploration and discovery of new features come into the picture. This side of the job is in complete contrast to wild dog control and is the part I love best, the chance to cover an untracked virgin landscape. I like to live beyond the boundary fences and enjoy the experience of being outside all tracks of domestic stock, this gives a real sense of isolation. Exploration is in my blood. It is a way of life from my earliest years as a young stockman in the cattle camps of South Australia out along the Birdsville Track. Isolation also, like the western desert fringe beyond cattle stations like Mount Doreen in the Northern Territory.

I know that some future reader will detest my regular reference to traps, poison and scalps, I dislike it too, however I am a dogger. These things needs must be, as must frequent reference be made in reports to head office at the end of each month. So bear with me future reader, you must suffer the bad aspects of this work as well as the good, if you wish to share with me the joys of new discovery.

We set off for Gregory Hills this morning, inspecting traps and baits en route. I found one dog in a trap and two poisoned near a roo carcase left before. All these dogs were male. I reset the traps and left the Gregory Hills behind.

From Peter Hill's junk yard we followed the sandalwood track east for twenty miles, bearing a little north of an eastern line all the way. The first few miles being mulga thicket, then at twelve miles light mulga and saltbush. This open aspect of saltbush then continues all the way around the southern end of Lake Wells. The road then takes a swing around the south side of some stony hills and begins a more northern, but winding course, for six miles. Once past the hills the road bears more to the north-east for the next fourteen miles, to a distance of forty-four miles out from the Gregory Hills starting point.

At the forty-four mile point, the "SG 51-15 THROSSEL" 4 miles to the inch, map runs out. Enter north then onto the sheet of ROBERT the number of which I cannot read through masking tape I edged the map with. I begin mileages on ROBERT at the fifty mile point, as my bearings don't seem to correspond with the position of Lake Wells as shown on the map. I got over this problem by drawing a line north-west to the only lake in the vicinity, where I ran a saltpan around its southern perimeter for two miles. We left the saltpan behind at it's north east corner and entered sandhills. These dunes occupy the country east and north-east for the next ten miles, or sixty miles north-east from the Gregory Hills starting point. The sixty mile point marks the position of a granite rubble rise. A large old campsite here where sandalwood pullers camped last year.

The road continues another ten mile through sandhills from the rubble rise, north-east past a remarkable isolated tabletop peak. This I think is the Peterswald Hill marked on the map and goes by the native name Manngu says Dooley, meaning a wedgetail eagle's nest. This country out here is all part of Walawurru Tjukurrpa (Eagle Dreaming) and is seventy miles out from the starting point. The road swings more to the east from the tabletop. It runs across laterite gravel flats for a few miles, then sandhills for twelve miles.

At the eighty-two mile point, a jutting breakaway of low profile and small but sheer cliffs, appears beside the track on north side. In shape the feature is like a long finger. The road runs along it's southern face, then swings north around the east end and west one mile along it's north side, to a small rough little gully. We got out to walk around here and found numerous gnamma holes, both small and large, on top of the low escarpment, all being dry. One hole is quite large. Odd ones have no bottom and go right through the caprock to small caves underneath.

This escarpment finger, native name mulkutu, represents an eagle's claw. The holes represent marks left by the claws or talons, native name miltji. This eighty-two mile point coincides with Peterswald Hill on my map and is a wonderful vantage point. Although low in itself, the finger breakaway called mulkutu, rests on top of high ground. This high ground begins it's rise from near the tabletop peak Manngu, that we saw earlier. From here the Ernest Giles Range, native name Tortu is visible, running away south and south-west into the distance. The Blaxland Range is evident too. Tortu is a bird Dooley calls a dove.

Satisfied with our day's achievement, we returned after dark to Gregory Hills. We found no evidence of water anywhere along the eighty-two mile stretch of road. I do not feel optimistic about surface water out there at all. The only sign of life was one emaciated kangaroo, one fox with the mange and one skinny dingo heading west. I had a shot at him but missed.

Despite its dry condition and starving animals, it is excellent pastoral country in some sections. I intend to follow this line of country out much further soon, but for the present will wait till I can afford a quantity of film. I wish to make a photographic record as it has historical and scenic value. Both Carnegie and Wells travelled through this region in 1896. From where we turned back today is only thirty miles or so west of Carnegie's Empress Spring, a place I must locate. He gave an excellent account of it in his book Spinifex & Sand. The air turned cool after dark and gave us an enjoyable trip out of the parched landscape. A strong wind blew all night with storm clouds rising. Quite a pleasant change from the unseasonable hot weather of late. A total of two hundred and forty-six miles today. It is no wonder the APB chides me for spending too much on fuel. Bless their hearts.

Saturday 11 - Mileage on the meter is now 1857. We resumed the trap run this morning after almost being blown away by the wind last night. Cold and cloudy today. One dog in trap at Gregory Hills. One dog near the lakes to the west and one in trap along the spinifex stretch south of Tjilpitjarra. A total of three dogs, all male. I reset all traps. We found an old well one mile west of Tui Claypans. The well is in a mulga thicket south of a big sandhill, about midway between the claypans and some stony hills to the west. There is not much sign of dog activity anywhere around the run now, apart from those caught in traps. We carried on back to our Ten Mile camp quite late after driving through the night. One hundred and fifty miles.

Sunday 12 - Man's third lunar landing mission commenced this morning launching APPOLLO 13 with three astronauts on board. They are now travelling through space to their destination.

Monday 13 - The Appollo Moon Party are half way on their journey. Warm last night. Hot today. Not much likelihood of rain. I cleaned the Landrover out this morning and repacked it again. Made some notes in journals and annotated maps in the afternoon. Dooley busy sewing a new dress out of red and yellow material. I'll have to watch out someone doesn't take a fancy to her when she wears it in town.

One of us left a stick in the fire at dinner time. There was great excitement in our camp later in the afternoon. We both rushed out of the caravan to see what was all the crackling and roaring noise. We found our cosy little brush windbreak going up like a bonfire. When we heard the roar we thought it was a motor vehicle.

Tuesday 14 - Mileage 2007. Warm last night again and a few scattered clouds this morning. Bush flies are numerous and troublesome of late. This seems unusual after a full summer free of the pests. It must be something to do with the lack of rain. We had a big washing day. Complete overcast this afternoon. The first promising sign of rain this month. I'll believe it only when I see and feel it. We stayed on camp all day. I finished reading Gillen's 1900-01 Diary.

The Lunar spacecraft has developed an electrical fault that may prevent the landing attempt. An oxygen bottle exploded in the landing nodule and damaged the electrical system. Looks like possible tragedy for the APPOLLO 13 crew. They have to go into Lunar orbit tomorrow morning at 10-30 am before they can begin their return to Earth with the crippled spacecraft slowly leaking oxygen.

Wednesday 15 - Overcast this morning and spitting rain. We went north-east past Bandya boundary and Urarey, to turn off the track at forty-three miles, near a granite outcrop north of Tharukati. We went in south-east through the spinifex along the faint wheel marks of an old sandalwood cutter's track. We followed it east for seven and a half mile over spinifex sand plain, to a small gnamma hole on a hard rubble rise. At a bit short of eight miles we passed a little sandstone knob on south side of the track, with a cave at south end of the knob. At eight miles we left the spinifex and entered hard country with an old sandalwood camp on an open flat. A link-wire Cyclone bed, tent poles, a heavy iron drag for bush road making, along with other odds and ends of abandoned camp gear. The camp is at the west end of a small saltbush flat. There was no sign of a motor track beyond this point so we returned south-west to Tharukati. The latter rockhole is two miles south of where we turned off the Urarey road earlier. Plenty dog tracks around Tharukati, also a little water in sand at bottom of the rockhole.

Back south to Urarey. We followed the old boundary fence east for three miles, then south for another four miles, south-west one mile, south four miles. Then turn west through fence at a corner and continue west three miles to an old gate. One fence goes south. Followed the other fence west one mile and reached the main Urarey track again, from there we went on to

Bandya's north boundary. I can't work out how we missed the Quondong Well subdivision, it may have been flat on the ground. Return to Ten Mile camp. One hundred and eighteen miles today. APPOLLO 13 got around the Moon okay and is now on its way back to Earth. The spacecraft is due to land in mid Pacific between New Zealand and Samoa early next Saturday morning.

Thursday 16 - There was a little spit of rain last night but it all cleared away by morning. After breakfast we travelled to Laverton for fuel. We find that this Landrover is doing twenty-four miles to the gallon. Excellent mileage and double that of the old vehicle. We met Roy Sullivan in town. Roy gave us some useful information regarding the sandalwood track that we followed east the other day from Gregory Hills, he says it goes out one hundred and forty miles north-east altogether, past a large detached ridge he calls Ida Range. He claims the rockhole where we turned back when we reached the eighty-two mile point, bears the native name of Kunan.

Roy went on to say that away from the drag track, at south end of the Ida Range and on its east side, is a large rockhole name of Wanan. Also a big rockhole where the track ends further north, but he doesn't know its name. He maintains Empress Spring is away east of where the sandalwood track ends, but this doesn't fit in with my calculations. I record Roy's information about Empress Spring with tongue in cheek. He also says the name of Empress Spring is Marul, but that is different to the name we have for it from Ngalia people. The Ngalia call it Reti. Roy Sullivan is one of the Wongawol halfcastes from Tommy Melon's time. He's lived in Laverton most of his life. He has a large family. Most of his sons work for the Shire. He does too. He says he was out in that country a few years back with Hunt Oil Company, from the east side of Lake Throssel. Roy also claims there is a string of big rockholes along the sixty mile length of Ernest Giles Range. He saw plenty of dingoes out there. Further south he maintains, that the Mount Grant I want to find, is in reality Punjadda Hill where I found a good soakage not long ago. That last bit of information is only for the record of interview with Roy Sullivan, I won't have a bar of that one. Punjadda Hill is miles away from where Carnegie's Mount Grant should be. I wrote all this Sullivan stuff down while we were talking in Laverton's main street, so there is nothing left to memory, it is all verbatim, right from his own mouth, with no embellishments

While I was writing notes of the conversation with Roy Sullivan, a white fellow name of Reg Absalom came along. He introduced himself as a brother of Happy Absalom, the talkative dogger. Reg bears no resemblance to Happy and is much younger. After Reg and Roy left, Dooley had a long yarn with Dorothy Shaw, Minting Chapman's wife. They talked all afternoon until we had to leave.

Travelling east on the Yamarna road, I had several shots at kangaroos but missed them all. This government issue 303 rifle never hits the same place twice, it sprays bullets all over the place. I got a kangaroo with Dooley's 22 Winchester in the end, not long after arrival at Ivor Rocks. Pulled up and camped so as to enjoy some fresh meat. Big storms to the east but doesn't look like any rain coming here. One hundred and eighteen miles.

Friday 17 - Mileage 2243. The Moon rocket is on a straight course to Earth again. Good light rain fell last night. Lots of lightning to the west, north, and east. Not enough rain fell to benefit the country. It's too late now for grass, and not enough rain fell to fill any rockholes. I'm undecided which way to move this morning. Most of the storm seemed centred over Punjadda

Soak. We stayed on camp roasting roo meat and potatoes for dinner, while waiting to see what the weather might do.

Bob Collard, known to the tourist trade as The Leonora Bushman, was on the ABC Regional News this morning. He says he discovered a ceremonial site between Laverton and Warburton recently while prospecting. I wonder what, and whereat, maybe he found some drawings in a cave. Maybe he found the site I photographed years ago myself, near Lake Throssel. That was in 1967 when I did a trip to Alice Springs via the Warburton and Petermann Ranges.

Max Harris the new owner of White Cliffs, came the bounce last night. He said I'm way out of my run, that he has dog troubles, that Karl Srb is not doing his job and has only caught one dog in the past eight months. Harris also says he swapped Karl three dog scalps for a bottle of strychnine and that Karl afterwards boasted in Laverton how he shot the dogs himself. Looks to me like Karl Srb had better watch his step else someone like this disgruntled squatter will give him a bad reputation. As for me, I suggested to Mister Harris that he put all his complaints into a letter and post it to the APB. I told him that I was not in any way out of my official run, and to the contrary am camping right on my south boundary. For his interest I also told him I'd caught fifteen dogs during the past fortnight and told him that his dog troubles on White Cliffs Station came under Karl Srb's jurisdiction not mine.

I finished by informing him that I would take especial care of all dog problems wherever my boundary passed through his property and then cut the conversation short with a "G' night to you Mister Harris." End of story. He left. We stayed.

The flies are so sticky this morning while writing this. They follow the biro's every movement across the page and get so much in the way I can't see what to write. Looking up from the writing task I see far too much rain to the east and it looks like more coming, so we returned to Laverton and turned north to Bandya. We ran into some heavy going, with water running all along the road from McKenzie Well. The road was like a creek all the way through Bandya. We got back to our caravan at the Ten Mile only minutes before the rain began to pelt down in real earnest. A deluge of tropical proportions, it really pelted down. The first good rains for I don't know how long. I'm glad we came back to the caravan. Much better than being bogged off the road out Punjadda Soak way. One hundred and eighteen miles today, with the last lap through flowing water.

Saturday 18 - Mileage 2361. I awoke at 1 am this morning to tune in the radio and follow progress of the crippled spacecraft. The astronauts landed safely in the Pacific Ocean. Only three seconds late and four miles off designated touch-down position. All personnel feeling fine. The rain cleared during the night and gave us a crisp cold morning with blue sky and south-east to south-west winds. I hope this is the start of winter. Our caravan now sits in a lake-like surround of water as a result of the heavy rainfall last night. The ground around camp is too boggy to move now, but should dry out soon, I hope.

Sunday 19 - The ground is still too wet and boggy to move. I wrote a letter to the owner Leo Boladeras of Wonganoo Station. He complained to the APB about his cattle eating my kangaroo baits. I never lay baits within a mile of station waters. I suggested his cattle were dying of botulism, or something like that. They get it from chewing bleached bones of their own long-dead species. I wrote an extra copy to send Jack Kerr as well.

I can't understand these squatters. They cry for the dogger to keep the dogs down, then complain to blue heaven when he does his job. Just like Bill Green of Cunyu Station. In the middle of the drought a few years back Bill Green cried for rain and when the rain came, he reckoned it was too much. I don't know, their perspective is sometimes beyond me.

Peter Hill came out to visit this afternoon. He almost got bogged on his way to our camp in the thicket. He got in okay, but now we have his wheel ruts right up to the caravan door and more deep bog ruts on his way out. Peter had an old map annotated by Wack Lloyd, a former packhorse dogger. He worked the same area I'm working now, plus Windidda country further north. I knew him when I was a stockman on Windidda in 1963, when Wack was the camp cook. That was before he got burnt to death under suspicious circumstances in Wiluna. Later Wack used an old Morris truck in conjunction with the pack horses. Oh, and I found out from Peter that the WC Hill inscription on tank near old well west of Tui claypan was that of his grandfather. A fine clear warm day. Cold nights now. Flies much less troublesome.

Monday 20 - Cold misty rain all the way south toward Laverton this morning. We pulled up for dinner in the shelter of a small thicket just north of the junction where our road from Bandya meets the one going east to Cosmo Newberry. From our sheltered position, the Cosmo road was quite visible through a gap in the trees. While the billy was still on the fire, a utility loaded with natives, all standing upright behind the driver's cab, came along. We could see their heads above the trees that sheltered our position, they didn't see us though. Three men got down from the utility to spray bullets at some kangaroos beyond our position. This shooting spree was a bit too close for comfort so I fired three rapid shots into the air from the 303 army rifle, to warn them of our presence in case they might fire toward us. They didn't. The moment they heard the three loud bangs they scrambled back onto their vehicle and sped off down the road in a great cloud of dust. We saw the comical side of it afterwards. They must have thought we were returning their fire shot for shot. After dinner we drove around the road to look at their tracks. The hunters had shot a kangaroo alright, but in their great haste to get away, left their kill behind. Maybe they thought the return fire came from a party of tjinakapi killers. Anyway we had the last laugh, plus some of the best cuts of fresh roo meat.

I took sixteen dog scalps to the Laverton Shire Office and told the clerk I wanted the $32.00 bonus for pocket money today. As usual he had no one on hand to sign a cheque so I got no money. He said he'll send it by mail in due course. A most unsatisfactory idea but unavoidable it seems. The Shire Clerk tells me also that he finds it impossible most of the time to get a quorum together for council meetings. I do believe him.

Laverton was alive with prospectors today. Customer service at the two Stores and Post Office is both antiquated and unsatisfactory. Not one bag of flour available in Laverton. We had to go to Leonora for supplies. This was just as well, as things turned out. I got a letter in the mail from Jack Kerr. He complains about me not being in town to meet him on the 9th.

Also unbeknown to me there was a baiting drive on at the time. Jack had left ten cases of baits at Karl Srb's place for me to pick up and of course I didn't, but will now have to do so. In the mail too, was a cheque for the amount of $23.00 to refund an overpayment on my account. A letter from the State Library as well, with notification that my 1965-68 Exploration Diaries are now on microfiche and the originals will be returned to me in the mail soon. One hundred and sixty-two miles.

Tuesday 21 - Mileage 2523. Bob Collard the local Central Safari Leader, was on the News again this morning. Bob says he found a sacred Aboriginal site just north of Cosmo Newberry and now the Native Affairs Department, together with a tribal elder, will investigate it soon. Old Bob is always finding something. He does it I think, to get his name in the News. Good publicity for his business I suppose, not to mention his ego. The rain cleared away by this morning. We are now in the middle of cold winter weather. No complaints from us about the cold either, after the unusual long hot summer we've had. I picked up the ten cases of baits at Karl Srb's place and had a good yarn with him. Later I took Dooley to hospital for another prenatal check. Doctor says the baby has about eight weeks to go.

When we got home, I contacted a Mr Wilson, the APB Transport Officer. He okayed the service already done on UQD-634. I then rang Kalgoorlie office about progress of repairs to the portable transceiver and find it is now ready to pick up. Next morning on Wednesday the 2nd we went down to Kalgoorlie to get the transceiver and return with it immediately to Leonora. Round trip of three hundred and ten miles.

Thursday 23 - Got going to Laverton and fill up with forty-one gallons of petrol in the big tank. It doesn't hold as much as I thought. Also three and a half gallons in the small tank. That makes a total of forty-four and one half gallons. In the street later I saw some cheeky nickel men talking about us. I told them to have a bloody good look so they'd know us next time, at which they stopped talking and looked away. It seems some people can't get used to the idea of a white man in the company of a fullblood Aboriginal woman. We left town for the Ten Mile camp. Shot a kangaroo for meat along the way. One hundred and eight miles.

Friday 24 - Mileage 2991. A cold night but clear and fine this morning. I rigged up the portable and tried it. Contact with the RFDS base in Kalgoorlie was loud and clear. Caught up on a bit of correspondence and bookwork today. Dooley did our washing.

Saturday 25 - We've had thoughts of late about shifting to a better place away from the main road. This morning we went east to Red Well and found a real good camp there beside a small thicket in spinifex country, about four miles east of the well. Returned to the Ten Mile to pack up and shifted the caravan across to the spinifex campsite. We travelled via Bandya homestead because of the better road that way. We got a surprise to see Hank Cominelli the White House publican from Leonora. Hank was at the homestead with a Landrover, going north to Jerry's Well on a prospecting trip.

Our run from Ten Mile to the new camp was twenty-five miles both ways. Cleaned spinifex away from around the caravan, then we settled in. I feel a lot happier here despite the presence of ants in great numbers. It is more isolate and only four miles from the best water in the country. Plenty of firewood near camp and a high thicket on both south and east side of the caravan to act a windbreak, and also helps conceal it from the road. We came half a mile in across an otherwise open spinifex flat from the road. Our position is completely open to the north. Our old camp back at the Ten Mile was too much in the thicket with no outward view at all. A long way from good water and far, far too much traffic up and down along the road to Hootanui. There must be something big going on at Hootanui in the mineral line.

Not long ago I removed a ewe from one of Peter Hill's traps not far from the house. The trap had no poison on the jaws, as is Peter Hill's usual custom. The poor ewe had two front legs caught. Today I recognised the same trap hanging on the fence near the house gate. I saw Peter and told him about it. Peter Hill reckons Roy Sullivan the Laverton grader driver, saw a live dingo walking along the road and that is why he set the trap where I found it with the unfortunate ewe. I don't believe Sullivan was telling the truth. There are no dingo tracks around Bandya homestead at all. The weather turned out warm again. It looks like more rain brewing by the look of the clouds. We still have a couple more loads of gear to shift yet. Eighty miles today.

Sunday 26 - Proceeded west to the Ten Mile. The reserve petrol tank is empty at mileage 3078. We went past Hootanui to have a look at Waterfall or Nganpa as it is known to Dooley. This time we found all the rockholes and waterholes full. Dooley of course knows the place from childhood days, but this is the first time I've seen it that way. It makes a beautiful picture. Red rocks, creek gums with stark white trunks topped by green foliage and the wider view backed by a cloud studded blue sky. The entire scene being repeated again in rippled reflections of the various pools. The equal of a Namatjira landscape, in the wilds of Western Australia, that is, it would be wilds if there weren't so many blasted nickel men running around it.

These nuisance prospectors have cutlines running every which way in the vicinity of Erlistoun Creek. This creek is full too. A veritable chain of water holes the entire length. Not to mention mosquitoes. I find the distance to Waterfall from our new spinifex camp, via the old Public Battery and Mulga Queen, is 37.7 miles. We had a bath, then ate dinner near the creek before returning to Ten Mile and pick up a load of gear. I filled both tanks at mileage 3127. A warm afternoon and looks like it might rain again. Flies are bad. Eighty-one miles today.

Monday 27 - We set off this morning and took some mileages from our new spinifex camp as follows:

NE to	Patapuka gnamma holes	8.8 miles	water present
NE "	Tjampan (Dumbung) soak	20 " "	dry
NE "	Miltji (Milgie) RH	24.2 " "	dry
NE "	Karu (Karo) soak	30.7 " "	water
NE "	Gregory Hills	50 " "	dry
Gregory Hills south to junction		11 " "	dry
Gregory Hills south to Gibson Hill		18.7 " "	dry

I had a bit of a look around Gibson Hill area east of the road and found a little dry gnamma hole on top of the breakaway at south side of an enclosed saltbush flat. This flat also has a small waterhole catchment near its open north end. The enclosure has low cliff walls around three sides, with numerous indigenous pine trees in the gullies. Not much sign of life at all. The place has a most funereal atmosphere. It fits the description of a campsite mentioned by Carnegie the explorer in his 1896 Journals, prior to his reaching the Ernest Giles Range.

Gregory Hills south to Point Pater RH 38 miles, rockhole full

We camped further south at 44.4 miles with a total for the day of Ninety-seven miles all told.

Tuesday 28 - Speedo 3249. I continue the list of mileages from the two windmills at Gregory Hills as follows:

Cosmo Newberry north boundary	48 miles
Cosmo Newberry settlement	55 " "

From Cosmo Newberry NW to:

Pinjarra windmill	4 miles
Turnoff to Jutson Rocks	17 " "
Blackboy Rocks	23 " "
Old shaft N of road	26 " "
Granite Sk N side	28 " "
Jutson Gov Well	30 " "

From Jutson Rocks I went north for ten and a half mile in search of Uhr Soak again. This time I located it on north side of Mount Cumming, over the range at southern head of a corktree creek running north. Boulders and rocks in the vicinity are remarkable for their rusty red colour, made richer by a tinge of black. First we came to a series of elongated slabs, set upright in prominent positions to either side of the creek and also along crests of ridges above the gully.

A large number of these upright slabs stand spread across the flat immediately in front of the soakage. This would be one of those rare occasions, that I have found such slabs first, before finding the water they point to. As a rule one finds the water catchment before even seeing any pointer slabs.

```
/I\
 G
D U
22/8/1
```

Two rocks, and one old of prospectors or this soakage in earlier

```
W.
FROST
94
J.
COOCH
```

cork tree close to the soak, bear the names explorers who obviously made good use of days.

The soak hole is evident as a circular depression in hard greyish coloured soil. It appears quite dry, with no promise of water near the surface, although a supply may rest at depth if dug for. I certainly did not feel energetic enough today to get the shovel and bar to work, just to try it out. The date under D U 22/8/1 is indistinct and could also be 22/8/4. Whether it represents the year 1901 or 1904 makes little difference now, over sixty years further down the track. There is also another mark of just the one letter, a big **W** by itself. I have no idea who that may be.

Also a government survey mark with broad
```
/I\
 T
 5
```
arrow.

Although non productive as an easy to get at water supply, I am still happy to find this elusive soakage site and its historical inscriptions. There is no indication of where it is, from southern side of the range. A person has to cross over the range first, then search the soakage out. Maybe in earlier days it was in regular use by native inhabitants of the country. No doubt fresh foot pads led into it from all directions. Back then, thirsty whitefellows had only to follow foot tracks to water.

We left Uhr Soak to its aridness and returned south to Jutson Soaks. Found one dead dog on an old kangaroo carcase I baited last time we camped here. We continued south along the old wheel track to Mount Shenton and thence via the old Warburton track to Uhr Rocks. Same Uhr but different locations.

I was now undecided whether to go south to Punjadda Soak, on account of threatening rain coming in from the north. It was spitting all the way from Jutson and the country down Punjadda way is that wandary type that is subject to boggy conditions after rain, not to mention several swamps to be crossed en route. After inspecting the place that I call Camel Saddle Soak and finding it full of good clean water, I decided to leave the Punjadda area alone for the time being. We proceeded instead back past Laverton, to camp about one mile north of town.

On the way through town we spent a couple of hours watching native girls in short skirts standing around outside the hotel, obviously waiting for whitefella pick-ups. The white men however seemed far more interested in drinking beer inside at the bar, than in those skinny black legs supporting the miniest of mini skirts out on the street. Most of the girls got sick of waiting and went home. We travelled one hundred and sixty-five miles all told.

Wednesday 29 - Speedo 3414. Misty rain still with us this morning, but forecast to clear away this afternoon. It has become quite warm again and not a bit like winter. We went back into Laverton about 9 am. The two stores and post office are busy with renovations.

Across the street an old stone building that looks like a former boarding house, is being painted and spruced up. The intention is to open it as a cafe, complete with juke box, to cater for the great influx of itinerants now in the country due to the nickel boom.

We went back to last night's camp for dinner, and took Dorothy with us as company for Dooley. Dorothy is Dooley's tribal sister. Coral and June followed us out too. After dinner Lumi and his wife turned up. They were on the way to town after the shearing cut-out at Erlistoun. They intend going on to Warburton for a holiday.

We took Dorothy back to town and finally left for our spinifex camp on Bandya around 3 pm. Water and bog all along the road to our spinifex camp after we passed Bandya. I'm glad we didn't go down to Punjadda and get stuck out that way. Oh yes, and we got a hunk of fresh beef from Peter Hill when we called in at the homestead, the first meat ever given us by him, what a shock that was. One hundred miles today.

Thursday 30 - Fine clear morning with heavy dew, and a low mist hanging over the spinifex. The scent of dampness on the air is something to tingle the nostrils. What a pleasant change this open spinifex scene is, in contrast to the confines of mulga scrubs back at the Ten Mile. A warm picture of tranquillity if ever there was. Clouds began to rise again this afternoon. I spent the entire morning on bookwork while Dooley rested. She is now heavy with child poor woman, and starting to feel her burden. She wishes to stop in town next week, as the off road travelling we do is much too rough and constant, and causes her great discomfort.

I know Dooley hates to leave me alone. She really loves me so. She is quite jealous too of all her dusky sisters and cousins, in both Laverton and Leonora. She asks me all the time lately not to play up when she goes to hospital for the baby. Of course I will not do that, because I love her more than anything in the world. Truly she is the one and only fullblood native woman I ever knew to show genuine love for her man. The fact she has this feeling for me is enough to make me true to her. Dooley and I have never been away from one another, even for one night, since we eloped in 1968. We are so compatible and we get on so well together, it will tear me apart to be away from her for the few weeks necessary for her to bear our child. I sometimes experience a horrible sense of foreboding that she might have trouble and something happen to her, but hope this is just normal human reaction to such things. Dooley has brought so much happiness to my life and been such a good mate over the past two years, I doubt I could bear to lose her. We have discussed such things together and she just laughs at my concerns. Maybe I am the real sentimental bloke. She says "Don't be like that Peter, I have plenty of sisters to take my place." Then in the next breath she says. "If anything ever happen to you Peter I won't ever have another man." This attitude and high moral ground, are entirely out of keeping with my previous knowledge of Aboriginal females, but then Dooley is a most unusual woman. She is of extremely high ethical and moral standard and most intelligent. If literate Dooley would be more than a match for any intellectual or academic.

I've been at bookwork all morning. It is now 2 pm in the afternoon. How time flies. We missed out on dinner today because I wished to let Dooley rest. She slept well and is just waking now so, enough of this sentiment, it's the last day of the month and time to have a feed.

Figure 14 A Doggers Camp

Chapter Fifteen - HOSPITAL ATTITUDE v. NUPTIAL AMPLITUDE

MAY 1970

Friday 1 - Mileage 3514. We still here at the new spinifex campsite. There was heavy rain all last night and overcast today. Dooley and I went for a long walk to the nearest sandhill this morning and found a mallee hen nest in a dense mulga thicket. The nest is old and abandoned but is a good sign that some of these rare birds may still live in this area.

We went back to camp and cooked the last of the beef Peter Hill gave us the other night. Looks like some big falls of rain to the north. On the RFDS session this morning Wongawol, Windidda, and Carnegie stations, all reported more than an inch. Bandya reported half an inch. Helicopters are out searching for two men north of Onslow. Big rains over there too as well as in the Gascoyne. This is an excellent wet weather camp. I'm glad we shifted out of that flood country around the Ten Mile. This spinifex marks the start of elevated country leading up to the De La Poer Range. It is quite noticeable after you pass through the north-east Bandya boundary. You can actually see the upward slope rising ahead as you drive along. The country falls away rapidly as you drive higher and higher up a long gradual rise. This long rise is a wide and open spinifex sandplain with an upward slant. It ends abruptly on the edge of a mulga thicket at the highest point of elevation.

Patapuka gnamma holes lie a bit beyond the highest point of the elevation just mentioned, these cylindrical holes are situated on a laterite gravel flat amidst mulga scrub. From where the spinifex rise and the mulga covered gravel flat begins, one can look back and enjoy a beautiful panoramic view of the falling country sweeping away to the western horizon. Most plateaus are marked by an abrupt line of breakaway cliffs. It is not usual to find a long gradual slope leading to an upland plateau with no rim, like this one does.

Weekend 2nd & 3rd. On Saturday I completed the April journals, reports and correspondence, ready for dispatch to the Kalgoorlie office. My notes state that I put in scalps of sixty-seven dogs for bonus payments so far to the end of April. I have sixteen still on hand not yet entered in the official journals. Nineteen of these went to the Leonora Vermin Board, the remainder to Laverton. Both boards say I have to date, caught more dogs than any previous dogger in either district. I wonder if they are kidding. I know that I do my best for the APB and that is the main thing.

Overcast all of today with a cold east wind, but no rain. On Sunday we decided to leave for Leonora as it looked like rain building up in the north. Onslow area is still suffering rain and floods. We travelled by way of Duketon. This track intersects the main Bandya road at Swanson government well twenty-two miles south of the old Duketon townsite. From spinifex camp to Laverton is eighty-two miles. Still a lot of surface water along the road in places but I managed to dodge around most of it and got through okay. No sign of life in Laverton at all. Not much to interest us in a deserted town. Dooley was born near Laverton, in Skull Creek, but apart from that has no love for the place at all, so we continued the seventy-four miles west to Leonora. Total mileage one hundred and fifty-six.

Monday 4 - Lots of changes in Leonora since our last trip to town. Two new buildings, one a dwelling, one an office in Tower Street. The cafe too, is now in larger premises. The old cafe is to house a re-opened National Bank Agency.

Our private Landrover has some water plug trouble in the engine block. I spent over a thousand dollars to get it reconditioned throughout, yet nothing but faults ever since. Vide the wheel hub with no oil problem I had some time back. I renewed Dooley's rifle license then put our Landrover into the garage for repair.

I took umbrage today at the large number of wangkayi stare-bears in the street. Anyone would think they never saw us before. I chatted several of them and they either put their heads down or turned to look the other way. I won't stand cheek from anyone, white or black. I never did and don't intend to start now.

The sky still wears a blanket of heavy overcast and it is really cold. The Leonora shire council will declare a large section of the town a first class residential area. All substandard dwellings and old buildings to be demolished.

Neil Johnson and his son ran into one another yesterday, the old man suffered a broken jaw. Our Landrover repairs were completed late this evening and I was able to take the vehicle home.

Tuesday 5 - It seems funny how the shire is to get tough on old houses only since I bought one. This town has been stagnant and full of dereliction for a generation. Oldtime residents had no such problems, yet soon after I appear on the scene they decide to demolish old houses. Well, they are going to have a battle on their hands if they think to push me out of the place.

When Bob Collard is not out bush on safari tours he fills in time as a painter and bush carpenter. I asked him today to have a look at some renovation and repair work on our stone house but he can't fit it in until he returns from an Alice Springs trip later this month.

Wednesday 6 - It rained all day and continued after dark. We lit a cosy wood fire in the big open fireplace then settled in for a wet night with rain pelting down on the tin roof, music for the ears as we unrolled our swag alongside the fire in readiness for a comfortable night.

I don't smoke but Dooley does, she rolls her own. We were having a quiet yarn in front of the cheery flames when Dooley's Log Cabin tobacco tin, resting on the cement floor in front of her, began to click. It was an eerie experience. We opened the tin once or twice to see if something inside was making the noise but it held only finecut tobacco and a packet of Tally Ho papers. There was no obvious reason we could find for the noise. The clicks continued at a regular beat. Click, click, click, went the tin. As time passed the clicks grew louder, **click, click, click.** As the clicks grew more vigorous the tin began to rattle up and down in the one spot on the floor. Not a high rise and fall, just a perceptible twitch up and down as it clicked. Both puzzled and perplexed we continued to speak in whispers as we watched the tin. It finally stopped after an hour or more had elapsed. What a strange experience it was and no explanation or even logical supposition other than a spectral source. I neither believe nor disbelieve the supernatural, although I have seen more evidence for than against, yet I remain an extremely materialistic person. I subscribe to no religious beliefs at all. On the other hand I am open to any intelligent clarification of things I don't understand. Dooley has no problem explaining her tobacco tin's extraordinary behaviour. She claims a korti (spirit) was responsible for the clicking noises. A message from the spirit world she said, so there Peter Muir!

Thursday 7 - Misty rain all day. Jack Kerr arrived from Kalgoorlie with what the APB refers to as stores. He left them with me, then set off on the return trip to Kalgoorlie almost immediately. Jack's address by the way is 69 Robert Street, handy to know in case I need to find him anytime. Before leaving he agreed it would be futile for me to return to the dogging area until after the country dries out. That's okay by me just so long as the pay check doesn't dry out.

Friday 8 - I was in the process of lighting the fire for breakfast this morning when Mark de Graaf surprised us with a sunrise visit. He is the last person I expected to see in Leonora. He and a companion named Bill somebody or other? We enjoy mutual interests in exploration, anthropology and anything historical, so had a long yarn before they departed for Wiluna about mid morning. He is strong in the belief that I should have my exploration records published. A proper book he said is better by far than to be content with just having them preserved on microfiche film at the State Library, as I have.

De Graaf says my achievements in the exploration field north of Wiluna deserve official recognition. While here, he made a short contact with the local wangkayi mob and arranged for a return visit to inspect ceremonial sites next summer before Xmas. During that proposed visit he says he'd like to accompany me through the G6 dogging area. Some more rain fell today but the clouds broke up and it was hot when the sun shone through the breaks in the afternoon.

Saturday 9 - I took Dooley to see the doctor today for prenatal checkup. To my utter astonishment he admitted her on the grounds she has a touch of sugar in the urine. Sometime after admission to the female ward they shifted her into the maternity wing. This was a bit of a puzzle as she is not due for another month yet.

I asked Bill Pense the local cop to hunt Frank Narrier out of town. I fear for Dooley's safety while he is around and she alone in a detached wing of the hospital. Pense runs this town like an American sheriff and he assured me it was no problem for him to shift Narrier, no trouble at all.

Dooley and I decided on alternative names for the coming baby. We decided that it will be Kado Rentan Muir if a boy, or Ruina Renette Muir if a girl. Dooley had her last monthly period around mid September 1969, or the end of that month, but we are not certain which. That would make the baby due around the 9th of June next. The due date would be around May the 25th if taken from the 15th of September. Dooley favours the mid June date and I agree. On a personal note I must mention how my parents gave me the staid Scottish names of Ronald Sibbald Muir when I was a babe and how when bigger, I detested all three of them. The names that is. As an adult I dropped the names Ronald and Sibbald in favour of only the one first name of Peter. This was an official change by deed poll to make it legal. I dislike the name Muir too, but retained it in order to preserve my ancestry. I considered that an alternative surname is only an alias that has no substance behind it. With strong personal feelings about inapt names and my own experience in mind, I decided years ago that if I ever had a son, not to saddle him with a burden similar to my own. Furthermore, I would defy convention and give a son of mine something befitting the space age in which we now live. I came up with the name KADO after prolonged and careful musings.

Dooley is unhappy about her involuntary hospitalisation and has no wish to stay in. I too am reluctant to see her remain without any apparent good reason, however we are as yet undecided about defying the doctor's orders. There was a good picture on at the drive-in tonight so we just took the bull by the horns and went off to see the show without asking permission. She was back in hospital around midnight to a lonely and empty maternity ward without as much as one duty nurse in sight. I hated to leave her there but she said it was alright, she'd put up with it.

Sunday 10 - I spent all day visiting Dooley in hospital and we both got into a row with the nurses for taking her away to the pictures last night before 7-30 pm. We don't know the implications of that time factor or why they got upset about it, but that is what they said. Dooley feels much better now. More rain coming with summer type clouds and a nice warm day.

Monday 11 - It turned out cold last night but is not too bad this morning. I'm doing okay during Dooley's absence. I had a good breakfast of bacon and eggs after rising before daylight to light the fire. It is too lonely without my mate and we hope she will be out today.

I went to the hospital to visit Dooley and find out but got jarred by the doctor and the matron for visiting outside the set hours. The only words I can think of in response is, **inconsiderate mongrels,** but I let it slide without comment. Came back to town and put UQD-634 in for 2000 mile service and maintenance. The vehicle has no faults and I took it home again when they finished. A warm fine day and the doctor took a blood sample from Dooley.

Tuesday 12 - I purchased a load of stores from Elders then off to the hospital. I asked the doctor for a report on Dooley's progress and he gave a most favourable one. The sugar all gone from her blood but still a bit loaded with protein so she has to go light on eating meat and such foods until after the baby is born. Doctor wishes to keep her in hospital a bit longer so after visiting her I decided to attempt a bush trip and do the trap run.

I went across to Laverton and filled up with petrol then proceeded north. After leaving Lancefield behind there was a great deal of water along the road and the country still boggy. I reckoned it useless to enter the open country, as much of it must still be under water. I returned from Laverton Downs and came back to Leonora to wait for the country to dry out. Proper summer type rain clouds today including a lot of willy willies. Two hundred and thirty-two miles travel.

Wednesday 13 - The doctor refused to let Dooley come out before Saturday. He also refused to allow me to see her outside visiting hours. These are only from three to four o'clock in the afternoon, and seven to nine o'clock of an evening. This time I vent my spleen and pointed out that I am being singled for treatment not meted out to others. I am being victimised. I reminded him there are no restrictions on natives visiting their relatives at the Leonora hospital. Such visitors come and go at will, all day long. I suggested his objection to myself might have something to do with my white skin, since they say to get going the moment one of the sisters see me anywhere near Dooley. The doctor was at a loss for an answer. He held his chin for a while then said he would henceforth insist on regular hours for all visitors, black or white. Furthermore he said that if I took Dooley away before discharge he would wipe his hands of her. He requested that we both sign a paper stating that we take all responsibility for her early release.

Dooley and I discussed the ramifications of what the doctor said and came to the conclusion there is no real reason for her being in hospital at all. She insists she receives no treatment at night whatsoever. She could easily stay home where I can look after her and report to hospital each day. The attitude of doctor and nursing staff seems aimed at splitting Dooley and me apart for a longer period than necessary. She feels fine, but being kept alone in an isolated six bed maternity ward is not only too lonely for her, she also feels frightened at night. She says the nursing staff did not visit her even once during the night while I was away out bush, yet when I am in town and visiting, they are up and down like blowflies just to see if I'm still there. Anyhow, after the argument with Doctor Rowe I defied him and went right ahead to visit Dooley and discuss all this with her. Afterwards I went off and put our private Landrover in the garage for more attention. I visited Dooley after dinner and again at 6-30 pm.

We asked the duty sister's permission for Dooley to go to the pictures but she refused. She says Dooley forfeited all privileges for going away too early for the pictures last week. Dooley says she received no treatment of any kind all day and she felt fine, so I told her to get dressed and we would go regardless. The doctor and staff are in our opinion, trying to detain her and prevent me visiting for some strange reason. I know they don't like the way I stand up and answer back in response to their arrogance. They want me to be meek and mild and behave like a good little boy. I cannot help thinking it may be racial prejudice on their part. An objection to our mixed race match. White on black and all that sort of rubbish. This is not paranoia on my part. The blacks still enjoy unrestricted access to their relatives, including Dooley, yet I am treated as persona non grata. One old bitch of a sister told me to stop haunting the place after telling one of the nurses, "Oh, here's that blooming Peter again, he should dip his head in the bread." It all makes me wonder, is it a hospital they are running, or a bloody penal institution, anyway, Dooley has just walked off, so bugger the lot of them. I'm taking her home and hang the consequences, if any. I wrote these bitter notes while waiting for her to dress and get her things.

Thursday 14 - Vera Bond, a niece of Dooley's, offered to look after her aunt while I make another attempt to do the trap run. Dooley is okay, nothing wrong with her at all, so I left for Laverton after dinner then north to the caravan without any trouble, reaching it just after dark. The country is much drier now. I had a mug of Milo and a packet of biscuits then travelled north-east inspecting traps along the Karu Soak road. The traps were all sprung from rain. No sign of dogs but I reset all the traps anyway. A lot of heavy rain fell out here. The ground is still wet. Moxon Creek is still running over the road at Karu crossing, it ran full width when the rains were on. All the waterholes are brimful now. The road itself is okay but boggy to either side.

I continued north-east past the turnoff to Earli Earli to find the spinifex country through there is heavy travelling and wet. Not far ahead the road itself became so soggy that I nearly went down. I just managed to reverse out of it in time, a good indication that the country further north toward Warren's Well might be impossible to get through. I abandoned the trip and turned back to the caravan, packed up, and took the van in tow. Proceeded south with it along the Duketon road. Halfway to Swansons the over-width caravan collected a dead tree branch. The stick pierced the van right through, knocking the sink and cupboard drawers out completely. What a mishap! Another branch holed the ceiling in two places. This accident occurred at 11-30 pm. Our $2500.00 caravan is no longer a nearly new luxury de luxe model. It is now a badly damaged second hand one worth $100.00 at the most.

Midnight Thursday saw me still on the road travelling into a new day. I passed through Laverton about 2 am. During the next hour three vehicles passed me coming from Leonora. I forgot to mention that the only sign of life in Laverton was at the hospital where every light was on. About eighteen miles out of Leonora I suffered a fuel blockage. It was too dark to do anything as I had no torch. Early morning chill was on the air, the cold intense and I had to wait until daylight to fix the blockage.

I arrived home in Leonora at 6-30 am. I sat in the vehicle to hear the Kalgoorlie Regional News bulletin. Dooley heard the engine stop when I pulled in near the house but didn't come out until certain it was me. She didn't expect me back so soon and was cautious in case it might be some drunken nickel man looking for a woman. The round trip took four hundred and six miles of day and night travel.

Friday 15 - I patched up the caravan damage as best I could with adhesive tape and white paint. It wasn't a perfect job but at least the interior looks normal again. Before the patch job it looked like bomb damage. The holes outside I covered with a sheet of aluminium plate. I will try and have a tradesman do a proper job on it at the first opportunity. After dinner I caught up on lost sleep for a couple of hours. Later on, Mick Healy the builder came around and gave me a quote of $335.00 to fit a new roof on our Leonora house. I suggested a flat roof rather than a duplicate of the original huge gable structure that is on the house now. The whole roof still lifts up and down like a parachute every time the wind blows. Although a bit unsightly and not in keeping with the building's architecture, I reckon a flat roof is much less susceptible to wind.

The weekend was dull with little to report. Dooley was sick and irritable all Sunday night but much better on Monday. Tuesday I filled all fuel tanks on our private Landrover. Wednesday I received an "AUTHORITY" card signed by Dick Tomlinson the APB chief executive officer. This innovation is Tomlinson's personal response to complaints by some doggers of being challenged when on pastoral properties. I don't have this problem but apparently others do. Some time ago I asked the Battye Library for photocopies of LAW Wells 1892 Journals and they arrived in the mail today too, so I can look forward to a good read about country I know, as well as some I don't.

Thursday 21 - Dooley says she'll stay with her niece while I go out bush next week. Wulapa or Ruby Grey to use her whitefella name, is Ken Miller's wife. Ken was the one I had a row with over his threat to use a gun against me at the Laverton pub some time ago. Wulapa was central to that argument so I don't fancy the idea of Dooley staying with her even if Ken Miller is away. Sullivan's $100.00 account for repairs to our Landrover was in the mail today. There is a sideshow in town for the races this coming weekend. On Saturday we went to the races. On Sunday I got ready for the bush. On Monday we departed for Laverton. Dooley decided not to stay behind after all, she likes to be with me, I like to have her along too, so along she came.

Tuesday 26 - The northern trap run is much too long to take Dooley in her condition so I left her at Mervyn Sullivan's place in Laverton until I return. I got a real early start at 3 am. Travelled north past Bandya then via Urarey to Tharukati for breakfast at daylight. A hundred mile trip. Got one scalp from the first trap, the next one near Paiyari further north was missing. I couldn't track it up. A lot of rain fell here and washed out all the tracks. The same thing happened at Kurumin. On to Warren's Well then south along the beef road to Nyiruru turnoff. A trap gone from there too. A big flood washed it away and the ground too boggy to pass, so came back to the beef road and travel south-west to Karu where was one dog in trap.

No more sign of dogs anywhere after that so returned to Laverton, arriving at 2 pm. Eleven hours to do over three hundred miles. Dooley in good spirits. She had Dorothy keep her company while I was away. I refuelled and started off for the bush again late in the afternoon. This time with Dooley, who insisted that Dorothy come along too and camp with us for a couple of days.

Wednesday 27 - Inspected a lot of Laverton Downs country but saw no sign of dogs. Came on as far as Ivor Rocks then return to Hammer Hill where I shot a euro for supper. We made camp near the waterhole. On Thursday we went back to Laverton to drop Dorothy off then Dooley and I carried on north past Lancefield to camp.

Friday 29 - Pondering over events of the last two days brings me to record a few salient points that I failed to record earlier. First off Dorothy was good. Dooley got on well with her all day Wednesday, but during the night got jealous of me although she had no reason to be so. Dooley kept nudging me in the ribs and telling me to sleep with Dorothy on her side of the swag that we three shared. When I didn't respond to this persuasion Dooley got up and walked off into the night leaving me behind with her tribal sister. About ten minutes later a fresh-lit fire broke the darkness about a hundred paces away and Dooley stood beside it until the flames died. She eventually came back and asked did I have a good time to which I answered no, nothing happened. Dooley didn't want to believe it. As a result I got little sleep while Dooley walked around the camp in the dark all night threatening to walk into Laverton and leave me alone with Dorothy. At one sage she stopped a passing motorist who proved to be the station manager of Laverton Downs coming back late from his windmill run. She asked him for a lift into town but he refused. Now I suppose he thinks we were on the grog at Hammer Hill although we had none. If Dooley continues this sort of behaviour I'll be getting a bad name. Anyway she got over her pique after a while, had a long talk with Dorothy before daylight, and they were soon okay again. We went back to Leonora.

Saturday 30 - Rain fell in Leonora all day. Widespread falls reported from all over the State. It is just as well we did come back. I wouldn't like to get bogged out bush and unable to return with Dooley when her time arrives. It looks like dogging operations will be in suspense for a long time too. The open country is still water-logged from the last rain.

Sunday 31 - A terrific storm came over Leonora last night. Wind blew the roof off our garage. Several other properties around town also suffered damage. This event prompted me to write the Insurance Company about damage to our caravan on the 15th. EMBANK INSURANCE BROKERS Capital House 10 William Street Perth. I also did some work on the APB journals and reports. All roads closed over a wide area in the north.

Figure 16 Kado makes Three

Figure 15 Dooley and Kado at Gnamma hole N of Ingitjingi

Chapter Sixteen - AND KADO MAKES THREE

JUNE 1970

Monday 1 - Dooley carried on about Dorothy all night again. I got no sleep. Every time I dozed off she'd wake me with that regular low drone of quiet reprimand so characteristic of Aboriginal women who wish to chastise their husbands. She kept at it until daylight. I don't know why she is so jealous. It was her idea to get one of her sisters for company in the first place. She is the one who coaxed me to ask Dorothy to live with us and as that sort of situation accords with native custom I took it in good faith. Now it seems Dooley doesn't want another female for company, which suits me fine as I don't want a second mouth to feed anyway. Somehow I think the whole thing has to do with her pregnant condition and imminent birthing. I make a lot of allowance for her and try never to get angry. Really we enjoy excellent relations despite these minor upsets. Maybe she is just trying me out before she goes to hospital.

Mick Healy came along today and says he'll start on the new roof when building material arrives on the train. I brought the APB bookwork up to date today ready to post. Rain clouds still hanging about. On Tuesday I cleaned up around the camp and on Wednesday put the government Landrover in the garage for a 4000 mile service and took delivery of it again in the afternoon. One of Dooley's nephews name of Kenny Hennessey escaped from the police lockup.

Thursday 4 - We heard that Kenny gave himself up again last night. Paid my $100.00 Sullivan account by cheque. Wrote another cheque together with order to post away for John Forrest's book "Explorations In Australia" then later in the afternoon gave the APB vehicle a thorough clean.

Friday 5 - Jack Kerr sent APB stores from Kalgoorlie with Karl Srb. Jack not coming to Leonora this month. Keith Biggs offered to buy our old stone house that we bought off his dad. I said he could have it for $4000.00. He just laughed and walked off. I've no idea what he wants the place for, possible speculation maybe, anyway time will tell. Today is THE BIG DAY for lifting the current pegging ban on all crown land. The ABC will broadcast the new mining regulations at noon. The main change when announced seems to be an increase in the minimum height of corner pegs from four feet to six. The length of trenches likewise will increase from four to six, plus the placing of boundary markers not less than fifteen chains apart.

Saturday 6 - Dooley is now heavy with child. I hope she delivers soon as the burden is knocking her about too much. I took her to hospital for a prenatal checkup. She is okay. One of Dooley's nieces Mabel MacArthur brought her new whitefella kuri along for us to have a look at today. He is a New Australian. We had dinner at Adeline's place and in the evening went to the Drive-In. Monday saw Mick Healy pulling the old roof off at last. His quote is now $360.00. After dinner we went across to Laverton to get out of the builder's way.

Tuesday 9 - We went out to look over the fabulous Poseidon prospect at Windarra north-west of Laverton. Then back via Lancefield in search of a kangaroo for meat but saw none. The only roos left in the country are around the town where it's not safe to shoot. I rang Jack Kerr's office in Kalgoorlie. They say he'll be away for a week but his actual whereabouts they don't know. Dooley had a feeling that her time is close so we set off immediately for the outskirts of Leonora and camped about ten miles north of town west of a grid on the Nambi Road. This area is notable for a sort of magenta coloured soil of fine gravel that makes a good soft camp. I made a brush shelter for the night behind a patch of low scrub to keep Dooley comfortable and warm. Around midnight she had her first labour pangs. I left our camp gear where it was and took her straight into hospital. They admitted her to maternity at midnight. Nothing for me to do but wait, so I went home to sleep in the caravan beside the now roofless town house.

Wednesday 10 - Rang the hospital early this morning. Dooley comfortable. Baby son arrived at 5 am. I visited her and she agreed that I should not hang around in town but go and do some work for the APB while she and baby are in hospital care. Before leaving for the bush I paid Mick Healy for the roof job, then went out to pick up the gear we left behind on camp last night. Continued to Laverton via Nambi to refuel then travel east to Uhr Rocks where I arrived to the tune of a flat tyre around 10 pm. It was a bitter cold night. I rigged a lean-to shelter to reflect the fire like Dooley always does with the APB tent, then settled down for the night. For company I had a half bottle of rum bought on the way through Laverton. Dooley's idea of tent rigging is as follows:

Lay a calico tent lengthwise on the ground. Pull a light rope through the two ridge holes. Leave the material double. Tie the rope ends to a pair of leaning trees the right distance apart then pull the rope tight. Push the bottom of the hanging fabric back far enough to make room for a sleeping space. Unroll the swag then tuck the bottom tent material in under it along the far side as well as head and foot ends. The weight of the swag keeps the bottom of the tent secure against any wind that might blow during the night. A few bushes placed behind also helps hold it together. The result is a canopy above the sleeper with one side open, facing toward a fire in front. The fire is best if placed central to the opening at a safe distance from the blankets and there you have it, the cosiest camp imaginable, after only ten minutes work. This type of shelter will keep the heaviest frost at bay, or the interior free of the wettest dew. It is not a perfect wet weather shelter, but it can nevertheless, withstand a light drizzle. Essentially it is a cold weather camp. An orthodox tent requires far too much work for a one night camp. Too many poles and stakes to cut and holes to dig for my liking. That is why I never used a tent until I saw Dooley's method and that I like, it is a great idea. A compromise between conventional tent and traditional native brush shelter.

Thursday 11 - It was a bitter cold night but lovely and warm inside the lean-to shelter. This is the first night I've spent alone in the bush for many years, I've always had my mate with me before. Kado Rentan has messed the routine up a bit I'm afraid. After a leisurely breakfast at the granites, I changed the flat tyre and set off again, this time east across country to Punjadda Soak. A couple of dead dingoes from baits were there but nothing of them left to scalp so I took the bare skulls. Fresh tracks of two more dogs are still there. No game has been near the soaks at all recently so there must be a lot of surface water about the country yet. I found another soakage three quarters of a mile east of Punjadda situated in the middle of a clear open flat with a stand of several corktrees growing close to the soakage. I later returned to the outskirts of Laverton and camped following a ninety mile day. Light rain fell after dark.

Friday 12 - Got up early and travel twenty-two miles north-east along the Cosmo road to Deepa Rockhole. There is a rockhole name of Wanda I want to find. On the maps it is situated three to four miles east of Deepa in some breakaway country. I turned off in that direction and found a rockhole in the approximate position marked by a survey peg **FY 53**. The distance doesn't coincide with the map. I came six miles along a wider route and reached this rockhole from the east, while travelling west up a small creek running off east side of the breakaways. These breakaways are I think, the Adam Range.

From the Adam Range rockhole I went six miles north-east to hit an old derelict windmill on the Cosmo road and from there it was four and a half mile south-west back to Deepa Rockhole. Saw one old dog track near the granites north of Wanda. Ten miles past Deepa on the Laverton side, I turned south-east off the road. Passed a large granite outcrop at one mile, and at six miles came to a windmill. At twelve miles further on is another mill on the White Cliffs road. From there it was seventeen miles back to Laverton.

Back in Laverton I refuelled first, then spent some time in town. It is not the same in the bush without Dooley. Travelled back toward Leonora and met a mob of natives camped near the road just short of the mission turnoff. Papulo was with them. They are on ceremonial business and say they walked nearly all the way from Warburton after their truck broke down miles from anywhere. I went on after that and camped near Mount Morgan. One hundred and eighteen miles.

Saturday 13 - Came on in to Leonora. Went to visit Dooley and Kado in hospital. They both well but have to stay in for a while yet. I went to the pictures by myself this evening. On Sunday I cleaned out the house. This diary is starting to read like some sort of domestic routine instead of a dogger's daily journal. Things should change soon when Dooley leaves hospital and I have my little family together out bush with me. I have got so accustomed to having Dooley with me all the time day and night, that I just don't seem to be able to settle down by myself out bush anymore. It feels strange when she is not present in the passenger seat alongside me. It is too lonely in the bush for a sane man these days and I certainly don't want to finish up being a hatter like most lone bushmen do.

Monday 15 - The beads on some of these new tyres are impossible to get off with ordinary levers. I put a difficult one into the garage for repair today. Although I usually manage to do all my own repairs I had to give this one best. Dooley is okay but baby Kado has to stay in hospital a while longer.

Tuesday 16 - Cold windy morning. It looks as if winter is here. It was too cold in the caravan last night. I had to sleep beside the open fireplace inside the house. Dooley and baby came out of hospital today. Dooley's niece Veronica arrived from Wiluna to stay a few days too. I fixed up all the official documents dealing with Kado's birth and paid Sullivan for yesterday's tyre repairs.

Wednesday 17 - Took Veronica out to Nambi to pick up some gear she left behind last time she worked there. Returned to Leonora and had dinner, then left for Laverton. I can't seem to take a trick lately. It rained all night in Laverton. How in hell can I take a newborn babe out bush in that sort of weather? I can't leave this dogging job it is the only work I like and I've tried everything. On Thursday morning we went back to Leonora for the caravan. No good taking Kado out bush with no protection from the wet weather. Came back with it to Laverton and camp there overnight. Roy Sullivan, his wife, and Sandra paid us a visit, he gave us some fresh kangaroo meat. The first we've had in a long time.

Friday 19 - Gone north with the caravan in tow, back to the spinifex camp north-east of Red Well. It was a slow trip and took all day to get there. Nickel men's tracks everywhere along the Karu Soak road. I wish they would all go away and leave the bush alone. This time I shifted the caravan further back behind the thicket to keep it out of sight from the road.

Saturday 20 - We had a washing day. The caravan was still visible from the road. It shows up like a beacon above the tree line. After filling the water tank at Red Well and inspecting country north-east to the boundary gate, I came back and shifted camp again. This time we found a god site half a mile north behind a big thicket of taller trees. I don't think anyone will see the caravan now. One nickel man passed by today.

Sunday 21 - Time to start work again. Travelled north-east and saw nothing but nickel men's tracks up and down the road. Set two traps at Tjampan and reset two at Karu. Got one dog from traps in the lakes plus two foxes. Set one additional trap, making four at that site now. On to Nyiruru where was one dog in trap. Reset the trap then continued on to the burnt country. Skinned a kangaroo we shot back at the lakes, took what we need for meat and used the rest for bait material. We camped near the first sandhill west of Nyiruru. It was well after dark by the time we pulled up and finished all the camp chores. There was a beautiful salmon pink sunset. It gets dark around 5-30 pm now. We are camping on the ground with a good half tent for shelter that reflects the fire's heat much better than a conventional brush windbreak. I feel great now after a good day's work and happy to be on the job again, after all the anxiety over Dooley and Kado these past five or six weeks. I hope there are no more holdups.

Monday 22 - A good comfortable night. Baby doing fine after his first night in the bush. We went north to Warren's Well then west to Kurumin where, after another good look around I found the trap I couldn't find last trip. From Kurumin we continued on to Wakulyakutjarra where I set two traps, then south past Jerry's Well. No sign of dogs. Further south was a fox in trap near Tjilpitjarra. Tracks of a nickel man with motorbike at Tjilpitjarra show how he swung around in a circle and deliberately ran over the trap bending it beyond repair. From there we returned to the caravan after a long day's run of one hundred and four miles. Kado has to go back to hospital tomorrow for inspection and weighing to ensure he is okay. He is such a small baby. We commenced the return journey to Leonora in my own time, during the evening hours, to arrive Leonora about 11 pm. Two hundred and sixty-four miles all told.

Tuesday 23 - Just for a change of dealers I got a drum of fuel from AMPOL this time. Took Kado and Dooley to hospital for the checkup and they okay. Loaded our stores then proceeded east to Laverton and put fourteen dogs scalps in to the Shire Office. Cheque in payment to be posted to Leonora later, as per usual. Came back to the caravan at spinifex camp, arrive 6-30 pm. Rain approaching. Big falls reported in the south. One hundred and seventy-one miles.

Thursday 25 - Stayed on camp all of yesterday. Travel north-east along Karu road this morning and set two traps near Miltji, two more on Lake Wells and two additional traps at Gregory Hills. One dried dog carcase in a trap I'd set there before. I now have twenty-two traps set out in the G6 Area.

Prospectors have been busy pegging all over the Ullrich Range. It seems a shame to see such frenzied activity out here. The prospectors are not here now though, they departed and left their mess behind. Dingoes are on the move. There are fresh tracks everywhere. We came back to Karu Soak. We picked a good camp near the edge of spinifex on south side of the creek. Eighty-two miles.

Friday 26 - Heavy dew last night. The cliffs of an unnamed range south-east of Karu in untracked country, stand out well this morning. It is strange how distant features seem to rise above the horizon during winter months. There is a likely looking place for a rockhole on a bearing of 160^0 by the compass. The rest looks uninviting with scrub cover all over. I would like to traverse the intervening ten or twelve miles and explore the area but Dooley is not up to such rough travel yet, also, she is not making enough milk for the baby so I'll have to forego exploration for the time being.

After breakfast I walked half a mile to a waterhole down Moxon Creek to fetch two buckets of water for washing. Just to have a look, I walked another half mile on the compass bearing taken earlier of the cliffs. I wanted to see if it might be okay to take a traverse toward them, but as anticipated, the spinifex is much too rough for Dooley to travel over in her present condition. We continued south and found a trap at Tjampan with a euro in it. Reset the trap and baited the carcase. Had a look around in the spinifex for emu eggs south of Patapuka but found none. Seem to be a lot of negativity in the air lately, our luck might change soon I hope.

Saturday 27 - Proceed north-west to Jerry's Well. Set one trap at Tjilpitjarra near some fresh dog scratches. From Jerry's Well I turned west to take some mileages and compass bearings to plot the back track to Paiyari. Commence at speedo reading 6603.

W	4 miles	
SW	5 " "	
NW	3 " "	reach hill with clayhole to west
SW	2 " "	saltbush flat with low breakaway
S	13 " "	turnoff west to dry breakaways
S	6 " "	limestone blows
S	6 " "	a sharp bend in road
SE then E	3 " "	a big rockhole called Paiyari
W	1 " "	to Mulga Queen road running south
SW	4 " "	turnoff west to Seven Sisters gnamma holes

That job done we returned via Mulga Queen east past Red Well, then north-east to the caravan and camp. Rain cleared away last night. One hundred and forty miles travel today.

Sunday 28 - A heavy fog this morning. Dooley still not fully recovered but feels much better now than she did. She should not have walked so far looking for emu eggs last Friday. She was quite weak when she got back to the Landrover and sorry she didn't take heed of my advice not to walk like that. I'm afraid the lure of emu eggs was too great for her to resist. The fog cleared away around nine o'clock. It turned out a lovely day. We stayed on camp. Big riots in Northern Ireland. On Monday we stayed on camp again. I did some research into Giles' and Michael Terry's journals, where they travelled through the Warburton Range area. We came into Leonora to end the month on Tuesday the 30th. One hundred and sixty-two miles.

Chapter Seventeen - A RANGE OF DRAGS & TRACKS SO STRANGE

JULY 1970

Wednesday 1 - The first day of July saw Dooley and Kado checked out as okay at the hospital. On Thursday I put UQD-634 into the garage for service and repairs. They tuned the motor and it seems to be running much better now. Later I got in touch with Jack Kerr by phone to Kalgoorlie and told him the clutch is beginning to pack up at only 6000 miles. He will come through this way around dinnertime tomorrow. Karl Srb delivered APB stores: tyres, tubes, poison, traps, and bullets, left for me by Jack last time he was in Leonora. I missed him then because I was out bush.

I opened the John Forrest's book "Explorations In Australia" today. I hadn't time to do so before. SA State Library receipt for my payment in the package, dated 10/7/70 same day Kado was born.

Friday 3 - I spent time cleaning the government vehicle while waiting for Jack Kerr to arrive. He didn't get here till two o'clock in the afternoon and didn't stay long. We did however have time to discuss various aspects of the G6 Control Area regarding wild dog movements and the possibility of additional access tracks. He is on the way to Sandstone for a Vermin Board meeting and to see that unpredictable man Basil Atkins. Basil is a former APB man (never to be re-employed by that department) but is now private dogger for a group of stations centred on Depot Springs and Kaluwiri. Jack wants to have a yarn with him. There are also two new Group Doggers employed by the APB in the Wiluna area. One based on Lorna Glen to the north-east, the other at Albion Downs in the south-west. Jack seems quite satisfied with everything. He is happy with my work and the fourteen dogs caught last month. He is also aware of the numerous setbacks I had, of domestic and official natures. I informed him That I had two drum butts containing twenty gallons of petrol each, stolen by nickel men in Laverton. He agreed that I purchase all future drum requirements in Leonora as the safest option.

Saturday 4 - I spent most of today loading the Landrover ready for departure tomorrow or Monday. We heard in town that some natives discovered a gold reef near Hootanui not long ago. Strange we never saw any sign of them. We got going on Sunday and travelled one hundred and seventy-eight miles from Leonora to the caravan. A lot of motor tracks up and down past our camp turnoff.

Monday 6 - A white frost this morning froze everything stiff outside, while inside the caravan everything was soaking as though by rain. Water vapour from our breathing inside the van condensed on the ceiling and fell in large droplets after sunrise. Damned stuff wet all the maps I left out on the kitchen table last night and our blankets are wringing wet. This is a new experience for me.

I never had anything to do with caravans before, but always thought them ideal protection from weather. Now it seems I made a mistake. An interior rainfall is the only way I can describe it. Looks like we'd be better off in a native wurlie. Maybe a gas heater might solve the problem. Anyway this is not good for the baby so I'll have to find a solution. Jack Kerr's mention of new access tracks prompted me to action. At the north-east boundary gate is the 'drag' with which someone cut the track to Gregory Hills. A good drag pulled over virgin country, cuts a track similar in appearance to a graded road. My first experience with drags was in the NT on Helen

Springs Station. There in earlier times, donkey teams pulled a heavy iron blade to cut tracks and firebreaks over the wide expanse of grass plains. Over there they call the thing a fire plough. Here in WA they call the same thing a drag. Donkey, horse, camel, bullock, or whatever type of animal team used, the same heavy iron drag can hitch on behind a motor vehicle and that is the method used here on Bandya.

Today I hitched on to the drag at the boundary gate and cut a traverse over virgin spinifex country due east from the gate for a distance of twelve heavy miles. Where the sand was soft and the spinifex thick, the vehicle laboured, but most of the way it purred along in low range without much trouble. The route was over sand and spinifex with small sandhills to either side the entire distance. Other vegetation being small wattles and desert gums. We came level with two little limestone outcrops and small thickets of low mulga at seven miles. A pad running from north to south at the seven mile point led straight toward one of the mulga thickets. Tracks of kangaroos, camels and emus on the pad indicated that it must lead to water.

At ten miles the breakaways near Miltji Rockhole became visible in the north. The scrub-clad line of an unnamed range midway between my starting point and the high point known as Gibson Hill, appears to be about six or seven miles further east of the twelve mile point. On the other hand it could be nothing more than a scrubby rise or sandhill. The range I'm making for is however on the map at about the place estimated above. The drag bogged down in a stretch of soft sand and was difficult to extricate. The engine began to overheat. The radiator boiled, so I unhooked the drag for the day and returned to camp for the night. No good camps out there anyway only spinifex, and firewood is scarce.

Saw a porcupine track where we left the drag. The drag is not as good as I'd like but at least it leaves a distinct mark to follow and in that respect is much better than faint wheel tracks alone. I wish to establish a distinct track into this area as no motor vehicles have been here before. There are about sixteen hundred square miles of untraversed spinifex country in this section. It is not a remote area in the real sense, as it sits just outside the station boundaries of Bandya on this side, and Cosmo Newberry to the south. The perimeter of the area has the Prenti Downs beef road skirting it on the east side and the Bandya to Gregory Hills track on the west. The main attraction for me is this unnamed range in the middle, that is what entices me. My proposed access track will cut the whole area in two from west to east. It was a long interesting day but only thirty miles travel.

Tuesday 7 - Mileage on the Landrover is now 7056. This morning we returned to the drag getting there by 11 am. I hooked up and did another five mile east by half past midday. We pulled up for dinner beside a small clump of low mulga bushes where was one fresh dog track. The unnamed range is still not visible ahead. The high ground I saw yesterday was only a rise in ground level. However after dinner we got a shock to reach hard ground and hills only half a mile from dinner camp. The intervening rise and mulga thicket behind which we sheltered, hid this change of country from view. I had to find a way to negotiate a three foot rock ledge at base of this hard country where it meets the sand. The drag here was quite an encumbrance but I managed to get it up and over after a bit of manhandling. It was a comparative easy pull for the next two miles up a gradual slope. Travel was over hard flats of red laterite gravel leading upward to the rim of sheer cliffs facing east along that side of the range.

These cliffs were too steep to descend so I turned north in search of a way out It was here where I turned north that the drag gave up the ghost. It more or less fell to pieces. I abandoned it as useless. I continued north with vehicle alone, parallel with the escarpment for two miles, then east down a broken gully that allowed passage, although an extremely rough one, to lower ground below the cliffs. Here we entered a dense wash thicket for one mile, then open spinifex for six miles. Limestone flats then for another mile, after which the way led through thicket country, with an underlay of scraggly spinifex. We came out into the open on the Cosmo road about two miles south of Point Gibson. This was twenty miles due east of our starting point in the spinifex west of the range this morning.

Once on the graded road, I drove north ten miles past Point Gibson to where another old drag lay beside the road just as left there by someone years ago. I examined it and hooked it onto the vehicle to try it out for a short distance. Satisfied that it might hold together for a bit more work, I unhooked it and left it there for the time being. I may use it later to go back over our track this side of the range. We went on a couple more miles north to camp in some saltbush country south of Gregory Hills. By this time it was dark.

In retrospect I feel certain that water exists in the range we came over today. A great number of game pads running north and south cut across our path about halfway up the laterite slope, not long before we abandoned the broken drag. I will follow the pads first chance I get but for the present must concentrate on the new road. We only did fifty-one miles today.

Wednesday 8 - I hooked onto the second drag this morning and pulled it twelve miles south along the Cosmo road to where we emerged from the bush yesterday. Dragged five miles of track and found the limestone wash we saw yesterday west of the range, is four miles east of the Cosmo road. The wash offered such level running I turned along it south-west for one mile to reach the point where we struck it yesterday. We halted at that point for dinner then afterwards I did a run back over the morning's drag mark at 15 mph. The first cut was a 5 mph job, so the drag makes a lot of difference.

I decided to give the drag a rest for a while and left it beside the road to travel north and do a bit of dog control work. Set a trap at Point Gibson along the way and later got two male dogs from traps at Gregory Hills. Lots of tracks made by nickel men running up and down past the two windmills. There was one female dog in trap west of Irve's Grave, one female at Karu Soak, and a dead cat nearby. Came on south to Miltji where I shot a euro, then camped.

It is just forty-five miles from the new track turnoff south of Point Gibson, around the road to Miltji here, via Gregory Hills. Baby Kado is playing up, he has had no bowel movements for two days now, although he seems well enough. If there is no change in his condition by tonight then we'll take him to hospital to see what's wrong. Did seventy-three miles today.

Thursday 9 - One female dog on bait near Miltji and one in trap a bit to the south. At Tjampan was another kangaroo in trap. I poisoned the carcase and removed the trap from the area. Only kangaroos seem to get caught there. A fox in the second trap. I've never caught a dog at Tjampan yet. They don't seem to favour the place. From Tjampan we came back to the caravan where I completed the APB journals and log book for the month of June then set off toward Laverton to camp north of town. One hundred and six miles.

Friday 10 - We took Kado to hospital where the matron told us that it is quite normal for a breast fed baby to go as long as a full week without bowel movements. That's a new one on me, but strange Dooley didn't know the score. Filled up with forty-two gallons of petrol then proceed north again back to Bandya. I asked Peter Hill for some trace chains and bolts for the broken drag that I abandoned five miles west of the Gibson Hill, on top of the unnamed range.

Peter Hill says he once discovered a rockhole more to the north of my new track in a line with Karu Soak, at about eight miles west of Gibson Hill. He seemed happy to know I was pushing some new tracks into the country and says he's had no dog problems since I came into the area. He claims he can't see any of my traps. I told him that this should be to my credit. A professional dogger sets traps in such a way that even a dog can't detect them. I could have told him a bit about his own shortcomings in respect to ill-prepared trap jaws but didn't want to be such a boor.

We had to run the gauntlet of a huge prospectors' camp located close to Bandya homestead, beside the aerodrome, and strung for a short distance along both sides of our road out to Red Well. We came on back to the caravan where upon arrival, Kado decided to mess his napkin. The first movement since last Tuesday. One hundred and three miles.

Saturday 11 - Wrote the usual special month's report for RVCO Jack Kerr, including an additional carbon copy for the JS Battye Library. After dinner we came to within a few miles south of Warren's Well to camp. A fox in trap near Lake Wells and one fox dead beside a poisoned roo carcase near where we camped at Miltji the other night.

Sunday 12 - Did the trap run south-west to Deleta, Tjilpitjarra, Tharukati and Urarey, then return past claypan and Red Well to the caravan. No sign of dogs and no traffic of any kind since we were last around that way. Ninety-four miles. Monday was cool and cloudy. Dooley did our washing. I checked off a list of faults that need attention on the Landrover. Rearranged some loading and counted a pile of dog scalps. On Tuesday the 14th we departed the caravan for Leonora, travelling a new route via Biddy Patch and Tarmoola. Shot a bird for dinner. The way we came was one hundred and ninety miles. On Wednesday I went to the Post office to open a savings account for both Dooley and Kado, also put $100 in my own book. This is the first deposit in my savings book since recommencing work with the APB. The pay goes direct to a cheque account each month. I didn't realise where all the money went until I remembered the caravan purchase and new roof on the house. Those necessary expenditures are now out of the way and henceforth I hope to put a few dollars aside. Saw Mick Healy about putting a ceiling in the kitchen. He'll be back tomorrow to give me a quote. Mick came back early Wednesday morning to take measurements for window glass and says he'll do the ceiling for $105. We stayed in town for the next four days.

Tuesday 21 - Dooley went into hospital at seven o'clock this morning to have a cervical loop fitted. She was out again by noon. In the afternoon I went to see the dentist. We left Leonora at 5 pm and travelled north-east via Banjawarn to camp near Milyirri Outcamp. One hundred and twenty-three miles. On Wednesday we went on to the caravan and had a washing day.

Thursday 23 - Dooley not well enough to travel yet. Hope we can get on with the job soon, it seems I still can't get anything done. On camp all day. I reinforced ten maps by binding the edges with sticky tape. Also repaired damage to the caravan wall and ceiling with Plastic Mastic. Dooley cooked a duff and custard. Today was quite warm with lots of blowflies. They blew the butter. First time I've known that to happen. There is rain in the air. I sent a memo over the radio to Bandya telling them to direct any visitors looking for me, to Red Well on the Karu Soak road.

Friday 24 - We had a lot of strong wind gusts last night accompanied by light rain. I cleaned up around the camp first thing this morning then settled down for the day to read an account of John Forrest's first two expeditions of 1869 and 1870. We not happy living in the caravan, it is not a natural environment. Maybe I should have considered that aspect before I bought the thing in the first place but at the time I thought it a good decision. Today Dooley built an excellent brush shelter. Personally I always did favour the traditional native lifestyle.

Saturday 25 - Frost painted the landscape a dazzling white this morning. Our camp being beside a shady thicket means no thaw could occur until well after sunrise so we got going early to enjoy a bit of warmth inside the vehicle rather than wait. Travel was along the north-east track. I got a scalp from one dog carcase at Miltji. Some prospector bastard had run his vehicle wheels over the trap plate and ruined it. Whoever the idiot was, he deserves a summons for destruction of government property, except that the APB to my knowledge has never laid charges against anyone anywhere at any time for interference with traps. South of Gregory Hills was a second ginger and white colour dog caught in trap near Point Gibson but no sign of travellers in that direction.

From the Point we went on to our new drag track turnoff. I sometimes use the name Gibson Hill as marked on the map but this hill is five miles or more east of the beef road. The mother range however extends north from the cartographer's nominated hill. The beef road skirts a prominent point of this range at its northern end and forms a sharp bend before resuming its southern course toward Cosmo. That bend is the place I often refer to as Point Gibson. Out new drag track lies about three and one half miles south of the Point and a sharp bend in the road.

We returned to where I left the drag last trip and pulled it five miles east to the unnamed central range. The thing fell to pieces and broke up just prior to completion of the job on that side. I unhooked it and went south to the other broken drag that fell apart above the escarpment on the first trip. I pulled it back to the one that broke today and had a late dinner there. After dinner I lashed the two broken drags together. This makeshift contraption accomplished only one more mile before it too fell apart and that was that. I thought it a pity because the thing was doing a good job until it disintegrated beyond repair.

I fear that both these implements are too old and are victims of metal fatigue. There is no real reason to complain though because there is now a well-defined drag track running from west to east through the spinifex and over the central range. It was just that I wanted to do a better job. There is a little dry gnamma hole near where I left the broken drags. It is on the escarpment edge above cliffs facing east. Some tall prominent mulga trees spilling over a promontory a bit to the south are a good indication of the gnamma hole's location. We abandoned the broken drags there so, for the present will call it Wantingu Gnamma Hole. The native expression wantingu being past tense for the word leave or left.

During late afternoon I went midway across the plateau to where we saw well-used game pads running from south to north across our original traverse, during the first week this month. I left Dooley with baby Kado and the Landrover then walked north along the pads. I located several good big rockholes full of water down a rough gully. The range falls away here from the upper gravel flats. The gully runs into a bigger gorge lower down. This gorge is not visible at all from where I left the vehicle. The southern approach is up a gradual slope and over a rounded crest, before any fall becomes apparent.

The rockholes lie concealed from outside view about a quarter mile north of the drag track. One contains the decomposing carcase of a not long dead camel. The water is already putrid and green. A larger catchment further down the gully however, contains fresh clean water. Pine trees growing along cliffs to the north mark the approximate position. We will call this place Dead Camel Rockholes for the time being. Maybe we can ascertain the correct native name later.

Further west and just after entering the range from that side, the drag track passes a native indicator stone or nintiranyi. A flat slab set at an angle in the ground. On the first trip I was anxious to complete the job in hand, so did not stop to investigate what the stone slab might indicate. This afternoon though I walked north from the indicator up a slope and found a magnificent gnamma hole full of fresh cool water. The remarkable thing about this cylindrical hole was the stone plug stuck in the opening, and how it bulges out into a much larger catchment below ground level. The mouth of the hole is only about ten inches in diameter but the interior expands to a greater width like a bottle. This hole sits on the edge of, and atop a low cliff or dry waterfall that spills down into a scrub choked gully below. I know several other gnamma holes of this type with stone stoppers, to the north of Wiluna, but find this one most remarkable. For a start there is no sign that any white man before me ever found it, not by motor vehicle anyway, our Landrover is the first. What fascinates me most is the presence of the stone plug still in place. There is no doubt whatsoever that the last native to drink here, put the plug back before he or she left, in the exact position I found it today.

The former inhabitant of this country may be long since dead, but the aura of stoneage human remains present here. We'll call this one Lid Rockhole. Kangaroo tracks and those of wild dogs are present around the gnamma hole but they can't get at the water so must get a drink at the big rockholes further east, midway across the range. We continued over the range to camp on the edge of spinifex to the west. I was too intent on the job in hand to write the full day's events before. I wanted to record all the work activities first. Now however we are on camp and I have time to mention other remarkable things seen today. There is a notable **Y** junction about seven miles north of Point Gibson where the Prenti Downs and Gregory Hills roads meet to form a single road running south past Point Gibson to Cosmo Newberry. This morning was fresh and clear with the ground still wet from thawed frost when we reached the junction just described. There was no sign of recent traffic on the roads running south past Point Gibson. No sign of vehicles other than our own on Wednesday the 8th this month. Well, this morning we saw crisp and clear in the damp sand, the distinct imprint of a strange unexplainable track or footprint, that began right at the **Y** junction apex. It didn't come south along either of the two roads, nor did it come from one side or the other. The track began like that of a bird that lands on the ground, then moves along. I describe the track as we saw it. No suppositions, no guesses as to its source, no evidence of its origin. The thing looked as though it came out of the blue and landed.

It was a large creature. The entire foot was at least twelve inches in length from toe to heel. The thing was all heel and toes. A round heel with two elongated toes sticking out in front. We tried to equate it with all the animals we know, without success. The heel did hold a faint resemblance to that of a camel pad, but was certainly not that of a camel. The imprint was too small and much too rough. Camels leave a smooth track print. This one was rough and coarse. The toes were twice the length of the heel and narrow, with a clear-cut leading edge that kicked the dirt forward rather than back, as most animals do. The toes being squared and sharp enough to cut into the ground. The tracks indicated an upright creature with two legs. There is no doubt about that because there was only the one pair of tracks. Not four tracks like those of horse, camel, or other beast of similar size.

This strange track we followed was a big creature indeed. It staggered south along the Cosmo road, weaving like a drunken person from one side to the other, but always onward, without any deviation off the road the entire distance we followed it. The strange tracks led all the way from the junction, south to the big bend in the road adjacent to Point Gibson. Here it turned off the road for the first time and headed south-west through the spinifex. We followed it in for a short distance to get a bearing on its direction. We left off following it where the track left a clearcut imprint on a flat area of termite ant bed. This antbed was as hard as concrete, yet the track was heavy enough to break the cement-like crust and leave a sharp imprint of the whole foot, toes and all.

Too terrified of what might be ahead, Dooley refused to continue another step. She refused to follow the thing anymore, so I gave it away and carried on with the drag work for the rest of the day as already described. Dooley is sure the thing is a monster or some other kind of native devil. Aborigines believe in several different species of gruesome creatures. Kunatarrkatjarra, ngayanyangalku, wutatji, kunaturrun, kukaparr, plus the more common mamu, to mention but a few.

Sunday 26 - I had no film for the camera yesterday at all. There is none back at the caravan either. What a pity I couldn't take photos of the weird track we saw. I will buy film when we go to town but by the time we get back here with a loaded camera the evidence may not be here. I just hope there is no traffic along that road until we get a chance to try photos anyway. This morning our twenty miles trip back to the caravan took three hours and a half. The dragged track is still rough and will take a lot of trips to wear it in to some semblance of a normal vehicle road. All the drag did was graze the tops off spinifex hummocks and leave a faint drag mark along the ground.

Once back at our main camp we loaded all the dirty washing onto the Landrover and came into Bandya where I gave Peter Hill the good news that his favourite drag was in pieces. He was not surprised though because of the drag's age. He promised to help repair the thing if I bring all the pieces into the homestead so he can get to work with the welder. He says I can borrow a station trailer for the cartage. We continued on our way to Hootanui and from there west to Waterfall to camp and do some washing tomorrow. The rockhole is still full so we have plenty of water. We shot a young bird along the way and cooked it for supper. This is a beautiful camp.

Monday 27 - Sent a telegram to:

Jack Kerr
9IK Portable
Please forward one set canvas canopy side flaps for Landrover.
Signature Peter Muir.

Last night was not so cold. Dooley started on the washing early. When the clothes were dry we came on to Leonora. On Tuesday I unloaded the vehicle in preparation for repairs.

Wednesday 29 - RVCO Kerr arrived, talked, and departed, but came back later in the day. After discussing the **G6** Area, he returned to Kalgoorlie. I put UQD-634 in for repairs. Three blackfellows gave us cheek as we drove along the main street but for what reason I don't know. I swung the vehicle around, went back to ask what they were staring at and told them to get about their own bloody business. Afterwards I informed the police as a precaution against possible false allegations. Constable Pense said he would back me to the limit if I had to defend myself, just so long as I didn't kill anyone.

This evening on our way to the Drive-In, I pulled up at the cafe in Tower Street to have a look at the window poster and see what programme was on. Cecily Harris was in the Landrover with Dooley. She wanted to come to the pictures with us. The three blacks I'd chatted earlier were coming through the cafe doorway as I was looking at the poster. One of the trio came at me. He shouted abuse and remarked "Oh you is it! You're just the bloke I want to see." Why he wished to see me was unclear, however, I dodged his haymakers and rushed to the Landrover to put my glasses away. The antagonist was right behind me. I turned to meet him head-on with a flurry of straight lefts to the face and right rips to the body, plus a good right hook to his left cheek. It was obvious he got a shock. This unexpected retaliation from me, sat him back on his heels and gave me time to take stock of the situation. He had apparently thought me an easy mark. The other two kept well back after they saw my response, but despite my opponent's consternation, he still showed plenty of inclination to continue the fight. I was by this time anxious to teach the bloke a lesson he wouldn't forget in a hurry.

I adopted the classical boxer's crouch and belted the unwelcome adversary across the street to Elder's store and back again. At one stage I cornered the bastard in a doorway. I gave him quite a good doing for a while but let him out of the doorway when I noticed a crowd gathering. Once assured my rear was safe I put more effort into the fight for the crowd's benefit. I paused a moment to remove my high heel boots. In bare feet I slogged him along the middle of the street until he'd had enough, although he continued to dance around at a safe enough distance to avoid my fists. At this juncture Eric James the local JP who is also the manager of Elder Smith's store, appeared. He said: "That's enough Peter, come on now calm down, you won the fight and we don't want to see you in any trouble." I took notice of Mister James and walked back to our Landrover. My erstwhile opponent rushed off in the other direction into the juke box to berate his two companions for not helping him double bank me. I'm not too clear on just what happened next but while still shaking a fist at his two mates he backed off and fell right through the plate glass window. This was when the police arrived and took him away. I told them they could find me at the pictures if they wanted to see me.

Thursday 30 - The police didn't want to see me about last night's incident after all, but I hear the blackfellow will face charges over the broken shop front. Some people in town say I knocked him through it and broke the glass, but this is not true. I was nowhere near the man when he lost his balance and stumbled back into the window pane. Dooley and I also learned the bloke's name, he is Sam Peterson from Jiggalong. It seems he got jealous when he saw Cecily in our Landrover and thought I was cutting him out for a girlfriend. He couldn't be more wrong. Cecily is Dooley's friend and mine too for that matter, but she is not my lover and never was.

Friday 31 - Sam Peterson has more reason to be jealous of Cecily than he thought. She stayed at our place last night and slept with Papila of Yakabindie, her old boyfriend. I still can't understand why Peterson picked me as a rival. I have no interest in girls other than Dooley.

We took Kado to hospital for circumcision today. He is a candidate for ceremonial law when he grows up, but I wanted the operation done now as a precaution. I fear old traditions may die out over the next few years and Kado might miss customary initiation. Sadie the halfcaste matron here at Leonora Hospital, is a leading opponent of the old ways. Her influence caused Ngalia people on the Reserve here to suspend all ceremonies. It would appear the catalyst was one Tarn Harris who went to hospital for treatment after an initiation ceremony went wrong. Sadie was so active against further ceremonies that the men no longer hold them near Leonora.

Figure 17 Homestead Palms "Town House"

Chapter Eighteen - THE RED WELL CAMP

AUGUST 1970

Leonora slid behind us about dinner time on Monday the 3rd as we left town in our private vehicle because the government UQD is still in the garage being repaired. We arrived Bandya around 5 pm after a one hundred and forty mile trip.

Tuesday 4 - We travelled around via Karu to the strange tracks seen last month on the 25th. This time I have plenty of film in the camera. There was a heavy dew this morning. The ground was quite damp. To my great delight the strange tracks were still just as clear and crisp as when first seen ten days ago. Most important of all there was no sign of any vehicles other than our own along the road. Traffic of any kind would obliterate the tracks. I took two rolls of 35mm film, one of colour slides and one of black and white. The tracks are still a puzzle. There is no animal we can equate with them. Camels leave a dinner plate size impression in sand that is always soft, smooth and shiny like a snake's track. The round heel of this one though, is rough and hard. The two elongate toes are quite distinct and clear. The leading ends are square and hard, almost as though tipped with metal. Unlike an orthodox track, they kick the dirt forward rather than back. We are at a loss for an explanation unless we offer something extraterrestrial, but that would only invite ridicule. I therefore commit such opinions to those who favour the exotic.

I inspected all the traps on the way back as we returned to the caravan. Dooley dropped a match or cigarette butt into a bundle of clothes in the Landrover and we nearly lost the lot. I smelt the smoke and was able to douse the flames in time. To lose our private vehicle like that would be a sad ordeal, just when we are getting back on our feet again financially.

Wednesday 5 - Compiling journals and reports for last month. I don't enjoy this bookwork anymore. It has become a real bore. Too much vehicle log book and all that sort of bureaucratic stuff. When doing exploration work like the 1965-68 Survey north of Wiluna, I used to love the write-up, but this job forbids offroad travel and the bookwork is too mundane. I worked on it all day but got too knocked up to put everything together ready for dispatch to Kalgoorlie office.

Thursday 6 - We went into Bandya homestead to get a $200 cheque from Peter Hill for the centrifugal pump I sold him. The same pump I used to clean out some long neglected Canning Stockroute wells as well as a few others along the old abandoned Rabbit Proof Fence. It stood me in good stead in those halcyon days, but is of little use to me now, not in this country of dry rockholes. We had a good yarn about the desert backblocks, Carnegie, John Forrest and other oldtimers, then left. From Bandya we came to Laverton to see Stan Bridgeman. Stan sent a message a while ago asking me to look him up when next in town. He wants information about the Canning Route and Lake Disappointment. His main concern being the whereabouts of access tracks. He is in the employ of Mount Madley Prospecting Company. This company has a Yank with them too, cowboy hat and all. He is the helicopter pilot. The chopper sits in front of Bridgeman's town house on a back street east side of town. To see a helicopter parked in a town street anywhere is a most incongruous sight. Bidding goodbye to Stan we travelled across to Leonora to see how the government Landrover is progressing. It is still not ready.

Mick Healy has not long finished renovations to our old house so I gave him the $200 cheque I got from Peter Hill and received $20 change from Healy. My big cheque lasted just that long. I posted the films away for processing then returned to Laverton where we camped just north of town.

Friday 7 - We are still using our private vehicle. We went back to see Stan Bridgeman and gave him some of the information he was after. Next I refuelled our vehicle with thirty gallons and booked it out to UQD-634 on government purchase order or LPO. With tanks now full we proceeded north to the Duketon turnoff and took the direct route back to our caravan. Packed up and shifted holus bolus from our spinifex camp west to Red Well. A much better camp and closer to water during the hot weather, if we are still here next summer.

On the way out from Laverton we met a nickel man with a flat tyre but no jack handle. I helped him out with mine. Further on we also picked up a lot of fresh fruit. Oranges, tomatoes and potatoes strewn for a mile or more along the road. No doubt the stuff fell from a moving vehicle. Tracks showed how a motorist turned around to pick up some of it but didn't see fit to go right back and collect the lot, much to our good fortune.

Saturday 8 - Washing day at the new camp near Red Well. Peter Hill came along from his Gregory Hills block to the north-east, on his way back to Bandya. I shifted the last of the gear from our old camp, then spent the rest of the day settling in here.

Sunday 9 - Poor fella me. I have a bad dose of the flu. Went around the Gregory Hills trap run. One dog in trap at Lake Wells south. One at Irve's Grave. One at Earli Earli The waterhole there is full but no sign of dogs anywhere near it and not much game. Dooley shot a bird at Tjampan on the way out. We plucked and cleaned it, wrapped it up well and carried it all day until return at nightfall to Red Well.

Monday 10 - We heard over the RFDS radio that someone died at Banjawarn last weekend. I reckon it might be old Ted James who used to be on Windidda Station with Norm Jeffreys, before Norm got the job managing Banjawarn. Old Ted followed him as they were good mates. Ted James loved his whisky poor old chap. I knew him from my time in the Windidda stockcamp. Ted cared for a vegetable garden while on Windidda, at Christmas Yard, some distance away from the homestead. He was also an accomplished tinsmith. Most of the Windidda camp utensils like billycans, camp ovens, and other tin wares were the produce of Ted James. He was what I would describe as a typical example of those old bush identities known as remittance men.

Outcasts from Old England's upper class families were in years gone by, paid a regular annuity to exile themselves in some far off land. The idea being that they never show their face back home in Old England again. I don't know whether Ted was one of those eccentrics, but I always got the impression that he was. The Northern Territory had its share of such men in earlier years and I can only presume that WA may have had remittance men also. Vale Ted James, I hope there is a plentiful supply of good whisky where you have gone.

Peter Hill sent a telegram to Sullivan's Garage for me. The text being: "Please advise immediately government Landrover ready. Don't forget side curtains from railway. Regards Peter Muir." I couldn't send it myself as the portable is in the government vehicle. We stayed on camp all day. Warm and fine. On the afternoon RFDS schedule. We heard a telegram going over the air to Glenayle Station from Stan Gratte saying he and party had just left Blythe Pool.

I studied it up in John Forrest's Journal and Carnegie's Spinifex & Sand. I find it easy to visualise the country from their respective descriptions. It seems to be a northerly extension of the fifty mile wide belt of undulating laterite gravel rises and low escarpments west of Warburton. Similar terrain also exists south of Jiggalong. Half his luck. I'd love to go all through that country. No reply from Sullivan so suppose he is still messing around with UQD's repairs.

Tuesday 11 - I listened in to the morning RFDS session but still no word from Sullivan. I'll have to go to Bandya and send another telegram to stir him a bit. I attended to some correspondence today, including a letter to Native Welfare demanding an apology from that department. They accused me of something I didn't do. The accusation is, **that I shot a camel and poisoned the carcase (in) a gnamma hole near Cundeelee Mission**. How in hell they reckon I did that when it is a hundred miles or more outside my jurisdiction is beyond comprehension. In anycase, I haven't even shot a camel in this part of the world let alone poisoned one.

Wednesday 12 - We went in to Bandya and sent two telegrams. One reply paid to Sullivan's Garage:

"Please advise immediately expected date complete repairs government Landrover. Reply to Bandya Station. Signature Peter Muir."

The second to: "Mr Kerr 9IK Portable Kalgoorlie. - Landrover still in garage stop. Been using private vehicle for full fortnight please contact Sullivan's per phone reason for delay and advise me care Bandya Station. Signature Peter Muir."

Booked both telegrams out to my government 8WQA Portable. Peter Hill gave us a quarter of mutton. This was a welcome gift as there are no kangaroos about lately. While we were at the homestead a plane landed near the nickel men's camp. We bid the Hills farewell. Came back to camp at Red Well to cook a roast and await response to the telegrams.

Reply telegram: "To P. Muir c/- Bandya Station. Mr Kerr in Perth until Monday. Stop. Contacted Sullivan. Landrover now ready. Signature Agriculture Department."

Also a telegram from Leonora: "Repairs completed today. Signed Sullivan."

We travelled in to Leonora and took delivery of the Landrover. I got to the garage just before closing time. We pulled up at the cafe to get something for supper and my erstwhile opponent Sam Peterson was there. He came at me again so I got the tjuna (native fighting stick) out this time and met him on the footpath but he retreated when he spotted the tjuna. He stepped back and took his high heel RM Williams boot off then approached me with it raised above his head with the intention of hitting me with the heel. I swung the tjuna to ward off this comical attack. At that stage the police van pulled up. A constable hopped out to intervene. I took immediate notice of the police direction to desist, but Peterson made an issue of it. He berated the policeman and told him he, Peterson, was from the north country where he and his ilk never dodged a fight until it was decided one way or the other. The policeman told him: "You are not in the north now, we do things differently here in Leonora and you better take notice or I'll have to run you in."

Peterson wouldn't calm down so the law put him under arrest and that was that. I went on home feeling far from calm and collected. I can't stand people picking fights without good reason, but if anyone does pick a fight with me, then they just have to take the consequences. I won't back down from anybody be they black white or brindle.

On Thursday I fixed Sullivan with official purchase order. Got our stores for the bush and everything else ready for departure. After all this, Dooley and I had a bender until Sunday, then we left Leonora for Laverton late in the afternoon. We had a few more drinks in Laverton to wean ourselves off, but didn't leave town for Red Well until Monday the 17th.

Tuesday 18 - I had a bastard of a night with a bad hangover. Dooley was the same, but refuses to recognise that too much grog is the cause of her illness. We had a big washing day and a general cleanup today. Too much bloody town is bad news. No good for our pocket either. Lucky I still have credit in the cheque book.

I went mad while there and got a telephone installed at the Leonora house. This cost thirty-eight dollars. Just what in hell I'm going to do with a telephone I don't know. The store account at Elders GM is over fifty-three dollars too. Perth Dental Hospital account is forty-one dollars seventy cents. Booze cost forty dollars. Food while in town cost several dollars and we went to the pictures once. There is only one thing to do. We should give up drinking I know, but life in town gets so miserable I can't help it. I don't really like the stuff after the first few, also I get too kind hearted and foolish when under the influence. I am always so happy when out in the bush though and when away from town I couldn't care less if I never drank another drop.

Wednesday 19 - I awoke with a touch of the flu again. Peter Hill came along and we yarned the morning through. On Thursday I stayed on camp all day with the flu but started off early to do the trap run on Friday. We only got a few miles along the road when the flu got the best of me so we had to return to camp. Peter Hill called in again. This time he brought me two drums of petrol from Laverton.

Saturday 22 - Flu gone at last so got going on the job again to inspect traps via Urarey northeast to Warren's Well then south. One dog in trap at Wakulyakutjarra. Reset some sprung traps along the way, also removed a few. There are twenty traps set now. Not much sign of dogs anywhere.

The only fresh tracks are at Nyiruru where a couple of dogs padded up and down several times past a sprung trap. I reset it. On the way north of Urarey tracks near Tjilpitjarra show how a nickel man, a real delinquent, made several deliberate attempts to run over one of my traps. The trap had a fox in it. The only thing that prevented him from running over the trap was a mulga tree that prevented him from getting close enough to the trap to ruin it.

This trip we found that fresh camel tracks are numerous right around the run. We saw three live camels feeding in the sandhills south of Nyiruru. The camels stood looking at us for a while before making off south to the lakes. We saw a few kangaroos too, but couldn't get a shot. One hundred and sixty-four miles on the clock by the time we reached Red Well again.

Monday 24 - A frost yesterday morning brought a fine warm clear day. I stayed on camp to repair a tyre. Today I inspected the country around Mabel Hill and Yultu a rockhole to the north-west. The rockholes are all brimful. Saw only one dog track. We found some green gemstone on the way out this morning, a couple of miles to the east of Mabel Bore. Cutlines and nickel pegs everywhere north of Hootanui so there must be something big in the wind. Came back to Red Well after an eighty mile run.

Tuesday 25 - Went to Laverton to fix Don Leahy with LPO payment for the petrol Peter Hill took out to Red Well for me the other day. The new Coach House Cafe is now open. It is a real beaut. We bought some pies there and drove out of town to boil the billy for dinner. The billy was still on the fire and not yet boiling when a mob of blacks pulled up. They began walking over to our camp. Dooley was apprehensive. She didn't want to see them, so I pulled the billy off the fire. I tipped the water out while Dooley chucked the tuckerbox onto the vehicle. We then drove away from the approaching men.

I might mention that no traditional fullblood native woman ever feels comfortable in the presence of an all male group when away from town or otherwise, when out in the bush. It is just not the done thing for a woman to be caught in such a position, whether her husband be present or not. I understand this concern and cooperated to the full. It is probable that this particular mob only wanted to see me because of my initiated status. That in itself is quite in order, but I must also consider Dooley's concerns. That is why we did not tarry to find out the whys and wherefores of the situation.

Peter Hill was in Laverton. We didn't see him when travelling to town this morning. He came south from Bandya while we came by way of German Well. After the midday upset, we continued right through to Leonora. We felt disgust at having our dinner spoiled by the advent of uninvited and unwelcome visitors. One hundred and seventy miles.

Wednesday 26 - The speedo now reads 8808. We had a general cleanup at the town house and purchased a large quantity of stores for the bush. Saw Stan Bridgeman and gave him some of the green stone samples we found near Mount Mabel the other day. He thought them good, but only lucrative if the ground is still unpegged. He is off to Lake Disappointment with the Mount Madley Prospecting Company helicopter next week.

Thursday 27 - Left town and this time travelled north via Nambi Station. We pulled up for dinner after shooting a fat kangaroo twenty miles south-west of Bandya. We needed one too because it is ages since we had fresh meat. We were fortunate to get a roo at all as the shooters have just about shot them all out. If allowed to continue, I can see the marsupial becoming extinct within my own lifetime, at their present rate of destruction. Travelled on to our new camp at Red Well after dinner.
We have plenty of stores now but I hesitate to guess what the bill from Elders GM will be. Cold cloudy afternoon. I put the annexe on the caravan. On Friday I read the journal of A Mason 1896, his report of an expedition in the south-east of WA. Dooley cooked a wonderful plum duff. Her best effort yet.

Saturday 29 - On camp near Red Well all day sorting out maps of the 1:250,000 Series 4 Mile to the inch. I find I need another hundred Four Mile Sheets to cover all my areas of interest in WA. At a cost of seventy-five cents each that makes a total of seventy-five dollars worth. At that price I'll have to spread the purchase over a two year period. I can't afford to buy the lot in one go. I don't really need them all, but like to have them for personal interest. There are far too many other essentials to consider first. Clothing, furniture for the house, more renovations, books and so on. A working man is not in the race at all as far as money goes.

I strung a clothes line for Dooley and cleared a wide space around it. We had to throw half our meat away this morning. It was flyblown. Blowflies are around us in millions since the last rain and don't look like going away for a while either. Since I rigged the caravan annexe they don't come inside so that is one consolation.

News items: Some sex fiend murdered two little girls age five and seven, over in Queensland, after stripping and assaulting them. Also a family missing in the bush between Alice Springs and Lake Nash.

Sunday 30 - Cold south-east winds blowing a gale day and night of late. The first time I've seen these strong relentless winds for years. Such gales were common at this time of the year once. August winds used to be a regular feature of the cattle country when droving was in full swing. Both along the Birdsville Track in South Australia and across the Barkly Tableland in the Northern Territory.

We came out to the Gregory Hills and I took mileages along the sandalwood track from the two windmills en route Ida Range. Left camp at 8951.

Reach two windmills north of Gregory Hills at 9006 or 53 miles.

From the two windmills it is sixty-two miles to the gravel rise with big old sandalwood camp, north from the east side of the Lake Wells south-east corner.

Eighty-two miles north-east from the two windmills to Mulkutu rockholes.

North-east from Mulkutu with occasional swings due north to the one hundred mile point, where numerous old vehicle tracks lead off in all directions. We travelled three miles along the most easterly of these tracks. It bore north-west then north. We returned two miles along this track to camp on an open stony flat one hundred and one miles north-east of the two windmills. One hundred and sixty-three miles for the day.

Monday 31 - I have no real way of knowing, but the stony rises and low hills visible this morning, could constitute the elusive Ida Range. The mileage and compass bearings relate to the position on the map of Ida Range, but there may be other features not yet in full view.
We proceeded at a slow pace back along the track to examine all possible leads to natural waters. I found none. I feel sure that water does exist in this area because euro tracks are numerous near our camp of last night. This morning we heard two dingoes howling. At about the ninety mile point we saw a kangaroo on the saltbush flats, also a large flock of galahs feeding. At the eighty-two mile point the Mulkutu gnamma holes are all dry. At the fifty-five mile point we saw fresh tracks of brumby horses. The presence of horses away out here leads me to think there might be a claypan or similar water in amongst the network of lakes there.

At the twenty mile junction, wheel marks lead north past hills about four miles off the main track. I followed the wheel marks eight and a half mile to where they disappeared. There is a prominent headland and tabletop about eight or ten miles further north-east from where I turned back.

We came home to Red Well. Peter Hill was a visitor while we were away. He left a copy of the Kalgoorlie Miner dated 27th August. It featured the strange footprints we found near Point Gibson last month. Before we went in search of Ida Range I left a note for Peter, telling him where we were going and when to expect us back. He added a note to mine to say he'd be back this way again next Wednesday. One hundred and eighty-two miles. This Red Well camp is our best yet and the most convenient to work out from. I wonder what changes Springtime has in store.

Figure 18 Peter Hill and Joey Munro

Chapter Nineteen - AN AXE KILLER ALLEGED

SEPTEMBER 1970

Tuesday 1 - The first day of Spring. A telegram for me on the morning RFDS session:

> To P Muir
> 8WQA Portable
> Would appreciate if you telephone the West Australian Perth 210161 extension 210 re footprints. Reverse charges authorised.
> Signed Chief of Staff WA
>
> I sent a reply Collect:
>
> To Chief of Staff WA
> 210161 extension 210
> Out bush now but will proceed to town, and ring from Laverton Wednesday 2nd. Stop. Also have some photos.
> Regards Peter Muir
>
> I also sent a memo to 8UJ to say I'd arrived back from the bush okay. Then completed the August journals.

Wednesday 2 - Proceed into Laverton and ring the West Australian. I gave them the information they require regarding the strange tracks we saw on July the 25th and again last month when I went back with film to take photos. It was a long contact involving four extensions of time on the phone. We did not get to finish the conversation. The switch girl asked us to desist and give someone else a go.

I'd noticed a queue forming as we spoke. Laverton is being invaded by nickel men and the local switch board is unable to cope with all the additional telephone traffic. They don't have enough trunk lines. The newspaper asked for a photograph of myself to complement those of the strange tracks. I said I had none on hand but would try to get something suitable.

I left the cluttered little Post Office and set off to find someone with a polaroid camera. John Leahy the storekeeper directed me to Frank Pearce, manager of the lately renovated Coach House Cafe. When I asked Frank he said, "No, I haven't got a polaroid but I've always wanted one. In fact all I need to make me happy is a polaroid camera. Just you hang on a minute mate, I'll go buy one right now." Sure enough Frank Pearce walked off immediately toward Collopy's Store and came out shortly after with a brand new polaroid camera in his hand. It cost him somewhere around twenty dollars I think. Too expensive for me anyway. He read the directions for a couple of minutes then took two splendid colour snaps of me and Dooley, with baby Kado on her hip. He developed the photos in the space of about two minutes, mounted them and gave them to me. This is our first experience with instant cameras. We know about them but never seen them in operation before.

Frank wouldn't accept anything in payment so I thanked him and promised to give him two copies of the strange tracks from my own collection. I bought a prepaid envelope, enclosed in it the two snaps, together with a note to the newspaper, asking that the photos be returned when finished with. Put them in the post then we left town immediately for Red Well. I also purchased a drum of petrol while in Laverton.

Thursday 3 - Strong gusty winds last night continued all day, only colder than it was during the night. News reports are of frosts in the South West and over an inch of rain at Esperance. The wind is blowing off the colder regions in the south. Esperance is the cause of it all. The weather is colder now during the official spring than it was all through the winter months. Dooley is not too good today. I was aching all over last night too. We will rest today and maybe again tomorrow. That should make us fresh and fit for another trip out north-east of Gregory Hills. Dooley made a big duff after dinner. Bush flies are sticky behind the windbreak but the blowflies are not so bad now. I hope we've seen the last of them.

Some future reader of this journal may think I have an easy time of it, but in reality such is not the case. My official duties are to hold wild dogs in check. The APB does not sanction any off road exploration work at all. This job is not like the Exploration and Survey I carried out north of Wiluna during the period 1965-68. The APB forbids exploration in the G6 Area. Dingo control is the only thing I am to do. At the present time wild dogs are not moving anywhere in the G6 Area so I have no official work to do. The occasional trips I make into unknown portions of my run are unofficial and off the record for the present. I sometimes feel that my regional officer Jack Kerr keeps me short of good rubber and fuel supplies on purpose so I can't travel too far afield. He's a bit of an old sod in that respect.

Friday 4 - Washing day at Red Well and fill all the water tanks in preparation for departure tomorrow. We will go have a look at country along the north-east side of Lake Wells. Put the camp in order and rake up all around so we can see tracks better when we come back. Not that anyone has come around our camp yet but you never know who is in the country these days with all these itinerants wandering all over the place in search of nickel prospects.

Saturday 5 - Speedo at Red Well 9455. Fifty-three miles to Gregory Hills whereat I turned the trip meter back to zero. Mileages are from the two windmills enclosure starting point as follows:

Travel through spinifex for, and enter first saltbush at,	12 miles
Little lake in samphire on left and limestone rise	14
Reach east end of lake and travel through saltbush from	16
Reach track turnoff to north at	18.8
Long low range about three miles north, runs from W to E terminates at	19
Hill on north side	20.4
Track runs around hill's S for one and half miles then turns from E to NE	21.8
Sandhills and white lake to the left at	22
End of sandhill and small quartz rise on righthand side	24
Small hills half a mile to one mile west at	25
Samphire pan on east side of track at	27.7
Crest of hight sandhill three quarter of a mile east	28.8
Track turnoff east	30
Northern point of large stony hill one mile east at	31
Quartz hill near track on east side	35.2
Quartz hill terminates at	36.3
High hill three miles west and wandary grass country	37.5
Enter spinifex and sandhills (Leave Duketon Sheet)	39.5

Description		
High bluff hill 1/2 mile S (track runs west) low hill 1/4 mile N (Enter Robert Sheet)	41.3	
Turn N and NE again. Saltbush and wandary with sandhills both sides	42.7	
Reach large samphire pan on left side		50.2
North-east through saltbush for one and a half mile	51.8	
East end of high bluff hill visible about three miles to north	56	
Enter spinifex and sandhills that occupy country NE to stony outcrops at	61.4	
More sandhills to stony hill at	63.1	
N end Ernest Giles Range 15 mile E. A turnoff to Range at	64.3	
Remarkable tabletop peak visible 20 degrees to the north of track at		66.8
Road runs north-east. Remarkable peak now to NW about one mile away	71.2	
End of stones and gravel country. Enter spinifex again at	73	
Reach Mulkutu rockholes and their host breakaway point at	82.6	
Mulkutu point runs horseshoe fashion to hit track again W side	84.7	
Hills run W of track and run into a big stony bluff coming in from W	86.5	
No hills E for 10 miles. Big red bluff 3 miles ENE. Low scrubby hill W side	88.4	
Sandhill to W half a mile then enter sandhills	89.4	
Red Bluff NE about three miles. Dark stony hills SW three miles	89.8	
Nothing but sandhills around rest of the horizon. These terminate at	91	
Saltbush, mulga, stony clay flats running E and W. Small knob half mile W	91.6	
Large grass swamp and small stony rise E side of track	92.6	
Rounded grass covered stony hill half mile NW	93.4	
Ranges visible. Track runs NE Draw level with Ida Range t two miles E	97.5	
Low hills two miles W	98.4	
N to big sandalwood camp and junction of two distinct tracks	100	
Enter hills. High cliff to W Reach first creek running E	101	
Leave hills, enter sandhills N of hill then mulga and grass take over	102	
Mulga wash. Wanan Gnamma hole at N end of laterite. Has water in sand.	105	

Two smaller gnamma holes half a mile north. One dry, one half full, but polluted by the decomposed carcase of a dead fox. Return to and examine a track leading NW from the junction we passed earlier. It appears to be merely an access track to where the sandalwood people stacked their produce ready for transport out of the country.

Satisfied with the day's work we turned back and on the way found that Ernest Giles Range is about ten miles south of the remarkable tabletop peak seen this morning. We travelled right through to Red Well arriving after dark at 8-30 pm. Three hundred and thirty-three miles that I am certain my boss would prefer not to know of.

Sunday 6 - Washing day at Red Well.
Monday 7 - Strong gusty winds made it a miserable day. Clouds rising. I did some correspondence and a few camp chores but nothing else.

Tuesday 8 - Wind blowing a gale from the south-west and overcast here. Clouds coming off rain. I read "Explorations In Australia" by John Forrest.

Wednesday 9 - Red Well to Leonora. Plenty of mail to collect including a number of the 1:250,000 Series maps I had on order.

Thursday 10 - I rang Jack Kerr and got jarred for using my private vehicle when the UQD was off the road undergoing repair. Thankyou so much Jack, now I definitely will not tell you about the good time we had east of Lake Wells last Saturday. I'd be the last one to want to cause you pain. I answered Michael Terry's letter first then wrote out several cheques to settle various outstanding accounts. My office work done, we packed up for the bush once more and departed for Red Well. Severe cold winds blew from the south-west and south-east all day. They eased off and it became a bit warmer late in the afternoon. Some big storm clouds are visible in the north. I hope we get some rain out of them.

Friday 11 - The speedo is now 10090. Rain it did. The hoped for fell last night and all of today, but cold, oh so cold.

Saturday 12 - I spent the entire day on correspondence including a further letter to Budge of Native Welfare. I want the name, and exact location of, the rockhole one of his black bastards claims I shot and poisoned a camel at, or in. It is a complete mystery to me. I want to get to the bottom of it. Bottom of the facts that is, not the rockhole. They can bottom that themselves and clean the bloody thing out if they like.

I wrote another letter to Michael Terry too, in answer to his query about the hieroglyph site I discovered in the Pingandy Creek area over in the Ashburton Fall on the 29th of December 1964. Michael's long quest for finance to make a scientific investigation of the site now appears to be reaching a climax. He has tried for six years to convince the Commonwealth government and the Institute of Aboriginal Studies, of the import and implications of such a discovery. The Institute is to chew the matter over and if agreeable, then we'll be off on a trip together next January.

Sunday 13 - Contacted VJQ the RFDS Base this morning and requested an appointment with Dr Roberts somewhere around the 23rd to 25th of September. I learned also that his surgery is at St John of God's Hospital. The base operator will put my query as a reply paid telegram.

I wrote a long letter to Professor RM Berndt of WA University regarding the strange tracks. Publicity in the newspapers to date has all been negative and full of ridicule. I doubt I would ever report anything unusual again, there are far too many smart-arses in the world. Next time anything out of the ordinary comes along I'll keep it to myself. One idiot wrote to the paper and said the track was a kangaroo with no tail. Another said it was a human with swim flippers. All manner of improbable explanations for the track saw print, but none gave me any credit for a lifetime knowledge of tracks in the bush, nor did Dooley's expertise in this sphere get a mention. Nothing but ridicule and more ridicule. If any logical person likes to go over the facts with me, in the way that Professor RM Berndt did, then I'll be quite happy to cooperate. Cold westerly winds all day.

Monday 14 - Cold and windy again today. I annotated the Four Mile sheets: BULLER, GUNANYA, and ROBERTSON that I got in the mail last time in town. If only I'd had detailed maps like these when exploring the Savory Creek in 1968. I find now that I've been well over one hundred and fifty miles along the downstream side of the Rabbit Proof Fence. The vehicle speedo broke during my last trip along the Savory when I travelled furthest and I had to estimate the mileage by calculating from an approximate speed of five miles per hour, the average rolling pace of a Landrover over virgin terrain. I didn't have the benefit of aerial maps in those days. Only an ancient ten miles to the inch map with the desert area shown as total blank space.

It now seems that the saltbush flood flats I reached after the last creek gums cut out, and all sign of a defined channel disappeared, was a good eight miles north of the McFadden Range. The name McFadden was unknown to me at the time I passed that range. I only learned its name after receipt of this GUNANYA sheet. I find now also that I was only about ten or twelve miles south of the McKay Range. I wanted to reach the McKay and would have done so if the exploration job didn't come to such an abrupt end. I never had a chance to go back out there after, although there was a great deal more country I wanted to see. I had plans for a shortcut across country, from Puntawari Creek to the Durba Range, but that idea also fell by the wayside after the APB pulled out of the project. Exploration is in my blood, but not in that of the APB. The Canning Stockroute lay only about twenty miles east of where I turned back on that last trip down the Savory. Lake Disappointment was within easy reach yet I never got there.

A telegram on the afternoon session from Dr Roberts wanting to know the reason for my requested appointment. I replied to the effect it is for an operation on an infant aged three months.

Tuesday 15 - Telegram fro Dr Roberts confirming appointment on evening of the 24th and to attend hospital on morning of the 25th.

We travelled around the trap run via Karu and Gregory Hills. South then to the illustrious Point Gibson (of the strange tracks) where was one fox in a trap. This was the only trap requiring attention, the remainder being undisturbed. As I said the other day there is not much wild dog movement at this time of the year. The only tracks seen today were those of two dogs chasing after a kangaroo near Point Gibson since the rain the other day. Travelled two miles south to the new drag track, then west to the central range, whereat we pulled up for dinner.

Untangled what I could of the twisted drag, then dismantled what I could of it for transport in back of the Landrover. I still had the bulk of it however to tow, and despite the dead weight managed to get it back to Red Well. The two V cutters on the broken contraption even cut a bit more track through the spinifex as we moved along, but will still need a lot more work to make a good defined track. The tow took three hours to cover twenty-one miles. Much too slow for this big dogging area. We arrived home after dark, had a late supper and went to bed. We both knocked up. One hundred and thirty-one miles.

Wednesday 16 - A cold morning gave way to a hot humid day. Flies were a torment all day and persisted until well after dark. Some scattered clouds to the north. I spent most of today sorting out various pieces of the broken drag. Placed them in position for reconstruction when I can find suitable nuts and bolts, plus a few new stays. We all had a bath and wash day. The first time in ages that it has been warm enough to expose wet bodies to the open air.

Thursday 17 - In to Laverton to post the mail and refuel from a full drum, forty-four gallons in all. Whilst in the Post Office The OIC Laverton Police came in and asked me to come around to the Station. He didn't say what for however I agreed to accompany him. I drove along as directed, pulled up outside and Dooley followed me in. There in the presence of two constables, and three rifles on the desk, (there only by coincidence I presume) The OIC questioned me in a most polite manner. He asked did I have a violent encounter lately with blacks, along the northern boundary of his police district, and my dogging run. The area he described stretched from Windidda Station south boundary all the way east to the WA border. I expressed surprise at his question. He in turn expressed surprise that I had no knowledge of such an incident. He told me his information was from a radio message sent by a Wiluna Mobile Police Patrol.

Wiluna blacks alleged that I had a violent encounter with a group of natives not long ago. They alleged that during the said encounter I had attacked one Sam Peterson with an axe and mortally wounded him, but to date no corpse has come to light.

Of course I knew nothing of any such incident. The police interviewed Dooley separately. She verified my statement, to the letter I learned afterwards. Dooley and I have not seen hide nor hair of Sam Peterson since the fist fight in Leonora. In the presence of Leonora police he threatened to get me if I ever put foot in Wiluna. He also told others the same thing. He'd get me in Wiluna. I thought nothing of his threats at the time but now it looks like something fishy is afoot. I feel quite concerned now because Laverton police told me to be on my guard at all times, whether out bush or in town. He says the Warburton blacks and the Wiluna blacks are all after my blood and threaten to get me. He and the two constables gave me instructions as to how I should react if confronted by an aggressive mob. I am not to shoot any natives unless my life is in danger. He advised that I should use only a 22 calibre rifle in preference to a 303. The police said to fire initial warning shots into the ground. I must try and avoid hitting any of them if at all possible. Just warn, then hold them at bay. Try to get away to the nearest station homestead and radio for the police. I must also wait at the said homestead until the police arrive. I assured the police that it is not my policy to point a firearm at anyone unless I feel prepared to pull the trigger. I never bluff with a gun. I always follow that principle.

The police took note of my portable radio call sign 8WQA and promised to inform me of any new developments. The conversation then turned to our discovery of the strange tracks. They gave me some casting plaster with which to take a mould in case I come across any more unusual tracks.

I wonder if some Wiluna blacks have done someone in, and are trying to implicate me. The blacks all the way from Cundeelee in the south, through Warburton to Wiluna, seem to have me in the gun for some unknown reason. I never had bad relations with blacks all my life, I always got on well with them until I took Dooley for my wife. Since we eloped there is nothing but trouble of one kind or another all the time. She is an independent woman and not beholden to any of them. She will stick to me too, no matter what. She has told me so, time and time again. No one is going to part us she says. I do have an idea that a lot of the problem is that I will not pamper the bastards. We live alone out bush. We don't live in a camp situation where all must share. No one shares anything with me so I reciprocate in like manner. Bill Pense the Leonora policeman told me that it is because I have a regular job with good pay, and they expect me to share the goodies. They can wait a long time to get anything out of me that's for sure, and if they don't like me because of my attitude then they can lump it. They are only a lot of parasites and bludgers anyway. I'll continue to live my life the way I want, and won't humour them at all. They are picking on the wrong man if they want to make an enemy of me. My conscience is clear. I'll defend my woman, my son, and myself at all costs, come what may.

I called in to the shearing shed on the way back to Red Well and told Peter Hill of the day's events. He agreed that blacks are a funny lot because one of his best workers Fred Turner, had just walked off the job without telling him. We passed a blackfellow by himself in an old car at a stock grid about twenty miles back along the road before we reached the shed. He didn't look to the right or to the left, just stared straight ahead through the windscreen and shot past us in a cloud of dust. We were curious then as to what his problem was. Now we know.

Peter Hill promised to come out to Red Well on Saturday and weld the drag together. When we got home I sent a memo over the radio to advise Bandya Station that water is escaping through faulty check valve at Red Well and to say I'd shut the trough off. Hot and humid all day with storms around the horizon.

Friday 18 - We travelled around the north boundary of Bandya to inspect the granite soak. It is full of water, but only kangaroos and emus drinking there. Not a sign of dogs. This granite outcrop is seven miles west of the north-east boundary gate that leads out onto the Karu road.

I sorted the dog scalps and find we now have seventeen on hand. That makes a total of ninety-eight dogs for the twelve months ending 15th of October next. Took the caravan gas cylinder off ready for transport to town to get a refill. Hot day again with some clouds and wind gusts. It is more like summer than springtime, although more cold snaps might occur yet. I wrote a letter to Stan Gratte in Geraldton in answer to the first letter he's written to me in eighteen months or more. We used to be regular correspondents with much in common in the bush context. Our respective occupations though are planets apart. He is a poultry farmer. Only twenty-three miles today.

Saturday 19 - Waited all day for Peter Hill to come along with his welding plant as promised. He failed to show. Some time ago I asked Mollie Lukis of the JS Battye Library for copies of Frank Hann's diaries. Frank Hann covered much of the country out from where I work. Hann camped for years not far east of Laverton. Miss Lukis told me that nobody can read the old explorers writing and that his diaries would not be of much use to me unless I could read them. I responded that I would like to try a sample page or two and if successful she might comply with my request for further copies. Today I translated half a sample page she sent last mail. His writing is indeed an illegible scrawl, just as she claimed. It reminds me of my own old grandmother's writing in many respects. All curved letters like M, N, U, V, and W, appear the same, as do many other letters of the alphabet. After a great deal of close scrutiny I was able to decipher most of the page, but admit it was a difficult task. I will do the other page and send my results back to the Library in the hope they will agree to send me more. Another change in the weather today. It was cold and windy with lots of rain and storms around the horizon. Hot one day, cold the next.

Sunday 20 - Completed what I could of Hann's document by making intelligent guesses as to the meaning of words that I could not decipher with any degree of accuracy. The letter **L** for the most part he wrote like an uncrossed **T** while his renditions of the letters **B, H, K, P, R**, and **I**, are all the same. Then **A, O** and **E**, are almost identical. The letter **S**, although often done the right way to look like a normal letter **S**, sometimes instead, looks more like the letters **A, O** and **E**. It was a difficult task to read his writing but I had a lot of fun. I put the finalised translation into an envelope with covering letter and also included copies of my July and August Reports. I asked Miss Lukis to quote the cost to me of complete copies of the Hann Diaries.

The rest of today Dooley and I discussed the mysterious allegations of my trouble with blacks out bush somewhere and my supposed killing of one with an axe. What the hell is this business of threats upon my life from places as far afield as Warburton and Wiluna. It has us perplexed. Being out bush ourselves most of the time and out of contact with what goes on elsewhere, we of course know nothing of what developments might be taking place. I will take the Laverton police warning seriously though, and go armed at all times when out of doors, even when going to the toilet. We always keep a rifle handy while eating too, and especially at night.

I don't want to finish up like old Joe Wilkins. He got skewered by a noble savage along the Canning Stockroute around 1936. A 1941 police report says it happened on or about the 7th of August that year. Wilkins often expressed contempt for those desert nomads he termed "niggers" and the puny little spear sticks they use. He'd been in Africa amongst bush Negroes he claimed, and despite their formidable iron tipped assegai spears, stood up to them unharmed. He took our Australian blacks much too cheap and lost his life as a result.

The men sent women to his camp as was often the custom in those days. In such circumstances a woman should stay with the recipient for only a short time. After an interlude with the whiteman she must return with gifts of tobacco, flour, tea, and sugar, in return for layback favours. In this case however, Wilkins took a fancy to one particular lubra and kept her all night. A night that turned out to be his last.

The husband took rightful umbrage at the violation of courtesy. He and others of the band were patient. They waited until next day for Wilkins to move away from his rifle by fifty paces or more. He'd leaned the weapon against a tree while packing his camels or horses ready to shift camp. The aggrieved blacks rushed in, flung spears at Wilkins, disabled him, then battered him to death and cut off his head. Wilkins was running a few head of cattle north-west of Weld Spring just off the Canning Stockroute. He went off on a trip in the vicinity of Numbers 14 and 15 Canning Wells. There is a stretch of good pastoral country thereabouts that Wilkins wanted to look at with a view to taking a lease on it from the government. It was during that trip that he got killed. Some of the natives involved in that incident are still alive in Wiluna today. Dangul Dangul is one, Shovel Shovel the other.

The lubra who shared the whiteman's bed was Yiniyampa, better known to me as Ruby Parker. She also is still alive. The man charged with murder was Tjanga, later known to the blacks as Gaolman, because of the time he spent in prison. I have had Dangul out bush with me and found him pleasant company, but most unreliable and deceptive. Shovel is more taciturn. His contemporaries treat him with extreme caution.

Monday 21 - The ABC News this morning had reference to Bill Brown the Rawlinna dogger. He and his old wife got caught in a flash flood, one hundred and fifty miles north of the Trans Line. His vehicle has water all around it. It appears the couple camped after dark on the dry expanse of a large claypan. Heavy rain fell overnight while they slept, and next morning the vehicle was in the middle of a lake full of water, two miles in length and a quarter mile wide. Two doggers from Kalgoorlie are on the way to rescue him. They are within one mile of the waterbound dogger this morning. A party of CSIRO scientists from Seemore Downs Station is also on the way to the site. The combined parties expect to get the stranded vehicle out of the lake today. The position is near the top righthand corner of the PLUMRIDGE SH 51-8 Sheet.

We went around the fence to Urarey and saw where someone became hopelessly bogged in a swamp to the south of there. It looks as if a huge storm passed through there not long ago. We came back to camp with a few bits and pieces of iron and some old bolts to try and fix the broken drag. After dinner we went west to Mulga Queen on a similar errand but drew a blank. There is not much in the way of scrap metal around there at all. I shot a bungarra on the way back. Later we went south to Duketon but no metal there either. In the end we found the type of oddments required at Claypan Yard two miles west of our Red Well camp.

I assembled the drag alright, but can only hold it together with wire twitches as I have no U bolts or clamps of any description. If only Peter Hill had kept his word and came out on Saturday with the welder. Maybe he had trouble with his blacks, or the sheep, or something.

The clouds cleared away by dark and cold south-west winds took their place. We will have to shift camp into a sheltered thicket before long. The caravan is much too open to the wind where it is here. The whole body rocks like a boat on choppy water. I have a feeling we are in for a cyclonic summer with strong winds. Eighty-two miles.

Tuesday 22 - Speedo is now 10496. I put a few more wire twitches on the drag then took it for a trial run. It appears okay and may hold together. Just after I came back to camp, a SWB Landrover came along with three blacks on board, all men. They claimed to be prospecting but had no swags or camp gear with them. I didn't make them welcome at all, and sat well back to one side with the 303 between my knees while Dooley spoke to them across a gap of seventy paces. They didn't attempt to get off their vehicle though and soon went on their way when they saw my attitude, and the 303. After the unwelcome visitors departed, I locked up and we went into Laverton where I put seventeen scalps into the Vermin Board. Later we saw our erstwhile friend Stan Bridgeman, and one Bill Escreet, an oldtimer aged eighty-four years. The Mount Madley Prospecting Company flew him over here from Pine Creek in the Northern Territory. They have been all through the Rudall River country and Lake Disappointment area since I last saw Stan. Bill Escreet guided them to his old copper show out from No 7 Well on the Canning Stockroute. He, or a brother it was, who sunk Escreet Well west of Earli Earli in the G6 Area. I have no idea how long ago that was, and I forgot to ask him. Maybe Peter Hill knows. Stan gave me a small compass, and in return I gave him some information. I also annotated a couple of his maps for the syndicate. Not that I'll ever get anything out of it, but I obliged anyway. They are off next week to have a look at Carnegie's Mount Elizabeth and another called Mount Dora, about fifteen miles east of Prenti Downs. We left Stan then and travelled across to Leonora, where I arranged to put the UQD vehicle in for a service tomorrow. One hundred and sixty miles.

Wednesday 23 - Sullivan's did the service job in quick time. I took delivery of the Landrover then went around to the police station and saw Bill Pense about an application for a high power rifle licence, my preference being 243 calibre. This will set me back about two hundred dollars if approved by the Firearms Branch. It is six years now since my licence got revoked, due to a shooting incident in Wiluna in 1964. Some rough-neck drunk invaded my camp and wouldn't leave when asked, so I took the law into my own hands and shot a bottle of beer out of his hand. He left faster than he came, but complained to the police. After an initial struggle with the police I later submitted to arrest that same night, for discharging a firearm within a dwelling. I pleaded guilty next day to get it over with, and got sentenced to one month hard labour in the local lockup. While serving the time in Wiluna I got a job with the APB from Meekatharra Regional Officer Alex Campbell, who came to see me in the gaol house. In those days the APB required potential doggers to have their own four wheel drive vehicles, so immediately after release I flew to Perth in the DC3 Mail Plane to buy a Landrover. Dooley and I still have it. Dooley holds the licence for our private gun, a 22 Winchester pump action. The 303 is official APB issue.

Bill Pense offers no objections to my application. He is a broad minded individual and says anyone can run amok after a belly full of booze. The alleged axe killing incident is a topic of conversation around Leonora too, but I can't find any more information as to why they link my name with it. Bill Pense doesn't have a clue either.

The PMG men came around to the house today to install the new telephone. Probably the loneliest phone in town. The call number is Leonora 49. The black handset sits on a small table alone in the corner of an otherwise unfurnished large empty room. One day this room will serve as my office, if I can afford to furnish and paint it. I gave the phone a test run and tried a call to Jack Kerr but got no answer.

Thursday 24 - A flat tyre to change this morning. I rang Kalgoorlie again, but Jack not in by 2 pm. I wrote out a list of several items to buy in Kalgoorlie if we go down there today:

360^0 Protractor	Office furniture
Bedroom furniture	Set of large dividers
Kitchen furniture	Set square
Lino	Rule

Jack Kerr got my message, he returned my call at 9-30 am. He requests that I take the Landrover down to Kalgoorlie for inspection by the APB mechanic on September the 30th. He also says the Department wants to see photos and colour slides of the strange track. I may send away for duplicates. I can't part with the originals. We went down today anyway and saw Jack. He tells me my annual leave is due, but I asked him to postpone it until November as I don't have any cash to spare for holidays. The pay is much less when on leave, as camping and district allowance pay come only when on the job. I saw Dr Roberts and all okay at that end. Paid a subscription to the Goldfields Medical Fund, up to and including the qualifying period. I was on the way back home when I got booked by a Traffic Inspector for turning left past a red light. I thought it was okay to drive into the traffic flow, but is seems I was wrong. There is no way I will ever go anywhere near a Kalgoorlie traffic light intersection again. Henceforth it is all back streets for me. I can ill afford the twenty dollars fine but have to pay.. We had a few drinks Dooley and me, and Jenny Thorpe with Beth Shaw, two tribal sisters of Dooley's, were with us some of the time. They slept at our place overnight on Saturday but left on Sunday morning. They were to come back but didn't.

Wednesday 30 - On the way into Kalgoorlie, around seven o'clock this morning, about four miles out of town, we got quite a surprise to see Inguka (Jenny Thorpe) and Beth Shaw walking along the road, being followed by two young Aboriginal men. We had no idea they were in Kalgoorlie. We thought them to be still back at Leonora. They must have hitched a ride with a truck driver. That is their way of life and not our concern. It looked as though they had a meet-on with the two men so we didn't pull up, just gave them a wave and continued along our way into town. We got to the APB Depot early and had the vehicle inspected by two plant engineers. Noel and Jim. They went all over it and thought it okay, then at the last moment, found a faulty manifold. This they replaced with a new one. We got away after that and were able to reach Leonora before dark. Return trip from Kalgoorlie, one hundred and forty-nine miles.

Figure 19 a & b The Strange Track 1970

Chapter Twenty - BREAK NEW TRACKS - OR SCREW A FEW NECKS

OCTOBER 1970

Thursday 1 - Speedo 10990. Old father Biggs the local butcher agreed to sell me some second hand furniture from a load of stuff he bought from one of Leonora's former boarding houses when it closed years ago. He has a shed full of period chairs and tables. Today we had a big cleanup at the house. I put enough furniture in the proposed office to serve my purpose. I call it an office, although it is pretty rough and ready by anyone's standards. One never knows, I may one of these days be able to afford an interior paint job, buy some curtains, and get some proper office furniture, but I don't know when. I can't seem to make ends meet at all these days. Later I purchased stores, refuelled, then we proceeded back to Red Well to camp. Two hundred and two miles this trip.

Friday 2 - I compiled September journals first, then hooked onto the refurbished drag and took it in tow north-east to the boundary gate. My intention was to do another drag east to the unnamed range, en route Gibson Hill. I only got three quarters of a mile done when the tow chain broke. Nothing else but return to Red Well and leave repairs until tomorrow. From Red Well I did a round trip via Walaru and Claypan windmill in search of a kangaroo for meat but had no luck. We didn't see even one roo, nor did we see any last night on the way out from Laverton. A man is reported missing along the back track from Leonora to Southern Cross. Thirty miles only today.

Saturday 3 - We set off to the north-east again. Shot a turkey before reaching the drag. Dooley prepared it for cooking while I fixed the broken chain. I hooked on again and we took off. A strong tail wind from the west. The going was heavy so we had to halt about every mile to cool the engine. Petrol kept vaporising in the fuel pipes and the drag tended to bog down in the soft sand. The drag being such a dead weight behind, made it difficult to get mobile again if I pulled up anywhere, for as much as a moment, even in low range with the four wheels engaged. It was best to keep moving forward all the time. We only accomplished about nine miles by dinner time. We cooked the bird in the ground while the overheated engine had a spell. The meat was juicy and delicious. We ate nearly all of it for the midday meal.

After dinner and on the job once more, we got into a bad patch of soft sand. Even after deflating the tyres to 15lb pressure I still had a lot of trouble to get any forward motion. The tow chain broke several times. It took more than six hours after starting the job this morning, to reach the eighteen mile point. This was about one mile short of the central range which is hidden behind a sand rise at this spot. I've mentioned before how rising ground west of the range hides it from view. During the entire eighteen miles of this new access track, the range is invisible from the west until right upon it. The long north-south stretch of rising spinifex and sand hides it from view. The range when reached for the first time comes as a complete surprise as one tops the last sand rise. Anyway why worry, I don't want to make good roads for all these blasted prospectors infesting the country. I turned around in the hope that anyone following our new track will dislike travel over the numerous sandhills along the way.

Hopefully they may give it away before they see the range. The return trip to the starting point took only a bit more than two hours. I only had to stop twice for minor repairs on the trip back. Also it was much better travelling into a head wind to keep the engine cool, in contrast to the strong tail wind we experienced on the way out. This track is now good enough to serve my purpose and will be of immense value as it forms a round trip from Red Well, north-east to Gregory Hills, southward past the Gibson Point, then west back to Red Well.

Kado has a sore eye, his first. He'll be four months old on the 10th of October. Dooley is okay in the daytime but coughs all night. The man reported missing yesterday between Leonora and Southern Cross is safe today. The authorities found him in Sydney, he certainly gets around a bit!

Sunday 4 - Strong winds blew a gale all night. This morning was too windy to light a breakfast fire near the caravan so we headed off and had a late breakfast along the north-east road instead. We picked up the drag from where we left it last night and continued along the road to Patapuka. There was a bit of trouble along the way when part of the drag fell off, I had to go back three miles to retrieve the thing.

The graded north-east road to Lake Wells and Gregory Hills turns east near Patapuka. I wore some wheel tracks in through open country to the north of Patapuka in October 1969 and now wish to pull the drag over them to form a distinct access to rockholes in that direction.

The country we traversed is mulga scrub for two miles then spinifex, with a few low sandhills to either side for three or four miles. Scrub again after that for the last couple of miles. Eight miles to the first rockhole, the trough-like catchment called Narrkal that I've mentioned before in these journals, it is located on the rim of a low escarpment and not easy to see from below. It is more of a ledge than an escarp. Narrkal is at the north end of a narrow inlet clothed with small saltbush. The name Narrkal means concealed and that is quite an exact description of the place.

We turned west along the saltbush flat for one mile, west-north-west and north-west next for three and a half miles through scrub covered gravel flats, to reach Pilki, a large round rockhole full of sand. The rockhole is right out in the open, central to a clear gravel flat. Some interesting breakaways sit back from it a bit to one side. The hole is about four paces in diameter. I gain the impression it might be quite deep if cleared of the sand that fills it close to ground level. It is now only a dry basin.

Pilki marks the termination of an old sandalwood track now almost impossible to discern, but which I was able to trace this far. Sandalwood getters must have camped here for some time years ago, judging by the compact heaps of discarded wood chips left behind. Looking around the area I found a small gnamma hole on top of a rise one quarter of a mile west of Pilki, it too was dry. It has three prominent upright stone markers to denote its location.

Camels are the culprits that keep all rockholes dry these days. Since those old beasts of burden lost favour to motor vehicles, they have become feral herds that drink every drop of water the moment they find a full rockhole.

Nomads would perish in this country nowadays if they still lived here. Thirsty camels wouldn't give them a chance. It is rare to find a full catchment of any kind anymore except for immediately after rain.

Unhooked the drag near Pilki for a while. Further to the west there is another set of old wheel marks running east off the Paiyari track, just north of Tharukati, that I wish to link to this one later. If it holds together long enough, I may use the drag to perform that task. The Tharukati track runs east for a distance of about seven miles, to terminate at another old sandalwood camp about five miles north of here by my reckoning. There is a prominent little rocky knob just north of where the other track ends. I went today to the a high point not far from Pilki to climb and see if the knob is visible from here. Conditions are not the best today. Wind gusts and dust wracks dominate the horizon about eight or ten miles west, but I did see a bluff hill to the north that could be the one with knob I wanted to locate. I came back to the vehicle and we set off once more to make new wheel marks in that direction.

Travel at first was through open scrub and good going for two miles where we encountered a tiny isolated saltbush flat with jet black stone outcrops in places. I took some samples of the black rocks. We reached the knob at exactly five miles, it was the one I saw earlier after all, but one can never be certain of things seen from a distance in this country until you reach them. My estimate of the distance from Pilki was spot on. I seem to get better at navigation and map reading all the time, since these new aerial maps came out. I decided to do the drag job today after all. I returned to get it immediately and drag the route just traversed, then turned around and pulled it back again to consolidate the new track. The distance is four miles from Pilki to the knob.

That was it for now, being finished with the drag I left it on a saltbush flat one mile north of Pilki. We returned seventeen miles and a bit to Patapuka then thirty back to our camp at Red Well. The wind still roaring with hurricane force when we got there. The caravan annexe was in the process of being blown to shreds. I dismantled it and stowed it away. Still too much wind to light a fire near camp so we adjourned to a low thicket five hundred paces away and lit one there. A most interesting day. We travelled a total of seventy-seven miles all told.

Monday 5 - Our open campsite is no good when the wind blows so we shifted everything into a thicket. The wind actually shifted our caravan several inches out of position. After dinner we went into Laverton to post the APB journals and refuel. The Post Office was closed for a public holiday that I didn't know anything about, it seems this holiday was on account of the Leonora Races. To make things worse I couldn't get any drum fuel so had to get forty-five gallons from the bowser.

On the way back to Red Well we found one station gate open and another flat on the ground. Maybe the posts were rotten and cattle knocked them over. I think it more likely though that some boozed up nickel man left one gate wide open and drove straight through the other.

Tuesday 6 - Speedo now 11494. Brought out ten cases of APB baits from Laverton yesterday. I detest strychnine but have to wear it. All part of the job and can't do a thing about it other than resign and I'm not about to do that. Got to be realistic about these things, if I don't do the job then plenty of others will. We are off to enjoy four days break as of tomorrow and won't commence the baiting drive until we get back. Proceeded via Laverton to Leonora. Two hundred and thirty-three miles. Looks like a cool change coming tonight.

Monday 12 - I just discovered this morning that today is a public holiday so can't leave until tomorrow as we need stores. After I wrote that, we decided to leave for Red Well regardless. We arrived there at 7 pm. One hundred and fifty miles.

Tuesday 13 - A telegram from Perth on the morning session to say Insurance Assessors will be at Bandya on the of 15th October to inspect the caravan damage. In the meantime I commenced the baiting drive from the north-east boundary gate. When near Karu Soak I had to shoot one kangaroo still alive in a dog trap, it was caught by one leg.

Nyiruru is full of water for a change. Earli Earli waterhole also full. Heavy rainfalls out that way since we were last there and wildflowers everywhere. We got a surprise to find a blue tent pitched near Tjampan on the way out north-east tins morning. Looks like two nickel men are camping there. They have lots of tinned food stacked in neat rows on the ground inside the tent, but no one home. Must be they don't know they are living alongside a good soakage as they are using drum water. I got rid of seven cases of baits and good riddance to them. One dog in trap at Miltji. Two at Karu. One at Nyiruru. Two at Earli Earli. A kangaroo got away with one trap from Karu. Cool east wind all day. I'm getting a sore throat. Dooley's had one for more than a week now. One hundred and forty-five miles.

Wednesday 14 - Continued baiting north past Wakulyakutjarra and all the way when returning to Red Well. Collected three old dogs' heads along the way. I get bonus money for skulls the same as for scalps. Two south of Tharukati and one near our point of return. Four miles north of Urarey in spinifex country is an old well hidden in a thicket east side of the road. We saw prospectors' tracks turning off there. Some woman left her period rags there hanging inside a bush in such a way as to entice some curious person to put a hand in and grab it to see what it is. I almost got caught but recognised the thing for what it was in the nick of time. Six miles further north near the granites, more of the period things lay discarded around an abandoned prospectors' camp. These people appear to have had a helicopter there, because they left an empty AV Gas drum behind. Further north again at a point about four miles south of the derelict Jerry's Well, we followed a fresh set of well-used wheel tracks east for two miles. Where it crosses over a high sandridge we found a Toyota spare wheel lying on the sandridge crest. One mile further on we came to a large, not long abandoned campsite. Much rubbish and sample bags lay scattered all over. An empty forty-four gallon water drum and lots of foodstuffs thrown away. Potatoes, onions, eggs, and other things too numerous to mention. The track continues south over another sandridge near the campsite before turning east again. What a strange place for a camp! We turned back as the road seems to go nowhere. I picked up the spare wheel seen earlier and left it leaning against a tree at the new turnoff in case someone comes back to look for it. Whoever that crowd was, they haven't a clue about how to tackle sandhills. We could see by tracks how they made many attempts with high pressure tyres before getting over.

Travelling north again, when we got near Deleta we found a new datum peg right beside the old well. I took the paper off and it seems the peggers are a Mr Schiller and Mr Acron. No sign of dogs anywhere. I removed and brought back with me all bar one trap. Not a place to set a trap around this area anymore. I'll have to find some fresh country. Return to Red Well. One hundred and thirty-four miles.

Thursday 15 - We drove into the homestead to meet the STEHN insurance assessor. He was there before us, having arrived by charter aircraft. I expected him to come by road. Took him out to Red Well to look over the caravan damage. He assessed it at $430.00 and will send a cheque for that amount. He was polite and genuine. He told of how some people try to put it over the insurance companies, but claimed he never doubted my story for an instant. I took him back to the homestead then returned to Red Well for a washing day, straighten things out in the Landrover, and fixed a puncture. It amazes me that an insurance company would send a chartered aircraft out bush just to assess a claim at four hundred dollars. It seems so illogical and expensive to me.

Saturday 17 - On camp all yesterday. The speedo now reads 12221. The mileage is creeping up. Clarry Cashen the Wiluna dogger is making me angry. He's set traps north from Bandya boundary all the way along west side of the Scholl Range in my area. To rub me up a bit more he wrote his name on one of my poison tickets. This was just out from Kulitjanu rockhole. Further north he has beaten a track into a dry gully south of Karli Rockhole. It looks like he's been looking for pups in the caves there. He won't get any though as we already beat him to it. We got five dead pups there not long ago, from a cave not far from where Cashen turned back. He doesn't appear to use APB approved methods. His traps are wide open, with no hint of any sort of a lead into them at all. His traps are all the cumbersome old Delamy type. The APB no longer uses these. All APB traps these days are either Lane's or Uneida brands. I see he's caught a few foxes but no dogs. We saw two dog tracks near Karli where he turned off to go back inside Wonganoo boundary, at the cattle yard and windmill on the fence.

I don't know what Cashen is coming at. This is my G6 Area not his. What makes me so wild is, I was gong to commence intensive operations in the Scholl Range area now the dogs are under control to the east, where I've been working to date. Now this newcomer has spoilt it all. Saw another two dog tracks running up and down the winding east-bound desert track north of the Scholl Range. They disappeared twenty miles out in the open country. No sign of dogs around Seven Sisters gnamma holes at twenty-eight miles, they are all dry. Eight miles further east however, there are dog tracks everywhere, including those of pups. This fresh activity is along east side of the breakaways. I shot a kangaroo but had no strychnine to poison it with so cut pockets in the carcase and stuffed them with commercial brisket baits. Dog tracks all the way east then, to the junction with Mulga Queen track

I don't know where the dogs are drinking as there is no surface water anywhere that we know. Plenty green herbage and lots of kangaroos this trip though. One hundred and fifty-two miles today. We camping near the junction.

Sunday 18 - Got up early and travelled five miles north to Paiyari. A little water in the rockhole but only one dog track. I want to cut a track east from here, so took a compass bearing of $80°$ and put some new wheel marks across the country. At half a mile into the new traverse, we came to a little dry gnamma hole. A few hundred yards further east we came upon two fair size rockholes, both dry. It was a pleasant discovery though, being unexpected so soon after beginning the new traverse. Also unexpected was the discovery of a dragged sandalwood track when we got in a bit. The track does not reach the Paiyari road. That is why we didn't find it before this.

The drag mark is faint but easy to follow. It goes the same way I wanted to go so we continued along it. The track ends not far from a prominent gap or divide in an unnamed system of low ranges of white quartz lying ahead. The range runs north and south with a wide sandy creek running through the gap. Not a gum creek but a wash type with deep sandy bed, choked in the gap with minga, karara, needle, and mulga bushes. The creek being the type that promises good possibility of soakage water. I searched for signs of a soak for about a mile along its length without success but will take a closer look further downstream later.

Continued on the $80°$ bearing and passed two more gnamma holes before leaving the hard stony ground to enter open spinifex and sand. Surprise again. Nickel prospectors came in here from the south-east and pegged the area. Their track did not lead in the preferred direction so I ignored it and continued on my own course. Reached the first sandhill on east side of the two mile wide spinifex sandplain just traversed. We passed a picturesque red sandhill adorned with dark green pine trees, then at eight and a half mile east of Paiyari, we suffered a puncture. We were fortunate to have a mulga thicket for shade while I changed the tyre.

From this puncture thicket we could see what I supposed to be the Yantakanngang hills about ten miles east and right on course. Those hills are where I wish to come out, and thus link two graded access roads, running north from the Bandya boundary, with an east-west track. The day was by this time getting too hot for comfort, and far too hot for the baby, so we turned back on our tracks for the present, quite satisfied with the morning's work. Came back to Red Well and camp. Sixty-nine miles.

Monday 19 - Speedo 12442. Sent a telegram to jack Kerr asking him to bring a new tyre and tube to Laverton if he comes tomorrow. This morning I decided to tackle the new track from the east end. We went north to Yantakanngang and took a bearing of 260^0 for two and half mile, to discover a group of little gnamma holes. This saw the end of the hard stony country. We entered spinifex next and passed several pine-clad, but otherwise bare red sandhills. They do make an attractive scene. Similar dunes are scattered all along our route.

At seven miles west of Yantakanngang we sighted the Paiyari hills in front and realised that today's western traverse was too far north, as the mileage put our present position well westward of yesterday's point of return, so I turned due south to the thicket where I changed a flat tyre yesterday. This leg was three quarters of a mile and of course, we also hit yesterday's track running east past the thicket. Turned east there along the track to yesterday's point of return, then north to reach today's westerly traverse again at half a mile.

Now we have a west-east track with a half mile kink in the middle. I will straighten that out later, but for the present it is good enough. After hitting this morning's track we returned along it east. Pulled up for dinner about one or two miles west of Yantakanngang, or a bit more than six miles from the puncture thicket where we linked the two tracks with a half mile kink. Reached this morning's point of departure Yantakanngang at a bit short of eight miles. After adding the seven and a half mile travelled east from Paiyari to the puncture thicket yesterday, it makes the total mileage between Paiyari and Yantakanngang fifteen and one half miles.

From Yantakanngang we next travelled north three miles to Tharukati granites, then east through the spinifex. Found it to be eleven and a half mile to where we turned back with the drag on Sunday the 4th and left it near Pilki. We came to the rockhole south-east of Pilki at twenty and a half mile, and reached Patapuka at twenty-eight and a half mile. A total of forty miles back to Red Well where once arrived, we did washing and cleaned the Landrover before dark. Eighty-six miles today.

Tuesday 20 - I first read David Carnegie's classic of exploration entitled "Spinifex & Sand" some years ago during the 1950s. Since absorbing the contents of that book I've been anxious to relocate one particular desert water he discovered during mid August 1896. This was the underground cavern he named Empress Spring. The copious water supply found on that occasion deep beneath the ground, almost certainly saved the lives of Carnegie and party, there is no doubt about that. His description of the place fascinates me. It enjoys an aura of remoteness. Carnegie remarked also on the lack of landmarks near its location. To the best of my knowledge no whiteman has revisited the site since Carnegie's time. This makes it even more of a challenge to go and seek it out. To find that underground cavern is to be my next project.

Amongst a batch of aerial maps I purchased not long ago is one called ROBERT. This has Empress Spring on a bearing of 105^0 and eighteen miles from the southern tip of Ida Range. Carnegie's only geological landmark Breadon Bluff, is not on this ROBERT Sheet, but there is a high point numbered 1526 on a bearing of 120^0 about thirty miles distant from Ida Range. This high point lies in the right direction to fit Carnegie's coordinates. Carnegie recorded his chosen landmark, Breadon Bluff, as being approximately twelve miles distant from Empress Spring on a bearing of 320^0 and described it as a red tableland. I am however, not comfortable with the cartographer's position for Empress Spring, because he has it positioned at the southern end of some lake country. Carnegie did not refer to any lakes in the vicinity of his find. I wrote the above notes for the pilot of the baiting plane. In the event I go up with the plane tomorrow, I would like the pilot to fly around and see if I can get a fix on Empress Spring. We went to Laverton but Jack Kerr not there. I put the Landrover in to the new garage for a 12000 mile service. After I got the vehicle out we went west to Leonora. A tyre blew out along the way. When we got to Leonora I had Sullivan fit a new one. Purchased a drum of fuel at AMPOL and took it home to fill the tanks. The surveyor Mark (somebody) who camped near us at Larkins Outcamp on Yundamindra when we worked there, is realigning building lots throughout the town. He found fault with the position of corner pegs around our two acre block. He reckons one corner post is right where the survey peg should be. I suggested he drop the new peg down inside the hollow post, so to my astonishment, he did just that.

Wednesday 21 - Return to Laverton. Saw Jack Kerr and informed him of how dogger Cashen is working my area along the Scholl Range. Jack thinks it more likely to be a Meekatharra group dogger based at Wonganoo. He agrees the fellow is out of bounds. All country outside the station boundaries is the sole province of APB government doggers like myself. Group doggers must stay within the fenced country. Jack says he'll look into the matter and fix the problem. We returned Red Well.

Thursday 22 - Depart Red Well for Leonora again. This time we travelled via Erlistoun and Nambi. I gave the government Landrover a thorough good cleanup, filled all the tanks and got it ready for departure to the bush on Monday next. On Friday I cleaned our own vehicle and tidied up around the camp.

We had a cold windy night. No telegrams for me on the Saturday RFDS session. Did a lot of work around the house and garden. Sunday overcast and cold in the morning. Light showers during the day. On Monday we packed up and proceeded via Laverton back to Red Well. Shot a kangaroo north of Laverton, the only one we saw all the way.

Tuesday 27 - North-west via Mulga Queen track to the Seven Sisters breakaways, where we saw a lot of dog tracks during our last trip out that way. I'd placed a roo carcase bait there but nothing ate it. Dogs have been smelling around though and are still active in the area. I set two traps at north end of the hills where the road makes a sharp turn south-west to the Seven Sisters gnamma holes. We came back to the east side below the escarpment and this time saw a young dog lying down in the shade of a bush. The dog took off helter skelter across the flats, but after a bit of a chase I got him with a head shot.

After that episode we followed a grassy wash upstream into the south end of the breakaways and discovered a good rockhole. No water visible but a good supply deep down in the sand. I probed it with the full length of a four foot iron bar through wet sand all the way without touching bottom. Upright native stone markers are numerous all around, atop every outcrop in the vicinity. These indicate it is an important site. There is no sign that any motor vehicle has ever been near this rockhole. It is not easy to find and no evidence of its presence from outside. We only found it by following fresh kangaroo pads in.

I chiselled my name and date on a rockface. One or two petroglyph bird track markings on the rock are almost too faint to see. It must be a long time since natives pecked them into the rock. I'll take photos next trip as I'm out of film again. From the new rockhole find, we returned east to Paiyari. From Paiyari we continued east along our recent traverse to the white quartz gap, and acacia creek, to camp out in the open near some low granites. One hundred and five miles.

Wednesday 28 - Cold south-east wind all last night and again this morning. We had to pack up and shift camp into the creek out of the wind to have breakfast. It was much too windy and cold outside in the open. After breakfast I examined the creek for two miles east of the white quartz gap. I'd hoped to find a soak but had no luck. I did find several good clayholes in the creek channel but all were dry.

There is also a shallow catchment outside the creek on a flat half a mile east of the gap. This catchment lies beneath a small cork tree, and a heap of dirt shows where natives dug here for water in the past. I thought it a good sign that no other soakage is available in the vicinity, else they would not have dug on this shallow basin looking for water. The basin is a rain time only type of catchment by the look of it. That is my opinion although I may be wrong. One day I might dig down to make sure, but the ground looks pretty hard to me, and not conducive of a soak. Continued east and found a patch of yellow gemstone on top of a rise a bit north of our track. This rise marks the end of the stony country and is just short of where spinifex sandplain begins a bit further east. Collected a few samples.

On the way east we took a more southerly tack across saltbush flats, out a bit from south side of the Yantakanngang breakaways. This is better travelling than out original traverse. We also found several dry gnamma holes not found before. Not a sign of dogs all the way until we reached Yantakanngang where we pulled up for dinner. Just before we got there we came across a hill we hadn't seen before. The hill is a type of heavy brown stone.

After dinner I set one trap, then we proceeded via Tharukati granites east to Pilki. Dooley tried it with a bar this time and to my surprise, struck water at a depth of four feet. I'd not thought it that deep as the surface is hard-packed clay, but once through the upper clay crust the bar went down with ease into a body of water-logged sand below. I didn't bother to open the soak as we don't require water now, but it is handy to know where to get a supply if ever in need. Further on we found some more interesting stone near Narrkal, the concealed ledge rockhole. We took samples then returned to Red Well to camp. Sixty-three miles and no sign of dogs.

Thursday 29 - Mileage on the clock is now 13317. We set off this morning to have a look at what the prospectors camped at Tjampan are up to. We saw their tent and supply of stores there before, but the campers were not present at the time. They have pushed wheel tracks out into the spinifex a distance of eight miles north-west. At six miles from Tjampan they have a turnoff going east, which if it continues in that direction, should come out near Karu Soak. They appear to be on foot most of the time by the look of tracks, but we saw no sign of them in the flesh. We came back to the main track, then on to the spinifex a bit south of Miltji for dinner.

After dinner we came to Karu. From the spinifex plain located one and a half mile west of the soak, I cut a new traverse. On a bearing of $35°$ we came at two miles to a small creek running off the De La Poer Range. I ran the creek up to where it heads in granite, to find a small dry rockhole but nothing else of interest. Discarded the compass bearing in favour of a direct route to north point of the range, at three miles.

From the three mile point we drove around the end of the range to the west side, where is nothing but spinifex and sandhills. No sign of water. No sign of dogs. No sign whatsoever of the dotted road that is marked in so clearly on current editions of the army four mile sheets. The road does not exist. The maps being quite wrong about the marked road, we ran a direct course south-west across country back to Karu. Beside the first pool of clean water in Moxon Creek, we pulled up for a spell and did our washing.

A couple of stranded travellers set the spinifex alight before Xmas last year to make smoke for a distress signal. It is still a barren burnt landscape of blackened tree trunks and skeletal leafless bushes. After the laundry job we came five miles east from Karu into this burnt country to take a bearing of 165^0 towards the central unnamed range. A job I've wanted to do for some time past. There is a prominent round knob along this central high ground, visible above the tree line both from Karu on the west side, and Point Gibson to the east. This knob is what I took the bearing on. At nine miles we came to the first line of granite boulders and left the sand behind. For the most part at this, its northern end, the range comprises granite outcrops, broken ridges, and small peaks. It is one mile from west to east in width. Within the folds of this central feature, numerous saltbush flats occupy intervening spaces between granite outcrops, across a sort of divide at this point. The eastern flank where we came out, has dense mulga thickets blocking the exit. For a number of reasons, I wanted to get out before dark.

On a direct bearing of 120^0 we hit the Cosmo road at four miles. This brought us out a bit north of Point Gibson as anticipated, after a lot of scrub bashing. We didn't see any water catchments, but there are lots of fresh euro pads running north and south in the middle of the granites. Also saw one fresh dog track. I would like to have followed the pads, but it was too late in the day. I don't like to camp too far from the road when baby Kado is on board in case of vehicle trouble overnight. Also I do not have the APB's blessing for these offroad trips. In the event of a breakdown I could suffer dismissal for defying instructions. They tell me all exploration is out of bounds. I am certain that is why Jack Kerr keeps me so short of good tyres, tubes, and spare parts. Another thing in my experience is that vehicles have a habit of giving trouble in the mornings, more than any other time. They seem to contemplate the previous day's hard work and pack it in overnight. This is almost always the case when the night stopover is on a dry camp far from known water. Eighty-four miles.

Friday 30 - Doing the right thing by the APB I inspected the traps as far north as Nyiruru. Not a sign of dogs. Natives now living in Leonora who used to roam this country told us of a soak in the creek downstream from Nyiruru. I found it today, but it was difficult to locate as there are no pads or other indication of its whereabouts. It appears to be a good one, located in deep sand. Later I shot an emu and we cooked it in the ground.

A telegram on the afternoon session:

Kalgoorlie
Bernie O'Driscoll expects to be Laverton Friday afternoon 30th. Stop. Meet him there earliest. Signature Kerr.

It was too late when I got the telegram to keep the appointment. We got going via Karu to Red Well then in to Laverton. By the time we arrived it was too late to catch him but will see him in the morning. Two hundred and ten miles today.

Saturday 31 - Topped up the tanks with seventeen gallons of petrol. We left for the north with O'Driscoll and a chap name of Brian Duggan, who is a Wiluna group dogger. He is coming out with us (experts) for the experience. Arrive Red Well at half past twelve. We stayed the day. It was an interesting time. We spent the afternoon showing Bernie O'Driscoll my collection of photos, including a batch of originals sent me by Michael Terry, covering his 1925-32 periods of exploration along the WA-NT border region and other areas. Bernie was enrapt with our photos of the strange track. He studied the prints for the best part of an hour but could offer no explanation as to what made the footprints. I'm afraid poor old Brian Duggan was on the outer.

Dooley's uncle Albert Jones came along with his family mob, from Erlistoun for an unexpected, and I might add, untimely visit, during the afternoon. He announced he was going to camp here. I told him to go camp somewhere else. He is okay, but I don't want his hangers-on anywhere near me. Not only that, his arrival when one of the bosses is here, made me look so silly. The APB will get the impression we have blackfellows out bush with us all the time and that will spoil the job. A thunderstorm brought a few spots of rain in the evening. Eighty-three miles travel from Laverton to here.

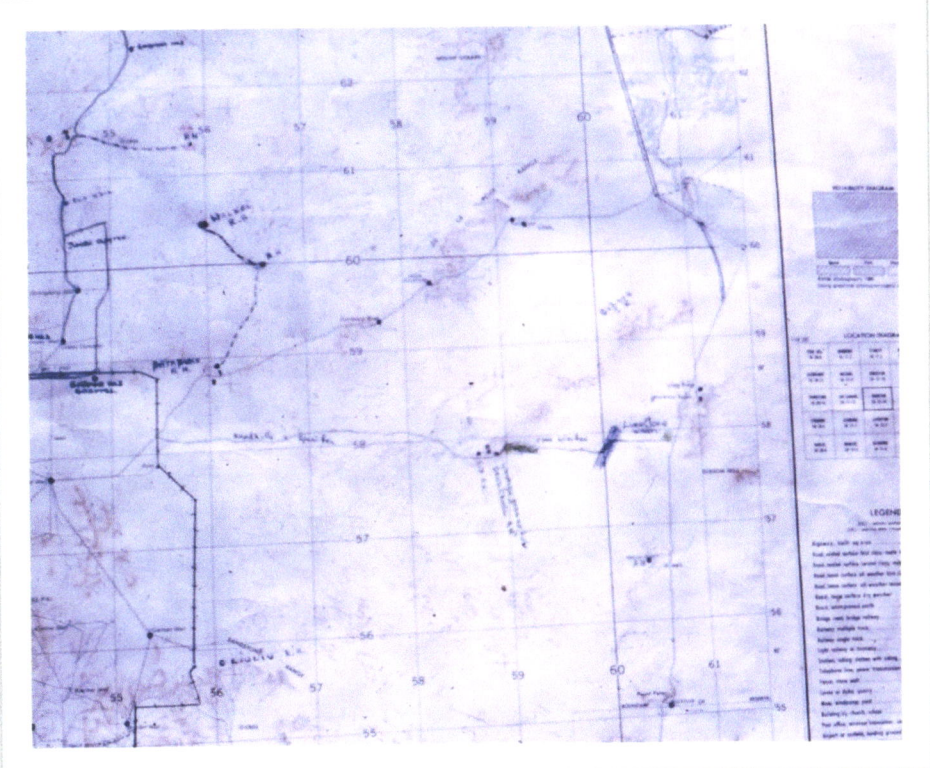

Figure 20 Filling in the Blanks – Duketon Mapsheet

Chapter Twenty One - THE MUIR GORGE & AN ANNUAL BREAK

NOVEMBER 1970

Sunday 1 - We set off this morning north-west along the Deleta track. In the lead was Dooley, baby Kado and me. In the second vehicle Bernie O'Driscoll. Brian Duggan brought up the rear. We made a neat little convoy of three. We didn't get too far, nor enjoy a good trip. We intended to go much further afield, but after dinner it rained all afternoon without let-up.

Our convoy turned east off the main track at Tharukati then southerly via the new Pilki and Narrkal drag track, coming out at Patapuka on the Karu road where by this time, the country was awash. It was much too wet to continue so we turned back to Red Well. The only sign of dogs seen was one track near Tharukati and one further east of the granites near the old "cyclone bed" sandalwood camp. Seventy wet miles travel today.

Monday 2 - We got going again this morning, this time along the Karu track. The big rain of yesterday ran the little creek a banker at Tjampan and filled the soakage depression in the creek to capacity. The two prospectors camping there were present today. The first I've seen of them in the flesh. Bernie O'Driscoll asked did I know the two men were camping there and I said yes, but he appeared sceptical when I told him I hadn't actually met them until today. He gave me quite a quizzical look of disbelief. I am not one to deceive anyone at anytime, and don't like it when people disbelieve things I say, but that was his attitude, so not much I can do about it. The two men told us how they nearly got washed away last night when the creek ran. They also showed astonishment when informed that their camp was right alongside a native water. They'd been camping there for some time, only fifty paces away from a soakage, and didn't know a thing about it until I told them today.

We bade them g'day and went on north-east to Miltji where Bernie gave a trap setting demonstration. After the demo we went on to Karu, but more rain coming up so we returned to Miltji for dinner. To date Bernie says my trap setting technique and general control work is okay. After dinner we came south-west to the Bandya north-east boundary gate and followed my new drag track east to the unnamed range. We left the spinifex and sand country at seventeen miles, then got bogged one mile further on while negotiating the west side of the range. Two tow ropes it took to get the bogged vehicle out of the muck after which we pulled up to camp near the lid rockhole at sundown. Eighty-one miles travel today.

Tuesday 3 - Had a look at what I call the lid rockhole after breakfast, then we went on to the central part of the range in order to inspect the (dead camel) water hole at head of the gorge there. Both these catchments are brimful now. We all walked a lot further down the gorge than I had done when alone, on the day of my first visit here. Every rockhole down the gorge is full. One has a profusion of green rushes. These rushes must have been green before the rain, indicating that either surface water was there before, or soakage water in the sand keeps them green. Strange there is no sign of dogs in the area.

We left the range and continued east to Point Gibson, then north to the two windmills at Peter Hill's junk yard beyond the Ullrich Range or Gregory Hills. Brian Duggan took a full roll of film to record the conglomeration of junk that Peter Hill stacked in neat piles within his two windmills' enclosure. He seemed impressed by the sign warning trespassers that the place is still of importance to the owner and not abandoned.

Brian says he'd never have believed it if the sign wasn't there to inform him of the fact. I agree fully with his sentiments. One dog track here, the only one seen all day.

Further west, the crossing at Lake Wells was treacherous and slippery. We got over it okay, but in a most comical sort of way. Me being in the lead, meant I had to take the brunt of slips and slides. The two following Landrovers got the benefit of me dispersing the upper slime-layer. My Landrover skidded across sideways the entire distance. The width is a good three hundred paces at the crossing and the sensation of sliding this way and that, instead of bonnet forward in the normal way, was sufficient to put one's heart in the mouth, as the old saying goes. It is not boggy just slippery. Vehicles don't sink in deep muck or anything like that. It is quite hard underneath, but the surface when wet is like skating on ice, or skidding on an oily bitumen highway.

The original plan was to continue right around the G6 dogging area, but Bernie now discovered he had only fifteen gallons of petrol left in his tanks. Then Brian Duggan found he'd run out of water, so we all returned to Karu Soak and camped on a high rise beside Moxon Creek. All the pools here are full since the rain. Beautiful water, clear as crystal. I thought to do the right thing and suggested to Brian Duggan that he top up his tank with some of this lovely water. He declined with a facial grimace. He claims he never tops up with natural waters at anytime. He only fills his tanks with tap water from town. I thought at first he was pulling my leg, but it seems not,: he was adamant that no bush water would ever see the inside of his tanks. He may he said, use windmill water if pushed, but only with reluctance. I said no more.

On a more interesting note Bernie O'Driscoll says the gorge where the dead camel rockhole is located, in the as yet unnamed range, will henceforth be known to all and sundry as Muir Gorge. I couldn't get over it. To the best of my knowledge, this is the first time any feature on the landscape is to bear my name. A rare honour indeed.

Wednesday 4 - Return from Karu to Red Well. My two visitors departed for Laverton. One for fuel, the other for water! After they left, Dooly and I went west to Wilson's Bore, then on to Yultu rockholes to the north-west of Wilson's after dinner. No fresh indication of dogs in the area, but I did get a couple of skulls from the two dogs Dooley and I shot here last year. We couldn't find the carcases at the time. The tails are still complete, but the skulls are broken and bleached white. We came back to Red Well by way of Hootanui. One hundred and sixteen miles.

Thursday 5 - The clock is now sitting on 14018. Came across to Leonora to meet Jack Kerr on his way through town en route Sandstone. On Friday I put the UQD vehicle in for service. I got it out on Saturday and fixed Sullivan with LPO payment. On Sunday I put last month's paper work in order. Later in the day Jack Kerr came back from Sandstone and told me Bernie O'Driscoll will be along tomorrow for another trip out bush with me.
Jack Kerr says that Leo Boladeras of Wonganoo is complaining about baits that he says I left along the Scholl Range, within half a mile of his windmills. Also that dogger Clarry Cashen, was quite within his rights working along the Scholl Range as it lies within the Wiluna Shire and not Laverton Shire as I had thought.

To top off the hate session, Cashen claims also that I left commercial baits on top of, and spread around his trap-sets. The instructions now are, that I no longer put an official foot along the Scholl Range. Henceforth I am to turn back from Seven Sisters gnamma holes when I come in from the east. That's alright by me.

Monday 9 - Refuelled, purchased stores, then got going again in company with APB Instructor Bernie O'Driscoll and his dogger companion Brian Duggan. This time along the Nambi road. We camped at sixty-five miles. Mosquitoes bad. On Tuesday we saw the manager Peter Hill at Bandya homestead. Leo Bonney, Peter's brother-in-law was there too. Dooley and I knew him when he managed Kaluwiri Station. We all enjoyed a cup of tea at Bandya then set off via Red Well, along the Karu track to Nyiruru. Had a look around there, then west to camp near the Tui claypans turnoff.

Wednesday 11 - Tui claypans are both dry. The rain did not fall this far. Carried on by way of the back track north to Warren's Well, Rock & Roll and Jump Up. We then cut across country to Panton Bluff in the Von Treur Tableland. Not a sign of dogs anywhere, other than one fresh track six miles north of Warren's Well. We came back to the latter well to camp. Seventy-four miles for the day.

Thursday 12 - South-west to Deleta and Jerry Well, then west and south-west to Paiyari, where we saw how a cunning dog exposed one of my traps. This gave our expert Bernie O'Driscoll a chance to demonstrate his technique for the capture of cunning dogs. He set the first trap and left a bit of paper showing over the plate to attract the dog's attention, he then set a second trap in front of the first, without any indication of its presence. Of course the cunning dog sees the paper showing on the first trap and stretches forward to sniff at it, thus putting an unaware foot in the blind set. Unfortunately my annual leave is overdue. I won't be back here until after the coming New Year 1971, so will not be able to examine tracks following the dog's next visit, to see just what it does do. Seventy-nine miles.

Friday 13 - I took a bearing of 170^0 to what appears like white quartz showing through the tree line, from a point about twenty miles south-west of Jerry Well. I haven't noticed it before. Today the sun was shining at just the right angle to reflect a glimpse of something white as we drove along. I am certain this is the same quartz ridge I saw away to the north-east of Paiyari breakaways, when pulling the drag east to Yantakanngang a while back.

O'Driscoll gave us another demonstration of his trapping expertise. He set two traps on an open saltbush flat near the turnoff to Seven Sisters. Not the sort of place I'd pick for a trap-set, so it will be interesting to see if anything gets caught. After that we returned south to Red Well, where we parted company with our visitors. Bernie and Brian went their respective ways via Laverton. I stayed behind to pack up everything laying loose around the campsite and secured the caravan, then we came into Leonora, arriving well after dark.

Saturday 14 - We came in a bit early. I should have come to town today, but did the trip in my own time last night instead. Leonora is cold, with bitter south-east winds blowing a gale. All last week we enjoyed lovely warm weather when out in the bush. I unloaded everything from the government vehicle and hosed it out in preparation for a thorough cleaning. Filled all the water and fuel tanks. It was an all day job. I finished the cleaning job on Sunday. Monday I spent on APB bookwork and got a surprise when Brian Duggan arrived for a visit. I settled him down with a book on Australian exploration then left him to his own devices and enjoy a good informative read.

Tuesday 17 - A letter arrived in the mail from Jack Kerr telling me to put UQD-634 into the police station while on holidays. I did as he bid today, although the police don't like the idea. They don't want the responsibility. Mr Kerr also stated that I should have a letter from the APB referring to the proposed trip north, to the Ashburton Fall with Michael Terry, and others from the Institute of Aboriginal Studies. No letters like that here yet.

Monday 23 - Official start of annual leave today. Time spent in town until now was time off in lieu. Doggers work a forty hour week. On Wednesday we left Leonora for Albion Downs, with the intention of going on to Wiluna for a holiday. After arrival at Albion Downs however, we lost interest in Wiluna and spent time on Mount Keith and Yakabindie stations, looking at various things of interest instead. One place we went to is an important Aboriginal site known to whites as Palm Spring. The native name is **Pii** pronunciation **pee**. The spring is the alleged habitat of a sacred water snake name of Tjila.

Tjiwal or Logan Spring is dry now and needs opening out, but judging by the size and length of the stock trough, this was once a good spring water. It reminds me of Pikilyi or Vaughn Spring, on Mount Doreen Station in the Northern Territory. Tjiwal is at the top end of a tight gully running out of the Barr-Smith Range. The gully runs south, as the range at this point takes a sharp turn from its north-south line, to run west for a few miles, before turning north again. Tjiwal is about half a mile west of the main road to Wiluna.

We also sighted several soaks in creeks running off the range, then paid a visit to Tjulpu, known to the whites as Mail Change Well. Tjulpu means a tuft of feathers. Such are native head adornments. Tjulpu is a native soak. The interior walls of the shaft have a curious feather-like appearance. During this sojourn along the Barr-Smith Range we sighted several soaks in gum creeks, all running west off the range at intervals. Jones Creek at extreme south end of the range, is the largest of these channels. The weather by this time was getting unbearable and too hot for baby Kado so we came back to Leonora. A letter for me from Michael Terry in the mail box. He is to approach the WA Premier and ask that politician to use his influence, to have me released from APB duties, along with the government vehicle, to do the Pingandy trip with Michael and company. They want me to guide them to my hieroglyph discovery of 1964-65 in the Pingandy area. Jack Kerr is dead-set against the idea, and the APB are notorious for non cooperation with any projects at all that lie outside their own narrow interests. The APB officials suffer from a sort of tunnel vision when it comes to things of interest outside dingo and vermin destruction. Michael wishes to do the trip right after the festive season.

Chapter Twenty Two - THE GUILE OF BUREAUCRATS DOTH PREVAIL

DECEMBER 1970

It was once, and probably still is, a popular expression for soldiers to say: "A man joins the army to be mucked around by experts." (Better spelt with an initial **f** instead of an **m**.) I could express similar sentiments about the APB. It is a self-important, top heavy organisation, that seldom cooperates with other government departments. It is lone doggers in the field who keep the APB in business. Without rank and file doggers the whole APB system would collapse. Doggers are the soldiers. Armed with 303 and 22 calibre rifles, traps, and bottles of strychnine, doggers are the APB's guerilla fighters in the bush. Like the defence forces, the APB is overweight with pompous desk-bound shiny-arse mostly quite ignorant, top brass, all filled with their own sense of self importance. For the most part though, these officials will leave the doggers to their own devices. They are content with the status quo, just so long as their doggers send in a detailed report of activities each month, and remain tight lipped about all operations. Doggers are essential to keep the bosses in a job, but are still of the lowest rank, and for the most part treated with contempt. The big shots at the top on the other hand, will not countenance any erosion of their authority. Like all government departments, the APB also, does not hold politicians in high esteem.

Michael Terry was probably the last Western Desert explorer. Between the years 1924 and 1932 he used a variety of vehicles, in conjunction with camels, to traverse large tracts of previously unmapped terrain, along either side of the WA-NT border. He wrote numerous articles for magazines, and at least seven books about his exploits. Why Michael Terry did not receive more plaudits for his accomplishments is a puzzle to me.

I first met Michael Terry over in the Northern Territory in the bar of a Tennant Creek pub. I was sixteen years old at the time, in town from Helen Springs cattle station, where I worked as a ringer in the stockcamp. Michael was on a return trip, to revisit former haunts and old acquaintances. A crowd of admirers stood at the bar as Michael recounted the noted massacre of Walpiri people in 1928. He didn't take any part in the killing spree, but was coincidentally present in the area at the same time. He was doing a cross country traverse between Hall's Creek and Alice Springs. I was enrapt with his tales of the desert and munjong blacks. I asked him for his opinion of whiteman-black woman cohabitation. His response was abrupt and to the point. "Renegades, nothing but renegades my boy." He said.

Before I continue with the main theme of this section, I should write a few introductory paragraphs to set the plot. The events that led to my recent battle with perverse officials occurred years ago, but those events are in themselves of sufficient interest to record once again:

Six years before writing the field notes from which this printed text is derived, I was a dogger in the Pingandy region, a jumbled area of rough country known to locals as the Ashburton Fall. That was in 1964. This is a fascinating stretch of rugged uplands, the principal features of which, are the Capricorn and Kenneth Ranges. The topography is a conglomeration of peaks, ridges, and tight gullies. It still holds more secrets than modern men have yet discovered. It was my privilege to find a few of these secrets. The scene described next, is near the head of an unnamed creek running from a spectacular gap in the Kenneth Range, north toward, and eventually into, the mighty Ashburton River. I now quote a few edited extracts from my old field notes of 29th December 1964:

"For one and a half miles I strolled in a south-westerly direction along a narrow saltbush flat. This flat extends away from Dingo Soak, toward, and eventually runs into, and borders, the south bank of a creek. [The creek since named Hieroglyph.] At the point where saltbush meets the south bank, I entered the creek itself and walked along a confined channel. The creek has high abrupt cliff banks to either side. At one quarter mile short of where the creek takes a sharp turn to the north-west, I sat on a boulder in the watercourse to rest awhile under a shady tree. The heat of day was oppressive enough in itself, but made more pronounced by the confined channel wherein I sat. Wet with sweat, I was weary from the walk. With elbows on knees I sat with cupped hands pressed across my forehead. I was in half a doze for the space of several minutes, after which I lifted my head to examine the surroundings in more detail.

Directly in front of where I sat, was a vertical cliff along the south bank. It rose about fifteen feet in height, and on the rim above, was the slender white trunk of a desert gum, silhouetted against a blue cloud studded sky. My eyes tight shut during the brief respite, opened to a dazzle of glare and stung from sweat. When clear vision returned I became aware of something strange about the cliff face in front of me. It was in full shade. I had to move closer to discern what had attracted my attention. Astonishment is too mild a word to describe what I saw. The entire cliff face was adorned with equal spaced parallel lines, like the ruled pages of a school exercise book. That was strange enough in itself, but between the lines I saw row after row of neat Sanskrit characters. To describe my reaction as astounded would be an understatement. I almost went into a trance-like state as I gazed in awe at this unexpected find." (Extract from my book Shattered Rocks & Shaded Waters published in limited edition 1988.)

That mysterious discovery led me to write one letter after another to Michael Terry, as I knew he had an avid interest in such things. During the mid to late 1960s he wrote numerous articles in magazines supporting his theory, that ancient civilisations entered Australia long before our present recorded history began. Letters went to and fro between Michael and myself for a full five years. Our mutual interest eventually reached a climax of non cooperation by the powers that be. A conflict that contributed to the theme of this December 1970 text. So much for the Michael Terry aspect.

On now to a second gripe: Around 1967 I was in another remote area, much further east, in the vicinity of the long-abandoned Rabbit Proof Fence. I located a rare animal thought to be extinct. I had a base camp and depot near a big rockhole, located a bit east of that old Rabbit Fence. I used to leave stores and other things under a rock ledge there at that depot, with the added protection of an old tarpaulin tucked in around the heap of gear. Sometimes I would be away on exploration work for long periods, and would not revisit this bush depot for weeks at a time. Once after a long absence, I returned and removed the tarpaulin in order to get at the stores stowed beneath its protective cover. I saw there a beautiful little animal looking at me with apprehension, from the shelter of the rock ledge. It was a lovely little creature, sleek and plump, with a beautiful fur coat of chocolate brown. It looked out at me from large limpid eyes, eyes that were almost black in colour. It showed no fear, just studied me for a while then moved off into the rocks. That is the one and only time I ever saw a sticknest rat.

I never said a word to anyone about the little animal until recent times. Something prompted me to inform the Fisheries and Wildlife Department. Of course they wanted me to guide them to the sticknest rat right away. I however am under legitimate restraint by the APB while on the dogging job and thus unable to leave on such a project, without special permission from the APB departmental brass. I applied for permission to go, and the Wildlife mob applied for a loan of my services. At this juncture, that is where the sticknest matter stands.

Michael Terry wants me to show him the hieroglyphs out Pingandy way. Fisheries and Wildlife want me to show them a living sticknest rat. The APB holds the scales and I don't feel heavy enough to weigh the pan down in my favour. Michael Terry has the ear of politicians. Fisheries and Wildlife are a Big Shot government department in their own right, and qualify as equals of the APB in that respect. A battle of the giants it was, but with me in the middle. That struggle is the theme of what I have yet to write.

Thursday 3 - Jack Kerr RVCO called in regarding my faulty transceiver. He was full of how the APB objects to other departments trying to get me on loan, to guide them to the Carnarvon Ranges north of Wiluna. He also mentioned objections to any involvement of myself with Michael Terry's proposed trip to the Pingandy area. I get the feeling that a lot of this is Jack's personal objection to my going. Jack's nature requires it to be his own idea before he'll condone anything, at least that is the way I've always found him, he is petulant all the time.

Monday 21- My annual leave expired today. I picked up the government vehicle from the police compound and got it ready to do four days work before Xmas. On Tuesday we came across to Laverton and camped a mile west of town. On Wednesday we did a run out to Farm Well, a few miles east of Laverton, and from there north to Crawford Soak. I have a desire to locate Frank Hann's old base camp. Also I wish to find which feature is Admiral Hill. Both places appear to be further east of Laverton. I may follow Skull Creek upstream later and search more.

Satisfied for the present, we returned to Leonora for Xmas Eve with speedo on 14980 and settled in for the festive break. All government employees in WA enjoy a holiday until December the 29th. On the 30th Jack Kerr rang at 11 am to advise me that the WA Premier had gone over the APB's head. The Premier had directed the APB Chief to instruct me to accompany Michael Terry to Pingandy, and guide him to my hieroglyph site, north of Not Riley's Gap. Kerr expressed surprise that I had not received written instructions from either the APB or the Premier's office. Personally I feel sure that both Kerr and the APB are now endeavouring to cover-up a deliberate delaying tactic, because I have not heard even a whisper of approval from either of them. I know for a fact that Jack Kerr and the APB have been against my participation in the trip all along. I'd love to make things difficult for them, but would most likely only make it harder for myself. Kerr sent a telegram at 1 pm to advise that the faulty transceiver now had new coils, and would be sent forward on Thursday's train to Leonora. I wrote a letter to Michael Terry to inform him of the cover-up tactics, and also sent him a telegram care of Pingandy Outpost Radio, in case he is there. It may not be too late for him to stir someone up in Perth, if he uses his political influence.

On another tack the bloody APB brass wouldn't even recommend my application to police for a point 243 high power rifle, and Jack Kerr wouldn't have a bar of it either. It is no wonder I'm so browned off with him, and with them. Being a government dogger is a good occupation though, I don't like to lose it. This evening in order to cool off, we took a run north to Agnew and back again.

Thursday 31- Spent the day compiling official journals to wind up the month, and preparing for departure next year. I rang Michael Terry and was most disappointed to learn that he'd already been to the Pingandy hieroglyph site without me. He'd been guided to there by the Scott family who of course knew its location from directions I'd given them before. Michael returned to Nedlands by plane from Mount Tom Price, much earlier than anticipated. He is disgusted with the whole project. A couple of academic experts also accompanied Michael to the site. They claim the hieroglyph characters to be nothing but natural dendritic markings. They say that what appears to be writing, is only a leaching of hard ironstone type mineral through the softer mass of host cliff face material. I had suggested to Michael years ago that the hieroglyphs were not in my opinion the work of human hands. Michael says he took samples of the formation for testing, then at that point, wished to cease the telephone conversation because of his hearing problem and a poor line connection. I've been corresponding with him for years, but never met face to face since 1946 in the Tennant Creek pub, when of course he was a much younger man and I but a mere youth. Today was our first voice contact in all those years. His well-modulated faint English accent, coming across quite clear to me over the phone, was something of an anticlimax. Michael was born in 1899 and will soon be 72 years of age. He would have been 47 years old that time at Tennant Creek.

Michael said he would like to put a bomb under my APB bosses and with that violent sentiment, I can only agree. May my strongest curse fall upon all who had a hand in the skulduggery and chicanery that prevented me from going on that Pingandy trip with the very last of the oldtime camel explorers. What a deceitful lot of bastards they turned out to be. However there is still plenty of new exotic interest out bush for Dooley and Me, despite the guile of the APB.

So much for the last days of 1970. As a family of three we are keen as ever to traverse the tribal lands east and north-east of Laverton. The exotic scent of untracked wilderness tickles our nostrils. The call of open country rings in our ears. The coming Year of 1971 is certain to bring further highlights to our privileged lives, with more than sufficient material for yet another book. For now it is farewell, as we pack up for the bush again. Who knows? We may catch up to you all again further down the desert track.

FINIS

Figure 21 Dooley and Peter

Errata

See Chp. 8
2nd para. p. 108

We returned to the Warburton track and followed it south-west to Nord Rockhole, in Mulgabiddy Creek. The name Mulgabiddy on the map is a misnomer, or rather an English corruption of the native word Palkapiti. The word palkapiti in dialect means, tail groove or the tail track of a kangaroo.

In addition to the above correction of translation it may be as well to mention also that the correct native pronunciation of the word **Nord** in Nord Rockhole above, is actually **Norr** with emphasis on the trilled letters **rr** which are frequently misheard by English speaking white people and more often than not recorded with the letters **t** or **d** in lieu of the trilled **rr**. There are numerous instances of this mistake at other places throughout the country east of Laverton.

EPILOGUE

In Loving Memory
Of
Pukungka Dolly Walker

Dolly was born in Skull Creek near Laverton WA circa 1930. She lived an eventful, happy, and productive full life until her last few years when she contracted and suffered a long illness that finally led to her death on the Tuesday evening of 29 June 2010 to the great sorrow and sadness of her partner and loving husband Nyingka Peter Muir who shared life together with Dolly for 42 years from 1968 to the time of her sad demise which period covered more than half this couple's respective lifetimes.

I Peter Muir hope to share this burial plot and the afterlife (If any) with you my beloved woman - when my time comes as it surely must. You Dolly were literally the only woman I ever really loved and oh how I miss you my darling one. I remain your soul mate forever. This headstone text was composed by me your loving mate:

Peter Muir - born 29 March 1929.

The APB
Dooley & Me
Recollections of Our First Two Years Together
1968-1970

NATIONAL LIBRARY OF AUSTRALIA
ISBN 0-646-41149-7

**First Edition
2000**

**Second Edition
2016**

www.ingramcontent.com/pod-product-compliance
Lightning Source LLC
Chambersburg PA
CBHW042055290426
44111CB00001B/14